THE LATIN
SEXUAL
VOCABULARY

J. N. Adams

The Johns Hopkins University Press
Baltimore, Maryland

470
Ad IL
144421
May 1988

First published in the United States of America by
The Johns Hopkins University Press,
Baltimore, Maryland 21218

First published in Great Britain by
Gerald Duckworth & Co. Ltd.,
The Old Piano Factory,
43 Gloucester Crescent, London NW1

Library of Congress Catalog Card No. 82–82629

ISBN 0–8018–2968–2

Printed in Great Britain

Contents

Preface

In recent years a good deal of interest has been shown in the sexual content of ancient literature. This book deals exclusively with the vocabulary of sex. My aim has been to describe and classify the varieties of language used in Latin to refer to sexual parts of the body, sexual acts and excretion. The sexual vocabulary of Latin is of both literary and semantic interest. Sexual behaviour has a place in numerous literary genres, such as epigram, satire, elegy, comedy, mime and farce, and the terminology in which that behaviour is described can vary revealingly from genre to genre, and also within a genre. The conventions of a genre, the tastes of its exponents, and the tastes of the age in which a literary work was composed, can all be illuminated by the study of sexual language. Some years ago I began to write a series of articles on different aspects of the Latin sexual vocabulary, and indeed a few of these have appeared. But it seemed worthwhile when the chance arose to bring the evidence together in one place.

The subject is a big one. Almost any object or practice can acquire a sexual symbolism in a suggestive context. More than 800 words are listed in the index of Latin words, and I should not wish to claim that I have been absolutely exhaustive. The book would be very much longer than it is if I had set out to translate the passages cited, or to discuss at length every crux containing a sexual usage. I have attempted to cover all the semantic areas from which sexual terminology in Latin was drawn, while restricting myself to reasonable limits of space. I have also tried to keep the book free from fanciful speculations, since I have no sympathy with the current mania for discovering obscene double entendres in unlikely places.

I have been particularly fortunate to have such learned and

wide-ranging colleagues as D. M. Bain and H. D. Jocelyn. Both have been intermittently engaged in researches of a similar kind, not all of which have yet been published. They have supplied me with much information, and discussed with me countless passages over the years. K.-D. Fischer gave me useful advice on various medical and veterinary passages.

I am grateful to the publishers for taking the book on, and for the impressive speed and efficiency with which it was seen through the press.

Manchester, 1982   J.N.A.

Abbreviations

Adams, 'Anatomical terminology'	J. N. Adams, 'Anatomical terminology in Latin epic', *BICS* 27 (1980), pp. 50ff.
Adams, *Culus*	J. N. Adams, '*Culus, clunes* and their synonyms in Latin', *Glotta* 59 (1981), pp. 231ff.
Adams, 'Euphemism'	J. N. Adams, 'A type of sexual euphemism in Latin', *Phoenix* 35 (1981), pp. 120ff.
Adams, *Pars pro toto*	J. N. Adams, 'Anatomical terms used *pars pro toto* in Latin', forthcoming in *PACA*.
Audollent	A. Audollent, *Defixionum tabellae quotquot innotuerunt* (Paris, 1904).
Brandt, *Am.*	P. Brandt, *P. Ovidi Nasonis Amorum Libri Tres* (Leipzig, 1911).
Brandt, *Ars*	P. Brandt, *P. Ovidi Nasonis De Arte Amatoria Libri Tres* (Leipzig, 1902).
CE	F. Buecheler – E. Lommatzsch, *Carmina Latina Epigraphica* (Leipzig, 1897–1926).
CGL	G. Goetz, *Corpus Glossariorum Latinorum* (Leipzig and Berlin, 1888–1923).
Chantraine	P. Chantraine, *Dictionnaire étymologique de la langue grecque* (Paris, 1968–80).
CIL	*Corpus Inscriptionum Latinarum.*
Citroni	M. Citroni, *M. Valerii Martialis Epigrammaton Liber Primus* (Florence, 1975).

Cohen	G. Cohen, *La «comédie» latine en France au XIIe siècle* (Paris, 1931).
Courtney	E. Courtney, *A Commentary on the Satires of Juvenal* (London, 1980).
Dover	K. J. Dover, *Greek Homosexuality* (London, 1978).
Ernout and Meillet	A. Ernout and A. Meillet, *Dictionnaire étymologique de la langue latine*[4] (Paris, 1959).
Fehling	D. Fehling, *Ethologische Überlegungen auf dem Gebiet der Altertumskunde* (Munich, 1974).
FEW	W. von Wartburg, *Französisches etymologisches Wörterbuch* (Bonn, etc., 1928–69).
FJGA	*Fontes iuris Germanici in usum scholarum (MGH)*.
Forberg	F. C. Forberg, *Antonii Panormitae Hermaphroditus, primus in Germania edidit et apophoreta adiecit F.C.F.* (Coburg, 1824).
Fraenkel, *Elementi Plautini*	E. Fraenkel, *Elementi Plautini in Plauto* (Florence, 1960).
Frassinetti	P. Frassinetti, *Atellanae Fabulae*[2] (Rome, 1967).
GL	H. Keil, *Grammatici Latini* (Leipzig, 1855–78).
Goldberger	W. Goldberger, 'Kraftausdrücke im Vulgärlatein', *Glotta* 18 (1930), pp. 8ff., 20 (1932), pp. 101ff.
Graffiti del Palatino	V. Väänänen (gen. ed.), *Graffiti del Palatino*: I, *Paedagogium*, ed. H. Solin and M. Itkonen-Kaila; II, *Domus Tiberiana*, ed. P. Castrén and H. Lilius (*Acta Instituti Romani Finlandiae*, vols. III-IV, Helsinki 1966, 1970).
Grassmann	V. Grassmann, *Die erotischen Epoden des Horaz* (Munich, 1966).
Herter, *De Priapo*	H. Herter, *De Priapo* (*Religionsgeschichtliche Versuche und Vorarbeiten* 23, Giessen, 1932).

Herter, 'Genitalien'	H. Herter, 'Genitalien', *RAC* X, 1ff.
Herter, 'Phallos'	H. Herter, 'Phallos', *RE* XIX.2.1681ff.
Hey	O. Hey, 'Euphemismus und Verwandtes im Lateinischen', *ALL* 11 (1900), pp. 515ff.
Housman, *Classical Papers*	J. Diggle and F. R. D. Goodyear, *The Classical Papers of A. E. Housman* (Cambridge, 1972).
Jocelyn	H. D. Jocelyn and B. P. Setchell, *Regnier de Graaf, On the Human Reproductive Organs* (*Journal of Reproduction and Fertility*, Supplement no. 17, 1972).
Krenkel	W. A. Krenkel, 'Fellatio and irrumatio', *WZ Rostock* 29 (1980), pp. 77ff.
Kroll	W. Kroll, *C. Valerius Catullus* (Leipzig and Berlin, 1923).
Lehmann	P. Lehmann, *Die Parodie im Mittelalter*² (Stuttgart, 1963).
Lewis and Short	C. T. Lewis and C. Short, *A Latin Dictionary* (Oxford, 1879).
L–S–J	H. G. Liddell, R. Scott and H. S. Jones, *A Greek-English Lexicon*⁹, with Supplement (Oxford, 1968).
Mariotti	S. Mariotti, 'Lo *spurcum additamentum* ad Apul. *Met.* 10,21', *SIFC* N.S. 27–28 (1956), pp. 229ff., = id. *Scritti medievali e umanistici* (Rome, 1976), pp. 47ff.
Marx	F. Marx, *C. Lucilii Carminum Reliquiae* (Leipzig, 1904–5).
MGH	*Monumenta Germaniae Historica.*
Nisbet and Hubbard I	R. G. M. Nisbet and Margaret Hubbard, *A Commentary on Horace: Odes Book 1* (Oxford, 1970).
Nisbet and Hubbard II	R. G. M. Nisbet and Margaret Hubbard, *A Commentary on Horace: Odes, Book II* (Oxford, 1978).
Oder	E. Oder, *Claudii Hermeri Mulomedicina Chironis* (Leipzig, 1901).

OLD   *Oxford Latin Dictionary* (Oxford, 1968–82).

Opelt   I. Opelt, 'Euphemismus', *RAC* VI, 947ff.

Otto   A. Otto, *Die Sprichwörter und sprichwörtlichen Redensarten der Römer* (Leipzig, 1890).

Pierrugues   P. Pierrugues, *Glossarium Eroticum Linguae Latinae* (Paris, 1826).

Pokorny   J. Pokorny, *Indogermanisches etymologisches Wörterbuch* (Bern, 1959–69).

Preston   K. Preston, *Studies in the Diction of the Sermo Amatorius in Roman Comedy* (Diss. Chicago, 1916).

RAC   *Reallexikon für Antike und Christentum.*

RE   *Paulys Real-Encyclopädie der classischen Altertumswissenschaft.*

REW   W. Meyer-Lübke, *Romanisches etymologisches Wörterbuch*[3] (Heidelberg, 1935).

Shipp   G. P. Shipp, *Modern Greek Evidence for the Ancient Greek Vocabulary* (Sydney, 1979).

Svennung   J. Svennung, *Wortstudien zu den spätlateinischen Oribasiusrezensionen (Uppsala Universitets Årsskrift* 1933, Band III, Bil. D).

Taillardat   J. Taillardat, *Les images d'Aristophane*[2] (Paris, 1965).

TLL   *Thesaurus Linguae Latinae.*

Tränkle   H. Tränkle, *Die Sprachkunst des Properz und die Tradition der lateinischen Dichtersprache (Hermes, Einzelschriften,* Heft 15, Wiesbaden, 1960).

Chapter One

Introduction

The Latin sexual language has never been exhaustively discussed, although useful collections of material and comments
on individual passages are to be found in various places. Of
older works those by Pierrugues and Forberg are worthy of
mention. Goldberger's often quoted articles contain much that
is interesting, but are marred by inaccuracy. Some other schol-
ars who have touched on the subject are Hey, Housman,
Hopfner,[1] Opelt, Herter, Grassmann and Jocelyn. Of commentators on individual authors I mention in particular Brandt,
Kroll and Citroni.[2]

1. Some types of sexual and excretory language

A language will generally have a set of words which can be
classified as the most direct and obscene terms for sexual parts
of the body and for various sexual and excretory acts. As a
rule basic obscenities have no other, primary, sense to soften
their impact.[3] They are unusable in polite conversation,[4] most
genres of literature, and even in some genres which might be
thought obscene in subject matter. Some of the Latin obscen-

[1] T. Hopfner, *Das Sexualleben der Griechen und Römer* I (Prague, 1938).
[2] On Greek, note Taillardat and Dover. J. Henderson, *The Maculate Muse*:
Obscene Language in Attic Comedy (New Haven and London, 1975) is so
inaccurate that I have chosen not to refer to it.
[3] They may of course in origin have been metaphorical, but metaphors often
fade.
[4] On the unacceptability of the direct terminology in Latin, see Arnob. *Nat.*
3.10 'genitalium membrorum . . . foeditates, quas ex oribus [*oribus* P, *moribus*
Reifferscheid] uerecundis infame est suis appellationibus promere' (cf. Cels.
6.18.1).

ities are well represented in the Romance languages, where their reflexes often retain a substandard flavour. There is not necessarily an exact correspondence between languages in the components of their sets of basic terms. *Irrumo*, for example, has no equivalent in English. Within the set, the various words may differ in offensiveness. In English the obscenity for the female parts would probably be considered by most speakers to be coarser and more emotive than any word for the male organ. In a dead language it is not possible to classify obscenities by degrees of offensiveness with any precision. One can set up a group of obscenities on the evidence partly of comments by Latin writers themselves, and partly of the distribution and use of certain words. But neither ancient comments nor distributions permit one to establish subtle distinctions of tone. Nevertheless there are signs that *mentula, cunnus, culus, futuo, pedico* and *irrumo* were more offensive than *coleus, fello, ceueo* and *criso*. And in the excretory sphere basic words for 'urinate' (*meio, mingo*) seem to have been less emotive than that for 'defecate' (*caco*; cf. *merda, pedo*), though *caco* itself may have been milder than the sexual obscenities (on excretory terminology, see the Appendix). The obscenities dealt with here are *mentula, uerpa, cunnus, coleus, futuo, pedico, irrumo, fello, ceueo, criso*. *Culus* I have discussed in detail elsewhere,[1] but a summary of the evidence is given in Chapter IV. Those words which can be identified as basic obscenities from the comments of Latin writers (notably *mentula, cunnus, futuo, pedico*) have a distinctive distribution: they are common in graffiti and epigram (Catullus, Martial, the *Corpus Priapeorum*), but almost entirely absent from other varieties of literature (including satire, if one excludes the first book of Horace's *Sermones*).[2] Certain sexual or excretory words not commented on in Latin literature which show the same distribution can plausibly be regarded as similar in status. It remains to add that various words of infrequent attestation are impossible to categorise (e.g. *muto, sopio, salaputium*). The important question to what extent the basic obscenities of Latin shed their primary senses and deteriorated into general abusive terms is dealt with below, pp. 132ff.

Metaphors and euphemistic designations provide the bulk

---

[1] Adams, *Culus*.

[2] Basic obscenities would also have been used in farce and mime: see p. 219.

of attested terms for sexual parts of the body and sexual acts in Latin. In a suggestive context almost any object or activity may be interpreted as a sexual image. The following general observations concerning the use of metaphors will be illustrated in the course of the book:

(*a*) Many sexual metaphors are not current in any variety of a language, but uttered off-the-cuff, particularly in jokes or to display linguistic inventiveness. Or a word used in a literal, non-sexual sense may be deliberately misunderstood, even though it possesses no established sexual meaning. Most sexual metaphors heard in a language may well be *ad hoc* coinages; certainly in Latin many metaphors seem to be of this type. The coining of metaphors was especially characteristic of Plautine comedy, Atellane farce and mime.

(*b*) The tone and implication of established metaphors varies. Some are slang terms with an offensive tone, others may be acceptable in educated parlance. The metaphor of ploughing in English, for example, has a literary flavour. *Anus* was a scientific term in Latin. The medical languages in Greek and Latin contain a number of anatomical metaphors of a sexual kind.

(*c*) Metaphors constantly fade; indeed basic obscenities may originate as metaphors (e.g. *irrumo*, perhaps *futuo*). In Greek γαμεῖν, originally a metaphor when applied to intercourse, eventually displaced the obscenity βινεῖν. By the time of Cicero *penis* had lost its literal sense; it is likely that some speakers did not interpret the sexual meaning as metaphorical.

Most sexual euphemisms refer to the sexual part or act by a name which is not its own (metonymy). In the case of the sexual organs the euphemism may strictly describe an adjoining part, or an extensive area of the body within which the sexual part is located (specialisation). In the case of sexual acts it is usually an act or event concomitant or associated with the sexual penetration which is mentioned. Another form of euphemism is ellipse, aposiopesis or the substitution of a pronoun for an indelicate noun, or pro-verb (*facio*) for an indelicate verb. I have dealt with euphemistic omissions elsewhere,[1] and offer here only a few examples.

---

[1] Adams, 'Euphemism'.

2. Some functions of sexual language in Latin

(i) Apotropaic and ritual obscenity

Apotropaic obscenities for the warding off of the evil eye or evil influences of an unspecific kind played an important part in various spheres of Italian life. Obscenities were shouted at triumphs.[1] Note especially Suet. *Iul.* 49.4 'Gallico denique triumpho milites eius inter cetera carmina, qualia currum prosequentes ioculariter canunt, etiam illud uulgatissimum pronuntiauerunt:

> Gallias Caesar subegit, Nicomedes Caesarem:
> ecce Caesar nunc triumphat qui subegit Gallias,
> Nicomedes non triumphat qui subegit Caesarem.'

The other couplet quoted by Suetonius from the same triumph contains *effutuisti* (*Iul.* 51); it is highly likely that basic obscenities had an important place in apotropaic verses. In the *carmen* quoted above there is a play on the double sense of *subigo*, and Suetonius speaks of the soldiers as singing *ioculariter*. Laughter and jokes often have a ritual function.[2] For the persistence of jests at triumphs under the Empire, see Mart. 1.4.3, 7.8.9f.

It was not only obscene language which was apotropaic, but also phallic representations and illustrations.[3] Sometimes the two, language and representation, go hand in hand. The *triumphator* had a phallic *bulla* (Macrob. *Sat.* 1.6.9 'quam in triumpho prae se gerebant inclusis intra eam remediis quae crederent aduersus inuidiam ualentissima'), and a phallus was hung under his car as a *medicus inuidiae* (Plin. *Nat.* 28.39).

Obscene verses (Fescennines) were sung at weddings: see Paul. Fest. p. 76 'Fescennini uersus qui canebantur in nuptiis, ex urbe Fescennina dicuntur allati, siue ideo dicti, quia fascinum putabantur arcere'. Such songs were sung especially by

---

[1] For the early period, see Livy 3.29.5, with R. M. Ogilvie, *A Commentary on Livy, Books 1–5* (Oxford, 1965), *ad loc.*

[2] See N. J. Richardson, *The Homeric Hymn to Demeter* (Oxford, 1974), pp. 214ff. for examples from various cultures of ritualistic jests, laughter and obscenity.

[3] See Herter, 'Phallos', 1719ff., especially 1733ff. For a phallic drawing accompanied by the words 'hic habitat Felicitas', see *CIL* IV.1454; on phallic statues in the forum and in gardens, see Plin. *Nat.* 19.50, where it is observed that they were placed 'contra inuidentium effascinationes'.

boys (Varro *Men.* 10, Fest. p. 284).[1] There was also a physical
representation of the phallus in the marriage ceremony (at
least in the early period). The bride was compelled to sit on
the phallus of the ithyphallic god Mutunus Tutunus (Lact.
Inst. 1.20.36, Aug. *Ciu.* 6.9, 7.24).[2] This rite was no doubt
intended to promote fertility as well as ward off evil.[3] These
two functions of an object or utterance, as apotropaic and
conferring fertility, are often impossible to separate: by ful-
filling the first the object assists in the second.[4]

At the festival of Liber phalluses were placed in carts and
displayed at crossroads in the country and even taken into the
city (see Aug. *Ciu.* 7.21 (cf. 7.24)).[5] At Lavinium a month was
set aside for the festival, a feature of which was the uttering
of obscenities (Aug. *loc. cit.* 'cuius diebus omnes uerbis flagi-
tiosissimis uterentur'). The two functions of the obscenities
(and phallic display) again cannot be separated (Aug. *loc. cit.*
'sic uidelicet Liber deus placandus fuerat pro euentibus sem-
inum, sic ab agris fascinatio repellenda').

At the festival of the Floralia in April mimes marked by
obscenity were performed by prostitutes, who took the place of
mimae: Lact. *Inst.* 1.20.10 'praeter uerborum licentiam, quibus
obscenitas omnis effunditur'.[6] The prostitutes also stripped at
the demand of the spectators (Lact. *loc. cit.*). It is a common
folk belief that indecent exposure may amuse and please a
god,[7] although there is no specific evidence that this was considered to be the purpose of the exposure at the Floralia.

Whatever the origin and function of the goddess Anna Perenna, at her festival on 15 March obscenities were chanted by
girls: Ovid *Fast.* 3.675f. 'nunc mihi cur cantent superest obscena puellae / dicere; nam coeunt certaque probra canunt' (cf.

---

[1] On Fescennine verses, see further G. Wissowa, 'Fescennini versus', *RE*
VI.2.2222f.
[2] Cf. Herter, 'Phallos', 1719f., *RhM* 76 (1927), p. 423, 'Genitalien', 15.
[3] Cf. Herter, *RhM, loc. cit.*
[4] So Priapus was both efficacious against the evil eye (Herter, *De Priapo*, p.
111, nos. 81–2) and also a god of fertility (Herter, *op. cit.*, p. 225).
[5] On Liber, see Wissowa, *Religion und Kultus der Römer*[2] (Munich, 1912),
pp. 297ff. On the festival, see Herter, 'Phallos', 1722; cf. 'Genitalien', 15.
[6] On the indecency of the Floralia, see also Val. Max. 2.10.8, Mart. 1.prooem.,
H.A., Hel. 6.5, Tert. *Spect.* 17.2–3.
[7] See Richardson (see above, p. 4 n. 2), pp. 215ff.

6   *The Latin Sexual Vocabulary*

695). There can be little doubt that these verses were intended in origin to be apotropaic or to promote fertility.[1]

Maledicta and *probra* were spoken when various herbs were planted (Plin. *Nat.* 19.120, Pallad. *Rust.* 4.9.14). Presumably these utterances were obscene (for the sense of *probra*, see Ovid, *Fast.* 3.676 above).[2]

Whether on non-ritual occasions obscenities were deliberately uttered as apotropaic, just as various obscene gestures could be made for the same purpose (the *fica*, the *corna*, the *digitus impudicus* extended),[3] is unclear. Note *Eph. Epigr.* III. p. 137 no. 111 'inuidiosis mentula' (accompanying a drawing of a phallus). Presumably the word might accompany a gesture, just as in the inscription it supports a drawing. At *CIL* III.10189.16 ('Dindari, uiuas et inuidis mentla', on a ring) the word appears to be apotropaic on its own.

(ii) Aggression and humiliation

Just as a sexual violation may be inflicted on an enemy as a punishment, so sexual threats or sexual abuse may be directed at someone as a means of venting aggression. I shall deal with the aggressive use of obscenities below (pp. 124, 128, 133f.).

(iii) Humour and outrageousness

Sexual language may have a humorous purpose. Dirty jokes probably have a place in all societies. For some sexual jokes made by Cicero, see *Att.* 2.1.5 and Quint. 6.3.75. Vespasian's jokes were sometimes in the most direct terminology (*praetextata uerba*) (Suet. *Vesp.* 22; cf. 23.1 for a sexual pun ascribed to the emperor). There is an interesting collection of jokes, some of them sexual, to be found at Macrob. *Sat.* 2.2–6. The humorous use of sexual language is to some extent linked with

---

[1] See K. Latte, *Römische Religionsgeschichte* (Munich, 1960), pp. 137f., J. G. Frazer, *Publii Ouidii Nasonis Fastorum Libri Sex*, vol. 3 (London, 1929), pp. 111f.

[2] See Henderson (mentioned above, p. 1 n. 2), p. 14.

[3] For apotropaic obscene gestures, see Ovid *Fast.* 5.433, and O. Jahn, 'Über den Aberglauben des bösen Blicks bei den Alten', *Berichte über die Vehandl. d. sächs. Gesellsch. d. Wiss. Phil.-hist. Klasse* 7 (1855), pp. 80ff., C. Sittl, *Die Gebärden der Griechen und Römer* (Leipzig, 1890), pp. 100ff., F. T. Elworthy, *The Evil Eye* (London, 1895), pp. 242, 255ff., 258ff., Herter, 'Phallos', 1739f., 'Genitalien', 18f.

the apotropaic and aggressive.[1] The obscenities spoken at weddings may have been apotropaic, but they were looked upon
as jokes as well (Catull. 61.120 *Fescennina iocatio*); indeed one
may wonder whether the apotropaic function was forgotten by
the late Republic, and the ribaldry enjoyed for its own sake
(as at modern European weddings). We have already seen that
the obscenities associated with triumphs were regarded as
jokes.

Martial insists again and again that his epigrams (he
usually has in mind those with a sexual content) are *ioci*, and
meant to provoke laughter (see 11.15.3). They were appropriate to the Saturnalia (see 4.14, 11.2.5), and the Saturnalia
was a time for *ioci* (10.18.3, 10.87.7). For *ioci* etc. see further
1. prooem., 1.4, 1.35.10, 13, 3.99, 4.49.2, 6.82.5, 6.85.10, 7.8.9f.,
8. prooem. In some societies at some periods oblique allusion
has been the only acceptable means of making jokes of a sexual
kind: direct language may be frowned upon as obvious and
tasteless. That Martial could use direct terminology in literary
epigram (unlike his predecessors in Greek) and still claim that
his work might be amusing to sophisticated readers (including
women: see p. 217) is something of a curiosity. To some extent
he was expecting to amuse by being deliberately outrageous
(see 11.16.7 for the *nequitia* of his verse contrasted with traditional *grauitas* (line 1); for *nequitia* as amusing, see 11.15.3f.,
and causing delight, 5.2.3f.; see also 6.82.5). The Romans (and
not only men) clearly enjoyed blatant sexual language on
special occasions (e.g. at the Floralia and at the festival of
Anna Perenna) as a means of letting down their hair in con-
travention of expected public behaviour. Even a character of
traditional gravity might be expected to abandon his *seueritas*
for a while on an occasion such as the *Saturnalia* (see 4.14).

(iv) Titillation

Obscene pictures and language may be intended to arouse the
viewer or the listener. Sexual illustrations are found in Pompeian brothels, and the role of language as titillating is recognised in the stress laid on the importance of words as an
accompaniment to intercourse (Ovid *Ars* 3.796, Mart. 11.60.7,

---

[1] See S. Freud, *Wit and its Relation to the Unconscious*, trans. A. A. Brill
(New York, 1916), pp. 138ff. for aggression and dirty jokes.

11.104.11, Juv. 6.406). Martial claims it as a function of his epigrams that they should arouse the reader. At 11.16.5ff. he speaks of the stimulating effect of his verse on both males and females. At 1.35.10f. he says that *carmina iocosa* should be arousing. And the pleasure which a woman receives from her husband's *mentula* is likened to that conferred by the word at 1.35.4f. Cf. Catull. 16.9.

Chapter Two

Mentula and its Synonyms

1. Basic obscenities

(i) *Mentula*

The basic obscenity for the male organ was *mentula*. The tone of the word is indicated by a few remarks which Martial makes. At 3.69.1f. he singles out *mentula* as the archetypal obscenity: the epigrams of a certain Cosconius are written *castis uerbis*, in that they contain no *mentula*. At 11.15.8ff. it is implied that *mentula* was the original word for the penis and the direct term *par excellence*. Martial argues that the word was in use in the time of King Numa: it was therefore akin to English 'four letter Anglo-Saxon words', the use of which, at least in dictionaries, is sometimes defended because of their antiquity. Martial avows that he will not use euphemisms for *mentula* (8 'nec per circuitus loquatur illam, / ex qua . . . '). Similarly at *Priap.* 29 *mentula* and *cunnus* are given as ideal examples of obscenities:

> Obscenis, peream, Priape, si non
> uti me pudet improbisque uerbis.
> sed cum tu posito deus pudore
> ostendas mihi coleos patentes,
> cum cunno mihi mentula est uocanda.

Cicero was not prepared to use *mentula* openly in his discussion of obscenity (*Fam.* 9.22). At *Fam.* 9.22.3 he refers to a diminutive form of *menta* (' "ruta" et "menta" recte utrumque; uolo mentam pusillam ita appellare ut "rutulam"; non licet'). In the next sentence ('belle "tectoriola"; dic ergo etiam "paui-menta" isto modo; non potes') the diminutive form of *paui-*

menta which he has in mind must be *pauimentula*.[1] Earlier
(9.22.2) he alludes to *mentula* as *id uerbum* (Paetus, the addressee of the letter, had clearly himself employed *mentula*):
'quod tu in epistula appellas suo nomine, ille tectius "penem";
sed, quia multi, factum est tam obscenum quam id uerbum,
quo tu usus es'. The offensive character of *mentula* is also
shown by the frequency with which some writers (e.g. Petronius) employ instead a feminine adjective or demonstrative un-
accompanied by the noun (see p. 62).

It is sometimes suggested that *mentula* was in origin a diminutive of *menta*, 'spearmint stalk'.[2] But it seems unlikely that
such an obscure plant would have provided such a common
name for the male organ. Sexual metaphors of any currency
owe their origin to the obvious sexual symbolism of the object
which serves as the vehicle of the metaphor. It is scarcely
conceivable that the spearmint stalk was so suggestive to so
many people that the metaphor should have caught on in the
whole community.[3] Certainly *mentula* was not felt by Cicero to
be metaphorical, though that is not decisive against a metaphorical origin for the word. His use of *suo nomine* at *Fam.*
9.22.2, quoted above, shows that for him it had no other more
basic meaning (whereas, for example, *anus* was strictly the
name for something else (= 'ring'): note *alieno nomine* in the
same passage: ' "anum" appellas alieno nomine; cur non suo
potius?'). His reference to a diminutive form of *menta* was not
offered as an etymology, but was a means of avoiding explicit
use of the obscenity.

Mentula is found 18 times in the Pompeian inscriptions and
3 times in the *Graffiti del Palatino*. It is the most common
word for the male organ in Catullus (8 times, twice in iambics
(29.13, 37.3) and 6 times in elegiac epigrams (94.1 twice, 105.1,
114.1, 115.1, 115.8); I include examples of the nickname *Mentula* given to Mamurra (?)). If one sought a literary precedent
for the use of basic obscenities in iambic invective, one need

---

[1] See D. R. Shackleton Bailey, *Cicero: Epistulae ad Familiares* (Cambridge,
1977), II, p. 333.

[2] See, for example, P. Kretschmer, *Glotta* 12 (1923), pp. 105ff., 283f., Goldberger (1930), p. 45, Jocelyn, p. 74, Herter, 'Genitalien', 3.

[3] Pokorny offers no etymology of *mentula*. For the possible connection of
mentula with *mens*, see Chantraine III, p. 693 *a*. Other affiliations which have
been suggested are with the root *men-* (cf. *mentum, emineo, mons*) and with
Skt. *mánthati*: see Ernout and Meillet, *s.v.*

think only of Archilochus and Hipponax.[1] But although Catullus may have looked upon 29 and perhaps some other abusive poems as written in the tradition of Archilochus or Hipponax, a good deal of his invective is not literary, but based, both in language and content, on real life. A good example of such 'Italian' invective is the *flagitatio*, 42. 37 and 59 too, both of them iambic, have a distinct smell of the streets. At 37.8 the hyperbolical threat to 'ducentos inrumare sessores' is distinctively Roman in spirit, even though the metre of the poem has associations with Hipponax. Caesar was deliberately misunderstood as making a similar threat in the senate (Suet. *Iul.* 22.2). An example of *mentula* in an epigram at 115.8, used *pars pro toto* as an empty term of abuse ('non homo, sed uero mentula magna miñax'), has parallels in graffiti (*CIL* IV.1776 add. p. 212 'Pilocalus mentula', 7089 'imanis metula es', 8931 'mentules' (= 'mentula es')).[2] It is in the sub-culture of low abuse that one should seek the models for Catullus' use of direct obscenities.[3]

---

[1] The sexual language of Archilochus was certainly metaphorical (see, e.g. μύκης = 'penis' at 252 West, κέρας = 'penis' at 247), but both Archilochus and Hipponax also admitted obscenities (see p. 220).

[2] See further Adams, *Pars pro toto*. For additional sexual terms emptied of their literal meaning in Latin, see pp. 124ff.

[3] Ordinary Latin speakers cast basic obscenities at one another, as the walls of Pompeii abundantly illustrate, and one can find constant parallels in graffiti for Catullan phraseology. But it was not only on walls that such sub-literary sexual abuse manifested itself, nor indeed was it the exclusive preserve of the lower classes. Scabrous *libelli* were circulated in the senate, and these, particularly if anonymous (see Suet. *Aug.* 55), might well have been couched in language far removed from that of formal oratory. An epigram of Augustus directed at Antony has survived (*ap.* Mart. 11.20), in which there are 4 examples of *futuo*, 1 of *pedico* and 1 of *mentula*. 'Fescennine verses' were composed by Augustus against Pollio (Macr. *Sat.* 2.4.21). Calvus abused Caesar in epigrams (Suet. *Iul.* 49.1, 73.1); a fragment contains the obscenity *pedicator* (Suet. *Iul.* 49.1). Otho and Vitellius exchanged sexual abuse in writing (Tac. *Hist.* 1.74 'mox quasi rixantes stupra ac flagitia in uicem obiectauere'). For examples of the language in which ordinary people might have vented their aggression towards men of distinction, see the Perusine sling bullets, *CIL* XI.6721, containing brief obscenities directed at Antony and Octavian. Note also *CIL* IV.8841 'Martialis, fellas Proculum', an inscription alleging sexual perversion on the part of some dignitaries of a *collegium*. We hear of interruptions and abuse by *operae* in the public assembly, and also of obscene verses drowning out a speaker (Cic. *Q.Fr.* 2.3.2 'uersus denique obscenissimi in Clodium et Clodiam dicerentur'). No doubt too *populi uersus* of the type mentioned by Cicero, *Phil.* 1.36 would on occasions have been obscene, as would the *probra* uttered by soldiers with a grievance against their general (Amm. 17.9.3).

In Greek epigram basic obscenities are rare (see p. 219). It was presumably Catullus who introduced such words to the genre: note Mart. 1. praef. 'lasciuam uerborum ueritatem, id est epigrammaton linguam, excussarem, si meum esset exemplum: sic scribit Catullus, sic Marsus, sic Pedo, sic Gaetulicus, sic quicumque perlegitur'. *Mentula* is by far the most numerous word for 'penis' in both Martial (48 times) and the *Corpus Priapeorum* (26 times); for an example in an epigram of Augustus, see p. 11 n. 3. *Mentula* is not admitted in satire or indeed in any other genre with a sexual content.

The tone of *mentula* varies. It is often employed in abusive contexts (e.g. Catull. 115.8; cf. the nickname *Mentula*), but it could also be used quite neutrally. A man might, for example, refer to his or someone else's *mentula* as desirable to women; if so he need not be speaking offensively, but only *Latine*. For neutral uses of *mentula*, see, e.g. Mart. 1.58.3, 6.23.2, 7.18.12, 7.30.8, 10.63.8, Audollent 135 A.8, p. 192, in a long list of anatomical terms used by the writer as the current *voces propriae*. πέος could be used in the same way in Greek (e.g. Aristoph. *Ach.* 1060, 1216, *Lys.* 124, 134, 415), as too could κύσθος (*Lys.* 1158). Basic obscenities should not be put on the same footing as either vulgarisms or terms of abuse. A vulgarism I should define as a usage restricted (largely) to lower-class speakers; an obscenity, on the other hand, is not confined to the speech of any one social class. A direct obscenity may be used by either a male or female when the circumstances of utterance are such (as, for example, in the private amatory language) that there is no need to cushion or distance the allusion to the body part in any way. When uttered in a context in which cushioning might have been expected, such a word may take on a highly offensive tone.

(ii) *Verpa*

Verpa can also be classified as a *vox propria* for the penis; it serves as a complement of *mentula*. *Verpa* is recorded in literature only in Catullus (28.12), Martial (11.46.2), the *Corpus Priapeorum* (34.5) and perhaps Pomponius (see below), but its currency in vulgar speech is established by its frequency in graffiti (see *CIL* IV.1655, 1884, 2360, 2415, 4876, 8617). It has derivatives reflected in Italian dialects.[1] In graffiti it is notable for its use, *pars pro toto*, as a term of abuse (e.g. *CIL* IV.1655 'Hysocryse puer, Natalis uerpa te salutat' (cf. 1375 'Natalis uerpe'), 1884 'qui uerpam uissit, quid cenasse illum putes?', 4876 'Regulo feliciter quia uerpa est');[2] it was undoubtedly offensive in tone. The dictionaries usually translate *uerpa* as 'penis', but the adjective *uerpus* as 'circumcised' (on the evidence of Juv. 14.104, where it is applied to Jews). It is not normally explained how two such disparate meanings could attach to the same root, or how an adjective meaning 'circumcised' could be applied to the name *Priapus* by Catullus (47.4). Kroll (on Catull. 47.4) was right to define *uerpus* as 'cuius glans nimia libidine nudata est' (= ψωλός). *Verpa* (= ψωλή; the equivalence can be seen if one compares *CIL* IV.1655 'Natalis uerpa' with 1363 'Antus ψωλή') indicated a *mentula* with foreskin drawn back as a result of erection, or, perhaps, excessive sexual activity, or, in the case of the Jews, circumcision (the Jews were also considered to be well-endowed and lustful: Mart. 7.35.4, 7.55.6ff.).[3] Given the sense of *uerpa* and *uerpus*, it is not surprising that they are often used when the performance of a sexual act is at issue (although at *Priap.* 34.5 *uerpas* indicates phallic figures). It was an aggressive homosexual act which seems to have been most appropriately performed by a *uerpa*, rather than mere *fututio*. This tendency to specialisation is probably due to the fact that *uerpa* was not a neutral technical term, but an emotive and highly offensive word. At Catull. 28.12 ('nam nihilo minore uerpa / farti estis') and *CIL* IV.2360 the allusion is (metaphorically) to *irrumatio*. At 11.94 Martial 4 times uses *uerpus* of a poet *qui pedicat*. *Verpa* used *pars pro toto* in the Pompeian graffiti seems to have indicated a *pedicator* or *irrumator* (note 1884), though it was subject to a weakening of sense.[4] *Verpus . . . Priapus ille* at Catull. 47.4 ('uos Veraniolo meo et Fabullo / uerpus praeposuit Priapus ille') may have been meant to suggest an image of Piso as an

---

[1] See *REW* 9237, G. Rohlfs, *Dizionario dialettale delle Tre Calabrie* (Halle-Milan, 1932–4), II, p. 371, s.v. *verpile* (= 'stirrup – strap made with the nerve of an ox or the member of a swine'). This derivative would suggest that in Calabria *uerpa* tended to be specialised to the animal anatomy.

[2] See Adams, *Pars pro toto.*

[3] For ψωλός used in reference to a circumcised state, see, e.g. Aristoph. *Aues* 507. Cf. Dover, p. 129.

[4] See Adams, *Pars pro toto.*

ithyphallic figure threatening his subordinates (metaphorically) with *pedicatio* or *irrumatio*. And at Pompon. 129 Frassinetti = 130 Ribbeck ('decedo cacatum. uerpa < num facta > est ueprecula?') *uerpa* is perhaps used in reference to *pedicatio*.[1] The speaker may have retired behind a bush to relieve himself, and found that he had suffered *pedicatio* from the bush. Much the same theme is found in an epigram from Pompeii: *CIL* IV.8899.3f. 'Vrticae monumenta uides, discede, cacator: / non est hic tutum culu aperire tibi'. The monument of Urtica (lit. 'nettle') seems to be threatening the *cacator* with *pedicatio*.[2] The *ueprecula* (a thorn bush) could 'sting' in the same sense as the *urtica*.

On the use of *uerpa* with verbs of eating and the like in slang (Catull 28.12f., *CIL* IV.1884, 2360), see p. 139.

2. Metaphors

(i) Sharp or pointed instruments

No objects are more readily likened to the penis than sharp instruments, and it is likely that metaphors from this semantic field abound in all languages. Most metaphors based on the symbolism of pointed objects in Latin seem to have been *ad hoc* coinages. But not all. A few words originally denoting some sort of sharp object live on in the Romance languages as designations for the penis. *Virga* ('branch, rod') is extensively represented in this sense (Fr. *verge*, etc.).[3] In the Latin versions of Oribasius (e.g. *Syn.* 1.21 La, p. 71.8 Mørland 'quibus paralysis in uirga patitur', = Aa 'ad beretri paralysin')[4] the usage is a calque on ῥάβδος,[5] but the reflexes in the Romance languages suggest that the metaphor appeared independently in popular speech: one would not as a rule expect a Grecising

---

[1] The text here is that of Frassinetti. For conjectures along the same lines, see M. Zicàri, *Hermes* 91 (1963), p. 123 ('uerpa est <profecto in> ueprecula') and p. 384 ('<nimirum in>'). The MSS. (see Nonius, p. 343 L.) have *uepra est ueprecula*.

[2] On this inscription, see W. D. Lebek, *ZPE* 22 (1976), pp. 287ff., L. Koenen, *ZPE* 31 (1978), pp. 85f.

[3] See *FEW* XIV, p. 500.

[4] See further Svennung, p. 142, A. Souter, *A Glossary of Later Latin to 600 A.D.* (Oxford, 1949), *s.v.*

[5] See *FEW*, loc. cit.

usage in the extremely artificial (if vulgar) language of med-
icine to achieve currency in everyday Latin.[1] *Virga* is fairly
common in both early and later Medieval Latin, in writers
who would have known it from the vernacular or popular
languages: Cassiod. *Anim.* 9, Migne 70, p. 1295 C 'nasus, os,
guttur, pectus, umbilicus, et genitalium uirga descendens' (=
'the descending rod of the genital parts'), *Lib. Leg. Langobard.
Pap., Leges Karoli M.* 81 (82) (*MGH, Leg. Tom.* IV, p. 502) 'si
quis alterum praesumptiue sua sponte castrauerit et ei ambos
testiculos amputauerit, integrum widrigild suum iuxta con-
ditionem personae componat; si uirgam absciderit, similiter'.
For an example in a twelfth century comedy written in France,
see William of Blois, *Alda* 468 'crebros in fine salientis senserat Alda / uirge singultus'.[2] In another comedy of the same
period, *Babio*, one manuscript (*P*) has *mentula uirga salax* at
338.[3] This phrase must have originated as a gloss on the metaphorical terminology used by the author ('captus non totus
abibit. / mecum deuenient funda petraeque simul'). For another late example, see *CGL* III.604.14 'pranton uirga uiralis'.
In one of the versions of the *Lex Salica* the diminutive *uirgula*
is used in the same sense: *Pactus Legis Salicae* 29.17 (rec. *C*)
'si quis hominem ingenuum castrauerit aut uiriculam suam
transcapulauerit, unde mancus sit . . .'. The misspelling may
be due to a conflation with *uirilia* (cf. rec. *B* 'uirilia transca-
polauerit'). The presence of *uirga* and ῥάβδος in medical writings is incidentally a good indication that metaphors from this
sphere are not necessarily risqué in tone. The sexual vocabulary of both Greek and Latin medical writings is full of metaphors; from this semantic field note *radius uirilis* = 'penis' at
Cael. Aurel. *Acut.* 3.115.

Two other words of this type reflected in Romance are *uectis*
(> Friul. *vet*) and **caraculum* 'stake', a diminutive of χάραξ,

---

[1] Although such a circumstance is not inconceivable. *Ficus*, apparently a
medical calque on σῦκον, σύκωσις, which indicated a sore on the genitalia,
became widespread in ordinary speech, to judge by the frequency of jokes in
Martial and elsewhere based on the metaphor (see Mart. 1.65.4, 4.52.2, 7.71,
12.33.2, *Priap.* 41.4, 50.2, and below, p. 113).

[2] For this work, see Cohen.

[3] For the *Babio*, see E. Faral, *De Babione, poème comique du XIIe siècle*
(Paris, 1948). The poem is also published in Cohen. There is a new edition by
A. D. Fulgheri, in *Commedie latine del XII e XIII secolo* II (*Università di
Genova, Pubblicazioni dell' Istituto di Filologia Classica e Medievale* 61, 1980).

which produced Sp. *carajo*.[1] *Vectis* is not attested in Classical Latin, but note *Lex Thuringorum* (ed. C. von Schwerin, *FJGA*) 18 'si uectem similiter' (sc. *excusserit*; cf. 16 'qui addingo unum uel ambos testiculos excusserit, CCC solidos componat').

While metaphors of our type undoubtedly had a place in popular speech and humour, one can sometimes speak of a general literary influence operating on a Latin writer. This is particularly the case in Priapic poetry, in which it was traditional to refer to the phallus of Priapus as a pointed object of some sort.[2] A Latin writer who coined such a metaphor in application to Priapus would presumably have had the tradition in mind, but his coinage would usually have been in keeping with native Latin sexual humour. It is not so much the individual metaphors which can be described as literary or Grecising, but the profusion of such images in Priapic poetry.

In Greek note Crinagoras, *A.P.* 6.232.7 εὐστόρθυγγι Πριάπῳ (στόρθυγξ = 'spike'), Erycius, *A. Plan.* 242.1 ὅπλον, Leonidas, *A. Plan.* 261.2 ῥόπαλον (for the imagery, cf. Aristoph. *Lys.* 553 ῥοπαλισμός). Horace applied *palus* ('stake') to the phallus of Priapus at *Serm.* 1.8.5 'obscenoque ruber porrectus ab inguine palus'. The metaphor is unique in Latin, but it has parallels in **caraculum* > Sp. *carajo*, and in a use of *terminus* in Pomponius, discussed below, p. 23. With the phrase *ab inguine* here, cf. ἀπὸ βουβώνων in Erycius, *A. Plan.* 242.2 ὡς βαρὺ τοῦτο, Πρίηπε, καὶ εὖ τετυλωμένον ὅπλον / πᾶν ἀπὸ βουβώνων ἀθρόον ἐκκέχυκας.

Martial, whose sexual vocabulary is not highly metaphorical, admits some comparable metaphors in Priapic epigrams: 6.49.3 *columna* (for which in the *Corpus Priapeorum*, see be-

---

[1] See *REW*, 1672 *b* (giving the etymon as **caraculum*), and C. D. Buck, *A Dictionary of Selected Synonyms in the Principal Indo-European Languages* (Chicago and London, 1949), p. 258, deriving *carajo* from *caracium* (<χαράκιον), which he erroneously gives as a hypothetical form (note *Edict. Roth.* 293 'de palo quod est carracio'). The derivation from **caraculum* is probably correct: see *FEW* II.1, p. 625. There may have been two separate diminutive forms of χάραξ in use in Vulgar Latin, the one with a Greek suffix, the other with a Latin. See further *REW* 1862, for reflexes of *caracium*.

[2] For the threatening appearance of the phallus of the god in art, see the illustrations given by Herter, *De Priapo*, opp. p. 96.

low),[1] 6.73.6 *inguinis arma* (metaphors from weaponry are dealt with separately below). *Columna* is in a non-Priapic poem at 11.51.1, but the referent is by implication likened to Priapus (line 2).

It is of course in the *Corpus Priapeorum* that most cases of such metaphors are found: 9.14, 55.4 *telum*, 10.8 *columna*, 11.3 *contus*, 25.1, 3 *sceptrum* (cf. *CIL* IV.1939),[2] 31.3 *uentris arma* (based no doubt on Martial's *inguinis arma*), 43.1, 4 *hasta*, 63.14 *pyramis*, 72.4 *bracchia macra* (see below, p. 37). With these examples compare Prudentius' use of *ramus*, discussed below, p. 28.

Augustine too was aware of the traditional method of describing the phallus of Priapus. At *Ciu.* 7.24 he calls the organ of Mutunus Tutunus, whom he confuses with Priapus, *scapus*, 'rod': 'in celebratione nuptiarum super Priapi scapum noua nupta sedere iubebatur'. Since an anatomical use of *scapus* is allegedly attested elsewhere, the word calls for further comment.

It has become the accepted view that *scapus* and *capus*, the latter supposedly a deformation of *scapus*, are found in veterinary writers with the sense 'penis'.[3] Indeed M. Niedermann[4] went so far as to introduce *(s)capus* in a gloss (*CGL* II.469.52 'φαλλός habus'); on the correct reading here, see below, p. 42.[5] *Capus* is not a predictable deformation of *scapus*; no such loss of *s* occurred as a regular change in Latin. *Clerocelicis* (*Mul. Chir.* 11) = σκληροκοιλίοις is not a parallel, since groups of consonants in initial position in foreign words were often reduced (cf., e.g. *Mul. Chir.* 81 *terrigia* = πτερύγια, 287 *tisanae* = πτισάνη). The form *capus* for *scapus* (as at Vitr. 3.3.12, *H*)

---

[1] A few sexual metaphors in Greek and Latin, like this, can be described as architectural: e.g. θριγκός ('clitoris'?) in Archilochus (R. Merkelbach and M. L. West, *ZPE* 14 (1974), p. 99 line 14), ἐκ τῶν καταγείων, of the anus, in Antipater or Nicarchus, *A.P.* 11.415.3, *pyramis* (*Priap.* 63.14). Note too the metaphor of the door (= '*cunnus*' or 'anus') (p. 89).

[2] Cf. the double entendre in Matthew of Vendôme, *Milo* 139 'oblitoque rigore / uultum demittit imperialis apex, / sceptra uerecundant' (*rigore* and *apex* too are probably intended as double entendres). For this work see Cohen.

[3] See Oder, index, p. 334, s.v. *capus*, *TLL* III.384.26.

[4] *Glotta* 2 (1910), p. 51.

[5] It is also a curiosity that Niedermann believed that an alleged example of *capus* in the *Mulomedicina Chironis* (461: see below) indicated the genitalia of a mare. In the passage in question the author is talking about horses in general; 'horse' rather than 'mare' is the predominating sense of *iumentum* in the work.

is more likely to be a haphazard scribal anomaly than a phonetic spelling.

At *Mul. Chir.* 487 (Oder: 'testes fumigato uel ligno uel oleo
cypressini scapi, uteris . . .'; MS. *cypressinis capi*) there is obviously no reason for introducing *capus*; indeed the false word
division in the manuscript shows how such a ghost word might
originate. Nor is the conjecture found in Oder's index ' . . . uel
oleo cypressi, in scapo uteris', which produces an example of
scapus = 'penis', necessary. For the adjective, see 110 *cupres-
sina* (MS. *cubresina*). At 463, where the text reads 'perungeto
eum a capo', there is no indication that the author had the
penis in mind.[1] The affliction in question might spread from
the head downwards (462 *a summo capite iumenti*); the author
is speaking of the greasing of the body, starting from the head.
For *capus* = *caput*, see *CIL* VI.29849a.

461, where there is another possible example of *capus*, is a
problematical passage. The first sentence of the chapter
('quando animal non potest stercorizare') does not square with
the second ('si quod iumentum loteum facere non poterit').
Since the other chapters in this part of the work begin *si quod
iumentum* + fut. / fut. perf., and since in the *tabula* (p. 130) it
is the second sentence which provides the title of the chapter
('loteum si non faciet'), it is likely that the first sentence is
secondary; perhaps it was added by someone who had found
the recipe useful for another purpose. The *quando*-sentence is
relevant to our passage (Oder: 'inde turundulam longam et
tenuem facito, ungito, intro in capum addito, ut anum impleat
et loteum facit'; MS. *capud adito*). The clause *ut anum impleat*
is curious, since one would expect the insertion to be in the
genitalia, or more specifically the urethra (see Col. 6.30.4
'melle decocto et sale collyrium tenue inditur foramini, quo
manat urina, uel musca uiua, uel turis mica, uel de bitumine
collyrium inseritur naturalibus'). *Anum* may be an emendation by the person who added the *quando*-clause (obelize, or
read *eum* or *totum*?).[2] *(S)capus* seems to be required by the
sense. In the corresponding passage Vegetius has *scapus* (*Mul.*
2.79.17 'in scapi ipsius foramen inserito'), and he must have
meant by that 'urethra', to judge from the correspondence with

[1] I am grateful to Dr K.-D. Fischer for advice about the subject matter and
composition of this passage and *c.* 461.
[2] These suggestions are Dr. Fischer's.

Col. 6.30.4. *Caput* (-*d*) can mean 'head' in the sense 'end' or
'opening' (note ps.-Theod. Prisc. *Addit.* p. 340.16 'suppones in
capite matricis'), but in the absence of a specifying genitive or
phrase it is unlikely to be the correct reading here. I conclude
that *scapum* (acc.) = 'urethra' should be printed. The passage
has been so tampered with that one would be unjustified in
bringing the form *capus* into existence on this evidence alone.
The metaphor is obviously different from that in Augustine's
scapus; the two usages are independent of each other.

In the above discussion I have largely restricted myself to
the terms 'sharp' or 'pointed object' as a general designation
for an important class of metaphors. Within this general class
it is of course possible to make further subdivisions (see, for
example, above, p. 17 n. 1 on architectural metaphors). Some
of these subdivisions are singled out below.

(a) Weapons
This is the largest category of metaphors of our general type.
No single word for a weapon seems to have become a banal
term for the penis in Latin, but the frequency of *ad hoc* metaphors both in Greek and Latin shows that the sexual symbolism of weapons was instantly recognisable in ancient society.
Words for weapons lent themselves readily to risqué jokes. I
begin with a few examples of such jokes.

Suetonius records a joke of Vespasian (*Vesp.* 23.1), who on
seeing a well-endowed man, quoted the Homeric verse μακρὰ
βιβάς, κραδάων δολιχόσκιον ἔγχος (*Il.* 7.213). ἔγχος of course
suggests the penis. It was not unusual in ancient humour for
epic verses and situations to be deliberately misinterpreted in
a sexual sense.[1] In the most protracted misinterpretation extant of epic lines, the *Cento Nuptialis* of Ausonius, various
words indicating weapons in Virgil are made to suggest the
mentula: see 92, p. 215 P., 120, p. 217 *telum* (for this word
with an anatomical meaning, see Justin 38.1.9, discussed below, and Mart. 11.78.6, *Priap.* 9.14, 55.4), 117, p. 217 *hasta* (cf.

[1] See Nicarchus, *A.P.* 11.328, Petron. 132.11, *Priap.* 68. See my article 'Ausonius *Cento Nuptialis* 101–131' forthcoming in *SIFC*.

Priap. 43.1, 4, in a similar context to that in Ausonius),[1] 121, p. 217 *mucro* (not found elsewhere with this meaning).

According to Justin (38.1.9), Mithridates, on being frisked by a representative of the younger Ariarathes, gave the warning 'caueret ne aliud telum inueniret quam quaereret' ('he should be careful lest he find a weapon other than the one he was looking for'). The remark provoked mirth (§ 10 'atque ita risu protectis insidiis . . .'). This joke is very similar to that at Plaut. *Cas.* 909 'dum *gladium* quaero ne habeat, arripio *capulum.* / sed quom cogito, non habuit gladium, nam esset frigidus'. The slave Olympio, while searching Chalinus in the dark for weapons, unknowingly handles his penis. The terms *gladius* and *capulus*, though innocent in his own eyes, could only be taken in a sexual sense by the audience.

Pomponius' expression *coleatam cuspidem* (69) (= 'the betesticled lance') would have been intended to sound comical. *Coleatus* is a Pomponian neologism based on the obscenity *coleus* = 'testicle' (cf. 40 'et ubi insilui in coleatum eculeum, ibi tolutim tortor'), and *cuspis* is nowhere else used in this sense. Sexual double entendre and metaphors must have been a prominent feature of *Atellana*.

Plautus shared such double entendre with farce. From the semantic field under discussion here note (in addition to *Cas.* 909 above) *Pseud.* 1181 'conueniebatne in uaginam tuam machaera militis'. *Machaera* implies the penis, *uagina* (another *ad hoc* metaphor) the anus. It is not surprising that *machaera* nowhere else has an obscene meaning, because the word was not in general use later. But in Greek one should compare the symbolism of the dream recounted at Ach. Tat. 2.23. As Clitophon enters the bedroom of Leucippe, Leucippe's mother dreams (2.23.5) that λῃστὴν μάχαιραν ἔχοντα γυμνὴν ἄγειν ἁρπασάμενον αὐτῆς τὴν θυγατέρα, where μάχαιρα is obviously meant to suggest the penis. The symbolism becomes more

---

[1] Note too the expression *hastam mei inguinis* in the medieval *spurcum additamentum* found in a manuscript of Apul. *Met.* 10.21. On the spurious nature of the *additamentum*, see E. Fraenkel, *Eranos* 51 (1953), pp. 151ff. (= id., *Kleine Beiträge zur klassischen Philologie* (Rome, 1964), II, pp. 391ff.), and Mariotti. For the genitive *inguinis*, cf. Mart. 6.73.6 *inguinis arma* (cf. *Priap.* 46.9 *fossas inguinis*), and, in Medieval Latin, William of Blois, *Alda* 485 *tumor inguinis ille rigentis*, 490 *tumor inguinis iste mei.* In the *spurcum additamentum inguinis* is conceivably (but not necessarily) a *genetiuus inhaerentiae* (and hence synonymous with *hasta*, = *mentula*), as Mariotti argues (p. 237 = p. 55). *Hasta* = 'penis' is found elsewhere in Medieval Latin: see Michael Scotus, *De Physiognomia* 22, 100.

explicit later in the sentence: μέσην ἀνατεμεῖν τῇ μαχαίρᾳ τὴν γαστέρα, κάτωθεν ἀρξάμενον ἀπὸ τῆς αἰδοῦς.

Other examples of metaphors from weaponry in Latin are *sicula* at Catull. 67.21, *gladius* at Petron. 9.5 in a possible double entendre ('gladium strinxit et "si Lucretia es" inquit "Tarquinium inuenisti" '), *arma* at Ovid *Am.* 1.9.26, Petron. 130.4, Maxim. *Eleg.* 5.77f., as well as at Mart. 6.73.6 and *Priap.* 31.3 above (cf. *inermis* at Ovid *Am.* 3.7.71), and *capulus* ('sword hilt') at *Priap.* 25.7 (see above on Plaut. *Cas.* 909). *Gesatus* (< *gaesum*) at CIL XII.5695.3, = *CE* 358 is possibly a humorous equivalent of *mentulatus* (so Buecheler *ad loc.*): 'Victoria: Balbus pedico uicit et gesatus / Actius erniacas qui ducet sa(e)pe choreas'. And the emperor Heliogabalus may have called men who were particularly virile *monobelis* or *onobeli*: *H.A., Hel.* 8.7 ' . . . ut ex tota penitus urbe atque ex nauticis onobeli quaererentur; sic eos appellabant, qui uiriliores uidebantur' (*monobiles* P, *monoboles* Σ, *monobelis* Salmasius, *onobeli* Lipsius). *Monobelis* would derive from μονοβελεῖς, 'with single weapon'. Lipsius' *onobeli* ('quasi asinino telo insignes') is very plausible (cf. *onon* at *Comm.* 10.9, of a well-endowed man).

Further examples in Greek are ξίφος at Aristoph. *Lys.* 632 (cf. Hesych. *s.v.* σκίφος), δόρυ at *Lys.* 985, and ὀξεῖα (sc. λόγχη) at ps.-Luc. *Asinus* 10 ὥστε τινάξας ὀξεῖαν ἐπίπρωσον καὶ βάθυνον: note *Sud.* ὀξεῖα ἡ λόγχη. καὶ παροιμία 'δι' ὀξείας δραμεῖν', ἐπὶ τῶν διακινδυνευόντων.

The metaphor of the bow can be classified as a metaphor from weaponry, but it is not exclusively of the same type as the above metaphors. At *Priap.* 68.33 Penelope speaks of Ulysses 'stretching his bow string' ('nemo meo melius neruum tendebat Ulixe'), and there is a similar metaphor at Apul. *Met.* 2.16 ('arcum meum et ipse uigorate tetendi' (*uigor attetendit* φ)). It was the capacity of the strings to tauten and relax which lay behind these double entendres (as behind the metaphor from lyre-playing at Varro *Men.* 368; cf. *Priap.* 68.16): for *tendo* and its derivatives applied to the state of erection, see, e.g. Catull. 80.6, Hor. *Serm.* 1.2.118, 1.5.84, 2.7.48, Mart. 6.71.3, 7.67.2, 11.58.1, 11.73.3, Juv. 11.169, *Priap.* 23.4, 33.5, Diomedes, *GL* I.376.10f., Eugraph. on Ter. *Eun.* 598. But in the double entendre at Ovid *Am.* 1.8.47f. ('Penelope iuuenum uires temptabat in arcu; / qui latus argueret corneus arcus erat') it is the 'horny' frame of the bow which suggests the male organ. Hence the one object provides two different types of metaphors, the second of which belongs among metaphors based on pointed objects. For the sexual significance of horn, see κέρας = 'penis' at Archil. 247 West and Meleager, *A.P.* 12.95.6; cf. Petron. 134.11 'nisi illud tam rigidum reddidero quam cornu', Cael. Aurel. *Acut.* 3.179 'tensionem autem fuisse ueretri nimiam . . . ut cornu putaretur'. Note too the popular belief mentioned by Pliny, *Nat.* 11.261 '(genitalia) urso quoque, simul atque expirauerit, cornescere aiunt'.

Ad hoc metaphors from weaponry continued to be coined in the Middle Ages. Note *Babio* 338 'captus non totus abibit./ mecum deuenient funda petraeque simul', where the sling, *funda* represents the *mentula*, and the *petrae* the testicles.

It is difficult to make generalisations about the tone of classes of sexual metaphors in Greek and Latin. But metaphors for the male organ derived from weaponry seem to have been risqué, and as such they were common in jokes and forms of comedy.

(b) Household objects

The house and its contents were a source of metaphors for the genitalia of both sexes. An early metaphor of this type for the penis is in a comic fragment of Naevius: 126 'uel quae sperat se nupturam uiridulo adulescentulo, / ea licet senile tractet detritum rutabulum'. *Rutabulum* literally means 'rake, poker' (see Fest. p. 318 'rutabulum est, quo rustici in proruendo igne, panis coquendi gratia'; note that the word had a rustic flavour). The presence of the metaphor in Naevius is of significance for the history of comedy in Latin. The manuscript of Festus, who quotes the fragment (*loc. cit.*), reads *Nauius* (*F*). Since the other example of the word quoted by Festus is from Novius (80 'quid ego facerem? otiosi [*otiose?*] rodebam rutabulum'), it is just possible that the couplet should be assigned to Novius. But the metaphor would not be out of character in *palliata*. Plautus, as we have seen, admitted anatomical double entendres of a sexual kind, and he may well have been anticipated by Naevius. There are other 'Roman' elements in the comic fragments of Naevius.[1]

[1] See Fraenkel, *Elementi Plautini*, pp. 20, 44 on frg. 129. On the numerous verbal similarities between Naevius and Plautus, see Fraenkel, *RE*, Suppl. VI, 628ff. See also J. Wright, *Dancing in Chains: the Stylistic Unity of the Comoedia Palliata* (*Papers and Monographs of the American Academy in Rome*, vol. xxv, Rome, 1974).

There may be a household term used metaphorically at Pompon. 96 'mulier ubi conspexit tam mirifice tutulatam truam' (for *conspicio* in such a context, see 69).[1] The literal sense of *trua* is 'ladle' (see Titin. 128). With *trua* Frassinetti compares τορύνη in a joke of Cleopatra's quoted by Plut. *Anton.* 62.6 ἡ μὲν Κλεοπάτρα σκώπτουσα 'τί δεινόν' ἔλεγεν 'εἰ Καῖσαρ ἐπὶ τορύνῃ κάθηται;' (Caesar had been delayed at a place called Τορύνη). If *tutulatam truam* is obscene, it is similar in type to Pomponius' *coleatam cuspidem* (above, p. 20): a metaphorical noun is accompanied by a bizarre adjective. *Tutulatam* ('having a head-dress, *tutulus*') would refer to the pubic hair.

Kitchen terminology is chiefly used suggestively of the female pudenda (p. 86).

(c) Poles, stakes and the like

A number of the metaphors which have already been mentioned fall into this category (**caraculum, uectis, uirga, radius, palus, contus, scapus, rutabulum*). To these can be added Catullus' *trabs* at 28.10 'bene me ac diu supinum / tota ista trabe lentus irrumasti'. *Trabs* is confined to Catullus with this meaning. Catullus is employing *irrumo*, in a grotesque metaphor, in reference to a non-sexual insult. *Trabs* was presumably adopted *ad hoc* as suitably drastic in the context.

Pomponius' *terminus* (126 'nisi nunc aliquis subito obuiam occurrit mihi, / qui oquiniscat, quo compingam terminum in tutum locum') is a more specialised image. The metaphor is from the rural activity of boundary marking (and as such it might also have been classified as 'rustic' or 'agricultural'). *Terminus* indicated a boundary marker, whether made of stone or wood (see *Grom.* pp. 89.18–90.4 Thulin). A wooden *terminus* could be described as a *palus*: see *Grom.* p. 102.18f. Thulin 'in quibusdam uero regionibus palos pro terminis obseruant'. *Compingam* in its literal sense would refer to the insertion of the sharp object into the ground (with *in tutum locum* by implication indicating the *culus*). *Terminus* in a sexual sense is unique to Pomponius, and it was no doubt his own coinage. For another type of boundary marking as a sexual symbol, see p. 85.

The use of *temo* ('pole') at *Priap.* 54.1 should also be men-

---

[1] For the sexual interpretation of the fragment, see V. Buchheit, *Hermes* 90 (1962), p. 252, Frassinetti, p. 105.

tioned here, though the symbolism there is of a special kind (see p. 39).

(d) Agricultural implements

The Latin sexual language is full of images which may be called 'agricultural' or 'rustic' (e.g. the similes at Lucil. 278, 330, *irrumo, glubo, molo, aro* = *futuo*, and in particular various words for the *cunnus* and *culus: ager, agellus, saltus, aruum, sulcus* and *aratiuncula*), which reflect the rural conditions of the Latin community over a long period. Various metaphors for the penis which have been seen above, and others which will be discussed in later sections, have a distinctly rustic flavour (e.g. *terminus, caulis* in Lucilius, *cucumis, radix, ramus, palus, rutabulum*). To these can be added certain words strictly denoting agricultural implements.

Vomer ('ploughshare') is used of the *mentula* at Lucr. 4.1273 'eicit enim sulcum recta regione uiaque / uomeris'. For the symbolism of the ploughshare, see also Artem. 2.24, p. 142.19f. Pack ἰδίως δὲ ἡ ὗνις, ὡς πολλάκις ἐτήρησα, καὶ τὸ αἰδοῖον τοῦ ἰδόντος σημαίνει. *Falcula*, diminutive of *falx*, 'sickle', must be an equivalent of *mentula* at *CE* 1900 'li[nge] Le[li, l]inge L[eli], linge Leli fa[lc]ula[m]'. The curved shape of the sickle might seem to undermine a metaphorical application of the word, but it was no doubt the pointed nature of the object which was in the writer's mind (cf. *falx* below). Similarly, as we have seen, in a suggestive context the frame of a bow might imply the *mentula*.

The above use of *uomer* was taken up much later by Matthew of Vendôme, *Milo* 184 'cultoris uacat egra manu qui uimina nulla / falce metit, nullo uomere tangit humum' (Milo is accused of not consummating his marriage; *humum* suggests the *cunnus*). Agricultural metaphors enjoyed a vogue in Medieval Latin. For *falx*, which also must be a double entendre here, see the satire *De Monacho Quodam*[1] 'misisti falcem in messem alienam' (the monk has committed adultery; *messem* is an agricultural metaphor for the *cunnus*). In this passage a Biblical phrase has been given an unintended sexual twist (see *Deut.* 23.25 'si intraueris in segetem amici tui, franges spicas et manu conteres; falce autem non metes'). The obscene

---

[1] The text can be found in the Appendix of Faral's edition of the *Babio* (see above, p. 15 n. 3), and in Lehmann, text no. 14, pp. 224ff.

misuse of Biblical phraseology is analogous to the misuse of epic phrases and of proverbs. For another example, see *De Monacho Quodam* 'ubinam est inimicus homo qui uenit, et superseminauit zizania, et cubile meum multa maculauit perfidia?' (cf. *Matth*. 13.25 'uenit inimicus eius et superseminauit zizania in medio tritici').

(*e*) Musical terminology
At *Cent. Nupt*. 127, p. 217 P. ('pectine pulsat eburno') Ausonius makes *pecten* ('plectrum' for playing the lyre at Virg. *Aen*. 6.647) indicate the penis. This metaphor has a parallel in a gloss (*CGL* V.252.28 'ueretrum percussorium'). *Percussorium* was a late word for 'plectrum' (*CGL* IV.145.14, 268.31). Cf. *pertunsorium* = '*penis*' at *CGL* IV.295.34, V.488.58. There is perhaps a comparable metaphor in the obscure graffito *CIL* IV.4862 'Berutius felator it [= *et*?] mames [< VL *mammaes*, = *mammae*?] et prethri'. The last word is uncertain (for the possible reading *plethri* see the editor *ad loc*.), but it may represent *plectrum*. If so it would be a musical metaphor which had found its way into slang. *Pecten* = 'pubic hair' (see p. 76) is irrelevant here.

Lyre playing also provided a sexual metaphor of another type: see Varro *Men*. 368 'et id dicunt suam Briseidem producere, quae eius neruia tractare solebat'. This metaphor is parallel to that of the bow string seen above, p. 21.[1]

(*f*) Nautical metaphors
Another innocent Virgilian word which is rendered obscene in the *Cento Nuptialis* of Ausonius is *clauus*, lit. 'tiller': 124, p. 217 P. 'clauumque adfixus et haerens / nusquam amittebat' (Virg. *Aen*. 5.852f.). The ship and seafaring served as the vehicle for various other types of sexual metaphors in Greek and Latin (p. 167). For a probable Medieval double entendre of a nautical kind, see *Pamphilus* 458 'nec sentire potest *anchora nostra* solum' (Pamphilus complains that he cannot achieve the object of his desires).

---

[1] For musical terminology used with an underlying sexual meaning in Greek, see Pherecr. 145.16ff. Kock (*Cheiron*), and E. K. Borthwick, *Hermes* 96 (1968), pp. 60ff., especially 67ff.

(ii) Botanical metaphors

Certain plants or vegetables, because of their shape or some other characteristic, may resemble the penis or one of its parts,[1] and hence they sometimes provide metaphors for the organ (for examples in Greek, note Archil. 252 West μύκης, Aristoph. *Ach.* 801 ἐρέβινθος, *Pax* 965 κριθή). But it should be stressed that some objects which are apprehended by some, if not all, speakers as sexual symbols do not give rise to a metaphorical usage. In the appropriate context the object may be interpreted as sexually significant, without the word for the object being formally equated with the word for 'penis'. Augustus' coinage *betizo* = *langueo* (Suet. *Aug.* 87.2) suggests that the plant *beta* was felt to resemble a *mentula languida*, and indeed the comparison is explicitly made by Catullus 67.21 ('languidior tenera cui pendens sicula beta'), but there is no evidence that *beta* was ever in use in an anatomical sense. For botanical similes signifying impotence, see Petron. 132.8 'ter languidior coliculi repente thyrso / ferrum timui', 132.11 'illa solo fixos oculos auersa tenebat, / nec magis incepto uultum sermone mouetur / quam lentae salices lassoue papauera collo' (= Virg. *Aen.* 6.469f. + *Ecl.* 5.16 and *Aen.* 9.436), and in Greek, Automedon, *A.P.* 11.29.3f. αὕτη γὰρ †λαχάνου σισαρωτέρη,† ἡ πρὶν ἀκαμπής / ζῶσα, νεκρὰ μηρῶν πᾶσα δέδυκεν ἔσω.

Plant metaphors are not common in recorded Latin, and some of those which do occur are special cases. *Caulis* (lit. 'stalk, cabbage stalk') deserves special comment. It is found first at Lucil. 281 'praecidit caulem testisque una amputat ambo' (cf. Petronius' use of *coliculus* in a simile at 132.8, quoted above). Later it is the standard word for 'penis' in Celsus (19 times), who adopted it as a calque on καυλός (also a botanical metaphor, 'stem of a plant'), a medical term.[2] καυλός is quoted once from the Hippocratic corpus (*Int.* 14), but it is more common later (e.g. in Galen: note, e.g. *VP* 14.12, II, p. 324.19f. Helmreich τοῦ καυλοῦ – καλεῖται δ' οὕτω τὸ ἀνδρεῖον αἰδοῖον: cf. Rufus *Onom.* 101, Pollux 2.171, Diod. Sic. 32.11.2).

---

[1] The potential sexual symbolism of plants is reflected in the naming of various plants with a suggestive appearance after the sexual organs. See, for example, J. André, *Lexique des termes de botanique en latin* (Paris, 1956), s.vv. *orchis* (note Isid. *Etym.* 17.9.43), *orchites* (*-a*), *satyrion*, *testiculata*, *testiculus*. Cf. *CGL* III.593.48 'Priapisce herba testiculis similis est'.

[2] Medical writers, as we have seen, were not averse from the use of sexual metaphors (see p. 15).

The relationship between the example of *caulis* in Lucilius and those in Celsus is open to question. It seems likely enough that Lucilius employed the metaphor as an *ad hoc* coinage, and that Celsus later introduced the calque in ignorance of the Lucilian passage. One might alternatively argue that Celsus made the calque with an existing Latin slang term in mind (in the manuscripts it is always the dialectal and no doubt vulgar form *colis* which occurs), given that, though at 6.18.1 he comments on the coarseness of the current Latin sexual terminology and the greater acceptability of the Greek, he also shows an awareness there of the need to be comprehensible. But his sexual language in general is recherché rather than slangy. It would be rash to conclude that *caulis* ever had any popular currency. Nor did it become established in the later medical vocabulary.[1] It occurs later only in Theodorus Priscianus (*Eup.* 1.78, p. 82.13), the *Mulomedicina Chironis* (474) and Vindic. *Epit. Alt.* 28 p. 479.17. The author of the *Mulomedicina* was influenced by his Greek source ('ad extremum cole iaculum interpunge', = *Hipp. Berol.* 48.1, *CHG* I, p. 223.16 κεντοῦντες τὸ παρὰ τὸν καυλὸν δέρμα). At 385, however, it is *ueretrum* which corresponds to καυλός ('ueretrum procadet et subinde arriget', = *Hipp. Berol.* 54.1, *CHG* I, p. 239.17f. καὶ ὁ καυλὸς προπίπτει καὶ ἐπαίρεται).

The sort of popular pun which may have been often heard in Latin, but seldom written, is illustrated at Plaut. *Cas.* 911 'num radix fuit? . . . num cucumis?'. Pardalisca leads Olympio on by suggesting that the object which he has touched in the dark (a *mentula*) may have been either a root or cucumber. The sexual symbolism of the cucumber is widely recognised, but there is no evidence for an established metaphorical use of *cucumis* = 'penis' in Latin.

---

[1] καυλός itself was obviously a rather recherché term. There is a misunderstanding of its sense at Cael. Aurel. *Gyn.* p. 4.91f. 'habet (matrix) os, collum, ceruicem, quorum congestio siue unitas ueretrum dicitur'. The Greek (Soran. p. 177.16f. Rose) has ἡ συνδρομὴ δὲ τούτων καυλός, where καυλός is used in another sense, 'neck of the womb' (cf. Aristot. *H.A.* 510 *b*). Soranus Lat. (Mustio) in the corresponding passage uses *caula* (lit. *caulae* = 'opening') as a calque on καυλός in this sense (p. 8.8 'ubi ergo est A posita, orificium dicitur. ubi uero est B, collum dicitur. ubi est C, ceruix dicitur. omnis autem horum concursus caula dicitur'), but Caelius took καυλός not in its technical gynaecological meaning but as equivalent to αἰδοῖον (for *ueretrum* = αἰδοῖον, see below, p. 52), as if καυλός = 'penis' had been generalised to include the female pudenda.

Cicer = 'penis' in the Oxford fragment of Juvenal (6.373 B 'mangonum pueros uera ac miserabilis urit / debilitas, follisque pudet cicerisque relicti'; on *follis* = 'scrotum', see below, p. 75) is a manifest calque on ἐρέβινθος. This and the loanword *chelidon* (χελιδών) (p. 82) in the passage are out of keeping with the normal sexual vocabulary of Juvenal (see p. 221). They raise doubts about its authenticity.

The alleged translation by Apuleius of a passage from an Ἀνεχόμενος ascribed to Menander found at *Anth. Lat.* 712 contains a botanical metaphor at 18: 'thyrsumque pangant hortulo Cupidinis' (*horto* S). Here *thyrsus* suggests the *mentula*; it was the literal meaning 'stem of a plant' which served as the vehicle of the metaphor, as is clear from the phraseology in the rest of the line. For the *thyrsus* of a plant mentioned in a simile describing impotence, see Petron. 132.8 above. The sexual vocabulary of *Anth. Lat.* 712 is extremely artificial, and not that of current slang. *Hortulo* is a calque on κῆπος, and *sulcus* and *aruum* (of the female external genitalia) in 17 ('arentque sulcos molles aruo Venerio') were taken from Virg. *Georg.* 3.136. But *thyrsus* (in its Vulgar Latin form *tursus*) must have been in use in its literal sense (> It. *torso*, etc.).

Ramus = 'penis' can be classified as a botanical metaphor. The sexual symbolism seen in the *ramus* is implicit in the fact that the grammarian Diomedes (*GL* I.451.7) found a *cacemphaton* in the Virgilian expression 'ramum qui ueste latebat' (*Aen.* 6.406). Ausonius, no doubt with the school interpretation of the line in mind, imposed a sexual sense on it at *Cent. Nupt.* 105, p. 216 P. The way in which the word is used at Novius 21 ('puerum mulieri praestare noenu scis, quanto siet / melior, cuius uox gallulascit, cuius iam ramus roborascit?') suggests that for the writer the metaphor was showing no tendency to fade. An example at Prud. *adu. Symm.* 1.115 ('turpiter adfixo pudeat quem uisere ramo') applied to the phallus of Priapus belongs with the other metaphorical designations of the god's *mentula* seen earlier. Nothing in the use of *ramus* indicates that the metaphor had been banalised. The word (in this sense) does not survive in Romance.[1]

---

[1] Goldberger (1930), p. 62 makes the claim that Sp. *ramera* and Pg. *rameira* = 'prostitute' are derivatives of *ramus* = 'penis'. The explanation of these two words can be found in J. Corominas, *Diccionario crítico etimológico de la lengua castellana* (Madrid, 1954), III, p. 987. They reflect a whores' custom of advertising their trade by placing a branch on their doors.

It has been suggested that a proverb at Catull. 94.2 ('Mentula moechatur. moechatur mentula: certe / hoc est, quod dicunt, ipsa olera olla legit') contains a double entendre.[1] The proverb must mean 'like finds like', 'those who are suited come together'. *Olla* may imply the *cunnus*, as at Apul. *Met.* 2.7 (cf. *ollula*, ibid.), and *olera* the *mentula*. This interpretation is by no means certain, given that *olera* is a generic term which does not suggest an object of any particular shape, and is plural.[2]

The only other botanical metaphor from this semantic field in Classical Latin is a calque (*glans*: see below, p. 72).

A remarkable example of protracted botanical symbolism in Medieval Latin is found in the comedy *Lidia* 510ff., the tale of the Enchanted Pear Tree, imitated by Boccaccio, *Dec.* 7.9. There the pear tree (*pirus*) symbolises the penis. Note 548 'nec Pirrus me mouet, immo pirus' (a double entendre, in reference to copulation'), 551 'ut dixi tibi, dux, uitium fuit *arboris*; illa, / esse potest, alios ludificabit adhuc', 554 'sit pirus excisa'. The pears from the tree seem to represent semen: note 544 'sepe quidem Pirro sunt pira missa piro' (certainly a double entendre; given that *piro* is the penis, the pears sent from it must be semen), 510 'iam meliore piro succute, Pirre, pira'.

(iii) Personification and animal metaphors

The penis is often treated as having a personality and life of its own, and partly for this reason it tends to be identified with various animals or birds. Visual symbolism may also lie behind such metaphors. Certain animals (e.g. the snake) have an obvious similarity to the organ.

Personification of the penis is widespread in Latin (for Greek see, e.g. Aristoph. *Thesm.* 1187 and below). The graffito *CIL* IV.1938 'metula tua iubet' shows the popular character of such personifications. Similar personification to this is found in Martial (e.g. 9.2.2 'queritur de te mentula sola nihil', 11.58.11f. 'lota mentula lana / λαικάζειν cupidae dicet auaritiae'; cf. 1.58.3),[3] and in various other writers (e.g. Hor. *Serm.* 1.2.68

[1] So Buchheit, *Hermes* 90 (1962), pp. 254f.
[2] Buchheit's view (*loc. cit.*) that *holus* is obscene at Petron 6.4 and *Priap.* 24.4 is totally implausible.
[3] For further personifications in Martial, see 9.37.9f., 11.78.2.

'huic si muttonis uerbis mala tanta uidenti / diceret haec animus . . .', *Priap.* 83.21 'o sceleste penis . . . licet querare'). The phraseology at Petron. 132.8 ('(mentula) confugerat in uiscera') is comparable with that at *Mul. Chir.* 681 ('ne refugiat (ueretrum)'), *ibid.* ('statim fugiet sibi') and 731 ('ne praecisus intus refugiat'). Both writers no doubt used popular language with an implicit personification. At Ovid *Am.* 3.7.69, Petron. 132.9f., *Priap.* 83.19, 38 and Maxim. *Eleg.* 5.87ff. a *mentula* is rebuked;[1] one might compare the address of the penis at Strato, *A.P.* 12.216 and Scythinus, *A.P.* 12.232. The organ can be said to have a head (e.g. Petron. 132.8, Mart. 11.46.4, *Priap.* 83.5) or an eye (Mart. 9.37.10, Auson. *Cent. Nupt.* 108, p. 216 P.);[2] it can drink (Auson. *Cent. Nupt.* 118, p. 217 P.; for the πέος eating in Greek, see Artem. 5.62, where a dream is reported in which a man fed his penis with bread and cheese as if it were an animal), weep (= 'ejaculate', Lucil. 307 'at laeua lacrimas muttoni absterget amica', *Hist. Apoll. Tyr.* 34 'non potest melius: usque ad lacrimas . . .', Scythinus, *A.P.* 12.232.5),[3] stand or sit (Mart. 3.73.2, Maxim. *Eleg.* 5.96, Apul. *Met.* 9.16 *desidia*),[4] and die (of impotence: Ovid *Am.* 3.7.65, Petron. 20.2, 129.1, Mart. 3.75.6, Maxim. *Eleg.* 5.83).

In Greek various animal metaphors are attested. In Strato the penis is a snake (ὄφις) at *A.P.* 11.22.2, and a number of times a lizard (σαύρα: 11.21.1, 12.3.5, 12.207.1; cf. *CGL* II.185.9 'sira σαύρα τὸ αἰδοῖον', and Isid. *Etym.* 12.4.34, 37 for *saura* in Latin). For κύων = πέος, see, e.g. Aristoph. *Lys.* 158, Argentarius, *A.P.* 5.105.4, Strato, 12.225.2, for ταῦρος in the same sense, see *Suda, s.v.* ταῦρος· τὸ αἰδοῖον τοῦ ἀνδρός, and for ἵππος, see Hesych. *s.v.* ἵππον· τὸ μόριον καὶ τὸ τῆς γυναικὸς καὶ τοῦ ἀνδρός.

The snake was felt to have phallic significance by Latin speakers (see Suet. *Aug.* 94.4, Firm. Mat. *De Errore* 10), but

---

[1] The personification in *Priap.* 83 is remarkably protracted (19ff.). For a similarly extended personification at a much later period, see William of Blois, *Alda* 499ff.

[2] For the 'one-eyed' penis in Greek art, see Dover, p. 132.

[3] For possible 'sobbing' of the *mentula* in Medieval Latin, see Vitalis of Blois, *Geta* 347 'sed sic dum crebro *singultu* colligit iram / ad curtum muto tenditur usque genu', William of Blois, *Alda* 468 'crebros in fine salientis senserat Alda / uirge *singultus*'. Probably, however, *singultus* has here been used in the transferred sense 'throbbing': cf. Pers. 6.72 'cum morosa uago singultiet inguine uena', which may be the source of the medieval usage.

[4] For 'sitting', see also William of Blois, *Alda* 509 'tunc sedet ille tumor'.

there is no certain example of the metaphor in Latin. At *Priap.*
83.33 a *mentula languida* is compared to an *anguis*: 'licebit
aeger angue lentior cubes'. *Natrix* (lit. 'water snake') is taken
in the sense 'penis' by Marx at Lucil. 72 ('si natibus natricem
inpressit crassam et capitatam'), and this interpretation is
certainly possible;[1] note in particular *capitatam*, and cf. p. 72
on *caput*. But it is at least as likely that the word indicated a
type of whip. For whips of this sort, see Isid. *Etym.* 5.27.15
'anguilla est qua coercentur in scolis pueri, quae uolgo scotica
dicitur' (cf. Plin. *Nat.* 9.77). A snake-name used metaphorically
of the penis might be expected to refer to a *mentula languida*
(see *Priap.* 83.33). If *natrix* does have a sexual sense in our
passage, it would have to indicate a *mentula rigida*, to judge
by the limited context. And it is slightly more plausible to see
in *natibus* a reference to the site of a beating than of a sexual
assault (though *nates* occasionally comes close to the sense
'*culus*': Mart. 12.75.3, *CIL* X.4483). Frassinetti (p. 106) inter-
prets Pompon. 113 (118 Ribbeck) ('mirum ni haec Marsa est:
in colubras callet cantiunculam') as a description of an *erectio
penis* ('she knows a charm for the snakes'), on the grounds that
snakes are a common phallic symbol. There is nothing in the
context, or in the use of snake terminology in Latin, to make
this view certain. The gloss *CGL* II.185.9 quoted above, in
which *sira* is equated with σαύρα = αἰδοῖον, is poor evidence
for the currency of *saura* (*sira*) in a sexual sense in Latin,
although it is taken as such by Heraeus (*loc. cit.*). One can
only deduce that *sira* had entered Latin (= 'lizard'), and that
the glossator was familiar with the use of σαύρα = αἰδοῖον in
Greek.

Various bird-names are recorded with the metaphorical
sense 'penis' in Latin. According to Festus (p. 410) *strutheum*
(neuter not masculine: see below) was in use in mime with
this meaning: 'strutheum in mimis praecipue uocant obscenam
partem uirilem, <a> salacitate uidelicet passeris, qui Graece
στρουθός dicitur'. This form must represent the diminutive of
στρουθός, στρουθίον, with the typical vulgar uncertainty concerning the aperture of the vowel in hiatus. *Strutheum* is one
of the few loan-words for a sexual organ in Latin. But in
lower-class speech the influence of Greek, imposed by slaves

[1] For the same interpretation, see W. Heraeus, *ALL* 12 (1902), pp. 265f.,
note.

and freedmen, was strong (witness the *Cena Trimalchionis* of
Petronius), and Greek would no doubt have left its mark on
the language of popular mime. Even in the fragments of Laberius there are a few words of Greek origin which are scarcely
found in Latin but were presumably current in the low social
circles to which numerous Greeks belonged. *Eugium = cunnus*
(p. 83) is especially worthy of mention alongside *strutheum*.
Both words look like lower-class slang terms of the type which
rarely found their way into the literary remains of the
language. They may have been introduced by Greek prostitutes (cf. *calo*, p. 173).

It is implied by *Schol. Pers.* 1.20 that *titus* ('dove') could be
used of the penis ('*ingentes ... Titos* dicit aut generaliter
Romanos senatores a Tito Tatio Sabinorum rege, aut certe a
membri uirilis magnitudine dicti titi'), and the word has reflexes with this meaning in the Romance languages.[1] The evidence of Romance is important in this case as corroborating
inadequate Latin evidence.

Turtur is also quoted with this meaning by a gloss (*cod.
Vatic.* 1469): 'turturilla loci in quibus corruptelae fiebant, dicti
quod ibi turturi opera daretur, id est peni' (see *CGL*, Index,
s.v. for this gloss and its variants). *Turturilla* may have been
soldiers' slang for a brothel: see *CGL* V.524.30 'purpurilla [*sic*]
dicitur locus in castris extra uallum in quo scorta prostant'.[2] A
pun has sometimes been found in *turturem* at Plaut. *Bacch.*
68 ('ubi ego capiam pro machaera turturem'),[3] but this interpretation is not compelling. For *turtures* at symposia, see
Most. 46.

I am also unconvinced by the view[4] that *passer* in Catull. cc.
2–3 and *passerem Catulli* at Mart. 11.6.16 were intended in a
double meaning. Lines 6f. in Catull. 3 ('suamque norat / ipsam
tam bene quam puella matrem') tell strongly against the presence of a double entendre in the poem. Verbs of knowing in
Latin could be used of carnal knowledge (see p. 190). If the
rest of the poem is covertly sexual, *norat* too would have to be

[1] *FEW* XIII, p. 362.
[2] See Heraeus, *loc. cit.*
[3] See F. Buecheler, *ALL* 11 (1885), p. 117, = O. Hense and E. Lommatzsch
Kleine Schriften von Franz Buecheler (Leipzig and Berlin, 1915–1930), III,
pp. 76f.
[4] See most recently E. N. Genovese, *Maia* 26 (1974), pp. 121ff., G. Giangrande, *Mus. Phil. Lond.* 1 (1975), pp. 137ff.

given an obscene sense. But if it were, the comparison *quam puella matrem* would become grotesquely inappropriate. That *passero* and *passera* in modern Italian are said to be capable of an obscene meaning is irrelevant to Catullus, unless it could be shown by late or Vulgar Latin evidence that there was continuity in this respect between Republican Latin and modern Romance. The slang of the modern languages is full of innovations. Mart. 11.6.16 is too obscure to assist in the interpretation of *passer* in Catullus.[1]

Gurgulio = 'penis' at Pers. 4.38 ('inguinibus quare detonsus gurgulio extat?') is probably an animal metaphor. At *TLL* VI.2.2365.31ff. the word is interpreted as the anatomical term *gurgulio*, which normally is used of the upper digestive tract, = 'throat, oesophagus' (so the *Schol.* ad loc.: 'gurgulionem autem nunc penem dicit, cum proprie in gutture sit gurgulio'). How the semantic change might have occurred is not explained. It is true that the penis and other sexual parts are sometimes likened to non-sexual parts of the anatomy (see below, p. 35), and indeed that a *mentula* is compared by Martial to the neck of a vulture (9.27.2 'uulturino mentulam parem collo'), but the *gurgulio* was an internal organ to which the male external genitalia could not be readily compared; such a word would be more appropriately applied to the vagina or rectum, like *guttur* at Plaut. *Aul.* 304 and Mart. 11.21.10. *Gurgulio* must be equivalent to *curculio* (a type of worm), as it is usually taken. The Romance reflexes of *curculio / gurgulio* derive from the form *gurgulio* (e.g. OIt. *gorgoglio*, Fr. *gourguillon*, Sp. *gorgojo*), and *gurgulio* is well attested (e.g. Schol. Juv. 6.276, Isid. *Etym.* 12.8.17, *CGL* III.431.59). The form may have been due to a popular etymology (*curculio* may have been associated with *gurges*, *guttur*, *gula*, or even the anatomical term *gurgulio* itself; note Isidore's statement that the *gurgulio* was composed of almost nothing but *guttur*: 12.8.17 'gurgulio dicitur, quia pene nihil est aliud nisi guttur'). It is impossible to tell whether this figurative use had a basis in popular speech. *Gurgulio* has a parallel in a use of *uermiculus* reported

---

[1] See further Jocelyn, *AJP* 101 (1980), pp. 421ff. I record here without comment the notion of Giangrande, reported (with apparent approval) by P. Howell, *A Commentary on Book One of the Epigrams of Martial* (London, 1980), p. 122, that 'Stella used *columba* as the equivalent . . . of Catullus' *passer*, i.e. *mentula*' (see Mart. 1.7).

in a gloss: *CGL* II.552.13 'uermiculus .. βάλανος ... ἀνδρείας φύσεως'.

There is no evidence that *equus* was used of the penis, despite ps.-Acron's comment on Hor. *Serm.* 2.7.50 'equum appellauit membrum uirile ab eo, quod supra illud sedet'. The passage of Horace has here been misinterpreted, no doubt because of the existence of ἵππος = πέος in Greek (see above, p. 30).

I do not accept that the grammarian Sacerdos (*GL* VI.462.1ff.) interpreted the obscure *sopio* in a remark directed at Pompey as a fish name applied metaphorically to the *mentula* (see below, p. 64).[1]

Proverbial expressions are often given an obscene implication in Latin (see above, p. 29 on Catull. 94.2), and it is this practice which accounts for the use of *lepus* in reference to the *mentula* at Petron. 131.7 ' "uides" inquit "Chrysis mea, uides, quod aliis leporem excitaui" '. *Lepus* would not have had any currency with this meaning, but the tendency for the male organ to be seen as an animal allowed Petronius to give the expression an obscene twist. For this type of double entendre, cf. Mart. 10.90.10 'noli / barbam uellere mortuo leoni', where *leo* suggests the *cunnus*.[2] For proverbial expressions put to a sexual use in various ways, cf. Petron. 25.6, 39.7, 43.8 ('non mehercules illum puto in domo canem reliquisse'; for the proverb, see *H.A.*, *Aurel.* 22.6),[3] *ibid.* ('omnis mineruae homo'), 134.9. The examples in Petronius are all in speeches; they no doubt reflect a form of popular humour. For an example in Greek, see Argentarius, *A.P.* 5.127.6.

I mention finally Ausonius' *ad hoc* use of *monstrum* at *Cent. Nupt.* 108, p. 216 P. 'monstrum horrendum, informe, ingens, cui lumen ademptum'. The creature to whom Virgil (*Aen.* 3.658) was referring was the one-eyed Polyphemus. Ausonius would also have had in mind the image of the penis as one-eyed (see above, p. 30).

---

[1] For this view see Heraeus, *loc. cit.*, Goldberger (1930), p. 46. See further Adams, *Pars pro toto*.

[2] For the proverb, see Otto, p. 190.

[3] See M. S. Smith, *Petronii Arbitri Cena Trimalchionis* (Oxford, 1975), *ad loc.*

(iv) Anatomical metaphors

Sometimes a non-sexual anatomical term is applied metaphorically to the penis (or another sexual part) because speakers spot resemblances between sexual and non-sexual parts.[1] A
similarity was observed, for example, between the penis and
both the nose (Mart. 6.36.1, Phaedr. 1.29.7f.; cf. *Priap.* 12.14,
where it is the clitoris that is called a *nasus*)[2] and the tongue
(Phaedr. 4.15.1, Tert. *Adu. Val.* 1.3), though neither *nasus* nor
lingua occurs as a metaphor for the male organ.

Not infrequently *uena* = 'penis' (Pers. 6.72, Mart. 4.66.12,
6.49.2, 11.16.5, *Priap.* 33.2, Lactant. *Op. Dei* 12.4, p. 43; for
φλέψ in this sense, see Alcaeus, *A.P.* 6.218.1, Leonidas, *A.
Plan.* 261.4). At *Serm.* 1.2.33 ('nam simul ac uenas inflauit
taetra libido') Horace implies by his choice of the plural that
passion causes all the veins of the body to swell (see Cels. 1
prooem. 19 'tum requirunt etiam, quare uenae nostrae modo
summittant se, modo attollant'), but he must primarily have
had in mind the *mentula*.

Penis (lit. 'tail': this meaning was obsolete by the classical
period: see Cic. *Fam.* 9.22.2) was metaphorical when used of
the penis (for examples, see Catull. 15.9, 25.3, Hor. *Epod.* 12.8,
and below; the capacity of the tail of some animals to become
rigid was partly responsible for the image: see *Mul. Chir.* 122
'rigidam caudam habebit'). The metaphor has parallels in
cauda (see below) and Gk. οὐρά (Soph. frg. 1078 Radt, Heysch.
s.v.) and κέρκος (Aristoph. *Thesm.* 239, Herod. 5.45). *Penis* is
described by Cicero as an obscenity (*Fam.* 9.22.2 'at hodie
"penis" est in obscenis'), but the fact that he cites it openly
implies that it was a milder term than *mentula*, which he
alludes to only in a roundabout way. Latin speakers were clear
about the existence of a set of basic obscenities, and about
most of the components of that set, but *obscenus* is used rather

---

[1] See further Adams, *Culus*, p. 249.

[2] It became a commonplace in the Middle Ages that the shape and state of
the nose reflected the nature of the genitalia. See *Flos Medicinae Scholae
Salerni* 1790, in S. De Renzi, *Collectio Salernitana* V (Naples, 1859), p. 51 'ad
formam nasi dignoscitur hasta Priapi', and Michael Scotus, *De Physiognomia*
22. I have not had access to either of these works. In the seventeenth century
see Regnier de Graaf, *Tractatus de uirorum organis generationi inseruientibus*
132 (with Jocelyn, p. 74, n. 152). Ancient caricatures often give the nose a
phallic appearance (e.g. *CIL* IV.7248, *Graffiti del Palatino* II.36). For mutilation of the nose as a castration symbol, see Virg. *Aen.* 6.497, Mart. 2.83.

loosely as an evaluative term in reference to the sexual language. One finds it employed on the one hand to describe a basic obscenity (*Priap.* 29.1), on the other a veiled sexual allusion (Sen. *Contr.* 1.2.23). Evaluative terms are characteristically vague. Cicero's assertion is undermined by the presence of *penis* not only in the annalist Calpurnius Piso (frg. 40, quoted by Cicero, *loc. cit.* to show that the word had once been decent) but also in Sallust (*Cat.* 14.2), neither of whom is likely to have tolerated an outright obscenity or vulgarism. It is also used by later satirists (Pers. 4.35, 4.48, Juv. 6.337, 9.43), who rejected the primary obscenities. At worst *penis* was probably a risqué colloquialism of educated speech. Its lack of currency, at least in the later period, is shown by its failure to survive into the Romance languages (there is one example in the Pompeian inscriptions, *CIL* IV.1939). Indeed in later Latin there are signs that it was upgraded into an acceptable educated term. Though it is avoided by early medical writers, there are examples in Marcellus Empiricus (7.20, 33.2, 33.36). It is the standard term for the male organ in the Scholia to Juvenal (12 times), and is also found in Arnobius (*Nat.* 5.18, 5.28), the *Historia Augusta* (*Comm.* 10.9), Porphyrio (on Hor. *Epod.* 8.17, 12.8) and the grammarian Sacerdos (*GL* VI.462.3). Arnobius in particular employed a highly decent sexual vocabulary. Augustine, commenting on Sallust's use of the word, implies that for him it was not sordid or vulgar: *Dialect.* 7, Migne 32, p. 1414 'unde enim fit, quod non offenditur aurium castitas, cum audit "manu uentre pene bona patria lacerauerat"? offenderetur autem, si obscena pars corporis sordido ac uulgari nomine appellaretur? in hoc autem sensum animumque utriusque deformitas offenderet, nisi illa turpitudo rei quae significata est, decore uerbi significantis operiretur, cum res eadem sit, cuius utrumque uocabulum est'. It is also an indication of the tone of the word, that whereas to call someone a *mentula* or a *uerpa* was to deliver an aggressive insult, *penis* could be used *pars pro toto* as an affectionate term: Suet. *Vit. Hor.* 'praeterea saepe eum inter alios iocos "purissimum pene<m>" et "homuncionem lepidissimum" appellat'.[1]

Cauda = 'penis' is securely attested only in Horace (*Serm.* 1.2.45, 2.7.49), who may have innovated in using the word thus, perhaps on the analogy of the semantic change which

---

[1] See Adams, *Pars pro toto.*

οὐρά, κέρκος and *penis* had undergone. The reflex of *cauda* in French (MFr., NFr. *queue*) can mean 'penis', but whether it reflects a Latin usage or is a French innovation is open to question, in view of the absence of examples in Old French and also of examples of *cauda* = 'penis' in later Latin.[1] The *TLL* (III.627.32ff.) and *OLD* (*s.v.*) mistakenly cite Cic. *Fam.* 9.22.2 'caudam antiqui "penem" uocabant' as evidence that the ancients used to call the penis *cauda*. What Cicero meant is that the ancients used to call the tail *penis* (whereas in Cicero's own day that word had come to be restricted to its sexual sense). The only other alleged parallels quoted by the *TLL* are glosses based on Cicero's remark (note *Gloss. Vat.*, *CGL* IV. praef. p. xviii 'penem antiqui codam uocabant, id est uere-trum'; the glossator has here made the same mistake as some modern lexicographers). Another possible example not found in the dictionaries[2] is in the *Testamentum Porcelli*: 'dabo don-abo . . . mulieribus lumbulos, pueris uesicam, puellis caudam'. But the piglet has already left what appear to be his sexual organs (*lumbulos*: see p. 48) to women, and he seems to have moved on to children (when *puella* is juxtaposed with *puer* it almost always means 'female child'). Boys are to get his blad-der and girls his tail as some sort of plaything. On balance it would seem best to treat *cauda* in Horace as an *ad hoc* meta-phor. Indeed one of the examples occurs in a description of sexual intercourse using the image of horse riding (*Serm.* 2.7.47ff.: see p. 165). In this context *cauda* is overtly figurative: it is appropriate on the literal level to the horse, and on the figurative to the man. One cannot argue from such an extended metaphor that *cauda* had passed into common parlance. In view of the limited attestation of the usage it is also unjustified to see in *codati* at *CIL* IV.7240 an allusion to the male organ (despite the editor *ad loc.*).

Bracchia macra is possibly applied to the phallus of Priapus at *Priap.* 72.4 'quia si furaberis ipse / grandia mala, tibi brac-chia macra dabo', but the passage is obscure. The writer may have had in mind the resemblance between an extended arm

---

[1] There are numerous examples of *cauda* = 'penis' in William of Blois (*Alda* 470, 486, 489, 492, 496, 510, 514), which might conceivably have been taken from the vernacular language, but it is equally likely that the highly literate author knew the usage from Horace. Note too Matthew of Vendôme, *Art. Versif.* 1.53.78 'cauda riget'.

[2] It is referred to by Herter, 'Genitalien', 3.

and an erect *mentula*, particularly of the type seen in grotesque caricatures in ancient art.[1]

Neruus (lit. 'sinew', 'tendon') = 'penis' (Cic. *Sest.* 16,[2] Hor. *Epod.* 12.19, Petron. 129.8, 131.6, 134.1, Juv. 9.34, 10.205; cf. Catull. 67.27 *neruosius illud*, and *eneruo* = 'castrate' at Aug. *Ciu.* 6.7 'homines [= *gallos*] infeliciter ac turpiter eneruatos atque corruptos'; cf. νεῦρον at Plat. com. frg. 173.19 Kock) should not be classed as a figurative usage of the above type. The penis could be regarded as a tendon or group of tendons: see Galen, *VP* 15.3, p. 344.24f. Helmreich τὸ νευρῶδες σῶμα = 'penis', and Vindic. *Epit. Alt.* 28, p. 479.14 'ueretrum est oblongum, natura neruosum ...' for its sinewy character (for the 'tendons of the penis', see Archil. 252 West ἀλλ' ἀπερρώγασι μύκεω τένοντες). It is a form of specialisation when the generic word for a tendon (*neruus*) or a group of tendons (*nerui*: for the plural referring to the penis, see the examples from Cicero and Petronius cited above) is applied to just one of the body's tendons or groups of tendons (see further below, pp. 44ff. on semantic specialisation as a form of euphemism). There is usually an ambiguity about the plural use; though the writer may have been thinking of the penis, his statement might be interpreted as referring to all of the tendons of the body, including those of the penis (note in particular the Petronian examples above).

It has already been seen (pp. 21, 25) that *neruus* in another sense ('string' of a bow or lyre) is sometimes used metaphorically of the male organ. One should not lump all sexual examples of the word together.

(v) Scholastic metaphors

Since any aspect of everyday life may generate sexual metaphors, it is not surprising that those with grammatical or scholastic tastes should have found sexual symbols among the objects of their interest. A combination of letters, *C* and *D*, is sexually significant at *Priap.* 54: 'CD si scribas temonemque

---

[1] Dover, p. 131 mentions a representation of a satyr's penis which resembles an arm.

[2] There is little doubt that Cicero was thinking of the penis here: '... nullis suis neruis – qui enim in eius modi uita nerui esse potuerunt hominis fraternis flagitiis, sororiis stupris, omni inaudita libidine exsanguis'. See Grassmann, p. 66, n. 154.

insuper addas, / qui medium uult te scindere, pictus erit'. The
penis and scrotum are formed by the combination of the two
letters, with an attached pole, *temo* (for *temo* = 'pole', see,
e.g. Col. 6.2.7). The author may have recalled Aristophanes'
use of δέλτα to signify the shape of the female pubic hair at
Lys. 151. Letter puzzles of various types are typical of the
preciosity of epigram (in Latin cf. *Priap.* 7, 67, Auson. *Epigr.*
85, p. 343 P.). Ausonius went a stage further in forcing a
sexual implication on the shape of letters (or combinations of
letters) at *Epigr.* 87, p. 344 P., and he also gave the practice
a more scholastic setting. The grammarian Eunus, a *cunnilingus*, sees in certain objects of his professional interest (letters)
a resemblance to the object of his sexual interest (the *cunnus*).[1]
The letter *rho* is also made to symbolise the penis and scrotum:
10 'quid, imperite, P putas ibi scriptum, / ubi locari I convenit
longum?'

It was above all in the Medieval period that grammatical
and scholastic sexual metaphors came into vogue. For metrical
terminology, see Matthew of Vendôme, *Art. Versif.* 1.53.79f.
'metri dactilici prior intrat syllaba, crebro / impulsu quatiunt
moenia foeda breues'. The first syllable of the dactyl, the long,
represents the penis, and the two short syllables, the *breues*,
the testicles. For the suggestive use of grammatical terminology, see *Magister Golyas de quodam abbate*[2] 'soloecizans partem
masculini parti foeminini generis associat', where the 'part of
masculine gender' has an obvious enough meaning: cf. the *De
Monachis*[3] 'ubi possunt hoc discerni, dum suppositum in genere
feminino et appositum in masculino et conueniunt in metro
dactilico ascendendo ex hoc in illud'. An extended parody of
grammatical phraseology can be found in Lehmann, text no.
13, pp. 223f., but anatomical terminology scarcely plays a part
in this piece (see p. 179).

In the twelfth century the language of logic is sometimes
employed in sexual double entendre. See *Babio* 441f. 'quo te
concludam, dabit entimema sophisma, / et quod non falles, tale
sophisma feres' (= 'I will castrate you'; the enthymeme was a

---

[1] I have discussed this puzzling epigram elsewhere: 'An epigram of Ausonius
(87, p. 344 P.)', forthcoming in *Latomus*.

[2] For a text of this work, see T. Wright, *The Latin Poems commonly attributed
to Walter Mapes* (London, Cambden Society, 1841), pp. xlff.

[3] See Lehmann, text no. 4, pp. 192ff.

syllogism reduced from three to two or even one proposition).[1]
At 406 ('cum duo de trinis planget adempta sibi') the image is
also typical of Medieval interests (two members of the 'Trinity'
may be lost); see further 451 'nunc erit eclipsis, non ludes
amodo ternis; / cimbala sola dabis; nolo nocere magis'.[2]

(vi) A medical metaphor

In Mart. 11.60 punning use is made of medical terminology.
The use of *aluta* = 'penis' requires explanation.

> Sit Phlogis an Chione Veneri magis apta requiris?
>   pulchrior est Chione; sed Phlogis ulcus habet,
> ulcus habet Priami quod tendere possit alutam
>   quodque senem Pelian non sinat esse senem,
> ulcus habet quod habere suam uult quisque puellam.

Aluta indicated a type of soft leather with various functions.
The predominating use of the word is medical: it refers to an
emplastrum, or plaster (e.g. Scrib. Larg. 81, 82, 229).[3] Phlogis
had an *ulcus* which could *tendere* ('stretch', or 'make erect')
even Priam's piece of soft leather (his plaster, or his *mentula*).
For the *mentula languida* likened to leather, see Petron. 134.9,
Mart. 7.58.3f., 10.55.5. An *ulcus* in medical terminology was
a sore (e.g. Marc. Emp. 33.3), in this case no doubt the sore of
satyriasis: note Serv. Virg. *Georg*. 1.151: 'nam proprie robigo
est, ut Varro dicit, uitium obscenae libidinis, quod ulcus uocatur'. This disease was believed to afflict women as well as men,
and female sufferers forced even strangers to satisfy their lust
(Cael. Aurel. *Acut*. 3.178 'haec omnia etiam mulieribus pas-
sione affectis, sed plus in ipsis praeualet prurigo ob naturam.
indecenter enim ipsa in loca manus mittunt prurientibus uerendis, atque omnes ingredientes appetunt et suae libidini ser-
uire supplices cogunt'). Satyriasis was not simply a state of
mind: it had physical symptoms, such as *dolor, incendium* and
tentigo (Cael. Aurel. *Acut*. 3.176 'sequitur autem aegrotantes
uehemens genitalium tentigo cum dolore atque incendio, cum
quodam pruritu immodico in ueneream libidinem cogente,
mentis alienatio, pulsus densitas . . .'; cf. *CGL* III.605.3 'sati-
riasis impetus desiderii circa ueretrum sine mensura cum do-

---

[1] See Faral (cited above, p. 15 n. 3), p. 62, and H. Laye in Cohen, II, p. 53.
[2] See Fulgheri (cited above, p. 15 n. 3) on both of the last two passages.
[3] See *TLL* I.1799.53ff.

lore et pruritu'), redness of the parts, and even fever (Cael. Aurel. *Acut.* 3.182). The burning sensation associated with the desire for intercourse in this disease is probably alluded to in Phlogis' name (< φλόξ, 'flame'),[1] whereas Chione is cold (< χιών, 'snow'). These puns are rendered the more likely by the fact that Martial makes an obvious pun on the name *Chione* in another epigram (3.34 'digna tuo cur sis indignaque nomine, dicam. / frigida es et nigra es: non es et es Chione': Chione is worthy of her name in that she is cold, but unworthy of it in that she is not white). Satyriasis was treated by the application of poultices or plasters to the affected parts (Cael. Aurel. *Acut.* 3.180, 181, 183, 184). At the literal level then Priam is envisaged as carrying out the appropriate medical treatment. But the treatment really required was sexual intercourse. Hence the usual female attendants (see, e.g. Cael. Aurel. *Acut.* 3.184) were useless; it was a male physician who was required (6 'ulcus ... / quod sanare Criton, non quod Hygia potest'). This line corresponds to 11.71.7f. 'protinus accedunt medici medicaeque recedunt, / tollunturque pedes. O medicina grauis!' (Leda has claimed she is *hysterica*, and 'queritur futui ... necesse sibi' (2)). Clearly the literal use of *ulcus* in 11.60 has nothing to do[2] with the metaphorical use at Lucr. 4.1068, indicating the festering sore of passion.

(vii) Tools, implements, vessels

Words for 'implement, tool, vessel' and the like are often used metaphorically of the penis: note, for example, Eng. *tool*, and σκεῦος at Antistius, *A. Plan.* 243.4. Some terms for specifically agricultural tools used metaphorically have been seen above.

Vas (lit. 'implement, vessel', with two handles) had a risqué ring over a long period, with the *ansae* perhaps suggestive of the testicles. It is first used in a pun (= 'male genitalia, testicles': on the failure of euphemistic and metaphorical language to make a consistent distinction between the penis and testicles, see p. 69) at Plaut. *Poen.* 863, where the speaker is carrying certain vessels ('refero uasa salua'; cf. 847 'nunc domum haec ab aedi Veneris refero uasa'). The sexual force

---

[1] See Buchheit, *Hermes* 90 (1962), p. 256.
[2] As suggested by Buchheit, *op. cit.*, p. 256 n. 3.

which the word is to be given is prepared in the previous line
('facio quod manufesti moechi hau ferme solent').[1] *Vas* is found
again in a double entendre (the context is Homeric) at *Priap.*
68.24 ('hic legimus Circen Atlantiademque Calypsun / grandia
Dulichii uasa petisse uiri'). It is also possible that there is a
double entendre in a freedman's speech at Petron. 57.8: 'tu
. . . uasus fictilis, immo lorus in aqua'.[2] The formulaic phrase
lorum in aqua is used in reference to impotence at Petron.
134.9 (cf. Mart. 7.58.3f., 10.55.5), and the speaker may have
identified the referent *(pars pro toto)* with a *mentula languida*
after inadvertently making an identification with a *mentula
rigida* in *uasus fictilis*. The sexual use of *uas* may have belonged in the classical period to that class of non-banal metaphors which tended to occur in jokes or puns (cf. *testis*).
Petronius shares various such words with Plautus (cf. p. 43 on
peculium, pp. 20f. on *gladius*). Further evidence for the currency of *uas* in a sexual sense is provided by *uasculum* (Petron.
24.7) and the derivative *uasatus* = *mentulatus* (*H.A., Hel.* 5.3,
8.6, 9.3, 31.6).[3] There is a late example of *uas* at Aug. *Ciu.*
14.23 'ita genitale aruum uas in hoc opus creatum seminaret';
here *aruum* is taken from Virg. *Georg.* 3.136.

Vas occurs in the form *basus* (with the typical vulgar misspelling involving *b* and *u*; for the ending, see Petron. 57.8
above) at *GL* VII.167.9: 'praeterea excipi cognouimus haec
quae subiecta sua cum interpretatione reddemus, quae nusquam nisi in diuersis cottidianis glossematibus repperi, . . .
basus φαλλός, τὸ αἰδοῖον τῶν βιολόγων'. At *CGL* II.469.52
('φαλλός habus') Heraeus' conjecture[4] *basus* = *uasus* is undoubtedly right; he points to a variant reading *babus* at *GL*
VII.167.9 which might have provided the intermediary between *basus* and *habus*. *Basus* = 'penis' is of course a ghost
word, if it is interpreted as anything other than a vulgar
misspelling of *uas(us)*. It is not clear what Frassinetti had in
mind when he printed 'oro te, base, per lactes tuas' at Pompon.

---

[1] On the 'Plautine' character of this passage, see Fraenkel, *Elementi Plautini*,
p. 46.

[2] See Smith (cited above, p. 34 n. 3) *ad loc.*

[3] Krenkel, p. 85 does not explain why he reads the graffito *CIL* IV.2268 in
the form 'Myrtale uassatos fellas'. The editor reads *Cassacos*, which is taken
at *CIL* IV, Index, p. 233 as a possible name.

[4] *Die Sprache des Petronius und die Glossen* (Gymn.-Programm Offenbach
a. M., 1899), pp. 42f., = J. B. Hofmann (ed.), *Kleine Schriften von Wilhelm
Heraeus* (Heidelberg, 1937), p. 136.

57 and argued (pp. 37, 103f.) that the *lar familiaris* appeared
in phallic form and was addressed as *base*.[1] In any case the
context does not permit the deduction that there is an address
of the phallus here.

A rough parallel to *uas* is provided by the use of *instrumentum* at Petron. 130.4 'non me sed instrumenta peccasse' (cf.
Arnob. *Nat.* 5.14), a usage not noted in the *TLL*. Cf. the double
entendre in William of Blois, *Alda* 483 'instrumenta, quibus
tam dulces utar in usus / edoceas, ubi sint inuenienda michi!'.

In the anonymous medieval comedy *Lidia*, *malleus* 'hammer'
suggests the *mentula* at 124: 'malleus incude terque quaterque
sonat' (for *sonare* used in a similar sense, see Mart. 7.18.12,
Priap. 83.37; cf. Auson. *Cent. Nupt.* 119, p. 217 P.).

I mention finally an interpretation by Forberg (p. 272 n.) of
Auson. *Epigr.* 77.8, p. 341 P., which he would print in the form
'Lucili uatis subulo pullipremo', deriving *subulo* from *subula*
(lit. 'awl'; hence *subulo* 'one who uses the awl') in a metaphorical sense 'penis'. But *subulo* is a conjecture (Ferrarius). *Subpilo* (*sub pilo* Z, *pilio* G), 'one who plucks from below', is
metrically possible (cf. *depilo*), but it does not carry conviction.
One should obelise.

(viii) 'Private property'

Peculium (lit. 'private property') = 'penis' tends to occur in
puns. At Plaut. *Pseud.* 1188 the pun is unintentional; it is the
next speaker, a *leno*, who gives the word a sexual force: 'mea
quidem haec habeo omnia, / meo peculio empta. BA. nempe
quod femina summa sustinent'. There may also be a pun in a
speech by Ascyltos at Petron. 8.3: 'prolatoque peculio coepit
rogare stuprum'. Just as *uas* (*uasculum*) is used in a sexual
sense by both Plautus and Petronius, and then taken up by
the *Historia Augusta* (in the derivative *uasatus*), so *peculium*
is used *sens. obsc.* at *H.A., Hel.* 9.3 (where *uasatus* also occurs):
'prodebatur autem per eos maxime, qui dolebant sibi homines
ad exercendas libidines bene uasatos et maioris peculii opponi'.
The author of the *H.A.* had a taste for risqué usages which he
had found in earlier comic writings (or in the current language

---

[1] The fragment is quoted by Priscian, *GL* II.213.5. The manuscript variants
are *baso, basso, base, basse* (*uaso* Ribbeck).

of risqué jokes). *Peculiati* = *mentulati* occurs at *Priap.* 52.7 ('pulcre pensilibus peculiati').

Sexual metaphors reflect the nature of the society in which they are coined. In modern societies machinery has often been interpreted as sexually symbolical,[1] whereas the rustic imagery that we have seen typifies a general feature of the Latin vocabulary. In Medieval Latin (particularly that of the twelfth century) some of the classical classes of metaphors are still in evidence, but current intellectual interests inspired certain coinages (see the section on scholastic metaphors above). Little sociolinguistic variation can be observed in the metaphors which have been discussed. Scholastic metaphors would have had a place only among the educated. Most of the other metaphors were no doubt readily comprehensible to all classes (but *strutheum, titus* and *turtur* seem to have been vulgar).

3. Euphemisms

(i) Specialisation

By 'specialisation' I mean the use in reference to the sexual organs alone of an imprecise word which might strictly have indicated either a large area of the body or other bodily parts as well as the genitalia. Such general terms are usually capable of suggesting both the male and female parts indifferently, though a few show a tendency to be used of the one part or the other. Often the general word will be complemented by a specifying adjective or phrase, as for example in the expressions 'the female parts' or 'the genital organs'. Strictly one should reserve the term 'specialisation' for those examples without specification (e.g. 'the parts'), but I have not completely excluded phrases with specification from the following discus-

---

[1] Even Latin speakers were conscious of a sexual symbolism in certain types of mechanical device. Hence the application of the terms *masculus* or *femina* to various parts of machines, depending on their function: Vitr. 9.8.11 'in eo autem minus tympanum includatur cardinibus ex torno masculo et femina inter se coartatis', 10.7.3 'ita de supernis in modiolis emboli masculi torno politi et oleo subacti conclusique regulis et uectibus conmoliuntur'. No anatomical metaphor from this sphere is known to me.

sion. It would also be pointless here to restrict oneself to examples which signify the male organ alone.

Pars (sing. and plural) usually has some form of specification. For examples without a complement, see, e.g. Pompon. 86 'partem insipui conclusi condepsui',[1] Petron. 138.7 'resipiscerent partes ueneficio, credo, sopitae', Cael. Aurel. *Gyn.* p. 11.254 *partibus* = Soran. p. 188.17 Rose τὰ μέρη. A common type of complement is a relative clause: e.g. Petron. 129.1 'funerata est illa pars corporis, qua quondam Achilles eram' (for the idea, cf. Antipater, *A.P.* 12.97.5f. εἰ γὰρ τῷ τά τ' ἔνερθε τά θ' ὑψόθεν ἴσα πέλοιτο, / ἦν ἂν 'Αχιλλῆος φέρτερος Αἰακίδεω), 132.12 'cum ea parte corporis uerba contulerim, quam . . .', Ovid *Ars* 2.707, *Priap.* 37.8f., 48.1f., *Anth. Lat.* 309.9f., 317.6f.[2] Examples of *pars* with adjectival complements strictly belong elsewhere, since *pars* + adj. is usually equivalent to the neuter substantival use of the adjective. For *pars genitalis* = *genitalia*, see, e.g. Cael. Aurel. *Acut.* 3.175, Porph. on Hor. *Serm.* 1.5.100, for *pars obscena* = *obscena*, see Ovid *Ars* 2.584, *Priap.* 9.1, and for *pars pudenda* = *pudenda*, see Ovid *Ars* 2.618. A special class of examples are those in which the complement is a demonstrative, as at Ovid *Ars* 3.804 *pars . . . ista. Ipsae partes* (and *ipsa loca*) are particularly common in late medical works, where they are probably intended as equivalents of τὰ μέρη (for which see above) or τὰ μόρια, with the demonstrative playing the role of the definite article. For *ipsae partes* see Theod. Prisc. *Eup.* 2.33, Soran. Lat. (Mustio), pp. 26.1, 53.15, 117.9, and for *ipsa loca*, see Cael. Aurel. *Acut.* 3.178, *Gyn.* p. 38.964, Soran. Lat. (Mustio) pp. 17.16f., 22.13.

Particula = 'penis' (Theod. Prisc. *Eup.* 2.32, p. 130.14 'satyriasis . . . tensionem particulae cum assidua patratione auidissimam facit') may be unique, but *pars* is so common in various sexual senses that it is not surprising to find a diminutive without diminutive force. Theodorus may have used the word as a calque on μόριον.[3]

---

[1] See Frassinetti, p. 104 on the possible interpretation of this fragment (which he prints as no. 82).

[2] It is not only *pars* which takes such complements. Cf., e.g. Plaut. *Cas.* 921 'saepit ueste id qui estis <mulieres>', Varro *Rust.* 2.4.10 'naturam qua feminae sunt', *Priap.* 37.2 'membrum . . . unde procreamur', ps.-Acron on Hor. *Serm.* 1.2.45 'dicitur enim membrum illud, in quo libido est, esse salsum'.

[3] See T. Sundelin, *Ad Theodori Prisciani Euporista Adnotationes* (Uppsala, 1934), p. 80.

Membrum is largely restricted to the male organ (but see Auson. *Epigr.* 78.4, p. 341 P., 87.3, p. 344 P., and perhaps Lucr. 3.346). For examples without a complement, see, e.g. Prop. 2.16.14 (plural, but the implication is unmistakable), Ovid *Am.* 2.15.25, 3.7.13, *Fast.* 4.221 (plural). *Membrum uirile* is not found until Tertullian (*Adu. Val.* 1.3). One combination which may be unique is *masculina membra* at Phaedr. 4.16.13.

In a suggestive context *corpus* could take on a precise anatomical sense. For the implication 'penis' see Ovid *Am.* 3.7.28 'languent ... / corpora'; cf. Lucr. 4.1056 'iacere umorem in corpus de corpore ductum', *Mul. Chir.* 177 'corpus earum, id est uirginalis' (of the female parts). For the sense 'testicles' see p. 69. Cf. Galen's νευρῶδες σῶμα = 'penis' (*VP* 15.3, p. 344.24f. Helmreich).

Sometimes the whole person is mentioned instead of the appropriate sexual part. At *Priap.* 47.4 ('illius uxor aut amica riualem / lasciuiendo languidum, precor, reddat') the author could have spoken of the *mentula* as *languida*, but he generalised the state of impotence to the whole body. The uses of *corpus* seen above are similar. For comparable descriptions of impotence, see, e.g. the use of *iners* at Catull. 67.26, Hor. *Epod.* 12.17, of *langueo* at Hor. *Epod.* 12.14, *Epist.* 1.20.8, and of *inutilis* at Sen. *Contr.* 2.5.14, Schol. Juv. 6.366 (cf. *utilis* at Mart. 11.81.3). For erection, see Catull. 32.11 'pertundo tunicamque palliumque', Hor. *Serm.* 1.5.83f. 'somnus tamen aufert / intentum ueneri', 2.7.47f. 'me / natura intendit', Mart. 6.71.3 'tendere quae tremulum Pelian Hecubaeque maritum / posset' (cf. 11.58.1, 11.73.3), *Priap.* 4.1 'rigido deo' (cf. 45.1),[1] 68.32 'ad arrectos ... procos'. And for castration, see Sen. *Contr.* 10.4.17 'exoletos suos ... amputant', Isid. *Etym.* 12.7.50 'ueteres enim abscisos gallos uocabant' (cf. *CGL* V. 559.3). The female parts are alluded to thus at (e.g.) *CIL* IV.10004 'Eupla laxa landicosa', Mart. 11.81.2 'et iacet in medio sicca puella toro', *Priap.* 18.2 'laxa ... femina'. This type of euphemism is also found in Greek: note, for example ps.-Luc. *Asinus* 51 περιβάλλεταί με καὶ ἄρασα εἴσω ὅλον παρεδέξατο, in which context Apuleius adopted a similar expression: *Met.* 10.22 'totum me prorsus, sed totum recepit'.

The use of *medius* with a personal noun or pronoun is a

---

[1] Contrast the (medieval) nominal usage *rigor* = 'penis', in William of Blois, *Alda* 509 (cf. 471).

common method of indicating inexplicitly the genital area of
male or female (or the *culus*: see p. 116). For the penis referred
to in this way, see Petron. 129.6 'medius [fidius] iam peristi',
Mart. 2.61.2 'lambebat medios inproba lingua uiros', 3.81.2
'medios lambere lingua uiros'; cf. Catull. 80.6 'grandia te medii
tenta uorare uiri'. For the female parts, see Mart. 7.67.15 'sed
plane medias uorat puellas'. This euphemism was at least as
old as Plautus: see *Cas.* 326 'ego edepol illam mediam dirruptam uelim'.

At *CIL* IV.5396 'Ccosuti fela ima' *ima*, in association with
fellare, is presumably meant to suggest the male genitalia.
Elsewhere *imum* is used of the buttocks / anus (Aug. *Ciu.*
14.24). Contrast *alta* (*Priap.* 28.5, Auson. *Cent. Nupt.* 105,
p. 216 P.) and *summa* (Mart. 11.46.6, *Priap.* 74.2) of the mouth
put to a sexual use.

For *loci* (*-a*), see p. 94.

(ii) Adjoining parts

Sometimes an explicit word is replaced by a word which
strictly designates a neighbouring part without sexual significance. Of words in this category *inguen* was the most common, and the most readily interchangeable with the *voces
propriae* for the sexual organs. Various words which might
seem on occasions to be used as synonyms of *mentula* or *cunnus*
can be shown to retain their literal sense, or at least to be not
genuinely interchangeable with the sexual terms. I discuss
below not only the genuine equivalents of *mentula*, but some
other words which have been falsely equated with it.

The euphemistic use of *inguen* (= *mentula* or *cunnus*) was
established in all types of Latin, from obscene graffiti (*CIL*
IV.1230 'Fortunatus futuet te inguine'), epigram (e.g. Mart.
3.81.5, 7.30.5, *Priap.* 1.6, 83.43, Auson. *Epigr.* 78.3, p. 341 P.,
86.1, p. 344 P., 87.1, p. 344 P.) and satire (e.g. Hor. *Serm.*
1.2.26, 1.2.116, Juv. 1.41), to high poetry (Virg. *Georg.* 3.281
'(hippomanes) lentum destillat ab inguine uirus', Ovid *Met.*
14.640) and educated prose (Suet. *Tib.* 44.1, *Nero* 29).[1] For

---

[1] *Inguen* enjoyed a vogue in the sense 'penis' in later Medieval Latin. See
Vitalis of Blois, *Geta* 363, 364, 365, anon. *Baucis et Traso* 251. The presence
of the usage in the *spurcum additamentum* at Apul. *Met.* 10.21 is not incon-
sistent with a twelfth century composition for that piece (see p. 230).

inguen as a substitute for *cunnus*, see Tib. 2.4.58, Mart. 3.72.5, Juv. 9.4, 10.322.

ὀσφῦς, a synonym of *lumbus*, is used of the penis twice in ps.-Luc. *Asinus* (9 καὶ ἡ ὀσφῦς ἰσχυέτω, 51 ἡ δὲ τῆς τε ὀσφύος τῆς ἐμῆς εἴχετο).[1] *Lumbus* too is sometimes said to be capable of signifying the sexual organs of male or female (or the *culus*),[2] but the equation is usually unconvincing in Classical Latin. In sexual contexts *lumbus* (generally in the plural) for the most part occurs in descriptions of the movements of seduction or copulation (e.g. Catull. 16.11 'duros nequeunt mouere lumbos', Mart. 5.78.28 'uibrabunt sine fine prurientes / lasciuos docili tremore lumbos', *Priap*. 19.4 'crisabit tibi fluctuante lumbo', Apul. *Met*. 2.7 'lumbis sensim uibrantibus spinam mobilem quatiens placide, decenter undabat'; cf. Lucil. 278, Lucr. 4.1267, Arnob. *Nat*. 2.42), where it should be taken in its original sense (note particularly *spinam* in the last passage quoted). A belief that the loins were the site of sexual desire (*Schol. Pers*. 1.20 'bene dicit lumbum et non animum; dicitur enim libido lumbis immorari', Isid. *Etym*. 11.1.98 'lumbi ob libidinis lasciuiam dicti, quia in uiris causa corporeae uoluptatis in ipsis est, sicut in umbilico feminis') would account for examples such as Pers. 1.20 'cum carmina lumbum / intrant et tremulo scalpuntur ubi intima uersu' and Juv. 6.314 'nota bonae secreta deae, cum tibia lumbos / incitat'. In a few other places *lumbus* seems to be used of a vaguely defined area within which the sexual organs might be situated, but not necessarily conterminous with them: Pers. 4.35 'penemque arcanaque lumbi / runcantem', Juv. 6.024 'saepius in teneris haerebit dextera lumbis', 8.16 'si tenerum attritus Catinensi pumice lumbum / squalentis traducit auos'. But it must be admitted that *lumbus* is often in ambiguous contexts (e.g. Juv. 9.59), and it might sometimes have been interpreted as a euphemism for a sexual organ. The diminutive *lumbulus* must refer to the male sexual organs in the *Testamentum Porcelli* ('dabo donabo ... mulieribus lumbulos'), and *delumbo* seems to mean 'castrate' at Sen. *Contr*. 10.4.2 ('alium distorquet, alium delumbat'). In Christian Latin *lumbus* is used of the loins (i.e. genitalia) as the source of procreation (e.g. Arnob. *In Psalm*. 7 p. 333D 'de lumbis meis egressus est').[3]

---

[1] This meaning is not noted by L-S-J.
[2] So Lewis and Short, *s.v.* II.A.
[3] *TLL* VII.2.1809.40ff.

Abdomen signifies the male genitalia at Plaut. *Mil.* 1398
('quin iamdudum gestit moecho hoc abdomen adimere, / ut
faciam quasi puero in collo pendeant crepundia'). The punishment in question is that dealt to adulterers (castration: puns
on *testis* occur repeatedly in the passage), but since the soldier's *abdomen* can be likened to the phallic amulets worn by
boys (1399; cf. Varro *Ling.* 7.97),[1] it is clear that the speaker
is thinking of the genitalia in general. For other sexual examples of *abdomen*, see *CGL* V.632.2 'abdomen ueretrum',
Don. on Ter. *Eun.* 424 'abdomen in corpore feminarum patiens
iniuriae coitus scortum dicitur' (one may doubt whether *scortum* had this meaning, but *abdomen* seems to be used as an
established term). The sexual use of *abdomen* must derive
from the meaning 'belly' (for which see Cic. *Pis.* 41, *Sest.* 110,
Sen. *Ben.* 7.26.4, Juv. 4.107).

Latus ('side') is often vaguely suggestive of the male genitalia, but it was subject to a contextual restriction and not
genuinely interchangeable with *mentula*. *Latus* is used particularly often to express the general site of the exhaustion
which might follow intercourse: e.g. *Priap.* 26.11 'defecit latus',
Suet. *Cal.* 36.1 'latera sibi contubernio eius defessa etiam uociferatus est', Apul. *Met.* 8.26 'defectis iam lateribus'. It is by no
means as narrow in reference as *mentula*. Sexually significant
examples of *latus* alluding to the male role are widespread (cf.
Catull. 6.13, Ovid *Am.* 2.10.25, *Ars* 2.413, Petron. 130.8, Mart.
7.58.3, 12.97.4, *Priap.* 83.45).[2]

In the Scholia to Juvenal *colyphia* at Juv. 2.53 ('luctantur
paucae, comedunt coloephia paucae') is interpreted as a term
for the *membrum uirile*: 'pulmentum siue membrum uirile'.
This is an appropriate place to mention the word, but I am not
convinced by this interpretation. A *colyphium* (κωλύφιον, a
derivative of κῶλον)[3] was a cut (or preparation) of meat eaten
particularly by athletes (Schol. Juv. *loc. cit.*, *CGL* V.55.39). It
can be deduced from Petron. 70.2 that it was a piece of pork

---

[1] See Herter, 'Phallos', 1733 on line 1399.
[2] It should be added that in allusions to sexual intercourse *latus* is sometimes
said to join *latus*: Lucil. 305 'tum latu componit lateri', Ovid *Her.* 2.58 'lateri
conseruisse latus', Matthew of Vendôme, *Milo* 123 'rex continuat lateri latus'.
Note too the grammatical parody in Lehmann, no. 13, p. 224.45 'iungatur
latus lateri'.
[3] See Chantraine II, p. 605, *s.v.* κῶλον; cf. Heraeus, *Die Sprache des Petronius
und die Glossen*, p. 19 = *Kleine Schriften*, pp. 85f. (cited above, p. 42 n. 4).

(cf. *Mul. Chir.* 495, 813).[1] Vegetius (who was not thinking specifically of the pig) defines it as the joint of the hip: *Mul.* 2.82.5 'uino et oleo calefacto colefium ipsum, hoc est iuncturam coxae, diutissime confricant'. On this evidence *colyphium* used as a culinary term might have indicated the whole or part of a ham. If the word could genuinely be used of the penis, it would have been transferred from one part of an animal's anatomy to a different (but adjoining) part of the human body. It is true that culinary terms were sometimes applied to parts of the human anatomy in Latin (e.g. *cerebellum* at Petron. 76.1), but one would at least like to have an intermediate sense (such as 'human hip-joint, haunches') attested as partial corroboration of the scholiast's note. The possibility cannot be ruled out that the scholiast was led astray by *comedunt*, in which he may have seen the common metaphor of 'eating' the genitalia (= *fellare* or *cunnum lingere*). For *comedo* used in this way, see *CIL* IV.2360 (see p. 139). The view advanced by some of the scholia and accepted by Herter[2] that *colyphium* could signify a phallic-shaped loaf (cf. ὀλισβοκόλλιξ) is at best dubious, since it would then have to bear a striking diversity of culinary senses.

Ile is sometimes said to be capable of referring to the pudenda,[3] but it does not genuinely display the semantic development seen in *inguen*. Medical writers thought of the *ilia* as arteries situated somewhere in the lower abdomen: note Plin. *Nat.* 11.208 'inter eam (uesicam) et aluum arteriae ad pubem tendentes, quae ilia appellantur'. It is impossible to determine what they had in mind.[4] There is another sense of the word, of indeterminate relationship to the first, in medical and other Latin. It could indicate the sides of the lower belly between the hip and the pubes ('flanks'):[5] Cels. 4.1.13 'ipsa autem ilia inter coxas et pubem imo uentre posita sunt. a quibus ac pube abdomen sursum uersus ad praecordia peruenit'. Hence there were two *ilia*: see Cass. Fel. p. 131.3 'iuxta umbilicum initians frequenter a sinistro ilio, aliquando a dextro', *id.* p. 118.20 'utraque ilia cooperies'. In this sense the

[1] See Heraeus, *loc. cit.*, J. André, *RPh* 40 (1966), pp. 48f.
[2] 'Phallos', 1744.
[3] See Lewis and Short, *s.v.* (= 'private parts').
[4] See A. Ernout and R. Pépin, *Pline l'Ancien, Histoire Naturelle, Livre XI* (Paris, 1947), *ad loc.*
[5] See *TLL* VII.1.325.61ff.

word sometimes appears in sexual contexts. The *ilia* could be described hyperbolically as 'bursting' as a result not only of emotion (see Virg. *Ecl.* 7.26 'inuidia rumpantur ut ilia Codro') but also of sexual activity: see Catull. 11.20 'nullum amans uere, sed identidem omnium / ilia rumpens',- 80.8 'clamant Victoris rupta miselli / ilia'. This use of *ilia* is not unlike that of *latus* above; it is based on the literal sense 'flanks', and does not reflect a change of meaning to 'penis'. For 'bursting' of this type, see p. 151.

At Catull. 63.5 *ile* comes closer to a narrow sexual sense: 'deuolsit ilei acuto sibi pondera silice'. *Ilei pondera* is a circumlocution = 'testicles'. There are no grounds for seeing in the use of *ile* here a development of a medical use of the word signifying an artery between the penis and testicles.[1] *Ile* has been used loosely of the lower belly or pubes within which the sexual part (*pondera* = 'testicles') is located, or to which it could be said to belong.

In Christian Latin *femur* sometimes expressed the organs of procreation, whether of male or female.[2] In Classical Latin the thighs are regarded as a sexually significant part, in that the space between them was the site of the sexual organs (for *femur* in various types of sexual contexts, see, e.g. Tib. 1.8.26, Ovid *Am.* 3.14.22, *Priap.* 83.25, Apul. *Met.* 8.25, 10.24, *Apol.* 33 (*interfeminium*), Auson. *Cent. Nupt.* 109, p. 216 P., *Epigr.* 87.5, p. 344 P.), but the word itself is not equated with either *mentula* or *cunnus*.

(iii) 'Parts of shame'

The standard euphemism for the sexual organs of male and female in Greek was αἰδοῖον. There are various comparable words and expressions in Latin, some of them inspired by the Greek word. I make no consistent distinction in the following pages between the senses 'penis' and 'female genitalia', because euphemisms of this type are not restricted to the one part or the other.

---

[1] See *TLL* VII.1.325.56f.
[2] See *TLL* VI.1.472.68ff.

(a) Veretrum

The first example of *ueretrum* in recorded Latin is at Varro *Men.* 282 'dein immittit uirile ueretrum'.[1] Its presence in Suetonius (*Tib.* 62.2 'repente ueretris deligatis') and Scribonius Largus (234 'ad ueretri tumorem lens ex aqua cocta et trita rosaceo oleo mixta prodest') suggests that it already had a polite and euphemistic flavour. These examples, along with that at Phaedr. 4.15.1 ('a fictione ueretri linguam mulieris. / adfinitatem traxit inde obscaenitas'), are specialised in the sense 'penis'.[2] The word was not always to have such a specific meaning.

Veretrum became very common in later medical Latin. Since it was interpreted as a derivative of *uereor*, it came to be regarded as an equivalent of αἰδοῖον. For the association of *ueretrum* with αἰδοῖον see, e.g. *CGL* II.206.32, III.311.60, 349.71, 351.55. So in Caelius Aurelianus' *Gynaecia* it is used to translate αἰδοῖον, as at p. 6.150 'femininum . . . . ueretrum', = Soran. p. 181.24f. Rose γυναικεῖον αἰδοῖον. See also Hippocr. *Aer.* 9, p. 21.10, 22, translating αἰδοῖον (-α). The derivation from *uereor* may be a popular etymology,[3] given the early restriction of meaning, and the fact that the word is generally in the singular: other Latin euphemisms of this type are regularly in the plural, unlike αἰδοῖον (an exception to this rule for Latin is at Jul. Obs. 25 'puer ex ancilla quattuor pedibus manibus oculis auribus et duplici obsceno natus').

Some glosses give *ueretrum* as a general equivalent of αἰδοῖον, but others restrict it to the male organ (*CGL* V.335.56, 398.42; cf. Isid. *Etym.* 11.1.103 'idem et ueretrum, quia uiri est tantum, siue quod ex eo uirus emittitur'). Clearly the earlier specialised sense tended to linger on. These variations of meaning suggest that the word had no place in ordinary speech. Theodorus Priscianus' glossing of *ueretrum* at *Eup.* 1.27, p. 82.1 ('de ueretri hoc est naturae causatione') implies that it was a learned and perhaps obscure term. It does not

---

[1] Despite the assertion of Ernout and Meillet, *s.v.* that the word is found first in Imperial Latin.

[2] The context at Phaedr. 4.15.1 is fragmentary, but it would seem that the tongue is being likened to the penis.

[3] *Veretrum* < *uereor* certainly looks like a possible formation (see M. Leumann, *Lateinische Laut- und Formenlehre⁶* (Munich, 1977), p. 313), but it does not seem to have the typical instrumental sense of such words (cf. *aratrum*, *feretrum*, *rutrum* (<*ruere*), *rostrum* (<*rodere*), *rastrum* (<*radere*); contrast *fulgetrum*).

survive in the Romance languages. The numerous different forms which the word has in vulgar texts may be partly due to its lack of currency: e.g. *CGL* II.206.32 *ueratrum*, Anon. *Med.* ed. Piechotta LV *beletrum*, Oribas. *Syn.* 1.40 Aa, p. 71.7 Mørland *beretrum*, Vindic. *Gyn.* 13 (*G*), p. 442 *deretrum*.

In medical writings one finds the same differences of meaning as in glosses. In the *Mulomedicina Chironis* and Vegetius' *Mulomedicina*, in both of which *ueretrum* is a favoured word,[1] it usually means 'penis' (note, for example, *Mul. Chir.* 385, where *ueretrum* translates καυλός: see above, p. 27), although occasional examples might be interpreted more generally, = αἰδοῖον. In both Theodorus Priscianus (in addition to the example quoted above, see *Eup.* 1.77, p. 82.2, 2.32, p. 130.9) and Vindicianus *ueretrum* indicates the penis (note Vindic. *Epit. Alt.* 28, p. 479.14 'ueretrum est oblongum, natura neruosum . . .'). Some writers in whom *ueretrum* means both 'penis' and 'female genitalia' (and hence = αἰδοῖον) are Caelius Aurelianus (e.g. *Acut.* 3.179 = 'penis', 184 *muliebre ueretrum*, *Chron.* 4.133 *uirilis ueretri*, 5.89 = 'penis', *Gyn.* p. 67.123f. *ueretri feminini*, 118.1522 *feminino ueretro*) and the Latin translator of Hippocr. *Aer.* (at 22, p. 43.26, = 'penis'; cf. 9, p. 21.22f. *ueretro femineo*; the Greek has αἰδοῖον (-α) in both places). At *CGL* III.248.57 *ueretrum* is given the narrower sense 'testicle' ('δυδίμων ueretrum'). It is not unparalleled for αἰδοῖον or its Latin equivalents to be applied to this part. Because of the generality of such euphemisms they could be made to suggest any taboo area. For αἰδοῖον = *testes*, see *Hipp. Berol.* 48.1, *CHG* I, p. 223.7 αἰδοῖον τὸ προπεσόν, εἰ μὴ δύναται πάλιν εἰς τὴν χώραν ἀποκαταστῆναι (cf. *Mul. Chir.* 473 *testis*).

Veretrum was not confined to medical Latin in the later period. Note, e.g., Arnob. *Nat.* 5.14 'amputationes uirilium ueretrorum', 6.26 'nuda corpora feminarum et ueretrorum magnitudines publicatae', *Lex Frisionum* 22.57 (*MGH, Leg. Tom.* III, p. 678) 'si ueretrum quis alium absciderit'.

(*b*) *Verenda*
Another close equivalent of αἰδοῖον was *uerenda* (note *CGL* III.248.61 'αἰδοῖα uerenda'). Like the Greek word, it carried no implication that the sexual parts were shameful or disgusting (lit. 'parts that inspire awe, respect'). *Verenda* is first used

---

[1] In Vegetius, see, e.g. 1.46.1, 1.51, 1.61.1, 2.79.6, 2.79.12.

extensively by Pliny the Elder, no doubt as a deliberate equivalent of αἰδοῖον. It is only from book 20 onwards that *uerenda* becomes common.[1] In book 11, for example, where there is a discussion of the parts of the body based largely on Aristotle, *genitale* (*-ia*) occurs a number of times (246, 261, 263), and indeed it is common elsewhere in the work (see below, p. 58). Since Aristotle's stock word was αἰδοῖον, it is clear that Pliny at this stage was content to employ an established Latin euphemism without seeking a close equivalent of the word in his source. Another early example of *uerenda* is in the Younger Pliny (*Epist.* 3.14.2 'alius os uerberat, alius pectus et uentrem, atque etiam (foedum dictu) uerenda contundit'). Although *uerenda* probably started as a calque, it must have found its way into popular speech (cf. *uirga*, p. 14 above), since it has reflexes in the Romance languages.[2] *Verenda* occasionally occurs in late medical works, but it is outnumbered by *ueretrum*. Marcellus Empiricus has it 7 times (*ueretrum* 43). In Caelius Aurelianus it sometimes (but not always) translates αἰδοῖον: e.g. at *Gyn.* p. 86.619, = Soran. p. 335.2 Rose τοῦ αἰδοίου; contrast *Gyn.* p. 66.92, where *muliebrium uerendorum* renders γυναικείων τόπων (Soran. p. 306.14 Rose). For a non-medical example in the later period, see Arnob. *Nat.* 5.27.

(c) Verecunda

Verecunda in various forms (positive, comparative) and combinations was probably regarded as an equivalent of αἰδοῖον. For *loca uerecundiora*, see Marc. Emp. 8.177, 10.82, 31.16, 31.23, *CGL* IV.596.31, 604.2. Cf. Arnob. *Nat.* 4.10 'ceteraque alia locis posita in obscuris et uerecundioribus partibus', Vict. Vit. 3.22 'uerecunda . . . membra'. For the substantival use, see e.g. Isid. *Etym.* 19.22.29 'uerecunda corporis his uelentur' (cf. 19.33.1, Vict. Vit. 2.24).[3] Like *ueretrum* and αἰδοῖον, *uerecunda* also turns up as an equivalent of *testiculi* (*CGL* IV.326.30 'culei uiriles testiculi uerecunda').

Verecundia is given the same sense as *uerenda* at *CGL*

---

[1] For examples, see O. Schneider, *In C. Plini Secundi Naturalis Historiae Libros Indices* (Gotha, 1857–8), *s.v.*; cf. A. Önnerfors, *Pliniana, in Plinii Maioris Naturalem Historiam Studia Grammatica Semantica Critica* (Uppsala, 1956), p. 23.

[2] *REW* 9227.

[3] For the genitive *corporis*, see Plin. *Epist.* 6.24.3 *uelanda corporis*, Justin 1.6.14 *obscena corporis*.

V.428.34 'uerenda uerecundia'.[1] The spelling may be a scribal slip for *uerecunda*, but it is at least as likely that, like various other abstracts (see p. 57), *uerecundia* had acquired a concrete anatomical sense. Indeed at Aug. *Ciu.* 7.24 ('sic dehonestatur nouae nuptiae uerecundia') it is in a context in which its meaning is transitional. The word still means 'modesty', but since the reference is to the ceremony whereby the bride sat on the phallus of the god Mutunus Tutunus, it could also be taken in a concrete meaning. Similarly *pudicitia* approaches the concrete sense '*cunnus*' at Mart. 10.63.8 'contigit et thalami mihi gloria rara fuitque / una pudicitiae mentula nota meae'. In Spanish *vergüenzas*, the reflex of *uerecundia*, can be used of the sexual organs.[2]

(d) Pudenda et sim.

The substantival use of *pudenda* is found first in Seneca, where it expresses indifferently the sexual parts of both sexes: *Dial.* 6.22.3 'totas in uiscera manus demittentium et non simplici cum dolore pudenda curantium'. The adjectival use is attested earlier: Ovid *Ars* 2.618 'conueniunt thalami furtis et ianua nostris / parsque sub iniecta ueste pudenda latet' (also general in sense). For more specific examples (= 'penis'), see [Auson.] *Per. Od.* 6, p. 395 P. 'ut erat nudus, erupit, foliorum oppositu pudenda uelatus', Aug. *Ciu.* 7.21 'pudenda uirilia'.[3] *Pudenda* is one of various words in imperial Latin which, unlike αἰδοῖον and the Latin words discussed above, were not neutral in tone, but (at least etymologically) implied an attitude of shame or disgust.[4] Nevertheless they may have been regarded by some users as Latin equivalents of αἰδοῖον: note *CGL* II.220.18 'αἰδοῖον penes [= *penis*] pudendum'. *Pudibilis* (used adjectivally) at *H.A., Hel.* 12.2 ('ad honores reliquos promouit commendatos sibi pudibilium enormitate membrorum') is simply a recherché variant for *pudendus*.[5]

Other words (or expressions) in this category are *turpia*

---

[1] Cf. H. Rönsch, *Semasiologische Beiträge zum lateinischen Wörterbuch* (Leipzig, 1887–9), I, p. 76.

[2] See C. J. Cela, *Diccionario secreto* (Madrid – Barcelona, 1968–71), II, pp. 587f.

[3] For *pudenda* = 'anus', see Min. Fel. *Oct.* 28.9.

[4] On the disgusting nature of the sexual organs, see Cic. *Off.* 1.126.

[5] Cf. *genitabilis* at Arnob. *Nat.* 4.28 ('genitabiles habuisse partes deum') for the commonplace *genitalis*.

(*membra*, etc.) (e.g. Sen. *Ben.* 7.2.2, Auson. *Epist.* 14.34, p. 246 P.; cf. Sall. *Jug.* 85.41 'uentri et turpissumae parti corporis')[1] and *obscena* (either accompanied by a noun or in the neuter plural).[2] For the singular use of *obscenum*, see Jul. Obs. 25, quoted above p. 52. See further Cels. 5.20.3, 5.28.14B, 6.18.1, Ovid *Met.* 9.347, *Priap.* 9.1, Suet. *Cal.* 58.3, *Dom.* 10.5, Justin 1.6.14. For *inhonesta*, see Isid. *Etym.* 11.1.102 'dicuntur autem ista et inhonesta, quia non habent eam speciem decoris sicut membra quae in promptu locata sunt' (cf. *membrum inhonestum* at Aug. *Ciu.* 7.21, Avell. p. 433.13; cf. *Vit. Patr.* 6.3.11).[3] More circuitously the genitalia are in various places called the 'parts which cannot honourably (*honeste*) be named': [Sall.] *Epist. ad Caes.* 2.9.2 '. . . quoius nullum membrum a flagitio aut facinore uacat? lingua uana, manus cruentae, pedes fugaces; *quae honeste nominari nequeunt, inhonestissima*', Inu. in Cic. 3.5 'cuius nulla pars corporis a turpitudine uacat, lingua uana, manus rapacissimae, gula immensa, pedes fugaces: *quae honeste nominari non possunt, inhonestissima*'. Whoever was imitating whom, the phraseology was hackneyed. R. G. M. Nisbet[4] compares Rutilius Lupus 1.18 (*Rhet. Lat. Min.*, ed. Halm, p. 11) 'membra quae non possumus honeste appellare', which is part of a translation of a lost speech of Lycurgus. Cf. Cic. *Phil.* 2.47 'sed iam stupra et flagitia omittamus: sunt quaedam quae honeste non possum dicere', [Cic.] *Inu. in Sall.* 8.22 'ut ea dicam, si qua ego honeste effari possim'.

Pars tegenda (*Priap.* 1.7, = 'penis') is not unlike the other usages discussed in this section (cf. Ovid *Met.* 13.479, where the same phrase is equivalent to *cunnus*). Cf. *uelanda* at Plin. *Epist.* 6.24.3, *secretum, -a* at Arnob. *Nat.* 5.23 ('secreta rimantem summotisque arbitris circumiectas prolibus diripientem membranulas') and Amm. 28.1.28 ('ne uelamen quidem secreto membrorum sufficiens retinere permissa est'), and *interdicta* at Hor. *Serm.* 1.2.96.

---

[1] E. Skard (*Symb. Osl.* 21 (1941), p. 100 n. 3) compares Dem. 18.296 τῇ γαστρὶ καὶ τοῖς αἰχίστοις.

[2] For *obscenus* = *pudendus* ('id quod pudorem mouet'), see *TLL* IX.2.159. 70ff.

[3] See further *TLL* VII.1.1597.37ff.

[4] *JRS* 48 (1958), pp. 30ff.

(iv) Abstracts

Elsewhere[1] I have shown that various abstract nouns take on the concrete sense 'penis' in Latin (see also above, p. 55 on *uerecundia*), usually when complemented in a suggestive way by a word more applicable to an anatomical term. For *uenus* (usually = 'sexual intercourse': see p. 189) = *mentula*, see (e.g.) Mart. 3.75.6 'non uiuit sollicitata uenus' (cf. Lucr. 4.1270, Mart. 1.46.2, Juv. 11.167, *Priap.* 83.4); note too Apul. *Met.* 2.16 'et iam saucius paulisper inguinum fine lacinia remota *impatientiam ueneris* Fotidi meae monstrans'. *Amor* is used in the same way at *Met.* 9.16 'amoris languidi desidia tuos uolentes amplexus discruciat'. For *libido* = 'penis', see Petron. 87.1, *H.A.*, *Hel.* 5.2.[2] Note too Vulg. *Is.* 47.2 'denuda turpitudinem tuam', of the *uirgo filia Babylon* (cf. *CGL* V.510.38, for the text of which see *CGL* VII.93).

At Maxim. *Eleg.* 5.84 ('nec uelut expositum surgere uidit puella opus') *opus* ('penis') could be derived from the common use of the word = 'sexual intercourse' (see p. 157); the semantic change would be identical to that in *uenus*. *Surgere* is the complement which facilitates the concrete interpretation. Editors (following Ommerenus) unnecessarily change to *onus*.

(v) Descriptive and functional designations

A few terms can be called 'descriptive' or 'functional', in that they refer to a physical characteristic or function of the organ. This property need not be inherently offensive or sexual. The antiquity of such designations is shown by *podex* (cf. *pedo* = 'fart') = 'anus'. Nevertheless descriptive anatomical terms are not common in Latin, and some of the sexual examples are *ad hoc* coinages with a humorous intention.

The author of the *Priapea* (52.7) innovated in applying *pensilia* (lit. 'the things which hang') to the male genitalia.[3] For a verb of hanging used in reference to the male genitalia, see Lucil. 536 'pellicula extrema exaptum pendere onus ingens'.

The commonplace *genitale* (*-ia*, *partes genitales*, etc.) can also be classified as a functional designation. *Partes genitales* occurs first in Lucretius (4.1044), where it may be a conscious

---

[1] Adams, 'Anatomical terminology', p. 52.
[2] At Sen. *Contr.* 1.2.23 *libido* is ambiguous between the senses 'semen' and 'penis': for the word in the first sense, see *TLL* VII.2.1334.34ff.
[3] Cf. *Babio* 446 'moechus es, et Fodio *pendula membra* dabis'.

rendition of γεννητικὰ μόρια, which is common in Greek medical writers (e.g. 18 times in the *VP* of Galen: see the index of
Helmreich, *s.v.*). But there is no need to interpret the substantival uses of *genitale* and *genitalia* as deliberately Grecising,
especially in view of their distribution. *Genitale* is found first
at Cels. 4.1.11 (of the female pudenda), but neither it nor its
plural form is admitted elsewhere by Celsus, and it remains
rare in later medical Latin (for an example, see Marc. Emp.
26.128).[1] It is used mainly by Pliny the Elder.[2] Pliny, as we
have seen (p. 54), seems to have accorded *genitale* and *genitalia*
much the same status as αἰδοῖον (-α) in book 11. He was not
followed by later technical writers, and indeed he himself
eventually turned to *uerenda* as an equivalent of αἰδοῖον (-α)
(see p. 54). For a non-technical singular example = 'penis'
Apul. *Met.* 10.22 is worth quoting: 'reputans . . . quo pacto
. . . mulier tam uastum genitale susciperet'. In the corresponding passage of ps.-Luc. *Asinus* (51) no such word occurs
(τοῦτό μ' εἰς δέος οὐχὶ μέτριον ἦγε, μὴ οὐ χωρήσασα ἡ γυνὴ
διασπασθείη).[3] *Genitale* was obviously a polite euphemism, but
it did not have a particularly scientific tone after the first
century. The distribution of the plural *genitalia* is much the
same.[4] It is especially common in Columella and Pliny, but
later is not markedly frequent in the medical language (but
see, e.g. Marc. Emp. 4.46, Cael. Aurel. *Acut.* 3.176). It became
an educated genteelism rather than a technical term after the
first century (it is, for example, common in Christian writers),
and even in the early Empire it is not confined to scientific
works (see, e.g. Tac. *Hist.* 5.5, Juv. 6.514).[5] Among the various
phrases in which adjectival *genitalis* occurs may be mentioned
(e.g.) *genitalia loca* (e.g. Col. 6.36.2, 7.3.16) and *natura genitalis* (Marc. Emp. 33.49). Such combinations too seem to have

[1] For examples, see *TLL* VI.2.1815.42ff.
[2] See *TLL*, loc. cit., citing some 16 examples.
[3] In much the same passage the *spurcum additamentum* (at Apul. *Met.* 10.21)
has the extraordinary *genius= genitale* ('inspiciens quod genius inter antheras
excreuerat'). This is based on the gloss *CGL* IV.588.32f. 'genium genitale
naturale numen uirgo seu uigor', which is a conflation of two separate glosses,
'genitale naturale' and 'genium numen uigor': see Mariotti, pp. 243f. = pp. 62f.
Nothing could better illustrate the spurious artificiality of the *additamentum*.
[4] See *TLL* VI.2.1815.59ff.
[5] In the second passage ('qui rapta secuit genitalia testa') *genitalia* could
mean 'genitals' in general, or 'testicles'. Designations of the male pudenda are
sometimes ambiguous between the senses 'penis' and 'testicles' (see below,
p. 69).

had a vogue after Celsus in the first century,[1] both in technical (Columella) and educated prose. They are not numerous in later medical writings. It was *ueretrum, uerenda* and certain equivalent words and combinations which achieved popularity in the later medical register.

For *tumor* and *rigor* = *mentula*, see William of Blois, *Alda* 509 'tunc sedet ille tumor, pendet rigor ante superbus' (cf. 470f.).

(vi) *Natura, naturalia, necessaria, sexus*

Natura was a widespread euphemism for the sexual parts of either sex (but note Pelagon. 153 'supra naturam, qua meiat', where it is closer to the sense 'urethra'). It was neither overtly technical nor vulgar, but generally acceptable in the educated language. There are examples in technical writers (e.g. Varro *Rust.* 2.2.14, 2.4.10, 2.7.8, Plin. *Nat.* 10.181, 28.176, Marc. Emp. 33.49, 33.71, *Mul. Chir.* 132,[2] Veg. *Mul.* 1.33, 2.53.2 (= 'penis'), Theod. Prisc. *Eup.* 1.77 tit., Cass. Fel. pp. 118.15, 22, 119.2 (= 'penis'), Pall. 14.60), but insufficient to establish the word as a technical medical term. Indeed it is avoided by Celsus. Examples in obscene literature are few (*Atell. nom. inc.* 4 Ribbeck, = Suet. *Tib.* 45, *Priap.* 38.2, in a pun). The use of the word by Cicero (*Nat.* 3.56, *Diu.* 2.145) shows that it had a polite tone.

Natura has an exact parallel in Gk. φύσις, and it is likely that learned users of the word sometimes had in mind the Greek usage,[3] even if *natura* did not necessarily originate as a calque. It is a mistake to say that the sexual use of φύσις is not securely attested until after the corresponding use of *natura*:[4] note the fourth century *defixio IG* III.3.89a.6[5] Δέσποτα Ἑρμῆ, κάτοχε κάτεχε Φ(ρύ)νιχον κ[α]ὶ τὰ ἀκρω[τήρ]ια αὐτοῦ το(ὺ)ς πόδας: τὰς χεῖρας ψυχὴν φύσιν τὴν π[υ](γή)ν. It seems likely that, because the sexual parts (and anus: note Jul. Obs. 40 'posteriore natura solidus', = *culus*; cf. 26 'solidus posteriore

---

[1] See *TLL* VI.2.1813.81ff.
[2] For further examples in this work, see the index in Oder, p. 396.
[3] So Shipp, p. 560. Shipp points out that in the modern language φύσις is probably used only of the αἰδοῖον.
[4] So A. Pellicer, *Natura, Étude sémantique et historique du mot latin* (Paris, 1966), p. 360.
[5] R. Wuensch (ed.), *Defixionum Tabellae Atticae.* Dr D. M. Bain drew my attention to this inscription.

naturae parte') performed certain 'necessities of nature' (cf. Cic. *Off.* 1.126), they came to be called 'parts etc. of nature' (Varro *Rust.* 3.12.4 'inspicere oportet foramina naturae', Phaedr. 4.16.5 'naturae partes'), and then more simply 'nature'.[1] There is little to be said for the view[2] that *natura* was associated by some speakers with *nascor*, indicating 'place of birth', i.e. 'female genitalia'. All the examples in Varro indicate the female parts, but Cicero uses the word indifferently of the penis (*Nat.* 3.56) and female parts.

Naturale (*-ia*) stands to *partes naturales* (Cels. 7.18.1) as *genitale* (*-ia*) to *partes genitales*. It is used for the first time by Celsus, in whom it is the standard word for the female pudenda. It was no doubt coined on the analogy of the existing sexual use of *natura*. Celsus seems deliberately to have devised recherché terminology for the sexual organs (cf. *caulis*). I deal with *naturale* for convenience here alongside *natura*, though it might strictly have been postponed to Chapter III. In the singular *naturale* is used by Celsus specifically of the vagina (e.g. 5.26.13 'at cum uulua percussa est, dolor inguinibus et coxis et feminibus est; sanguinis pars per uulnus, pars per naturale descendit'; cf. 7.26.1C, 7.26.4). In the plural it could have a slightly less specific sense ('female pudenda', including the labia): e.g. 2.7.15 'feminae uero oras naturalium suorum manibus admotis scabere coguntur' (cf. 7.18.1). Celsus also employed *naturalia* sometimes as an inclusive term for the sexual parts of both sexes (e.g. 1.9.3, 5.20.4), and in the Toledo fragment there are two examples of the singular *naturale* used in the same way: line 37 'subestque, ut in prioribus, iunctarum quoque partium dolor simulque naturalis ipsius maxime dum urina descendit' (cf. 19).[3] *Naturale, -ia* is not used unambiguously by Celsus in the sense 'penis',[4] though there is an example

[1] See Pellicer, pp. 363f.
[2] Pellicer, pp. 361f.
[3] See U. Capitani, *Maia* 26 (1974), pp. 161ff. (see p. 170 for *naturale*).
[4] Though I should interpret both examples in the Toledo fragment as meaning 'genitalia, urethra' (of male and female indifferently), a case might be made that Celsus primarily had in mind an affliction of males. Similarly at 4.28.1 ('est etiam circa naturalia uitium, nimia profusio seminis; quod sine uenere, sine nocturnis imaginibus sic fertur, ut interposito spatio tabe hominem consumat') Celsus may have been thinking above all of males, but since gonorrhoea was believed to be an affliction of both sexes he could have intended *naturalia* quite generally of the genitalia of both sexes.

I am grateful to the Director of the *Thesaurus Linguae Latinae* for supplying me with some of the examples discussed here.

of *partes naturales* at 7.18.1 indicating the male genitalia in general.

Naturalia (along with *partes naturales*, etc.) continued to be used occasionally after Celsus, mainly in technical prose, and sometimes as a result of one writer imitating another. It never again had the status that it was given by Celsus. Columella, who knew the work of Celsus, has it twice, once as a general term (6.30.4 'de bitumine collyrium inseritur naturalibus'), and once of the pudenda of a mare (6.27.10). Pelagonius, who drew on Columella, has *naturalia loca* twice (152, 162), the second time ('aliud Columellae . . . e bitumine collyrium insere naturalibus locis') in a passage based on Col. 6.30.4. The example at 152 ('spongias calidas locis omnibus naturalibus admoueas') is general in sense. In the *Mulomedicina Chironis* *naturalia loca* is also used of the sexual organs of a mare (748). An example in Theodorus Priscianus (*Eup.* 3.8, p. 230.2 Rose), referring to the female pudenda ('fumigiis bene olentibus ad inferiora naturalia prouocabo'), was mistakenly changed to *naturam* by Rose.[1] One non-technical writer who admitted the usage (again of the female pudenda) was Justin: 1.4.2 'hic per somnum uidit ex naturalibus filiae . . . uitem enatam'. See further Nonius p. 153 L., Isid. *Etym.* 4.7.34, *CGL* IV.460.33, V.511.13; note also Firm. Mat. *Math.* 8.4.6 *naturale corpus = cunnus*.

Occasionally in late Latin *naturalia* is used of the male genitalia: Pallad. *Hist. Mon.* 1.14 (Migne 74, p. 292) 'postula enim quaedam, quam carbunculum uocant, nata est in ei ipsis uerendis, ac tanta per sex menses aegritudine laborabat, ut naturalia ipsius putrefacta radicitus caderent', *Mythogr.* 1.102, p. 33 Bode 'Iuppiter patri naturalia resecauit et in mare proiecit', ps.-Tit. *Epist.* 409 (*Rev. Bénéd.* 37 (1925), p. 58) 'naturalium dolor utique adulteri sunt et pederasti'.

φύσις occasionally found its way into technical works as a loan-word: e.g. Anon. *Med.* ed. Piechotta LXXXI 'delabet sibi fisin' (= *cunnum*).

The genitalia are sometimes 'necessary parts' or the like in Latin: *necessariae partes* (Gaius *Inst.* 3.193, Firm. Mat. *Math.* 8.31.7), *loca necessaria* (*Mul. Chir.* 52, 179, 364, Firm. Mat. *Math.* 5.3.26), *necessaria* (Firm. Mat. *Math.* 4.19.19). Cf. ἀναγκαῖον at Artem. 1.79, p. 95.22 Pack τὸ ἀναγκαῖον (τοῦτο γὰρ τὸ

[1] See Sundelin (cited above, p. 45 n. 3), pp. 67f.

αἰδοῖον καλεῖται): cf. 1.45, p. 52.5, *Suda, s.v.* ἀναγκαῖον. These Latin expressions have been taken as calques on the Greek usage,[1] but it is impossible to be certain; one would not expect such a calque in Gaius. The sexual organs performed certain 'necessities of nature' (cf. ἀναγκαῖα at Xen. *Cyr.* 8.8.11), and hence they were 'necessary parts'. The euphemism might have developed independently in both languages.

Sexus comes close to the concrete sense 'sexual part' at Plin. *Nat.* 22.20 'radicem eius alterutrius sexus similitudinem referre'. Cf. *CGL* IV.241.14 'genitalia sexus uirilis et femine' (cf. 588.17).

(vii) *Res* and elliptical usages

Res (cf. Eng. *thing*) is used both˙ of sexual intercourse (see p. 203), and of the sexual organs of either sex (= *culus* at Mart. 11.43.11; = 'penis' at Arnob. *Nat.* 3.10 'Priapum inter deas uirgines atque matres circumferentem res illas proeliorum semper in expeditionem paratas' (cf. 5.26)). Similar to this usage is the employment of a neuter pronoun instead of a specific noun for the male organ (e.g. Catull. 67.27 'neruosius illud'; cf. Petron. 134.11). This is not the only elliptical method of alluding to the part. For feminine adjectives with *mentula* deleted, see, e.g. Catull. 56.7 'hunc ego, si placet Dionae, / protelo *rigida mea* cecidi', *CIL* IV.760 'oblige *mea*, fela . . . mentlam elinges . . . destillatio me tenet', Mart. 9.47.6; cf. Catull. 80.6 'grandia te medii tenta uorare uiri' (sc. *membra*?). I have collected further examples of this and similar phenomena elsewhere.[2] It is almost always the male organ which is referred to by means of an ellipse.

4. Miscellaneous

(i) *Muto, mutonium*

Mut(t)o is of unknown etymology. The word is related to the name of the marriage deity Mutunus Tutunus, and it seems

---

[1] See G. Carlsson, *Eranos* 25 (1927), pp. 189f., E. Löfstedt, *Late Latin* (Oslo, 1959), p. 100.

[2] Adams, 'Euphemism'.

to have provided the cognomen *Mutto* (*CIL* V.1412, 8473; for this type of *cognomen*, cf. *Penis* at *CIL* VIII.27237).[1] Hence it must once have been in general or vulgar use. *Muto* may have survived in Italian dialects with a derived meaning,[2] but there is no evidence that it had a prolonged currency in the period of recorded Latin.[3] The first example of the word is in Lucilius (307 'at laeua lacrimas muttoni absterget amica'). Elsewhere it is found only in Horace (*Serm.* 1.2.68), who would certainly have taken it from Lucilius (cf. Porph. *ad loc.* 'muttonem pro uirili membro dixit Lucilium imitatus'); indeed both Lucilius and Horace personify *muto*. There are no grounds for thinking that it was still in popular use in the Augustan period. But the derivative *mutonium*, which Lucilius also uses (959),[4] turns up in Pompeian graffiti (*CIL* IV.1939, 1940), and its derivative *mutuniatus* is found in Martial (3.73.1, 11.63.2) and the *Corpus Priapeorum* (52.10). *Mutonium* may have replaced *muto*. The exact tone of the two words is impossible to determine, but their distribution suggests that they were vulgar or obscene.

(ii) *Fascinum, phallus*

A *fascinum* was an amulet with the shape of a phallus worn around the neck for the purpose of warding off the evil eye (see Porph. on Hor. *Epod.* 8.18, and on such objects in general, Varro *Ling.* 7.97). *Fascinum* was sometimes transferred to the human penis (Hor. *Epod.* 8.18, Petron. 92.9), but it usually indicated representations of the organ. It is used thus twice in the *Corpus Priapeorum* (28.3, 79.1, of the phallus of statues of Priapus), twice at *CIL* XIV.3565 (= *CE* 1504) (lines 4, 20), and at *Catalept.* 13.20. Petronius employs it of a dildo at 138.1

---

[1] On *muto* and *mutonium*, see Herter, *RhM* 76 (1927), pp. 418ff., especially pp. 424ff.

[2] *TLL* VIII.1730.8ff., C. Battisti and G. Alessio, *Dizionario etimologico italiano* (Florence, 1950–57), IV, p. 2540 (*mutone* = 'mucchio grande'). It is not certain that *muto* lies behind such dialectalisms: see Rohlfs, *Dizionario dialettale delle Tre Calabrie* (see above, p. 13 n. 1), II, p. 73, s.vv. *mutoni, mutugnu* (< **tumugnu* < **θημόνιον?*).

[3] An example in Vitalis of Blois, *Geta* 348 ('sed sic dum crebro singultu colligit iram / ad curtum muto tenditur usque genu' (A; *membrum* B, *mentum* C, *uenter* DEF, *priapus* G)) could have been taken over from Horace.

[4] See *CGL* II.131.61 'muttonium προβασκαντον λουκιος' (edd. προβασκάνιον Λουκίλιος). It is impossible to say whether *mutonium* originally indicated a phallic amulet.

('profert Oenothea scorteum fascinum, quod . . . paulatim coepit inserere ano meo'). In Arnobius it is the standard word for an artificial phallus (4.7, 5.39, 7.33), and Augustine uses it in the same way at *Ciu.* 6.9. One of the two examples mentioned above with the meaning 'human penis' (that at Petron. 92.9) is applied to a grotesquely endowed man in a type of expression ('the man seemed to be an appendage of the penis': 'ut ipsum hominem laciniam fascini crederes') paralleled at *Priap.* 37.8f. 'fer opem, Priape, parti, / cuius tu, pater, ipse pars uideris'. Eumolpus, the speaker, may be suggesting that the man resembled ithyphallic statues.

The rare loan-word *phallus* (< φαλλός), which in Greek was largely restricted to the designation of cult objects,[1] and was also so used in Latin by Arnobius (*Nat.* 5.28), seems to have turned up in a Pompeian graffito in application to the human penis: *CIL* IV.10085 'phallus durus Cr(escentis), uastus'. The word was no doubt familiar enough to educated Latin speakers (note Cic. *Rep.* 3 frg. 4 'Sardanapallus ille uitiis multo quam nomine ipso deformior'), but it would not have been domiciled in any variety of Latin. The Pompeian example, if it has been read correctly, must be an isolated transfer.

(iii) *Sopio*

The obscure word *sopio* at Catull. 37.10 ('frontem tabernae sopionibus scribam') may well mean 'penis': the sentence would be a threat to draw representations of the phallus as a mark of contempt. Phallic drawings warded off the evil eye, and any apotropaic instrument could be used with hostile intent against a person. *Sopio* is also attested at Pompeii in a context which shows it to have been offensive: *CIL* IV.1700 'diced nobis Sineros et (?) sopio'. In at least one other hand is written 'ut merdas edatis, qui scripseras sopionis'. The insult aimed at Pompey quoted by Sacerdos (*GL* VI.461.30–462.3 'illud de Pompeio, qui coloris erat rubei, sed animi inuerecundi, "quem non pudet et rubet, non est homo, sed sopio". sopio autem est aut minium aut piscis robeus aut penis') would

---

[1] See Herter, 'Genitalien', 3.

also seem to require the sense 'penis' for *sopio*.[1] The penis could be described as both red (e.g. Mart. 2.33.2, Arnob. *Nat.* 7.33) and shameless; and for the structure of the remark, cf. Catull. 115.8 'non homo, sed uero mentula magna minax'.

(iv) *Salaputium*

Another obscure word in Catullus is *salaputium* (53.5), which was applied to Calvus by a member of the audience at one of his speeches ('Di magni, salaputium disertum!'). *Salaputium* has been derived from *salax* + *putium*,[2] but the derivation is not convincing. The interpretation of the word as meaning 'penis' is based mainly on the fact that Calvus was of notoriously small stature. *Penis* was used *pars pro toto* by Augustus of Horace (see above, p. 36), who was also small. Small boys are sometimes likened to the penis, and both Augustus and the speaker quoted by Catullus may have used the terminology appropriate to children.[3]

(v) A nonsense word?

The only possible case of a nonsense word = *mentula* in Latin is *xurikilla* at *CIL* IV.8380,[4] but the reading has been challenged (*Auricilla?*).[5]

(vi) A glossator's mistake

CGL V.493.32 ('cadurdum [*sic*] membrum uirile; nam proprie cadurda dicuntur summitates naturae femineae sicut uirorum

---

[1] This passage has always been thought to contain an unexplained word *ropio*, but A. Lunelli, *Aerius, storia di una parola poetica (Varia neoterica)* (Rome, 1969), p. 125 has demonstrated that the *s* was misread as *r*. S. Mariotti, *ap.* Lunelli, p. 126 noted that the quotation is a trochaic septenarius without its initial syllable. Lunelli (pp. 129ff.) also makes some interesting, but inconclusive, remarks on the reading and interpretation of *CIL* IV.1700, and on the text at Petron. 22.1. In view of the offensive character of *sopio* (whatever its meaning), it seems most unlikely that Petronius would have admitted it. The vocabulary of the narrative of the *Satyricon* is extremely decent.

[2] See E. Bickel, *RhM* 96 (1953), p. 95 (*putium <praeputium* (?)).

[3] See Bickel, *loc. cit.*, E. Fraenkel, *Horace* (Oxford, 1957), p. 19 n. 4; cf. Adams, *Pars pro toto*.

[4] This interpretation is that of the editor (M. Della Corte).

[5] See J. Svennung, *Studi in onore di Luigi Castiglioni* (Florence, 1960), II, pp. 973ff.

praeputium') is based on a misinterpretation of Juv. 6.537 ('magnaque debetur uiolato poena cadurco'). The glossator saw in *cadurcum* a term for 'clitoris', and assumed that the word could also indicate the *membrum uirile*.

5. Some specialised terms

(i) Testicle

The obscene word for 'testicle' was *coleus* (etymology obscure). Its tone is commented on by Cicero, *Fam.* 9.22.4 ('et honesti "colei Lanuuini", "Cliternini" non honesti'), but the implication of the passage is uncertain. *Coleus* occurs in epigram (Mart. 9.27.1, 12.83.2, *Priap.* 14.8, 25.7, 29.4), but not in satire. It is attested at Pompeii, in what appears to be an offensive collocation (*CIL* IV.4488 'seni supino colei culum tegunt'), and it survives in the Romance languages (Fr. *couille*, etc.).[1] There are two examples in freedmen's speeches in Petronius, one in a proverb (44.14 'si nos coleos haberemus', 'if we were virile men'),[2] the other used *pars pro toto* of lecherous men (39.7 'in geminis autem nascuntur bigae et boues et colei'). This latter usage was idiomatic: cf. Mart. 12.83.2 'omnes quem modo colei timebant'. Fabianus, the subject of the poem, made a habit of deriding men with a hernia; he would have been feared by lechers, because a rupture was a hazard of lecherous behaviour (Varro *Men.* 192, *Catalept.* 12.7f., *Querolus* p. 19.13–16 Ranstrand). It is possible that *coleus* was not as offensive as *mentula*, *cunnus* and *futuo*. Cicero admits the word in *Fam.* 9.22, if only in certain (obscure) combinations. The freedmen in Petronius do not as a rule use obscenities (but note *caco* at 71.8, and see the Appendix). But it could be said that both examples in Petronius are in special contexts in which the tone of the word may have been softened. *Coleus* is found once in the fragments of mime, juxtaposed with *caco* in an expression which must have savoured of gross indecency (Laber. 66 'in coleos cacas'). The derivative *coleatus* is used twice by Pomponius (40, 69); it was probably a humorous neologism (note

---

[1] *REW* 2038.
[2] For the proverb, see Otto, p. 87.

especially 69 'coleatam cuspidem', where *cuspis* is an *ad hoc* metaphor: see p. 20).

The alternative form *coleo*, which also survives in Romance (It. *coglione*, Fr. *couillon*, etc.),[1] is reported in a gloss: *CGL* II.579.46 'famex spado contusis culionibus'. For this suffix in anatomical terms, cf. late Latin *testo* = *testis* (*CGL* V.516.46 'testones testiculi'; cf. 559),[2] and also *posterio* = *posteriora* (*CGL* III.596.7 'anum posterionem', > OIt. *postione*, OFr. *poistron*).

Testis (lit. 'witness') exemplifies the tendency to personify the male organ or its parts (for such a personification, cf. παραστάτης = 'testicle',[3] and see below on δίδυμοι). When used as an anatomical term *testis* never wholly lost its literal sense in the classical period. Hence it is common in puns (Plaut. *Curc.* 31, *Mil.* 1420, 1426, Phaedr. 3.11.5, Mart. 7.62.6, *Priap.* 15.7;[4] cf. Plaut. *Curc.* 30, 622, *Mil.* 1416, 1417). It obviously had a risqué and jocose quality, which would explain Cicero's characterisation 'non nimis (honestum)' (*Fam.* 9.22.4). Similarly it is described by Arnobius as vulgar: *Nat.* 7.24 'polimina porro sunt ea quae nos proles uerecundius dicimus, a uolgaribus autem adsolent cognomine testium nuncupari'.[5] *Testis* is however occasionally found in sober prose (e.g. Plin. *Nat.* 11.263, Suet. *Nero* 28.1, Porph. Hor. *Serm.* 1.2.43). On some late medical examples, see below.

The diminutive *testiculus*, unlike *testis*, was specialised in the anatomical sense with its etymology no longer felt, and it achieved currency in scientific prose. Celsus, who does not use *testis*, has *testiculus* 33 times. Scribonius Largus has *testiculus* twice, *testis* not at all, and Marcellus Empiricus prefers *testiculus* by 23 : 5. On the other hand veterinary writers made free use of *testis*, perhaps because they were prepared to tolerate a more slangy vocabulary (Columella, *testis* 4 times, *testiculus* 5 times, Pelagonius, *testis* 7, *testiculus* -, *Mul. Chir.*,

---

[1] *REW* 2036.

[2] See further Svennung, p. 130.

[3] παραστάτης occasionally has this sense (e.g. Plat. com. frg. 174.13 Kock), but in the medical language it had certain more technical senses (epididymides, vasa deferentia (κιρσοειδεῖς παραστάται), seminal vesicles (ἀδενοειδεῖς παραστάται)): see Jocelyn, pp. 67, 69, 70.

[4] *Testis* is found only here in the *Corpus Priapeorum*. The author preferred *coleus*, just as he had a taste for the other obscenities.

[5] The glossing of *testes* by *testiculos* at ps.-Acron, Hor. *Serm.* 1.2.45 merely shows that *testiculi* was the more commonplace word.

testis 31, testiculus 25, Vegetius, *Mul.*, testis 17, testiculus 9).[1]
Testiculus is also used by later satirists, who favoured a euphemistic vocabulary. Persius has it at 1.103 ('haec fierent, si
testiculi uena ulla paterni / uiueret in nobis?'), in an expression of proverbial character in which, as we have seen (p. 66),
a freedman in Petronius has *colei*. Persius toned down the
proverb, just as at 1.112 (' "hic" inquis "ueto quisquam faxit
oletum" ') he tones down an inscriptional prohibition, normally containing *caco* (cf. Petron. 71.8).[2] Juvenal preferred *testiculi* to its synonyms (6.339, 372, 11.157, 12.36).

A Greek personification of the testicles is seen in δίδυμοι,
'twins' (e.g. Philodemus, *A.P.* 5.126.6, Argentarius, *A.P.*
5.105.4 οὐρανὸς ἐντὸς ἔχει καὶ κύνα καὶ διδύμους).[3] *Gemini* turns
up with this sense in later Latin, where it is presumably a
calque: Amm. 16.7.5 'etiam tum paruulus abstractis geminis
Romanis mercatoribus uenundatus', Solin. 13.2 'testiculi eius
adpetuntur in usum medullarum: idcirco cum urgeri se intel-
legit, ne captus prosit, ipse geminos suos deuorat'. But the
implication of Petron. 35.3 ('super geminos testiculos ac ri-
enes') and 39.7 ('in geminis autem nascuntur bigae et boues et
colei') is that *gemini* would readily have been understood as
having an anatomical implication (cf. Plin. *Nat.* 26.162 'arsen-
ogoni autem semen geminum esse testibus simile'), even if it
was not at the time a current metaphor. Another possible
calque on δίδυμοι is *pares* at *Priap.* 50.6 ('totam cum paribus,
Priape, nostris / cingemus tibi mentulam coronis');[4] but it would
not be an exact rendition.

Proles is said by Arnobius to be a euphemism for 'testicles':
Nat. 7.24 'ea quae nos proles uerecundius dicimus' (for the full
quotation, see above, p. 67; note that the word is here treated
as plural). Cf. *CGL* IV.529.58 'inprolis nondum uir' (i.e. =
impubes). This must have originated as a learned substitute
for *pubes*, which among its various uses could be applied to the
testicles (*Anth. Lat.* 109.1 'incertum ex certo sexum fert pube

[1] It is worth noting in this connection that Pelagonius (unlike medical
writers) was prepared to use *caco* and *merda*: see the Appendix.
[2] For *oletum facio*, see also Paul. Fest. p. 221 'oletum stercus humanum.
Veranius: "Sacerdotula in sacrario Martiali fecit oletum" '.
[3] δίδυμοι was also in use in the medical language, to which it may have been
introduced by Herophilus: see Galen, *VP* 14.11, p. 323.22 Helmreich ... τῷ
καθ' ἑαυτὴν διδύμῳ· καλεῖ γὰρ Ἡρόφιλος οὕτω τὸν ὄρχιν. Cf. Jocelyn, p. 66.
[4] The text here is doubtful: see Buecheler, *RhM* 18 (1863), p. 398, = *Kleine
Schriften* (see above, p. 32 n. 3), I, p. 345.

recisa'). For *proles*, see further Arnob. *Nat.* 5.6 ('proles cum ipsis genitalibus'), 5.23, 5.35, 5.37.

Polimen = 'testicle', which Arnobius mentions in the same passage, was strictly applicable to the anatomy of pigs: cf. Paul. Fest. p. 267.9 'polimenta testiculi porcorum dicuntur'. J. André[1] has made the attractive suggestion that *polimen, polimentum* were derivatives of *pol(l)ire* (= 'play ball') attested only at Paul. Fest. p. 279 'pollit pila ludit'. The authenticity of the verb has not been widely accepted, but André associates it with πάλλα 'ball', πάλλω and perhaps *pello*. As instrumental derivatives *polimen* and *polimentum* might originally have meant 'ball'. Used of the testicles they would have been metaphorical (with abundant parallels in other languages: e.g. Eng. *ball, ballock*). Indeed the scrotum of the pig might have served as the casing for the type of ball in question.

There are many vaguer ways of indicating the testicles, usually by means of blanket euphemisms which could also designate the penis or even the female pudenda. In the appropriate context the sphere of reference of such a word might be narrowed down to just one part of the genitalia. It has already been mentioned (pp. 53f.) that *ueretrum* and *uerecunda*, both equivalents of αἰδοῖον, are sometimes given the sense 'testicles' (*CGL* III.248.57, IV.326.30). *Corpus* was used with the testicles apparently in mind by Horace (*Serm.* 1.2.43 'dedit hic pro corpore nummos') and Phaedrus (3.11.3 'damnum insectatus est amissi corporis'). *Genitalia*, as we have seen (see p. 58 n. 5), is sometimes ambiguous between the meanings 'penis' and 'testicle' (cf. Apul. *Met.* 1.9, 7.23, Arnob. *Nat.* 5.39). *Membra genitalia* at Ovid *Am.* 2.3.3 and Col. 7.11.2 ('duobus membris genitalibus'), and *genitales partes* at Col. 6.26.2 indicate the testicles. For *membrum* with this implication in another combination, see Tib. 1.4.70 ('et secet ad Phrygios uilia membra modos'). Note too ps.-Acron on Hor. *Serm.* 1.2.43 'pro corpore autem: pro obscena parte corporis'.

Virilitas (lit. 'manhood', an abstract which became concrete)[2] and *uirilia* are common euphemisms for the male organ, but because they usually occur in contexts in which castration is at issue, it is possible that they were often thought of as

[1] *RPh* 40 (1966), pp. 51f.
[2] Cf. Artem. 1.45 διὸ ἀνδρεία πρός τινων καλεῖται.

referring to the testicles.[1] At Petron. 108.10 ('Giton ad uirilia sua admouit nouaculam'), Plin. *Nat.* 7.36 ('mox barbam et uirilitatem prouenisse'; cf. 24.18), Mart. 11.29.1 ('languida ... uirilia') and Paul. *Fest.* p. 84.27 ('ut se priuent uirilitatis parte') the sense is closer to 'penis' or 'genitalia' in general, but in at least some of the following passages the writer may primarily have been thinking of the testicles: Plin. *Nat.* 35.165 'uirilitatem amputare', Mart. 9.5.5 'uirilitatis ... ereptae', Quint. 5.12.17 'uirilitate excisa', Apul. *Met.* 7.25 'uirilitatis lanienam' (cf. 1.13, 8.15), Arnob. *Nat.* 5.11 'uirilibus spoliaretur abscisis', ps.-Acron on Hor. *Serm.* 1.2.46 'multis etiam uirilia amputata sunt', Isid. *Etym.* 8.11.79 'uirilia amputasse'. *Virilis pars* at Col. 7.11.2 means 'testicle' ('cum uirilem partem unam ferro reseratam detraxeris': the reference is specifically to one of the testicles), whereas at Fest. p. 410 the phrase indicates the penis ('strutheum in mimis praecipue uocant obscenam partem uirilem').[2] In Spanish *verija*, the reflex of *uirilia*, has been generalised to cover the sexual organs of both sexes, but it is still used specifically of the testicles in appropriate contexts.[3]

Comparable with the above words are various phrases in different genres expressing the 'deprivation' or the 'loss of the man' in someone (with *uir*): Catull. 63.6 'itaque ut relicta sensit sibi membra sine uiro', Lucan 10.133 'ferro mollita iuuentus / atque exsecta uirum', Arnob. *Nat.* 1.41 'Attin Phrygem abscisum et spoliatum uiro', 5.13 'ut ille se uiro ... priuaret', 5.39 'arboris, sub qua sibi Attis uirum demessis genitalibus abstulit', Luxorius, *Anth. Lat.* 295.1 'exsecti ... uiri'. Cf. ps.-Luc. *Asinus* 33 ἐγὼ δὲ ἤδη ἐδάκρυον ὡς ἀπολέσων αὐτίκα τὸν ἐν τῷ ὄνῳ ἄνδρα.

Another word discussed earlier which varies in meaning

---

[1] It is of course not always possible to be certain what part of the anatomy a writer has in mind when he speaks of unmanning. Castration might be effected by excision of the testicles (note the puns on the double sense of *testis* at Plaut. *Mil.* 1416–26), but a mutilation could involve the removal of the whole organ. For removal of the *mentula* (or *mentula* and testicles), see, e.g. Plaut. *Mil.* 1398, Hor. *Serm.* 1.2.45f., Mart. 9.2.14. On castration and mutilation, see Herter 'Genitalien', 24f.

[2] Another circumlocution, *nota uirilis* at *Priap.* 66.1 ('tu, quae ne uideas notam uirilem, / hinc auerteris'), refers to the penis. Cf. Euenus, *A.P.* 9.602.4 ἀνδρὸς ... τύπους.

[3] See Cela (cited above, p. 55 n. 2), I, p. 268, II, p. 588.

between 'penis' and 'testicles' is *uas*. At Plaut. *Poen.* 863 (see above, p. 41) it seems to imply the testicles.

The testicles may be described as a 'weight' or 'burden', as at Lucil. 536 'pellicula extrema exaptum pendere onus ingens' (*testibus* in the previous line makes it clear what Lucilius had in mind). Note too Catull. 63.5 'deuolsit ilei acuto sibi pondera silice'. On the other hand at Mart. 7.35.4 ('Iudaeum nulla sub cute pondus habet') the allusion is to someone *bene mentulatus*, and the weight is primarily that of the *mentula*. Cf. Ovid *Fast.* 4.241 'onus inguinis aufert, / nullaque sunt subito signa relicta uiri' (of a mutilation of both parts), Petron. 92.9 'habebat enim inguinum pondus tam grande, ut ipsum hominem laciniam fascini crederes'.[1] For the theme of the weight of the genitalia, see Mart. 10.55, *Priap.* 69.4, Erycius, *A. Plan.* 242.1 ὡς βαρὺ τοῦτο, Πρίηπε, καὶ εὖ τετυλωμένον ὅπλον.[2] Conversely, for the *leuitas* of the organ, see Schol. Juv. 6.369 'tunc faciunt eunuchos, quando iam pubuerint et penem maiorem ferant, ut licet *leuis* sit, tamen idoneus ad concubitum'.

See also above, p. 57, on the possible use of *onus* at Maxim. *Eleg.* 5.84. I can see no reason to take *mala* at Virg. *Ecl.* 2.51 ('ipse ego cana legam tenera lanugine mala') in a secondary sense 'testicles'.[3] In later Medieval Latin various *ad hoc* metaphors for the testicles were coined. On *petrae*, see above, p. 22; on *breues (syllabae)*, see p. 39; on logical terminology, see p. 39. Cf. Matthew of Vendôme, *Art. Versif.* 1.53.77f. 'Venus excitat aegra *bilibres / fratres*, membra tepent cetera, cauda riget' (for *bilibres*, see Juv. 6.372 'ergo expectatos ac iussos crescere primum / testiculos, postquam coeperunt esse *bilibres*'), *Babio* 452 'non ludes amodo ternis. / *cimbala* sola dabis : nolo nocere magis' (*cimbala* BCP, *symbola* D).

---

[1] Another sense of *pondus* was 'rupture' (so *ponderosus* = 'ruptured'): see Arnob. *Nat.* 7.34, Aug. *Ciu.* 22.8, *Querolus* p. 19.14 Ranstrand 'sume Paphien Cytheren, Briseiden, sed cum pondere Nestoris' (Nestor is said to have had a hernia at Juv. 6.326; the implication of the passage is that Querolus, with girl friends like these, will suffer a rupture from excessive sexual activity: see above, p. 66).

[2] A fresco in the entrance of the house of the Vetii at Pompeii shows Priapus weighing his *mentula*. A photograph can be seen in M. Grant, *Erotic Art in Pompeii* (London, 1975), p. 53. For *pondus* in allusion to the penis in Medieval Latin, see William of Blois, *Alda* 495 'impar erat precium pro ponderis imparitate'.

[3] See Goldberger (1930), p. 35. Goldberger's view that *mala* at *Priap.* 72.4 has a sexual sense is absurd.

(ii) Glans

The frequency of *caput* used of the glans suggests that it was in common use: Petron. 132.8, *Anth. Lat.* 696.4 (Petron. frg. 37 Buecheler), Mart. 11.46.4, *Priap.* 83.5, 32, 37, Auson. *Cent. Nupt.* 107, p. 216 P., Cass. Fel. pp. 118.15, 22, 119.2, Maxim. *Eleg.* 5.98.[1] This usage reflects the tendency for the organ to be personified: indeed in some of the above passages the *mentula* is said to 'raise its head' or the like (e.g. Mart. 11.46.4 'nec leuat extinctum sollicitata caput', *Priap.* 83.5 'nec uiriliter / iners senile penis extulit caput'). Cf. *uertex* at Maxim. *Eleg.* 5.100, and below on *cacumen*.

The medical technical term was *glans*, a calque on βάλανος (the loan-word *balanus* is found at Marc. Emp. 33.67, Soran. Lat. (Mustio), p. 75.20), used almost exclusively by Celsus (e.g. 6.18.4, 7.25.1A, 7.25.2). But Martial puns on this anatomical sense at 12.75.3 'pastas glande natis habet Secundus' (the buttocks (or anus) of Secundus 'feed on' the *glans*). Here *glans* has tended to shift its reference to the whole organ. Note too *glandula* at Fulg. *Aet. Mund.* 8, p. 157.21 Helm (= 'penis').

Vindicianus mentions *caulus* and *dartus* as alleged terms for the glans at *Epit. Alt.* 28, p. 479.16f. Rose: 'cacumen eius dicitur caulus siue dartus'. *Cacumen* seems to have been used here in much the same way as *caput* above. καυλός usually referred to the penis as a whole. One cannot say whether Vindicianus used it loosely, or whether it genuinely shifted to the glans in Greek medical terminology. The case of *dartus* is more puzzling. In the Greek medical language δαρτός (lit. 'skinned, flayed', < δέρω) usually denoted one of the tunics surrounding the testicles (the one that could be 'stripped off'): see Rufus, *Onom.* 197, Cels. 7.18.2 'super ea ualentior tunica est, quae interiori uehementer ima parte inhaeret: darton Graeci uocant'.[2] It is difficult to see how it could have changed meaning in the required manner in the genuine medical language. Vindicianus may have misunderstood it as denoting that part of the organ which could be 'skinned', viz. the glans. It is most unlikely that either of these usages in Vindicianus had entered the Latin medical language.

---

[1] *Inguinis cephalum* in the *spurcum additamentum* at Apul. *Met.* 10.21 was no doubt an artificial creation based on this use of *caput*. See Mariotti, p. 239 = p. 57.

[2] The term may have been coined by Herophilus: see Jocelyn, p. 67.

The corona of the glans is called '*circulus*' by Celsus: 7.25.1C 'sub circulo glandis scalpello deducenda cutis ab interiore cole est . . . ubi iam sine inflammatione est, deligari debet a pube usque circulum'.

(iii) Foreskin

Praeputium, an obscure formation,[1] was not a medical technical term, but it must have been inoffensive (it is found in Christian Latin, as well as at Juv. 6.238, 14.99). Celsus speaks simply of the 'skin', *cutis* (7.25.1A, 1B, 1C, 2, 3; for δέρμα with this sense in Greek, see below, and Aristoph. *Eq.* 29, Plat. com. 174.18 Kock, *CGL* II.206.49 'uerpus . . . ὁ λειπόδερμος'), and such phraseology seems to have been commonplace:[2] cf. Mart. 7.35.4 'Iudaeum nulla sub cute pondus habet' (cf. 7.30.5 *recutitorum*), Porph. on Hor. *Serm.* 1.5.100 'urbanissimum nomen Iudaeo inposuit "Apella" dicens, quasi quod pellem in parte genitali Iudaei non habeant', *id.* on Hor. *Serm.* 1.9.69 'curtos Iudaeos dixit, quia uirile membrum uelut decurtatum habent recisa inde pellicula', ps.-Acron on Hor. *Serm.* 1.5.100 'finxit nomen, quasi sine pelle, aut certe Apella [circumcisus Apella], qui praeputium non habet',[3] Schol. Juv. 14.104 'Iudaeos, qui sine pellicula sunt', Marc. Emp. 33.21 'et tumor sedabitur et uitium omne reducta pellicula sanabitur'. Similarly in Celsus *tergus* ('hide') is a few times used of what appears to be the outer surface of the foreskin: 7.25.2 'subter a summa ora cutis inciditur recta linea usque ad frenum, atque ita superius *tergus* relaxatum cedere retro potest. quod si parum sic profectum est, aut propter angustias aut propter duritiem *tergoris*, protinus triangula forma cutis ab inferiore parte excidenda est sic, ut uertex eius ad frenum, basis in *tergore* extremo sit'. The sexual use of *excoriare* in the *spurcum additamentum* at Apul. *Met.* 10.21 is based on the metaphorical application of words for 'hide' and the like to the foreskin.

Cucutium (Diosc. II. p. 207.12 'uerpis cucutium crescere facit') seems to be a remodelling of *cucullus* ('hood' for the head; the 'head' in this case is the *caput*, 'glans') by means of the

---

[1] See F. Bader, *La formation des composés nominaux du latin* (Paris, 1962), p. 378 n. 26.

[2] See Housman, *Classical Papers*, pp. 1181f. for some examples.

[3] An Old French derivative (*pelete*) of the reflex of *pellis* means 'foreskin' (*FEW* VIII, p. 167 *a*).

suffix of *praeputium*.[1] For *cucutium* = *cucullus*, see *S.H.A.*, *Claud.* 17.6 'cucutia uillosa duo'.

For a vague phrase used of the foreskin, see *Mul. Chir.* 474 'stantis equi in ipso *ad extremum cole* iaculum interpunge'. That the allusion is to the foreskin is clear from *Hipp. Berol.* 48.1, *CHG* I, p. 223.15f. ἑστῶτος τοῦ ἵππου, ῥαφίδι λεπτῇ ἀκροθιγῶς κεντοῦντες τὸ παρὰ τὸν καυλὸν δέρμα (note δέρμα).

At *Anth. Lat.* 696.4 (Petron. frg. 37 Buecheler) the foreskin is called *inguinis ora*: 'ni tamen et ferro succiderit inguinis oram / et nisi nodatum soluerit arte caput'.

When at *Cent. Nupt.* 116, p. 217 P. Ausonius wrote of the *hasta* of the bridegroom as possessing *cortex*, 'bark' ('et super incumbens nodis et cortice crudo / intorquet summis adnixus uiribus hastam'), he introduced a metaphor of his own for the foreskin. *Glubo* ('skin, peel off bark') had been used metaphorically by Catullus (58.5) of the act of retracting the foreskin (by intercourse or masturbation?: see p. 168), and this metaphor probably led Ausonius to speak of the organ as having 'bark'. Catullus' use of *glubo* was imitated by Ausonius at *Epigr.* 79.7, p. 341.

Celsus introduced the term *frenum* to indicate the ligament connecting the foreskin to the bottom of the glans (7.25.2, quoted above).[2] In Greek this part was called κυνοδέσμη (Pollux 2.171, Hesych. *s.v.*) or (perhaps) σειρά: see *GL* I.548.26 'hi freni χαλινοί; sed et frena et frenum inuenimus, λέγεται δὲ καὶ σειρὰ φύσεως, freni'.

(iv) Scrotum

Celsus names *scrotum* as the current term for this part at 7.18.2: 'communis deinde utrique omnibusque interioribus sinus est, qui iam conspicitur a nobis: oscheon Graeci, scrotum nostri uocant'. Whatever the etymology of *scrotum*,[3] it is obviously the same word as the (hyperurbane?) *scrautum*, which is said by Paul. Fest. p. 449.7ff. to denote a type of leather

---

[1] See Ernout and Meillet, s.v. *cucullus*; for a different explanation (< Gall. **kukka*), see *FEW* II.2, p. 1461. But it seems necessary to assume a contamination involving *praeputium* to explain the sense in Dioscorides Lat., and the suffix.

[2] I do not accept (see Jocelyn, p. 75) that *frenum* had any connection with an alleged use of *equus* = 'penis' (see p. 34).

[3] For a possibility, see Pokorny, I, p. 947.

quiver: 'scrautum pelliceum, in quo sagittae reconduntur, appellatum ab eadem causa, qua scortum'. It is not surprising that words indicating containers, bags and the like should provide terms for the scrotum (cf. πηρίς, 'leather bag', = 'scrotum' at Erotian π.58).[1] *Scrotum*, despite Celsus' remark, never caught on in the popular language. It did not enter Romance except as a learned loan-word, and it is scarcely attested in Latin itself. The scrotum is rarely mentioned in popular speech. The testicles rather than their container provide a fertile source of popular humour. The words for 'scrotum' in Latin are all of infrequent attestation.

Folliculus occurs a few times:[2] see Arnob. *Nat.* 5.21 'arietem nobilem bene grandibus cum testiculis deligit, exsecat hos ipse et lanato exuit ex folliculi tegmine', *Mul. Chir.* 677 'si intelligis folliculum ipsum et testiculos sanos sine tumore esse', Cael. Aurel. *Acut.* 3.165 'quibus intestinum . . . in folliculum fuerat lapsum' (cf. *Chron.* 3.104), *Lex Frisionum* 22.86 (*MGH, Leg. Tom.* III) 'qui utramque coxam cum folliculo testium telo traicerit'. *Folliculus* survives as OFr. *forcel*, 'scrotum', attested in the thirteenth century.[3] *Follis* itself is used in this sense in the manuscript *O* at Juv. 6.373 B: 'mangonum pueros uera ac miserabilis urit / debilitas, follisque pudet cicerisque relicti'.

For *fiscus* ('money bag'), see Isid. *Etym.* 11.1.105 'fiscus est pellis in qua testiculi sunt', and for *suffiscus*, see Paul. Fest. p. 403.11 'suffiscus folliculus testium arietinorum, quo utebantur pro marsuppio, a fisci similitudine dictus'.

Bursa (< βύρσα) was more influential, though it does not appear in the sense 'scrotum' until the Middle Ages. The Greek word means 'leather, hide', and this is the meaning that the earliest examples of the loan-word in (Medieval) Latin have (e.g. Aldh. *Virg.* 1.35, p. 279.11, *Gloss., St.-S.* III.294.59). The meaning 'scrotum' is quoted first from the thirteenth century by the *Mittellateinisches Wörterbuch*,[4] but it is found somewhat earlier in the *Elementarium* of Papias (s.v. *pyga*, which is glossed by 'nates uel bursa mentula').[5] *Bursa* survives all over

---

[1] See Jocelyn, p. 67.

[2] For *folliculus* in another anatomical sense of a sexual kind ('utricle' of a horse's penis), see, e.g. *Mul. Chir.* 148, 184 (cf. *TLL* VI.1.1015.80ff.)

[3] *FEW* III, p. 687.

[4] Ed. O. Prinz and J. Schneider, vol. I (Munich, 1967), 1627.29ff.

[5] See p. 229 on *pyga*, and cf. Mariotti, p. 233 = pp. 51f.

the Romania. Its reflexes can generally indicate the scrotum; Rum. *boş*, however, has shifted slightly to the sense 'testicle'.[1]

(v) Pubic hair

In Classical Latin there was a distinction between *capillus* ('hair of the head') and *pilus* ('hair of the body', including 'pubic hair': note Plin. *Nat.* 29.26, Mart. 11.22.7, and cf. *pilosus* (?) at *CIL* IV.1830 add. p. 212 (= *CE* 230)), which was maintained in some areas of the Romance-speaking world (Fr. *cheveu* / *poil*). In other areas (Rumania, Sardinia, S. France) *pilus* assumed the function of *capillus*.[2] Sometimes even in Latin there is a blurring of the distinction between *capillus* and *pilus*. For *pilus* used of the hair of the head, see, e.g. Petron. 109.9, Sen. *Dial.* 9.8.3, Plin. *Nat.* 11.130.

Persius, who had something of a taste for *ad hoc* sexual metaphors (see above, p. 33 on *gurgulio* = *mentula*), coined two plant metaphors for the pubic hair at 4.39–42, *plantaria*, 'cuttings, plants', and *filix*, 'fern': 'quinque palaestritae licet haec plantaria uellant / elixasque nates labefactent forcipe adunca, / non tamen ista filix ullo mansuescit aratro'. Ausonius imitated this use of *plantaria* at *Epigr.* 93.3, p. 346 P. ('sed quod et elixo plantaria podice uellis', = 'hairs of the *podex*'), but neither metaphor would have been established in the spoken language. Various metaphors in which foliage or down (or the like) suggests the pubic hair are found in Greek: χνοῦς (Aristoph. *Nub.* 978), λόχμη (*Lys.* 800), βληχώ (*Lys.* 89).

The original sense of *pubes* may have been 'pubic hair'. Certainly that is the meaning which the word has at Cels. 7.19.1 'idque iam pube contegitur'. But it came to be used of the parts covered by the pubic hair, viz. the external genitalia (e.g. Cels. 2.3.1, 2.4.3, 2.7.12, 4.1.11). It is possible that this secondary sense was a calque on ἥβη, but the semantic change could have taken place independently within Latin itself.[3]

Pecten, lit. 'comb', came to mean 'pubic hair, pubes' (Plin. *Nat.* 29.26, Juv. 6.370), probably as a calque on κτείς. *Pecten* does not retain this sense in the Romance languages, but the

---

[1] See *FEW* I, p. 669, *REW* 1432.
[2] For further details, see A. Zauner, *RF* 14 (1903), pp. 410ff.
[3] See Adams, 'Anatomical terminology', n. 6.

diminutive *pectiniculus* means 'pubic hair' in Ibero-romance (Sp. *pendejo*, Pg. *pentelho*).[1]

6. Attitudes to the male genitalia

More than 120 designations of the penis have been discussed above, though not all are genuine, and some can denote the sexual organs of both males and females. In this figure no account is taken of the numerous different adjectival combinations with nouns of extreme generality such as *locus*, *membrum* and *pars*; *membrum*, for example, is counted only once. In the recorded language there are considerably more words for 'penis' than for 'female pudenda'. This disproportion must be due to the greater freedom with which the male organ was spoken about by some writers (Catullus, for example, often mentions the *mentula*, but *cunnus* occurs only at 97.8, and the part belongs to a mule; *gremium* at 67.30 and *infima inguinum pars* at 60.2 are the only certain substitutes for the word; on *olla* at 94.2, see p. 29), and in particular to the greater readiness of comic writers to make jokes about it. In Plautus, for example, most of the punning allusions to sexual organs concern the penis, and in the fragments of Atellane farce (which admittedly may be unrepresentative) there are various metaphorical designations for the penis obviously used for comic effect (*coleatam cuspidem, ramus, terminus, tutulatam truam*), but no comparable metaphor for the *cunnus*.

It is indeed possible to see in Latin writers a difference of attitude to the organs of the respective sexes. Roman modesty or 'repression' was not exactly comparable with that of today. The open display of representations of the phallus, for apotropaic and other purposes, in houses, streets and gardens, as well as in various special processions and ceremonies, seems to have rendered the male organ less shameful than the female. In Latin writers the *mentula* is not treated as exciting disgust, so much as fear, admiration and pride. It was a symbol of power which might present a threat to an enemy,[2] although that threat was usually manifested in linguistic aggression (see below, pp. 124ff.).

---

[1] *REW* 6331.
[2] See Fehling, pp. 14ff.

There is a constant preoccupation in Latin writers with the size of the male genitalia, a preoccupation which variously reflects pride, admiration and envy. Grotesquely endowed individuals might be the butt of jokes or cultivated as curiosities, but the attitude to them was one of amusement or awe rather than disgust. Admittedly admiration for the size of the *mentula* is usually ascribed to homosexuals or women, but male writers rarely express comparable admiration for the *cunnus* (contrast the epigram of Rufinus, *A.P.* 5.36, a mock judgement of Paris, in which the genitalia of three women are described in lavish similes; for the attractions of the κύσθος in Aristophanes, see *Ach.* 792, 795f., *Pax* 891, 1352, *Lys.* 88, 1158, *Thesm.* 289).[1]

For the admiration inspired by a well-endowed man, and the influence which his endowments conferred on him, it is worth consulting the anecdote told by Eumolpus at Petron. 92.8–10. The emperor Commodus is said to have had a favourite 'pene prominente ultra modum animalium', whom he enriched and appointed to a priesthood (*H.A., Comm.* 10.9), and Heliogabalus is alleged to have advanced to high honours men noted for the size of their genitals (*H.A., Hel.* 12.2). These stories were no doubt fabrications, but they at least indicate the obsessions of Roman voyeurs. A well-endowed character in Martial is said to have evoked applause in the baths (9.33). It is often assumed that the *mentula* is an object of concern, admiration or pleasure to women (Petron. 108.10, Mart. 1.35.5, 7.14.9f., 9.40.5, *Priap.* 39.7f.). For a woman's concern about the weight of the *mentula*, see Mart. 10.55, and about its size, Juv. 1.41, *Priap.* 80.3. So too the size of the *mentula* was of interest to *cinaedi* (Mart. 6.54, Sen. *N.Q.* 1.16.3). Various themes are combined in Mart. 11.63: the admiration provoked by large genitalia (a certain Philomusus stares at Martial's *tam mutuniati pueri* at the baths), and the threat which they pose (the well-endowed youths are prone to *pedicare* onlookers). Further preoccupation with large genitalia is to be found in Martial at 6.36 and 11.51. The sexual potency of a man was supposed to be reflected in the *mensura penis* (e.g. Juv. 1.41, *Priap.* 80.3).

---

[1] However these passages in Greek are unusual. In Greek art there is only a minimal interest in the female genitalia (see Dover, p. 135), compared with an obsessive interest in the attractions of the male (Dover, pp. 125ff.).

The attitude to the *cunnus* was remarkably different. It posed no threat, and did not arouse the same indulgent admiration. The *cunnus* which was *laxus* was an object of abuse and shame (see *CIL* IV.10004, Mart. 11.21.1, *Priap.* 18.2, 46.5). The *cunnus* might contain *lutum* (*CIL* IV.1516, *Priap.* 83.37), and it could have various other repulsive characteristics (note Mart. 7.18 on the *poppysmata* of a *cunnus*; on the *canus cunnus*, see Mart. 2.34.3, 9.37.7, and for an *osseus cunnus*, see Mart. 3.93.13). Excessive size of the clitoris also provoked abuse (*CIL* IV.10004, Mart. 1.90.8, *Priap.* 12.14).

Chapter Three

Designations of the Female Genitalia

In this chapter I discuss the designations of the female sexual organs and of their parts in Latin. Words for 'womb' are included, partly because the chronological and stylistic variations within the semantic field are of some interest, and partly because there is a degree of overlap between terms for the uterus and those for the vagina. Metaphorical designations in particular can often be interpreted as denoting either or both organs indifferently. I shall have little to say here about those terms for the female organs which could also indicate the male parts; such blanket euphemisms I have dealt with earlier.

1. *Cunnus*

Cunnus was the basic obscenity for the female pudenda. At *Priap.* 29 it is put on a par with *mentula* (line 5). The only reference to the word at Cic. *Fam.* 9.22 is concealed beneath the cacemphaton *cum nos* (§2); cf. *Orat.* 154 '. . . cum autem nobis non dicitur, sed nobiscum? quia si ita diceretur, obscenius concurrerent litterae, ut etiam modo, nisi autem interposuissem, concurrissent'. At *CE* 1810 it is by implication classified as 'plain Latin' (cf. *Priap.* 3.9f. 'latine / dicere'): 'hic ego me memini quendam futuisse puellam. / cunno non dico curiose'. Buecheler quotes Quint. 8.1.2 'multos . . . inuenias quos curiose potius loqui dixeris quam latine'; the writer seems to have meant 'I mention the *cunnus*' (or 'I call her a *cunnus*'), 'using plain Latin' (*cunno = cunnum?*). See also Soran. Lat. (Mustio) p. 9.4 'intus autem est spatiosissimus, foris uero angustus, in quo coitus uirorum et usus uenerius efficitur. quem uulgo connum appellant'. *Cunnus* is probably related to the Greek primary obscenity κύσθος,[1] but a connection with *cutis* (< *cut-nos?)[2] is uncertain.[3]

The tone of *cunnus*, like that of other basic obscenities, was not uniform. Such words occur in the speech of all classes when the speaker wishes to create an impact by using a word which has a strong taboo character. Hence they are not unusual in abusive and derogatory utterances (e.g. Catull. 97.8, Mart. 10.90.1). *Cunnus* was no doubt particularly offensive when used *pars pro toto* of male pathics (*CIL* IV.10078). On the other hand we have suggested that obscenities can occasionally be used neutrally as *voces propriae* in circumstances in which taboos do not operate, as between lovers or intimates. In the *defixio* Audollent 135B *cunnus* is listed, without an inherently offensive implication, as one of a number of *voces propriae* for parts of the body: 6 '. . . crus os pedes fronte[m] / un[gue]s di[g]itos uent[r]e / umlicu[m] cunu[m] / ulua[m]. . .'.

Cunnus occurs mainly in graffiti and epigram. In the published inscriptions from Pompeii and Herculaneum I have noted 35 examples (11 in the supplementary volumes to *CIL* IV). Horace uses the word 3 times early in the first book of *Sermones* (1.2.36, 1.2.70, 1.3.107), but thereafter it is not found in satire. It occurs once in Catullus, in an elegiac epigram (97.8), 31 times in Martial (I include 4 examples of the compound *cunnilingus*), and 6 times in the *Corpus Priapeorum* (22.2, 29.5, 39.8, 46.10, 68.9, 28; cf. 78.2 *cunnilinge*). The phraseology of epigram, as we have seen, often recalls that of obscene graffiti. With the vocative at Mart. 7.35.8 ('secretusque tua, cunne, lauaris aqua?'; cf. 11.61.9) can be compared *CIL* IV.3932 'cunne superbe'. *Cunnum lingere* at Mart. 1.77.6, 2.84.3 was a formula of graffiti (e.g. *CIL* IV.2400, 4304), and no doubt of the coarsest form of sexual abuse.

[1] See Chantraine, II, p. 603.
[2] See Pokorny, I, p. 952.
[3] But for *cutis* with a sexual implication (of a different kind), see Cato *Orat.* frg. 60, Gell. 13.8.5, Paul. Fest. p. 98, and below, p. 147.

2. Metaphors

(i) Animal metaphors

More metaphors of this type for the male parts than for the female are recorded, but a chance remark of Varro's serves as a warning against the assumption that recorded Latin does justice to the variety of the sexual language. According to Varro, *porcus* was a nursery word used by women, especially nurses, of the pudenda of girls: *Rust.* 2.4.10 'nam et nostrae mulieres, maxime nutrices, naturam qua feminae sunt, in uirginibus appellant porcum, et Graecae choeron, significantes esse dignum insigne nuptiarum'. The image has parallels in Greek, as Varro notes (cf. χοῖρος at Aristoph. *Ach.* 781, *Thesm.* 538, Nicarchus, *A.P.* 11.329.2, χοιρίδιον at Aristoph. *Vesp.* 573; cf. Hesych, *s.v.* δελφάκιον· χοιρίδιον. οὕτως ἔλεγον καὶ τὸ γυναικεῖον). Varro's remark provides a glimpse of the private language of the nursery, about which we know little. Nevertheless, there is some indirect evidence for the existence of this use of *porcus*.[1] The derivative *porcellana* survives in Romance (Fr. *porcelaine*, It. *porcellana*) as a designation for a type of shell which had the shape of the female external pudenda (the shell was called *ueneria* by Plin. *Nat.* 9.103, 32.151).

Only one other metaphor of this type is attested in Latin, and that is a loan-word introduced by Juvenal(?) and apparently used in a derived sense (of the mouth of a *fellator* which is by implication likened to the *cunnus*): 6.06 'et uasa iubent frangenda lauari / cum colocyntha bibit uel cum barbata chelidon'.[2] For χελιδών see Aristoph. *Lys.* 770, *Suda* s.v. λέγεται χελιδὼν καὶ τῶν γυναικῶν τὸ μόριον.

On the use of *leo* at Mart. 10.90.10, see p. 34.

(ii) 'Fields' and the like

The frequency (in Latin and other languages) of the metaphor of the field, garden, meadow, etc. applied to the female pud-

---

[1] See J. André, *Latomus* 15 (1956), pp. 299f.

[2] On *barbata chelidon*, see Housman, *Classical Papers*, p. 482. For the female parts as 'bearded', see Mart. 10.90.10, *Priap.* 12.13f. Nevertheless some doubt remains about the interpretation of *chelidon*. For some scepticism, see Courtney, p. 305. For another bird metaphor in Greek, see ἀηδονίς at Archil. 263 West (Heysch. *s.v.*), and M.L. West, *Studies in Greek Elegy and Iambus* (Berlin-New York, 1974), p. 138.

enda reflects in part the external appearance of the organ, and
in part the association felt between the fertility of the field
and that of females. The metaphor complements the verbal
metaphors of sowing and ploughing used of the male role in
sexual intercourse. Nominal metaphors of the type in question
were readily transferable to the (male) anus.[1]

Eugium, one of the few loan-words for the male or female
genitalia in Latin (< εὐγεῖον), can be classified as an agricultural image (cf. εὔγειος, 'having good soil, fertile'). *Eugium*
is restricted to a few texts in which vulgarisms were admitted:
Lucil. 940 'sine podice Hymnis, <si> sine eugio', Laber. 25 'an
concupiuisti eugium scindere', 139 'quae deleritas uos sub pol-
lictoris facit / <aduentum> cum cano eugio puellitari
<turpiter>';[2] cf. Non. p. 153 L. 'eugium media pars inter na-
turalia muliebria'. The primary sense of the word has been
taken to be 'hymen',[3] perhaps because of its juxtaposition with
scindere in Lucilius. But its etymology and the antithesis with
podex in Lucilius make it certain enough that it was equivalent to *cunnus*. *Scindo* was not a technical term for the breaking of the hymen, but a metaphorical substitute for *futuo* or
pedico (see p. 150). εὐγεῖον is not recorded in Greek; hence the
word must have entered Latin as a vulgar borrowing. Its generic restriction, and the fact that the passage of Lucilius manifestly has to do with prostitution, suggest that it would first
have been heard in brothels in the mouths of Greek prostitutes
(cf. *strutheum*, p. 32, *calo*, p. 173).[4]

It is an indication of the special character of the Latin of
Lucilius that no other satirist uses the word. It is also of note
that in this respect Lucilian usage can be compared with that
of mime. The sexual vocabulary of both farce and mime was
more vulgar and obscene than that of the later satirists (Persius, Juvenal). It is possible that Lucilius anticipated Horace
(in the first book of the *Sermones*) in admitting basic
obscenities.

Both Lucretius (4.1272 'eicit enim sulcum recta regione
uiaque / uomeris') and Virgil (*Georg.* 3.136 'nimio ne luxu
obtunsior usus / sit genitali aruo et sulcos oblimet inertis')

---

[1] See Adams, *Culus*, pp. 245ff. and Chapter IV.
[2] On the text here, see M. Zicàri, *Hermes* 91 (1963), p. 125.
[3] See Pierrugues, p. 197.
[4] See Zicàri, *loc.cit.*

used *sulcus* of the female pudenda in conjunction with the metaphors of sowing and ploughing. Clearly the word had an inoffensive tone. Later it was picked up by the author of *Anth. Lat.* 712 (17f. 'arentque sulcos molles aruo Venerio / thyrsumque pangant hortulo Cupidinis'). *Aruum*, which appears in two of the above passages, must also have had a literary flavour, to judge by its distribution (Lucr. 4.1107, Tert. *Anim.* 27, Ambros. *Exp. Luc.* 1.44. A, Aug. *Ciu.* 14.23; cf. the adjective *aruos* at Plaut. *Truc.* 149 'non aruos hic, sed pascuost ager': 'this is not arable land but pasture land'; again the metaphor of ploughing is used in conjunction with the nominal metaphor, as becomes explicit in the next line).

Ager implies the *cunnus* at Plaut. *Truc.* 149 above. The closest parallels to this usage are furnished by the use of *ager* and *agellus* as designations of the anus by Martial (9.21.1f., in a double entendre, 12.16.3; cf. Juv. 9.45). But there can be little doubt that in suggestive contexts *ager* would readily have been employed in reference to the *cunnus*.

Plautus has some similar words as *ad hoc* metaphors for the part: *Asin.* 874 'fundum alienum arat, incultum familiarem deserit', *Cas.* 922 'illum saltum uideo opsaeptum', *Curc.* 56 'pandit saltum sauiis', *Truc.* 148 'uolo habere aratiunculam pro copia hic apud uos'. *Fundus*, *saltus* and *aratiuncula* are not used elsewhere in this way, but such symbolism was so widely recognised that metaphors could obviously be coined freely.

In Greek κῆπος is sometimes equivalent to κύσθος (e.g. D.L. 2.116).[1] *Hortus* is not so used in Latin (note however *hortus* = *culus* at *Priap.* 5.4; for the semantic change, see (perhaps) *pratum* = *culus* at *Priap.* 52.9,[2] and cf. λειμών = κύσθος at Eur. *Cycl.* 171), but *hortulus* (a conjecture for *horto* S) has the same sense as *cunnus* at *Anth. Lat.* 712.18, quoted above. It was no doubt a calque on κῆπος.

In later Medieval Latin, particularly that of the twelfth century from France, metaphors of our type continued to be used and also coined: note Matthew of Vendôme, *Milo* 68*d* 'quo fodiatur ager non habet, uxor habet' (cf. anon., *Babio* 386 'incultus non erit eius ager'), 184 'falce metit, nullo uomere tangit *humum*' (*falce* and *uomere* are also double entendres),

---

[1] See Taillardat, p. 77.
[2] See Housman, *Classical Papers*, pp. 1176f.

Lehmann no. 14, p. 229 'misisti falcem in *messem* alienam' (on the Biblical parody, see p. 24).

(iii) Caves

The identification of the *cunnus* (or rectum) with a cave is an obvious enough image. It is exploited at length in the Priapic poem numbered 83: note 28 'inter atra cuius inguina / latet iacente pantice abditus specus', 35 'triplexque quadruplexque compleas specum'. For *specus* see further Diom., *GL* I.512.28 'Priapeum, quo Vergilius in prolusionibus suis usus fuit, tale est, "incidi patulum in specum procumbente Priapo" ' (= *cunnus* or *culus?*), Auson. *Cent. Nupt.* 113, p. 216 P. 'hic specus horrendum' (a Virgilian phrase). *Antrum* is attested only in the sense 'anus' (Auson. *Epigr.* 106.9, p. 351 P., Fulgent. p. 38.25 Helm). For comparable metaphors, see Auson. *Epigr.* 79.7, p. 341 P. 'deglubit, fellat, molitur per utramque cauernam' (= *cunnus* + *culus*),[1] *Cent. Nupt.* 119, p. 217 P. 'insonuere cauae gemitumque dedere cauernae'. *Cauerna* (of various bodily parts, including that here) achieved some currency in scientific prose.[2]

(iv) Ditches, pits and the like

The symbolism of the ditch (*fossa*) is implicit in Verrius (?) Flaccus' argument that, since it was permissible to clean old ditches but not new on festal days, it was more appropriate that widows should marry on such days than virgins: see Macrob. *Sat.* 1.15.21 'sed Verrium Flaccum iuris pontificii peritissimum dicere solitum refert Varro, quia feriis tergere ueteres fossas liceret, nouas facere ius non esset, ideo magis uiduis quam uirginibus idoneas esse ferias ad nubendum'. The type of ditch which Flaccus had in mind was perhaps a boundary marker; hence the image may be drawn from the same sphere as Pomponius' *terminus*. For *fossa* in this sense, see *Grom.* pp. 102.17, 111.19 Thulin; for some of the religious observances associated with such *fossae*, see p. 105.10ff. Later *fossa* was used metaphorically by the author of the *Corpus Priapeorum*: 46.9 'erucarum opus est decem maniplis, / fossas

---

[1] See R. Penella, *Hermes* 104 (1976), pp. 118ff.
[2] See *TLL* III.646.41ff.

inguinis ut teram' (for the genitive *inguinis*, see Mart. 6.73.6);
cf. *Priap.* 83.32 'uoret profunda fossa lubricum caput' (for *fossa*
= *culus*, see Juv. 2.10, where the word is used *pars pro toto* of
a *cinaedus*). It is not unlikely that *fossa* (= *cunnus* or *culus*)
was in use in the colloquial language, especially given that
the related *fodio* could be employed of the male role in sexual
intercourse (see p. 151). But *scrobis* at Arnob. *Nat.* 4.7 ('uirginalem scrobem effodientibus maritis') was probably an *ad
hoc* metaphor.

The applicability of words for 'hole, pit' and the like to the
vagina is illustrated by Martial's joke at 11.21.11f. ('hanc in
piscina dicor futuisse marina: / nescio; piscinam me futuisse
puto'), where the *laxus cunnus* of Lydia is identified with a
piscina. A similar coinage by Martial is *barathrum* at 3.81.1
'quid cum femineo tibi, Baetice Galle, barathro?'.[1] For a
Medieval coinage, see anon. *Lidia* 111 'pruritum scit queque
suum sudatque *lacuna* / omnibus'. Tertullian's *fouea* (with
genitalis) (*Anim.* 19) refers to the womb.

(v) Household terminology

We have seen that household terminology provides metaphors
for the male parts. The symbolism of the hearth (= 'external
female pudenda'?) and oven (= 'vagina / womb') was recognised by Artemidorus, 2.10, p. 116.21 f. Pack ἔοικε γὰρ καὶ ἡ
ἑστία καὶ ὁ κλίβανος γυναικὶ διὰ τὸ δέχεσθαι τὰ πρὸς τὸν βίον
εὔχρηστα. For the hearth, see also Aristoph. *Eq.* 1286 κυκῶν
τὰς ἐσχάρας. Apuleius made use of such imagery in a double
entendre at *Met.* 2.7 'discede . . . miselle, quam procul a meo
foculo discede'. In the corresponding passage in ps.-Luc. *Asinus*
(6) no equivalent to *foculus* is found, but there is one notable
correspondence between the two passages. In the Greek story
Palaestra has a pot (χύτρα), and the motions of her buttocks
as she handles it excite Lucius, who comments: ὡς εὐρύθμως
. . . τὴν πυγὴν τῇ χύτρᾳ ὁμοῦ συμπεριφέρεις καὶ κλίνεις (κινεῖς
Jacobs). The χύτρα has the secondary sense 'pudenda' (cf. Eu-
pol. frg. 52.2 Kock λοπάδων τοὺς ἄμβωνας, = τὰ χείλη τῶν
αἰδοίων? (Meineke)). In Apuleius' version it is an *olla* (or *ol-*

[1] The argument of Henderson, *The Maculate Muse* (see above, p. 1, n. 2)
p. 139 that βάραθρον was in use with this sense in Greek is unconvincing, on
the evidence offered.

lula) which stands for the female parts (cf. *CGL* II.138.26 'olla χύτρα'): 'quam pulchre quamque festiue . . . *ollulam* istam cum natibus intorques'; cf. *ibid.* 'nam si te uel modice meus igniculus afflauerit, ureris intime nec ullus extinguet ardorem tuum nisi ego, quae dulce condiens et *ollam* et lectulum suaue quatere noui'. On the use of *olla* in a proverb at Catull. 94.2, see p. 29.

I mention finally a double meaning given to *ara* at *Priap.* 73.4: 'quae tamen exanimis nunc est et inutile lignum, / utilis haec, aram si dederitis, erit'. *Ara* was a generic term indicating any type of altar; the author need not have had in mind a domestic altar. Since the altar could be a raised platform, *ara* here may be intended to suggest the external pudenda, whether the mons veneris, labia or clitoris. It would certainly have been coined off-the-cuff, but the author may have recalled the use of ἐσχάρα at Aristoph. *Eq.* 1286, quoted above (cf. schol. τὰ χείλη τῶν γυναικείων αἰδοίων). *Ara* and ἐσχάρα overlapped in meaning.

In most of the above metaphors it would have been not only the shape of the object which was suggestive, but also its heat (a theme on which Apuleius elaborates). For the 'fiery' character of the female parts, see also Auson. *Cent. Nupt.* 111, p. 216 P. 'est in secessu, tenuis quo semita ducit, / ignea rima micans: exhalat opaca mephitim'; cf. *CIL* IV.1830 add. p. 212 'futuitur cunnus [pil]ossus multo melius [qu]am glaber: / e[ad]em continet uaporem . . .'.

(vi) Containers

Some of the metaphors above could be included in this section; here I deal with those containers which are not necessarily kitchen utensils. The metaphor of the bag or container can be employed to designate the womb as well as the vagina; indeed it is not always possible to be sure which of these parts a writer had in mind.

In Greek note Aristoph. *Lys.* 824 σάκανδρος, Hesych. *s.v.* σάκαν τὸ τῆς γυναικός; cf. Eng. *bag, old bag*, which may originally have been used *pars pro toto*. Lucilius uses *bulga* ('leather bag': see Fest. p. 31 'bulgas Galli sacculos scorteos appellant') of the womb at 623 'ita uti quisque nostrum e bulga est matris in lucem editus'. There is no context at 73 ('in bulgam penetrare pilosam'), but he may have been describing a sexual act; for a possible example of *pilosus* referring to the female pudenda, see *CIL* IV.1830 add. p. 212, quoted above. Lucilius no doubt coined the metaphorical use of *bulga* himself. Tertullian is the only other writer who uses the word in a similar anatomical sense (*Nat.* 1.10.36 'omitto quae bulgae aut sacrilegae gulae uidebantur. . .' (= 'belly' > 'gluttony'?)).

In his note on Virg. *Georg.* 3.136 Servius glosses Virgil's *aruum* with *folliculus*, by which he meant the womb: 'genitali aruo pro muliebri folliculo, quem uuluam uocant, ut etiam Plinius docet: nam ante folliculus dicebatur'. He alludes here to Plin. *Nat.* 11.209 ('quod alio nomine locos appellant, hoc in reliquis animalibus uoluam'), but it is not clear what the authority for the last remark is. In medical Latin *folliculus* is sometimes used of the membrane which encloses the foetus (Gk. χόριον) (e.g. Cael. Aurel. *Gyn.* p. 32.829 '(corion) nos etiam folliculum appellamus, siue quod intra se fetum claudat, siue quod acceptum contegat ac ministrat spiritum',[1] Soran. Lat. (Mustio) p. 23.22 'si uero folliculus diu non fuerit ruptus'), but it never seems to have been a regular designation of the womb itself (but see Fulgent. p. 150.23 Helm).

Vas ('vessel, container') is used suggestively with the womb in mind by Julius Valerius, p. 7.27 'quod enim signari uidisti uirginal feminae, fidem rei uisae testatur. consignatio enim fides est atque ueritas, ex quo praenosti, quod illa conceperit; nemo enim uas uacuum consignauerit'. Here he was following ps.-Callisthenes fairly closely: 1.9.3, p. 9.10 Kroll οὐδεὶς γὰρ κενὸν ἀγγεῖον σφραγίζει. *Vasculum*, like *folliculus*, was used in the same sense as χόριον in the medical language (e.g. Cael. Aurel. *Gyn.* p. 32.822 'uocatur etiam hec membrana regio, et uasculum, et secunda, et preruptio'; cf. Soran. Lat. (Mustio) p. 18.14).

The malapropism *uter* ('bladder') for *uterus* in late Latin (*Mul. Chir.* 224 'similiter et tiniolae in utri, quae pediculi ab alis appellantur', *CGL* III.248.34 'γαστήρ uter') may be attributed to a popular tendency to look upon the womb as resembling a bladder. Pliny associates *uterus* with *utriculus*, 'little blad-

---

[1] The *Gynaecia* of Caelius Aurelianus (translated from a work by Soranus) is here quoted by page and line numbers from the edition by M. F. Drabkin and I. E. Drabkin, *Caelius Aurelianus, Gynaecia* (Baltimore, 1951). For further examples of *folliculus*, see their index, p. 129 (where the sense is given as 'afterbirth').

der', at *Nat.* 11.209: 'feminis eadem omnia praeterque uesicae iunctus utriculus, unde dictus uterus'. Cf. Isid. *Etym.* 11.1.135. See below, p. 90 on *sinus*.

(vii) Doors and paths

The external female pudenda may be likened to a door, and the vagina to a path or passage. The symbolism of the door is implicit in Isidore's remarks at *Etym.* 8.11.69 ('Iunonem dicunt quasi ianonem, id est ianuam, pro purgationibus feminarum, eo quod quasi portas matrum natorum pandat, et nubentum maritis') and 11.1.137 ('uulua uocata quasi ualua, id est ianua uentris, uel quod semen recipiat, uel quod ex ea foetus procedat'). For such metaphors in Greek, see Aristoph. *Vesp.* 768 θύρα, *Lys.* 250 πύλη, Antiphilus, *A.P.* 9.415.6 σανίδες, Eratosthenes, *A.P.* 5.242.3ff. πυλεών, πρόθυρον. Most examples of the metaphor in Latin refer to the anus (e.g. Catull. 15.18, Pers. 4.36; cf. *Priap.* 52.5), but that must be a matter of chance. Note Auson. *Cent. Nupt.* 112, p. 216 P. 'nulli fas casto sceleratum insistere *limen*' (= 'entrance to the vagina'). For the metaphor of the path, see Serv. on Virg. *Georg.* 3.136 ' "sulcos oblimet" claudat meatus', Auson. *Cent. Nupt.* 110f. p. 216 P. 'est in secessu, tenuis quo semita ducit, / ignea rima micans', 115 'huc iuuenes nota fertur regione uiarum', 126, p. 217 'itque reditque uiam' (for the anus or rectum described in such terms see Arnob. *Nat.* 2.16, Isid. *Etym.* 11.1.105). In Greek note the double entendre in στενωπεῖον at Ach. Tat. 8.9.3.

(viii) *Nauis*

The sense 'pudenda muliebria' is sometimes ascribed to *nauis* at Plaut. *Men.* 401f. and *Rud.* 354,[1] but there are no grounds for this view.[2] However *nauis* was used metaphorically of the womb in a joke by Julia quoted at Macrob. *Sat.* 2.5.9 (discussed below, p. 167). A word denoting any hollow object or container (in this case the hollow hull of the ship) can readily be used metaphorically of the womb or vagina.

---

[1] See Pierrugues, *s.v.*, Lewis and Short, *s.v.*, Grassmann, p. 28.
[2] See Adams, *Culus*, pp. 251f. (with examples of *nauis* = 'rump of chicken').

(ix) Topographical imagery

At *Anth. Lat.* 382.2 ('post mille complexus, post dulcia sauia penem / *confiniis laterum* retortum suscipe, posco'; cf. 253.124 'non omnis resupina iacet, sed corpore flexo / molliter et *laterum* qua se *confinia iungunt'*) the 'common boundary' of the *latera* (of a female) is obviously the *cunnus*. Similar topographical imagery can be seen in Tertullian's *fines*, lit. 'extremities, frontiers', = 'genitalia' at *Anim.* 38.2: 'fines suos ad instar ficulneae contagionis prurigine accingit'.[1] Cf. *terminus* (Pompon. 126), = 'boundary marker', > 'penis'.

3. Some euphemisms

(i) *Sinus (muliebris)*

Sinus is used of the vagina or womb by Tibullus, 1.8.36: 'teneros conserit usque sinus'; cf. Ovid *Fast.* 5.256 'tangitur et tacto concipit illa sinu'. As an anatomical (or near-anatomical) term *sinus* strictly denoted the space between the chest and the arms held in front of the chest as if to clasp an object (= 'bosom'). It is not from this usage that the above anatomical examples could be derived, but from its use in application to any hollow space or cavity.

Tibullus' expression anticipates, but is unconnected with, a later medical use of *sinus* (+ *muliebris, femininus*, et sim.), of the vagina. The medical usage was introduced as a calque on γυναικεῖος κόλπος, which was in use in later medical Greek. For the sense of γυναικεῖος κόλπος see Rufus, *Onom.* 196 εἶτα τὸ κοίλωμα τὸ ἐφεξῆς, γυναικεῖος κόλπος, καὶ αἰδοῖον τὸ σύμπαν σύν τοῖς ἐπιφανέσιν (making a distinction between γυναικεῖος κόλπος, 'vagina', and the αἰδοῖον in general); contrast Soran. p. 181.24f. Rose, where γυναικεῖος κόλπος is equated with γυναικεῖον αἰδοῖον: τὸ δὲ γυναικεῖον αἰδοῖον καὶ κόλπος ὠνόμασται γυναικεῖος. Soranus uses γυναικεῖος κόλπος constantly. The calque *sinus muliebris* is found often in his translators Caelius

---

[1] This passage has been elucidated by J. H. Waszink, *Quinti Septimi Florentis Tertulliani De Anima* (Amsterdam, 1947), pp. 436f. I should not be inclined, however, to relate Apul. *Met.* 2.16 *inguinum fine* to this usage; *fine* is 'prepositional', = 'as far as'.

Aurelianus and Soran. Lat. (Mustio).[1] The use of the expression
as a translation can be seen at (e.g.) Cael. *Gyn.* p. 4.79f. 'toto
sinu muliebri' = Soran. p. 176.17f. Rose ὅλῳ τῷ γυναικείῳ . . .
κόλπῳ (cf. Cael. *Gyn.* p. 7.157 = Soran. p. 182.6f., Cael. *Gyn.*
p. 9.215 = Soran. p. 187.23), Cass. Fel. 78, p. 191.3 'in sinum
mulieris infundes, quem Graeci colpon appellant'. For the
sense of *sinus muliebris*, see also Soran. Lat. (Mustio) p. 9.3
'(sinus muliebris) quem uulgo connum appellant'. The form of
the expression is not invariable. Sometimes *sinus* is used without *muliebris* or an equivalent (Cael. *Gyn.* p. 114.1412), and
femininus is often substituted for *muliebris* by Caelius;[2] note
too Vindic. *Epit. Alt.* 32, p. 480.14 'quod Greci genicion colpon
uocant, hoc est feminum [*sic*] sinum'. For *sinus mulieris* see
the passage of Cassius Felix quoted above, and Mustio p. 8.15,[3]
and for *feminarum sinus* see Cael. *Chron.* 5.71. A more striking variant is that of Mustio p. 89.9 'inmissa manu sua obsetrix
omnes in sinum uuluae repellat'. It is impossible to tell
whether the author of *Anth. Lat.* 144.2 'uirgineos ardens pan-
dere fraude sinus' was influenced by medical terminology, or
had in mind poetic usages of the type seen above.

Lactantius at *Inst.* 1.20.36 used the expression *sinu pudendo*
when he must have had the penis in mind: 'Tutinus, in cuius
sinu pudendo nubentes praesident' (for the implication, see
Aug. *Ciu.* 6.9 'super cuius inmanissimum et turpissimum fascinum sedere noua nupta iubebatur'). But it would be a mistake to say that he has employed *sinus* = 'penis'. He has
spoken loosely of the bride sitting in the god's 'lap' or 'bosom'
to avoid anatomical exactitude.

(ii) Adjoining parts

I have shown earlier that the sexual organs may be referred
to by the name of a nearby part of no sexual significance
(pp. 47ff.). A use of *uesica* (lit. 'bladder') at Juv. 1.39 ('in cae-
lum quos euehit optima summi / nunc uia processus, uetulae

[1] For Caelius Aurelianus, see the edition of Drabkin and Drabkin (cited
above, p. 88 n. 1), index, p. 134; for Mustio, see, e.g. pp. 8.16, 14.19, 96.4,
96.19, 97.2f., 107.3 Rose. Examples are quoted by J. Medert, *Quaestiones
criticae et grammaticae ad Gynaecia Mustionis pertinentes* (Giessen, 1911),
pp. 25, 75, 78.
[2] See the edition of Drabkin and Drabkin, index, p. 134.
[3] On the text here see Medert, p. 25.

uesica beatae') seems to be of the same type: Juvenal may deliberately have failed to make a distinction between the bladder / urethra and the vagina (for the position of the *uesica* note Cels. 4.1.11 'in feminis (uesica) super genitale earum sita est'). There is a superficially similar example at 6.64 ('Ledam molli saltante Bathyllo / Tuccia uesicae non imperat'), but Juvenal was perhaps coarsely suggesting that the referent was becoming *uda* with desire.[1] Just as male semen could be called *urina* (Juv. 11.170; cf. the use of *mingo*, *meio* and their derivatives of ejaculation, p. 142), so female secretions (considered in antiquity to be a form of semen) might be vulgarly looked upon in the same light.

There is a curious use of *rene* (abl. sing., formed from the usual plural *renes*, 'kidneys'; *renis / ren* are not usual as nominative singular forms) at Auson. *Epigr.* 34.2, p. 324 P. 'utere rene tuo: casta puella anus est'. The kidneys might have been thought of by Ausonius as a seat of sexual desire (for the sexual desire of the male located in the *lumbi*, see *Schol. Pers.* 1.20), but no reader could fail to take *rene* as a euphemism for *cunnus*. In this case the 'neighbouring part' might be thought to be on the opposite side of the body to the sexual organ. Such a usage is not without parallel. ὀσφῦς ('loins') is used of the penis by ps.-Luc. *Asinus* 9, 51, and *lumbulus* seems to refer to the male sexual organs in the *Testamentum Porcelli* (p. 48).

Gremium is sometimes used of the uterus or vagina: e.g. Catull. 67.30 'qui ipse sui gnati minxerit in gremium' (cf. Ter. *Eun.* 585, Stat. *Theb.* 1.234).[2] The word literally denoted the lap. In this case a word for an adjacent area (as distinct from an adjacent part of the body) was transferred to the genitalia. The semantic change has a parallel in the transfer of *sinus* ('bosom') to the adjacent chest (Tac. *Hist.* 3.10 'opposuit sinum Antonius stricto ferro'; cf. Fr. *sein*).

Euphemisms of the type under discussion are quite common in Biblical Latin, where they ultimately reflect Hebrew usage. Jerome (*Epist.* 22.11.2) attributes to *umbilicus* at Job 40.11 the sense 'female genitalia', and he goes on to make some observations on the phenomenon (*lumbi* and *femur* are given as further examples): 'Iob deo carus . . . audi quid de diabolo suspicetur: "uirtus eius in lumbis et potestas eius in umbilico".

---

[1] For *uda* of a woman in a state of arousal, see Mart. 11.16.8, Juv. 10.321.
[2] See further *TLL* VI.2.2322.36ff.

honeste uiri mulierisque genitalia immutatis sunt appellata nominibus'.

Apuleius' coinage *interfeminium* (*Apol.* 33; lit. 'the space between the thighs') can be mentioned here;[1] compare the circumlocutions at *Met.* 10.24 'titione candenti inter media femina detruso crudelissime necauit', 7.28 'ardentemque titionem gerens mediis inguinibus obtrudit' and 8.25 'nam si faciem tuam mediis eius feminibus immiseris'. There is no question here of the word for an adjacent body part being equated with *cunnus*. But the sexual organ is named by reference to its position in relation to another, non-sexual, part of the body.

(iii) 'Female parts', etc.

There is a variety of designations for the female genitalia comparable with designations such as *uirilia, uirilitas, membrum uirile* for the male. Some of these are substantival, others are adjective + noun combinations.

Muliebria is rare, but found in Tacitus: *Ann.* 14.60 'ex quibus (ancillis) una instanti Tigellino castiora esse muliebria Octauiae respondit quam os eius';[2] cf. Soran. Lat. (Mustio) p. 108.5 'haemorroides raro quidem in muliebribus inueniuntur' (text doubtful). Note too *loci muliebres* (*loca muliebria*) (Varro *Ling.* 5.15, Scrib. Larg. 156, Marc. Emp. 25.2, Soran. Lat. (Mustio) pp. 67.18, 107.1), *muliebre membrum* (Auson. *Epigr.* 87.3, p. 344 P.), *partes muliebres* (Soran. Lat. (Mustio) pp. 50.11, 99.7).

Feminal was coined by Apuleius: *Met.* 2.17 'glabellum feminal rosea palmula . . . obumbrans'. The adjective *fēminalis* is not attested elsewhere,[3] and hence *feminal* would have been

---

[1] For anatomical terms deriving from prepositional expressions, see Svennung, pp. 112ff.

[2] This is one of the few references to the sexual organs in Tacitus (cf. *genitalia* at *Hist.* 5.5).

[3] H. D. Jocelyn points out to me that *feminal* is possibly a derivative of *femur* (cf. *interfeminium*). Nevertheless there was a marked tendency for adjectives of the base *fēmin-* to be applied (in various combinations) to the female parts. For *femininus* combined with *sinus*, see p. 91; cf. *ueretrum femininum* at Cael. Aurel. *Gyn.* p. 6.150, = Soran. p. 181.24f. Rose γυναικεῖον αἰδοῖον; cf. *Gyn.* pp. 67.123, 118.1522. Note too *feminee partes* at Cael. Aurel. *Gyn.* p. 33.855, = Soran. p. 236.12 τοὺς τῆς γυναικὸς τόπους, and *feminea natura* at Jul. Obs. 51. *Feminium* (= *femineum*, substantival) appears in a Medieval medical text, the *Tractatus de cura omnium causarum matricis* (*Cod. Vendôme* 175 (s. XI)). Note *fol.* 101 r, XXIIII tit. 'mulier si in feminio uermes habuerit' (see Henry E. Sigerist, *Bull. Hist. Med.* 14 (1943), p. 106). This example was drawn to my attention by Dr. K.-D. Fischer.

euphemistic because of its recherché quality. There is some
alternation between the endings *-ale* and *-al* in the neuter of
-alis adjectives. *-al* sometimes serves as the nominal ending,
-ale as the adjectival. The neuter nouns *capital* and *cubital*
stand in the same relationship to the adjectives *capitalis, -e*
and *cubitalis, -e*, as *feminal* to **feminalis, -e. Tribunale* is
attested alongside *tribunal* (Quint. 1.6.17), and both *penetrale*
and *penetral*, and *ceruicale* and *ceruical*, are found.

Both *uirginal* and *uirginale* were used in Imperial and late
Latin. For *uirginal* see Jul. Val. p. 7.18, 25 (the Greek original
did not influence Valerius here: see ps.-Callisthenes 1.8.3, p.
9.9 Kroll φύσις), Prud. *Peristeph.* 14.8, *CGL* V.254.3 (?), and
for *uirginale*, see Phaedr. 4.16.12. The *uirginal* at Prud. *Peristeph.* 14.8 belongs to a virgin, but *uirginal(e)* was also employed even when the referent was not 'virginal'. It could be
classified as hyper-euphemistic, in that it is based on a refusal
by the user to contemplate that the sexual parts might have
been used for sexual purposes. In the *Mulomedicina Chironis*
another form of the word, *uirginalis* (sc. *pars*), is the standard
term for the pudenda of a mare.[1] At 761 *uirginalis* corresponds
to αἰδοῖον at *Hipp. Berol.* 14.11, *CHG* I, p. 84.6: 'oportebit
autem uirginalem eius manu tractare et ipsam uuluam', =
δεῖ δὲ κατὰ τοῦ αἰδοίου ἐνθεῖναι τὴν χεῖρα καὶ παρεῖναι εἰς τὴν
μήτραν.

(iv) Specialisation

Euphemisms of this type tend to be capable of signifying both
the male and female parts. I have discussed these at length
earlier, and hence there is no need here to give more than a
few special examples.

Loci (*loca*) with or without specification was from early Latin
used of the female parts: e.g. Cato *Agr.* 157.11 'et si mulier eo
lotio locos fouebit',[2] *Mul. Chir.* 769 'ad loca imponito'; cf. Varro
Rust. 2.7.8 'contra ab locis equae nares equi tangunt', Ovid

[1] See Oder, index, s.v. *uerginalis*, where 17 examples are quoted.
[2] Cato presumably had in mind here the external female pudenda. *Loci* could
also indicate the womb (Plin. *Nat.* 11.209; cf. 26.152, where the word is
probably used of the external surface of the womb, i.e. the lower belly). There
is nothing surprising in the application of such a vague word to two different
parts. In any case a lexical distinction is not always maintained between the
vagina and womb.

Ars. 2.719 'cum loca reppereris, quae tangi femina gaudet'. For the unusual meaning 'penis', see Lucr. 4.1034, 1045.

Some other general words or expressions applied to the female genitalia are *inferior pars* (Cels. 4.27.1D) and *infima pars* (Catull. 60.2). *Viscera*, a vague term for the internal organs, was applicable to the female internal pudenda or to the anus / rectum (see p. 116). For the first sense see Ovid *Am.* 2.14.27 'uestra quid effoditis subiectis uiscera telis / et nondum natis dira uenena datis?', *Priap.* 66.4 'intra uiscera habere concupiscis (notam uirilem)', Aug. *Ciu.* 14.26 'feminea uiscera'. Similar euphemisms are found at Sen. *Contr.* 2.5.4 'uerberibus corpus abrumpitur exprimiturque <sanguis> ipsis *uitalibus*', ps.-Theod. Prisc. *Addit.* p. 343.5 'mulier supra dimissis uestibus apparata sedeat, ut ipse uapor ad eius *interiora* perueniat'.

On *naturale*, see p. 60

4. Miscellaneous usages

(i) *Rima* and the like

According to Rufus (*Onom.* 110; cf. Pollux 2.174) σχίσμα was used of the opening of the vagina (ἡ τομὴ τοῦ αἰδοίου). The existence of the term in the medical language (though it is not elsewhere attested) is an indication that such designations are not necessarily indecent. Nevertheless the comparable words found in Latin had no place in learned prose. Juvenal's description of the external genitalia at 3.97 ('uacua et plana omnia dicas / infra uentriculum et *tenui distantia rima*') was recalled by Ausonius when he wrote the *Cento Nuptialis*: 110f., p. 216 P. '*tenuis* quo semita ducit, / ignea *rima* micans'. Note too the pleonastic expression at *Epigr.* 87.6, p. 344 P. 'fissi rima qua patet'. *Fissa* survived with this sense in Italian dialects (e.g. Sic. *fissa*).[1] For *rima*, see also *CGL* II.174.49 'rima ῥαγάς, ῥύμη, γυναικεία φύσις'. It is impossible to determine the status of *rima*, but it is not unlikely that Juvenal adopted the usage off-the-cuff and was imitated by Ausonius.

Two examples of *hiatus* in Martial and the *Corpus Priapeo-*

---

[1] See *FEW* III, p. 582.

rum refer specifically to a *laxus cunnus*: Mart. 3.72.5 'infinito lacerum patet inguen hiatu', *Priap.* 12.13 'qui tanto patet indecens hiatu'. That at Claud. *Carm. Min.* 43.7 ('spurcos auidae lambit meretricis hiatus') is more nearly equivalent to *cunnus*. This nominal usage corresponds to the use of the verb *hio* in reference to bodily orifices: Hor. *Epod.* 8.5 'hietque turpis inter aridas natis / podex uelut crudae bouis', Cels. 7.29.5 '(uolua) hiante'. The offensive tone of *hiatus* is unmistakable: the *laxus cunnus* was a common topic of obscene invective. In the passages of Martial and the *Priapea* above, as at *CIL* IV.10004 'Eupla laxa landicosa', the defect is associated with an enlarged clitoris.[1]

(ii) *Longao* and *culus*

There is a good deal of interchange between words (particularly metaphors) for 'anus / rectum' and those for 'vagina' (see, e.g., p. 84 on *hortus*/ κῆπος, and p. 89 on the metaphor of the door: see also Chapter IV). On the use of *cunnus* = *culus*, see p. 116;[2] conversely, *culus* survived as an equivalent of *cunnus* in some French dialects.[3] A parallel semantic change is perhaps to be seen in the use of *longao* (strictly 'rectum') of the vagina at Vindic., *Epit. Alt.* 32, p. 480.18: 'huius ceruicis uel cornu in tribus foraminibus porrigitur usque ad longaonem, in qua res uenerias perficitur'. It is not clear what lies behind this usage, but it is not impossible that an epitomator, faced with a corrupt text of Vindicianus, misunderstood his meaning.

(iii) *Spurium*

According to Isidore, *spurium* was once a designation of the female pudenda: *Etym.* 9.5.24 'quia muliebrem naturam ueteres spurium uocabant'. Plutarch (*Quaest. Rom.* 103) reports a theory that the adjective *spurius* derived from a Sabine word (σπόριον) for the female parts, which was allegedly applied to illegitimate children as a term of abuse: λεκτέον δὲ καὶ τὸν ἕτερον λόγον, ἔστι δ᾽ ἀτοπώτερος· τοὺς γὰρ Σαβίνους φασὶ τὸ τῆς γυναικὸς αἰδοῖον ὀνομάζειν σπόριον, εἶθ᾽ οἷον ἐφυβρίζοντας οὕτω

---

[1] See Jocelyn, *LCM* 5.7 (Jul. 1980), pp. 153f.
[2] See also Adams, *Culus*, pp. 262f.
[3] See A. Zauner, *RF* 14 (1903), p. 522.

προσαγορεύειν τὸν ἐκ γυναικὸς ἀγάμου καὶ ἀνεγγύου γεγενημέ-
νον. It seems certain that both writers were drawing on a
common source, probably Varro. If Varro did indeed provide
the information, it would be reasonable to suppose that *spurium* had once, somewhere, had the sense in question. Ernout
and Meillet (s.v. *spurius*) suggest that the word may have been
Etruscan in origin (cf. the Etruscan name *Spurinna*). If so, it
might once have been used by Etruscan prostitutes in Rome,
just as *eugium* seems to have been used by Greek prostitutes.

(iv) *Coitus*

The use of *coitus* in a concrete sense (= *cunnus*) at Jer. *Epist.*
84.5.3 ('quod si dederimus, statim expetunt uuluam et coitum
et cetera, quae in uentre sunt et sub uentre. singula membra
negant et corpus, quod constat ex membris, dicunt resurgere')
is similar to the concrete use of *uenus* (lit. 'sexual intercourse',
> 'penis') and a few other words (see p. 57).

5. Parts of the female genitalia

(i) Clitoris

The function of the part was well understood, and it is often
mentioned in connection with sexual acts. *Tribades* were
thought to employ it as a male might employ the *mentula* (see
Mart. 1.90.7f., Phaedr. 4.16.13). The clitoris that was exces-
sively large provided a topic of abuse (see p. 79).

The *vox propria* was *landica*, a word which, at least in Classical Latin, was so indecent that Cicero alludes to it only by
means of a *cacemphaton* at *Fam.* 9.22.2 ('hanc culpam maiorem
an *illam dicam?*'). Its currency in the vulgar language is shown
by *CIL* XI.6721.5 'peto [la]ndicam Fuluiae' and *CIL* IV.10004
'Eupla laxa landicosa' (this derivative is not attested elsewhere). It was also used by the author of the *Corpus Priapeorum*, a work in which the basic obscenities are freely admitted:
78.5 'nunc misella landicae / uix posse iurat ambulare prae
fossis'. By contrast Juvenal, who alludes to the clitoris a few
times (see below), avoids *landica*. The sense of *landica* is established by the second inscription above, in which the woman

must surely be abused for the size of the part,[1] and by its use in later medical Latin: Soran. Lat. (Mustio) p. 9.6 'quem uulgo connum appellant. cuius foris labra graece pterigomata dicuntur, latine pinnacula dicta sunt, et a superiore parte descendens in medio dicta est landica'; cf. Cael. Aurel. *Gyn.* p. 113.1392 'quibusdam landicis horrida comitatur magnitudo et feminas partium feditate confundit et, ut plerique memorant, ipse adfecte tentigine uirorum similem appetentiam sumunt et in uenerem coacte ueniunt'. *Landica* survived in Old French (*landie*).

Nymfe, which Mustio uses at p. 106.3 ('turpitudinis symptoma est grandis yos nymfe'; cf. *landica*, p. 106.1), was taken over from Soranus (νύμφη). It would not have been in use in Latin. Medical writers (particularly translators) had a habit of carelessly introducing a Greek word from their source even when there existed a native Latinism (cf. *fisis*, p. 61, and *balanus*, p. 72). For νύμφη, and its synonym μύρτον, see Rufus *Onom.* 112. . . ταῦτα δὲ Εὐρυφῶν καὶ κρημνοὺς καλεῖ· οἱ δὲ νῦν τὰ μὲν μυρτόχειλα, πτερυγώματα, τὸ δὲ μύρτον, νύμφην (see also Pollux 2.174).

Various other designations, *ad hoc* metaphors and the like, are recorded for the part in Latin. One such, *nasus* at *Priap.* 12.14 ('barbato macer eminente naso'), is an 'anatomical' metaphor of a type I have discussed above (p. 35). The usage reflects the similarity which was observed between the clitoris and the penis. For the use in application to the clitoris of a term more normally applicable to the penis, see *uenus* at Mart. 1.90.8: 'inter se geminos audes committere cunnos / mentiturque uirum prodigiosa uenus'.

Juvenal employed *crista* as an *ad hoc* metaphor at 6.422: 'callidus et cristae digitos inpressit aliptes / ac summum dominae femur exclamare coegit'. Similarly for a derivative of *crista* (*cristatus*) used of part of the penis, see Maxim. *Eleg.* 5.98. For metaphors in Greek, see Hesych. *s.v.* κυσθοκορώνη· νύμφη (= Com. adesp. 1060 Kock), Nicarchus, *A.P.* 11.329.2 δεινὴν χοῖρος ἄκανθαν ἔχει(?).

On *uolua* at Juv. 6.129, and *ara* at *Priap.* 73.4, see pp. 103, 87.

---

[1] For the 'laxness' of the *cunnus* (note *laxa* in the inscription) associated with an enlarged clitoris, see above, p. 96.

(ii) Labia

Orae is used a number of times by Celsus of the labia (e.g. 2.7.15 'oras naturalium', 7.26.1C 'inter imas oras', = 'labia minora'; cf. 7.26.4, 7.28.1 twice). It may have been an attempt to render the Greek κρημνοί, which is employed thus at Hipp. *Loc. Hom.* 47, and is mentioned by Rufus as a term used by Euryphon (*Onom.* 112, quoted above, p. 98; cf. Pollux 2.174).

According to Mustio, p. 9.4f. (quoted above, p. 98) the labia (*labra* is the word which he uses, but it is not otherwise recorded in this sense) were called *pinnacula*, 'little wings'. To this passage corresponds Caelius, *Gyn.* p. 7.152ff. 'interior ergo pars collo matricis connectitur, exterius uero fibris adnexa est quas pinnas uocant feminini sinus'. Despite the use of *dicta sunt* and *uocant*, neither writer was employing current Latin terminology (cf. καλεῖται at Soran. p. 183.17 Rose), as is clear from the variant terms *pinnacula* and *pinnae* which were allegedly in use. Both words are calques on πτερυγώματα, as Mustio states. For this word in Soranus, see, e.g., pp. 182.2, 183.17 Rose. It is quoted from Galen (19.114) as well as Soranus, and is described by Rufus as a modern term (*Onom.* 112, quoted above, p. 98; cf. Pollux 2.174). For *pinnacula* elsewhere in Mustio, see, e.g., pp. 96.4, 19, 107.2. The same word is found in Caelius at *Gyn.* p. 118.1527, but usually Caelius prefers *fibrae* (at, e.g., *Gyn.* p. 114.1411 – 'nascitur thimus aliquando in fibris' – this word corresponds to *pinnacula* at Mustio p. 107.2: 'clauuli uero nascuntur et in pinnaculis et ...').[1] It is impossible to tell whether *fibrae* had any currency. It is not quoted from any other writer in this sense,[2] although Goetz proposed to introduce it in two glosses (*CGL* V.456.45 'fibre partes iecoris pecodis uenas sanguinum'; cf. V.500.62) by changing *sanguinum* to *inguinum*.[3] But the conjecture is not certain, and even if it were accepted *inguinum* need not necessarily signify the female genitalia. There seems to have been no standard word for the labia in Latin. Mustio's *labra* was

---

[1] For further examples of *fibrae*, see the index in the edition of Drabkin and Drabkin, p. 129.
[2] See *TLL* VI.1.643.52ff., quoting only Cael. Aurel. *Acut.* 3.184.
[3] See *TLL*, loc. cit.

influenced by χεῖλη (see Soran. p. 183.18 Rose; cf. Hipp. *Mul.* 1.40).[1]

(iii) Womb

In the Republic *uterus* was in use as a designation for the womb, alongside *uenter* and *aluus*, which, though they were general in sense (= 'belly'), were readily applicable to this part (cf. γαστήρ and νηδύς in Greek). Indeed *uterus* itself may originally have meant 'belly'.[2] It has this meaning at (e.g.) Lucil. 541, Cels. 1. introd. 42, 3.21.14, 4.1.4, 4.1.5, 7.14.5, 7.21.1. But whereas *aluus* and *uenter* continued to have a wide range of uses, *uterus* from an early date showed a strong tendency to be specialised. Plautus uses it 8 times in the sense 'womb' (I include in these figures the examples at *Stich.* 163, 387), and there are 4 other examples with this meaning in comic fragments (Turp. 179, Afran. 337, 345; cf. Caec. 94 *uter*). The word has only this sense in Cicero (*Nat.* 2.128) and Varro (*Rust.* 2.2.14). Nevertheless, though *uterus* may have been the *vox propria*, Republican writers were as likely to use *aluus* or *uenter* (on the difference between these two, see below): note, e.g. Plaut. *Curc.* 221, *Stich.* 159, Lucr. 5.225, Cic. *Cluent.* 34, *Pis.* frg. 14, *Diu.* 1.39, Varro *Rust.* 2.8.6, 3.12.4. *Vterus* may have been developing a rather formal tone by the early Empire. It is common enough in epic (Virg. *Aen.* 8 times, Ovid *Met.* 16, Statius 11, Lucan 3, Silius 2, Valerius Flaccus 2), but unusual in satire (Lucil. 541, Juv. 6.599, 10.309). Certainly it must eventually have fallen out of everyday use, since it leaves no trace in the Romance languages.

I have elsewhere shown[3] that by the early Empire *aluus* (in all its senses) had acquired a recherché tone, whereas *uenter* remained in everyday use. It is not surprising to find *uenter*

[1] It is perhaps worth mentioning here the absurd notion of Judith P. Hallett (*Hermes* 105 (1977), pp. 252f.) that *os* and *labra* at Mart. 1.83.1. ('os et labra tibi lingit, Manneia, catellus: / non miror, merdas si libet esse cani') indicate parts of the female pudenda. One cannot legitimately argue that Martial based a pun on an obscure medical calque which is only attested in a very late translation. There are various calques for unseen parts of the female genitalia which seem to have been totally unknown in the ordinary language (see below, p. 108).

[2] Cf. the possible cognates Skt. *udáram* = 'belly', Gk. ὅδερος=γαστήρ (Hesych.). See Ernout and Meillet, *s.v.*

[3] See Adams, 'Anatomical terminology', p. 54.

used of the womb in works of colloquial or vulgar flavour (e.g.
Rustius Barbarus, *CPL* 304.9[1] 'habio . . . / fratrem gemellum
qui de unum / uentrem exiut', *Mul. Chir.* 745, 765), and its
reflexes in Romance can bear this sense.[2] But it was never fully
specialised, and it came to be outnumbered (in our sense) by
more specific terms.

Vulua came into rivalry with *uterus* as the specialised word
for the womb in the early Empire. According to Pliny (*Nat.*
11.209), *uulua* was the term for an animal's matrix: 'feminis
eadem omnia praeterque uesicae iunctus utriculus, unde dictus uterus. quod alio nomine locos appellant, hoc in reliquis
animalibus uoluam'. It is not impossible that the word was
originally applicable to the anatomy of animals, and then, like
various other words (e.g. *pellis*, *rostrum*, *gamba*), transferred
to humans. Certainly it was in use as a culinary term for a
sow's matrix (Hor. *Epist.* 1.15.41, Petron. 70.2, Mart. 7.20.11,
13.56.2, Juv. 11.81), and it survived with this meaning in the
old dialect of Sassari.[3] But outside the culinary language there
is little sign of a restriction to the womb of animals (but see
below on the *Mulomedicina Chironis*). Pliny himself uses
uulua twice elsewhere in book 11 of an animal's matrix (210
twice), whereas *uterus* indicates the human womb at 11.270,
but he does not consistently make such a distinction. *Vulua* is
extremely common in the *Natural History*, of the human womb
(see below).

The first example of *uulua* (in any sense) in prose is at Varro
Rust. 2.1.19 'dicuntur agni cordi, qui post tempus nascuntur
ac remanserunt in uoluis intimis . . . uocant chorion, a quo
cordi appellati'. Here *uolua* is used as an equivalent of χόριον,
the membrane which surrounds the foetus. Varro has given
uolua his own special sense ('wrapping, enclosure'), based on
a popular etymology (< *uoluo*; cf. *inuolucrum*). It is in Scribonius Largus and Celsus that *uulua* makes its first appearance meaning 'womb'. In Celsus the word outnumbers *uterus*
by 30:11, and in Scribonius by 2:0 (see 121, 126). *Vulua* usually
means 'womb' in Celsus (note particularly 7.29, where *uulua*
occurs 10 times in an account of the method of delivery of the
stillborn foetus, and 4.1.12, where the womb (*uulua*) is de-

[1] R. Cavenaile, *Corpus Papyrorum Latinarum* (Wiesbaden, 1958).
[2] See *FEW* XIV, p. 251.
[3] *FEW* XIV, p. 648.

scribed precisely: 'ea (uulua), recta tenuataque ceruice, quem
canalem uocant, contra mediam aluum orsa, inde paulum ad
dexteriorem coxam conuertitur; deinde super rectum intestinum progressa, iliis feminae latera sua innectit'). *Vterus*,
however, is not used as an unmarked anatomical term with
this precise sense. Often, as we have seen, it means 'belly'
(internal or external), whether of male or female. At 2.10.1 it
has taken on the meaning 'foetus': 'feminis uterum non ger-
entibus' (cf. e.g. *uenter* at Liv. 1.34.3). And a few times the
phrases *in utero* and *ex utero* are used in roughly the senses
'before birth' and 'after birth, after childbearing' (7.17.1,
7.28.1, 7.32). At 7.28.1 *ex utero* means 'inherited from the
womb', i.e. 'congenital': 'si ex utero est, membrana ori uoluae
opposita est'. Celsus thus restricts *uterus* to certain idiomatic
and special senses, and brings *uulua* into service as the regular
anatomical term.

In later medical Latin (see below), when *uterus* is used at
all, it tends to be restricted to one or two phrases (notably *in
utero*). Celsus would appear to be partially anticipating the
usage of later writers. Presumably *uterus* was already obsolescent in everyday speech, and hence showing a tendency
(later to become more marked) to be restricted to a few idioms.
Celsus seems to have taken *uulua* from popular speech, re-
taining *uterus* as a semantically marked term.

There is sufficient evidence to establish a stylistic distinction
between *uterus* and *uulua* (I leave aside culinary examples of
the word) in the early Empire. *Vterus*, unlike *uulua*, was freely
admitted both in the higher genres of poetry (see above on
epic; cf. Hor. *Carm.* 3.22.2) and in formal prose (e.g. Tacitus
and Apuleius have *uterus* 10 and 11 times respectively, *uulua*
not at all; Seneca the Younger uses *uterus* 18 times, but has
uulua only at *N.Q.* 3.25.11; Pliny the Younger, Suetonius and
Justin all use *uterus*, but not *uulua*, except as a culinary term).
Vulua, for its part, appears in literature in satire and epigram
(on technical prose, see below), both genres which drew on the
everyday language. For the sense 'womb', see Mart. 11.61.11
'nam dum tumenti mersus haeret in uolua', Juv. 2.32 'cum tot
abortiuis fecundam Iulia uuluam / solueret'. The currency of
the word in ordinary speech is shown by its use in *defixiones*.
Note in particular Audollent 135 B.7 'umlicu[m] cunu[m] /
ulua[m]', where its juxtaposition with *cunnus* suggests that it
was the established *vox propria* for the part. Cf. Audollent 300

(= *CIL* VIII.19525 (B).2) 'q(uem) p(eperit) uulua',[1] Audollent 265 A.6 'Victoria / quem [= *quam*] peperit sua / uulua' (cf. 264).[2]

Vulua was not used only of the womb in the early Empire. It tended to shift its reference slightly to other parts of the female genitalia. In the vocabulary of popular speech no rigid distinction is necessarily made between the womb, the internal genitalia (vagina) and the external pudenda (see p. 94 n. 2). Similarly there is some interchange between words for 'anus' and those for 'rectum' in Latin.[3] At 4.1.12, where Celsus describes the outlet of the female urethra in relation to the vagina, he must have meant by the phrase *uuluae ceruicem* not 'neck of the womb', but 'entrance of the vagina': 'tum in masculis iter urinae spatiosius et conpressius a ceruice huius descendit ad colem: in feminis breuius et plenius super uuluae ceruicem se ostendit'. Hence *uulua* must mean 'vagina', or perhaps, more generally, 'vagina + womb'.[4] At 7.28.1, a passage which deals with the affliction of sealed labia (note 'earum naturalia nonnumquam inter se glutinatis oris concubitum non admittunt'), *os uoluae* obviously has much the same sense (for the same expression with the same implication, see Vulg. *Prov.* 30.16; cf. *CGL* III.606.50 'uulua os matricis'): 'si ex utero est, membrana ori uoluae opposita est'. At Pers. 6.73 *uulua* comes close to the sense 'vagina': 'patriciae inmeiat uoluae'. In later Latin note Fulgent. p. 158.18 Helm 'Salomon adulterinae uuluae contagione turpatus'. And at Juv. 6.129 the word has almost certainly been used of part of the external pudenda, viz. the clitoris: 'adhuc ardens rigidae tentigine uoluae, / et lassata uiris necdum satiata recessit'. Both *tentigo* (Hor. *Serm.* 1.2.118, Mart. 7.67.2, *Priap.* 23.4, 33.5) and *rigidus* (Petron. 134.11, Mart. 11.16.5, *Priap.* 4.1, 45.1) were typically used of (male) erection. Such terminology might be applied to the

[1] See David R. Jordan, *Philol.* 120 (1976), pp. 127ff., suggesting a restoration which is certainly right (Audollent tentatively took *puuluam* as equivalent to *puluerem*).

[2] On the text, see Jordan, p. 131 (Audollent *Suauulua*). Jordan points out that in Greek *defixiones* μήτρα sometimes occurs in similar contexts.

[3] See Adams, *Culus*, pp. 238f., and below, p. 116.

[4] Similarly *uterus* may indicate the vagina at Sisenn. *Miles.* 10 'ut eum penitus utero suo recepit'. Sexual penetration was probably being described here, but it is just possible that someone was spoken of as taking refuge in the womb (cf. Justin 1.6.14 'sublata ueste obscena corporis ostendunt rogantes, num in uteros matrum uel uxorum uellent refugere').

clitoris (see Cael. Aurel. *Gyn.* p. 113.1394 for *tentigo* used of an erect *landica*: 'quibusdam landicis horrida comitatur magnitudo et feminas partium feditate confundit et, ut plerique memorant, ipse adfecte tentigine uirorum appetentiam sumunt et in uenerem coacte ueniunt'), but scarcely to any other part of the female genitalia. Similarly the etymology which Isidore offers at *Etym.* 11.1.137 ('uulua uocata quasi ualua, id est ianua uentris, uel quod semen recipiat, uel quod ex ea foetus procedat') suggests that he thought of the word as including the cervix and perhaps the vagina.

Scribonius Largus and Celsus were not alone among technical writers in admitting *uulua*. Columella, it is true, largely rejected *uulua* in favour of *uterus* (*uulua* occurs at 7.9.5 only, compared with 10 examples of *uterus*), but Pliny the Elder, who has only a handful of examples of *uterus*,[1] used *uulua* with extreme frequency (e.g. in 26.151–61 there are 14 examples of *uulua*, against 2 of *uterus*).[2]

If one is right in seeing in *uulua* a word from the popular language in the early Empire, one is faced with the need to explain its acceptance by a few technical writers. Celsus' Latin, though syntactically correct, presents a curiously mixed vocabulary. *Abdomen*, for example, which also seems to have started as a term for a part of an animal's anatomy (see Plin. *Nat.* 11.211), and which occurs only in abusive contexts in formal prose (Cic. *Pis.* 41, *Sest.* 110, Sen. *Ben.* 7.26.4; like *uulua*, the word is avoided in high poetry, but found in Juvenal (4.107)), was freely admitted by him (10 times) in application to the human anatomy. Pliny's language is often artificial, but he too allowed colloquialisms.[3] Technical writers were less selective in their choice of words than orators, historians and other non-technical prose writers. In any case the womb is not a part which might be expected to attract outright vulgarisms. Whereas the external female pudendum, as an observable and manifestly sexual part, is often the subject of comment in coarse speech, the womb, as an internal organ which has no obvious part in sexual intercourse, is infrequently mentioned

---

[1] Schneider, *In C. Plini Secundi Naturalis Historiae Libros Indices* (cited above, p. 54 n. 1), *s.v.* quotes only 6 examples, but his collection is not complete (add, e.g. 28.247).

[2] Schneider's collection of examples runs to about five columns.

[3] See A. Önnerfors, *Pliniana, in Plinii Maioris Naturalem Historiam Studia Grammatica Semantica Critica* (cited above, p. 54 n. 1), pp. 43ff.

in ordinary speech. It does not generally serve as a source of ribald jokes. Though one can legitimately speak of *uterus* as a word of higher status than *uulua* in the early Empire, and though *uulua* was probably the term which an ordinary speaker would have chosen to designate the womb should he have had to name the part, the word would scarcely have had an overtly vulgar or offensive tone. The terms 'popular' or 'colloquial' as applied to it must be given a more restricted sense.

Vulua seems to have been the *vox propria* for the womb in the eyes of the early Latin Bible translators, as far as one can judge from the published portions of the *Vetus Latina*. *Vulua* appears to be the usual rendition of μήτρα (*Gen.* 29.31, 30.22, *Luke* 2.23), whereas *uterus*, which is often in the phrase *in utero* (*Gen.* 25.22, 25.23, 38.24, 38.27, *Luke* 1.31, 1.41, 1.44), was chosen to render γαστήρ (*Luke* 1.31) or κοιλία (*Luke* 1.15, 1.41, 1.44). This would suggest that *uulua* had the specific sense 'womb' during the second century, whereas *uterus* was regarded as less specific (because it no longer had the status of a *vox propria*, having fallen out of regular use?). *Vterus* is more numerous (72 times) than *uulua* (33 times) in the Vulgate, presumably partly because the tastes of the learned Jerome manifest themselves in the Old Testament (where *uterus* occurs 59 times), and partly because γαστήρ and κοιλία were particularly common in the Greek version. The frequency of *uulua* in Tertullian (see, e.g. *Carn.* 17, 19 (6 times), 20 (5 times)) is probably a reflection of the importance of the word in the *Vetus Latina*.

At some stage during the Empire *uulua* itself was rivalled as the popular term for the womb, by *matrix*. The first alleged example of *matrix* in this sense quoted by *TLL* VIII.483.3ff. is at Sen. *Contr.* 2.5.6 'fac iam ne uiro placeat matrix', but there the word could have its original meaning, 'breeding animal' (= 'see that she no longer pleases her husband as a breeder'). It is possible that such a sentence might have been interpreted to mean 'see that her breeder [i.e. womb] no longer pleases her husband', with the womb personified. Hence *matrix* might be described as transitional in sense, or at least as used in the sort of ambiguous context which would tend to generate the new meaning. Another ambiguous example quoted by the *TLL* supposedly meaning 'uterus' is at Tert. *Carn.* 17: 'si ex humana matrice substantiam traxit'. The new sense definitely appears in the *Vetus Latina* (though *matrix* was probably outnumbered in early translations by *uulua* and *uterus*): see *Judith* 9.2 (*ap.* Lucif. *Non Parc.* 10, p. 230.20) 'coinquinauerunt matricem' (= μήτραν). Often in translation literature of later antiquity, as in this passage, *matrix* renders μήτρα, and it is not impossible that the phonetic similarity between the two words was one of the factors which lay behind the semantic change in the Latin word. Crude Latin translators of the late period sometimes chose a Latin word not because it had the same meaning as the Greek word before them, but because it was phonetically the nearest equivalent to it, and was roughly of the same semantic field.[1] In addition there is a close relationship between the meanings 'mother, breeder' and 'womb'. Lat. *mater* is widely reflected in Romance in the sense 'womb';[2] and in the *defixio* Audollent 265A. 6, quoted above, p. 103, *sua uulua* (used *pars pro toto*) is virtually equivalent to *sua mater*.

Matrix is extremely common in late medical works. It is found 15 times in the section on gynaecology in Theodorus Priscianus, in which *uterus* and *uulua* do not occur. The short anonymous medical work edited by Piechotta has only *matrix* (3 times, at CL (twice) and CLXIII). In books II and IV of Dioscorides Lat. *matrix* is used 27 times, *uterus* twice (both times in the expression *in utero*: II, p. 197.2, IV, p. 65.15), and *uulua* not at all. In the first book of the Latin versions of Oribasius only *matrix* is admitted (p. 49.6 Aa Mørland, p. 49.8 La, p. 66.18 Aa, La, p. 75.18 Aa, La, p. 78.21 Aa, p. 78.23 La).

---

[1] In the Latin Bible translations, for example, *poto* was sometimes used to render ποτίζω (e.g. *Matth.* 25.27, in codd. *r*[1], *d*, *f*, *h*, *q* of the *Vet. Lat.*); hence it was converted into a transitive verb.

[2] See *FEW* VI.1. p. 478. Indeed *mater* = 'womb' is attested in Latin as a rendition of μήτρα at Oribas. Lat. p. 355.8 La ('infrigidata matre non concipit'; Aa has *matrix*), quoted by F. Arnaldi, *Latinitatis Italicae Medii Aevi Lexicon Imperfectum* I (Brussels, 1939), s.v. *mater*. This example could well be a scribal slip (for *matrice*). There is possibly another example in a popular name for a plant recorded by Isidore, *Etym.* 17.9.51 'eadem et *matris animula*, propter quod menstrua moueat'. I cannot see why a plant which induced menstruation should be called 'soul, life of the mother', since it is not only *matres* as such who menstruate. But the womb could be personified in popular speech (note the popular incantation recorded by Marc. *Emp.* 10.35 'item carmen hoc utile profluuio muliebri: "stupidus in monte ibat, stupidus stupuit. adiuro te matris [*sic*], ne hoc iracunda suscipias" '), and it seems plausible that a plant which activated its natural function should be called its 'soul'. A comparison of (e.g.) Paul. *Dig.* 36.1.83 (81) 'qui *ex eadem matre* erant' with Rustius Barbarus, *CPL* 304.7ff. 'habio ... fratrem gemellum qui *de unum uentrem* exiut' illustrates the type of context which might have generated the new meaning for *mater*.

Cassius Felix uses only *matrix* (25 times). The Latin translation of Hippocr. *Aer.* has *matrix* 3 times (rendering both μήτρα and ὑστέρα; for the former translated see 21, p. 41.7, and for the latter, see 7, p. 13.15). *Vterus* outnumbers *matrix* (4 times), but 3 times it is in the phrase *in utero* (rendering ἐν γαστρί: 7, p. 13.13, 10, p. 23.22, 21, p. 41.14). The fourth example (7, p. 13.7 'difficile uterum accipiunt') also corresponds to ἐν γαστρί (ἐν γαστρὶ ἴσχουσι μόλις), and it is possible that the text is corrupt. In Caelius Aurelianus' *Gynaecia matrix* is very common (I do not have full statistics, but there are 31 examples in the first 13 pages of the text), but *uulua* occurs only once (p. 25.632, in its culinary sense). Caelius has the phrase *in utero* a few times (pp. 3.72, 44.1134, 50.1295), but unlike most late medical writers he also admitted *uterus* sometimes in other forms (13 times). Finally, Soranus Lat. (Mustio) uses *matrix* 142 times, *uterus* 9 times (for *in utero* see pp. 12.13, 15.4, 16.8, 28.7, 33.8; cf. p. 10.10 *intra uterum* and 85.12 *de utero*). He has *uulua* 19 times.

A few writers stand apart from the rest. Marcellus Empiricus has *matrix* only once (in the form *matris*: 10.35), but *uulua* 7 times. *Vterus*, in the phrase *intra uterum*, occurs at 7.23. And in the *Mulomedicina Chironis* there are 8 examples of *uulua* = 'womb' (742, 745 3 times, 747, 761, 771 twice), compared with 4 of *matrix* (176, 177, 745 twice); cf. *uenter* at 745 and 765, and *uter*, a malapropism for *uterus*, at 224 (with *in*; see above, p. 88).

In only three of the works mentioned above (Mustio, Marcellus Empiricus and the *Mulomedicina Chironis*) is *uulua* at all common, and in one of these (Mustio) it is greatly outnumbered by *matrix*. Though the Latin of all three writers might be classed as particularly vulgar, one cannot deduce from their taste for *uulua* that it was still the standard word for the part in all or most areas. It is a fair assumption that the great frequency of *matrix* in late medical works considered as a whole reflects its wide currency at the time. It survives in Gallo-romance and Italian (*matrice*) meaning 'womb', as well as in other Romance languages with a variety of different senses,[1] whereas *uulua* (= 'womb') had a more limited survival (OLog. *bulva*, Jud.-Fr. *borbe*).[2] The anatomical vocabulary of

---

[1] See *FEW* VI.1, p. 502, *REW* 5422.
[2] See *FEW* XIV, p. 648, *REW* 9470.

the *Mulomedicina* is by no means drawn exclusively from the everyday language (*uirginalis* = *cunnus* is perhaps unparalleled). Those late writers who preferred *uulua* probably did so out of personal idiosyncrasy or under the influence of their sources. It is also just possible that *uulua* had a lingering tendency to be used in application to the anatomy of animals. But since Pelagonius and Vegetius do not speak of the womb, one cannot be certain that the author of the *Mulomedicina* was employing a veterinary usage.

In veterinary writers *matrix* is often used in another sense, of a vein (apparently the jugular) in the neck from which blood was let. Note *matricalis uena* at Veg. *Mul.* 1.10.7 'postea ex ceruice de matricali uena sanguinem detrahes' (cf. 1.13.2, Oribas. Lat. *Syn.* 1, p. 49.1 Aa Mørland), and compare (e.g.) Pelagon. 17 'sanguinem de matrice detrahe'.[1] Much the same phraseology occurs repeatedly: Pelagon. 24, 37, 291, 302, *Mul. Chir.* 15, 16, 262, 965, Veg. *Mul.* 1.23, 1.25.1, 1.34.2, 1.55.1, 1.56.25, 2.5.3, 2.6.1, 2.68, 2.76.2, 2.94, 2.136, 3.7.2 (cf. 3.7.3 *dematricare*).

Ordinary speech does not distinguish parts of the womb, but in some Latin medical writings certain specialised terms, derived directly from Greek, are recorded. Soranus *Gyn.* p. 177.14ff. Rose names the στόμιον, τράχηλος, αὐχήν, ὦμοι, πλευρά, πυθμήν and βάσις of the womb. In the corresponding passage (p. 8.5ff.) Mustio uses the terms *orificium, collum, ceruix, umeri, latera, fundus* and *basis*. Most of these words occur elsewhere both in Caelius Aurelianus and Mustio. For *orificium*, see Mustio pp. 14.18, 18.1, 20.6, 84.9; Caelius uses *osculum* = στόμιον (28 times in the *Gynaecia*, according to the index of Drabkin and Drabkin: e.g. p. 72.265). For *fundus* = πυθμήν, see, e.g. Mustio p. 18.13, Cael. *Gyn.* pp. 4.81, 6.130, 72.265.[2] For *collum*, see Cael. *Gyn.* pp. 4.80, 5.122.[3] *Ceruix* is

---

[1] See K.- D. Fischer, *Pelagonii Ars Veterinaria* (Leipzig, 1980), p. 97 (against *TLL* VIII. 483. 19ff.).

[2] See further *TLL* VI.1.1575.35ff.

[3] *Collum* in a gynaecological sense is a medical term in recorded Latin, but the popular belief that the neck (*collum*) of a virgin increased in circumference after intercourse (see Catull. 64.376f. 'non illam nutrix orienti luce reuisens / hesterno collum poterit circumdare filo') would seem to be based on a view that the stretching of the 'neck' of the vagina by intercourse had a reflection in a swelling of the external neck. We have seen that a similarity was often observed between internal organs and prominent external parts of the anatomy (note, for example, Martial's comparison of the *cunnus* of Lydia to the

found in a number of medical and veterinary works (Cels. 4.1.12, *Mul. Chir.* 228, Veg. *Mul.* 1.46.2) in various senses.

---

throat (*guttur*) of a pelican at 11.21.10). Hence *collum* might well have been transferred occasionally in popular speech to the vagina. In the medical language, however, *collum* is rather more specialised: it does not indicate the vagina.

Chapter Four

Culus and its Synonyms

I have dealt elsewhere[1] with *culus* and its synonyms, and also with words for 'buttocks' and 'rectum'. Here I include a summary of the evidence relating to *culus* and its substitutes.

1. Basic words

Culus (of uncertain etymology) was the basic word for 'anus'. As such it is found mainly in graffiti and epigram. There are 5 examples in the Pompeian graffiti, as well as a case of the artificial compound *culibonia* (*CIL* IV.8473);[2] cf. *CIL* XI.6721.7, 14 (the Perusine sling bullets). Catullus has the word 6 times, in both hendecasyllables and elegiacs, Martial 16 times, and the *Corpus Priapeorum* 4 times. It is also found at Phaedr. 4.19.36; Phaedrus admits various basic words (see the Appendix). The drastic tone which *culus* was capable of bearing is nowhere more obvious than in Catullus 97 (note, for example, 11f. 'quem siqua attingit, non illam posse putemus / aegroti culum lingere carnificis?'; cf. *CIL* IV.4954 'linge culu'). *Culus* is very widely reflected in the Romance languages.[3]

The currency of *culus* in Vulgar Latin is confirmed by its productivity as the base of derivatives, a productivity which is shared by its reflexes in the Romance languages. *Culibonia* (= 'ea quae bonum culum habet') was obviously a humorous formation, designating perhaps a whore who offered anal in-

---

[1] Adams, *Culus*.
[2] On which see F. Munari, *RCCM* 3 (1961), pp. 105ff.
[3] See *REW* 2384.

tercourse. Its termination must be modelled on that of female names such as *Scribonia, Antonia, Pomponia*, etc., with vowel quantity disregarded.[1] It would no doubt have sounded anomalous, with its adjectival element second and termination *-ia*. A similar derivative is *culiola (CGL* II.164.9), which, though it is glossed by τριβάς, must have had much the same implication as *culibonia* (of a woman who offered the *culus*). Marius Victorinus, *GL* VI.8.9 refers to a nickname *Sesquiculus* given to Iulius Caesar Strabo: '. . . donec Iulius Caesar, qui Vopiscus et Strabo et Sesquiculus dictus est'. The force of the name must be 'qui ita magnis est praeditus natibus, ut uideatur habere culum cum dimidio' (= εὐρύπρωκτος).[2] The verbs *culo* (Petron. 38.2 'arietes a Tarento emit, et eos culauit in gregem') and *apoculo* (Petron. 62.3, 67.3) are more problematical.[3] A derivation from *culus* has not always been accepted for *apoculo*;[4] recently, for example, Shipp (p. 88) has suggested that *apoculo* was a borrowing from some such verb as Gk. dial. ἀποκολώνω, 'disappear from view, go away'. This theory would do nothing to explain *culo*, which must surely be associated with *apoculo*. And *apoculo*, like *culo*, is a transitive verb. I see no insuperable difficulty in deriving *culare* from *culus*[5] and

---

[1] See Munari, p. 105.

[2] See E. Bickel, *RhM* 100 (1957), p. 4, quoting Forcellini-De Vit.

[3] The text is certain at 38.2, but there are variants in the other two passages.

[4] See E. V. Marmorale, *Petronii Arbitri Cena Trimalchionis*[2] (Florence, 1961), p. 123 (on 62.3) for various explanations.

[5] There was no uniform semantic relationship between the rare first conjugation denominative verbs based on nouns for parts of the body, and their nominal base. *Magulare* 'eat' (see G. Rohlfs, *Die lexikalische Differenzierung der romanischen Sprachen* (Munich, 1954), p. 37 and map 20: surviving as *magliar* in Grisons, Switzerland), apparently a denominative of *magulum* 'jaw' (see Schol. Juv. 2.15 and the loan-word μάγουλο 'cheek' in NGk.), would mean literally 'use one's jaws'. *Maxillare*, on the other hand, which at *CGL* II.438.23 glosses στομοκοπῶ, must refer to an action directed at someone else's jaw ('hit (someone) in the jaw'). Smith (*Petronii Arbitri Cena Trimalchionis*) on 38.2 translates *culauit* 'got them to bash his ewes', as if it were a causative correspondent of πυγίζειν. But such a causative would be unlikely to have a prepositional phrase (*in gregem*) as its complement; and if it were a sexual causative, it would have to refer to *pedicatio*, not *fututio*, which would be inappropriate. The verb must mean 'push (someone) by, in the *culus*', i.e. 'drive, impel'. Its relationship to *culus* would be much the same as that of *maxillo* to *maxilla*.

apoculo from ἀπό + *culare*.[1] The interpretation of *reculo* at
CGL V. 329.5 is doubtful. For verbal derivatives of *culus* in
Romance, cf. Fr. *reculer*, Ital. *rinculare*.

Podex is sometimes interpreted as gross in tone,[2] but one
should not be led astray by its etymology (cf. *pedo* 'fart').[3] It is
unattested in the Pompeian graffiti, is hardly used by Catullus, Martial or the author of the *Corpus Priapeorum* (note
Mart. 2.42.1, 6.37.1, *Priap.* 77.9), and does not survive in the
Romance languages. But it is used by Juvenal (2.12), whose
lexical mildness has been commented on earlier, and also by
Ausonius (*Epigr.* 93.3, p. 346 P.). Later it is admitted in medical Latin (11 times in both the *Gynaecia* of Caelius Aurelianus
and in Cassius Felix, and 4 times in Marcellus Empiricus).
Note too Cass. Fel. p. 178.15 'alia quae appellatur a Graecis
dactylice, id est *podicalis*, siquidem podicis uitia emendat',
where *podicalis* is given as an equivalent of δακτυλική, though
δακτύλιος ('ring' > 'anus') had an exact parallel in *anus* (see
below), which had various adjectival derivatives (e.g. *anularis*,
-arius). Cassius Felix is according *podex* the status of the
proper educated word. I should interpret its distribution as an
indication that it was obsolescent in the classical period, and
obsolete by late antiquity. Its connection with *pedo* probably
ceased to be felt. An obsolete word which had once been offensive might be expected to undergo an amelioration of tone (cf.
penis).

2. Metaphors

It has been pointed out that metaphorical designations of the
culus are much the same as those of the *cunnus*, and numerous

[1] Compounded denominatives based on anatomical terms (e.g. *delumbo, dematrico, decollo, depilo*) usually mean either 'take away the body part (from
someone)' (e.g. *delumbo* 'castrate') or 'take something from the body part'
(*dematrico* means 'let blood from the *matrix*, jugular vein'). *Apoculo* (reflexive),
which in both passages means in effect 'leave', does not fit into either of these
categories. It must be based on *culare*, rather than directly on *culus* (= 'drive,
impel oneself (someone) away'). For a hybrid in Latin with a Latin base and
Greek prefix, cf. *catafrico* (?) at Cass. Fel. p. 8.10, and note *catafalicum* (<
fala: *FEW* II.1, pp. 486f.), *catamodicum, -e* (*TLL* III.591.8ff.), *catalectus* (<*lec-
tus*: *REW* 1759). Hybrids more often have a Latin base and a Greek suffix:
e.g. Plaut. *Rud.* 310 *hamiota*, Petron. 42.1 *baliscus*, 62.14 *exopinisso* (?).
[2] See Courtney, pp. 45f.
[3] See Pokorny I, p. 829.

examples of such substitutes for *culus* have been quoted in Chapter III. Here I refer to the relevant places in that Chapter, and discuss a few metaphors which did not come up there.

Perhaps the largest category of images for the *culus* could be described as 'agricultural': *ager* and *agellus* (p. 84), *fossa* (p. 86), *hortus* and perhaps *pratum* (p. 84), based on κῆπος and λειμών (words indicating not the *culus* but the *cunnus* in Greek), and *saltus* at Plaut. *Cas.* 922 'ubi illum saltum uideo opsaeptum, rogo ut altero sinat ire' (in the second clause *saltu*, understood with *altero*, has the implication 'anus'; for *saltus* = *cunnus*, see p. 84). The calques *hortus* and *pratum* (?) were obviously literary.

Comparable with, but not identical to, the above images was the important metaphor of the fig. The fig had a widely-felt symbolism in antiquity.[1] In Greek, words for 'fig' are sometimes used metaphorically for the anus (e.g. ἰσχάς at Philip, *A. Plan.* 240.8, Argentarius, *A. Plan.* 241.5). The usual metaphorical sense of a sexual kind borne by Latin *ficus* and comparable words was 'anal sore' (usually thought to have been induced by anal penetration): e.g. Mart. 6.49.11 'nascetur, licet hoc uelis negare, / inserta tibi ficus a cupressu', 14.86.2 'stragula succincti uenator sume ueredi: / nam solet a nudo surgere ficus equo' (here the *ficus* is caused by horse riding), Juv. 2.13 'sed podice leui / caeduntur tumidae medico ridente mariscae' (a *marisca* was a large fig, apparently considered insipid: see below). This use of *ficus* etc. may have been a calque based on σῦκον, σύκωσις, perhaps introduced originally into the medical language. But at 12.96.9f. Martial goes beyond the current metaphorical use of such words: 'non eadem res est: Chiam uolo, nolo mariscam: / ne dubites quae sit Chia, marisca tua est'. A husband desiring to *pedicare* boys might say that *pedicatio* of his own wife would not be the same thing: he wants the Chian fig (*Chia*), not the insipid *marisca*. The suggestive phraseology here was adopted with Greek usage in mind; one cannot deduce that *ficus* et sim. were regularly used of the *culus* in the Latin of Martial's day. But it is worth pointing out that in late popular Latin *ficus* may have taken on the sense 'female pudenda'. Ital. *fica* = 'pudendum muliebre' is usually taken as a late Latin calque on σῦκον in another of its

[1] See V. Buchheit, *RhM* 103 (1960), pp. 200ff.

senses (see Aristoph. *Pax* 1354).[1] Evidence for a corresponding late use of *ficus*= *culus* is lacking.

A 'topographical' image for the anus has been mentioned earlier (see p. 23 on *in tutum locum* at Pompon. 126; with this compare *uicinis . . . locis* at Sen. *Contr.* 1.2.22, quoted below, p. 162). A rather more striking topographical metaphor is found at Auson. *Epigr.* 93.4, p. 346 P. 'sed quod et elixo plantaria podice uellis / et teris inclusas pumice Clazomenas'. Clazomenae is a small island roughly round in shape, and hence of suggestive appearance to those accustomed to such bizarre jokes (with the surrounding sea representing the buttocks). A parallel for this type of image may be provided by Εὐρώτας = κύσθος at Rufinus, *A.P.* 5.60.6. The river Eurotas might be thought to resemble the κύσθος, because it flows straight down into the Laconian sea between two peninsulas which look (on a map) like thighs. Ausonius himself uses a similar metaphor at *Epigr.* 106.9, p. 351 P. 'luteae Symplegadis antrum'; it was based on Mart. 11.99.5 'sic constringuntur magni Symplegade culi'. The metaphorical use of geographical terms had long had a place in ancient sexual humour (cf. Aristoph. *Thesm.* 647). One cannot help noticing that the anus attracted a variety of Grecising metaphorical designations in Latin epigram.

The most common metaphor for 'anus' is *anus* itself, lit. 'ring', an etymology felt by Cicero (*Fam.* 9.22.2) and no doubt by many others at different periods. Some sesterces, for example, of the year A.D. 192 contain the inscription 'Herculi Romano Augusto' (of Commodus), written in three lines divided down the middle by the club of Hercules;[2] hence the right-hand column reads 'culi ano usto'. In this phrase *anus* must be given its etymological sense (= 'with the ring of his anus burnt', *sc.* 'by *pedicatio*'). Some metaphors retain a figurative force over a very long period. *Anus* had a polite tone, and was the standard term in medical writings of all periods (e.g. 15 times in Celsus); *podex* (see above) was no more than an occasional rival. The metaphor was old: note the diminutive *anulus* at Cato *Agr.* 159. *Anus* has a parallel in Gk. δακτύλιος

[1] See Battisti-Alessio, *Dizionario etimologico italiano* III, p. 1632. See also M. Cortelazzo, *L'influsso linguistico greco a Venezia* (Bologna, 1970), pp. 88f. on *figa*, 'pudendum femminile'. Cf. *REW* 3281.

[2] For the coins, see W. Derichs, *RhM* 95 (1952), pp. 48ff.

(e.g. Pollux 2.210), but the Greek usage, which seems to be fairly late, need not have determined the Latin. We have seen some other sexual metaphors in the Latin medical language (*uirga, radius, caulis*).

The lack of uniformity in the Latin medical / technical vocabulary is well illustrated by Pliny the Elder's taste for *sedes* (e.g. *Nat.* 22.143, 23.75, 23.83), which was almost certainly a calque on ἕδρα (e.g. at Hdt. 2.87 and in medical works).

Some other metaphors which have been seen are the 'anatomical' image *inferior guttur* at Plaut. *Aul.* 304 (p. 33), *uagina*, 'sheath', used in conjunction with *machaera* at Plaut. *Pseud.* 1181 (p. 20), and the images of the cave (p. 85), door (p. 89) and path (p. 89). At Pers. 4.36 I accept Housman's *ualuas* for *uuluas*,[1] a certain emendation which has not received proper recognition. *Vuluas* (plur.) could not possibly be used of the *culus* of a pathic, but *ualuae* is regular in the plural (cf. σανίδες at *A.P.* 9.415.6).

3. Euphemisms

It is a curiosity that the standard euphemism for the *culus* (*anus*) was not only metaphorical in origin, but was still felt to be metaphorical in the historical period, at least by some speakers. But there are also attested numerous less common, non-metaphorical substitutes for the direct word. Any word indicating the back or its lower part could of course be used as an occasional euphemism (specialisation). Words for 'buttocks' sometimes replace a more specific term for 'anus':[2] e.g. *CIL* X.4483 'caca, ut possimus bene dormire ... et pedicare natis candidas' (cf. Mart. 12.75.3). At Mart. 9.47.6 ('in molli rigidam clune libenter habes') *clune* might be treated as ambiguous between the meanings 'buttocks' and 'anus', but the choice of the singular hints strongly at the second sense. For *tergum* implying the anus, see Auson. *Epigr.* 93.6, p. 346 P. 'tergo femina, pube uir es', and for *postica pars*, Lucil. 119 'non peperit, uerum postica parte profudit'. Cf. *posterio*, glossed by *anus* at *CGL* III.596.7 (> OIt. *postione*, OFr. *poistron*). Here

---

[1] See *Classical Papers*, pp. 1178f.

[2] Conversely words for 'anus' are sometimes used of the buttocks: e.g. Eng. *arse*, Ital., Sp. *culo*, Fr. *cul*.

again one sees the close relationship between the meanings 'buttocks' and 'anus'. The Old French reflex has both senses, and the closely connected *posteriora* is used of the buttocks at *H.A., Hel.* 5.4.

Viscera, which we have seen in the sense 'female pudenda' (p. 95), is used as a synonym of *culus* at Juv. 9.43 'an facile et pronum est agere intra uiscera penem' (here *agere penem* is a graphic circumlocution for *pedicare*). For *pudenda* = 'anus', see p. 55, n. 3, and for *(posterior) natura*, p. 59. With this latter expression, cf. Vulg. *Iud.* 3.22 'statimque *per secreta naturae* alui stercora proruperunt'. *Medius*, finally, could be used of any taboo part; for the implication 'anus', see *Priap.* 54.2 'qui medium uult te scindere, pictus erit'.

4. Miscellaneous

The use of *cunnus* = *culus*, of a male pathic, was highly pejorative: *CIL* IV.1261 'futebatur inquam futuebatur ciuium Romanorum atractis pedibus cunus' (interpretation doubtful: see p. 121), IV.10078 (with *cunnus* apparently used *pars pro toto*, of a *cinaedus*; contrast the masculine derivative *cunnio* at *CIL* IX.6089.2, on a *tessera*). The transfer to a male of terms strictly applicable to a female suggests the effeminacy of the referent with extreme forcefulness. One might compare *futuo* = *pedico* (p. 121), and also the use of various feminine nouns and names in application to males: e.g. Cic. *Att.* 1.14.5 *filiola*, 4.11.2 *Appuleia*, *De Orat.* 2.277 *Egilia*, Juv. 2.120 *noua nupta*, Suet. *Iul.* 22.2 *femina*, Apul. *Met.* 8.26 *puellae*.

I mention finally the occasional overlap between words for 'anus' and those for 'rectum': e.g. *CGL* III.604.12 'podicem stalem' (*stalis* here is a vulgar form of *extalis*, 'rectum'; for this meaning, see *Mul. Chir.* 476). It is only in the most precise medical prose that a distinction is consistently made between the anus and the rectum. Metaphorical designations in particular may refer indifferently to the one part or the other (note *inferior guttur* and *uagina* above). It is doubtful whether speakers and non-technical writers consciously consider the precise implication of the metaphors and euphemisms which they might use for this general area of the anatomy.

The *culus* was clearly a common topic of jokes both in ordinary speech (note *culibonia* and the name *Sesquiculus*) and in certain varieties of literature (comedy, farce and epigram), and as such it inspired a surprising frequency of metaphors (more than 20 examples have been mentioned above). In epigram there was something of a convention of seeking bizarre metaphors for the part.

In the lexicon of the language little distinction is drawn between the *cunnus* and the *culus* as the site of sexual acts; metaphors and euphemisms for the two parts constantly interchange.

Chapter Five

The Vocabulary Relating to Sexual Acts

It would scarcely be possible to discuss all the designations of sexual acts attested in Latin, but I have attempted to deal with the most important categories, with the exception of euphemistic omissions. Various commonplace verbs and expressions are scarcely illustrated here, especially if the relevant article in the *TLL* is adequate. On the other hand for rare, little noticed or important phenomena I sometimes quote all the evidence known to me.

1. Basic obscenities and some other direct words

(i) *Futuo*

The basic obscenity for the male part in sexual intercourse with a woman was *futuo*. The tone of the word is indirectly commented on by Martial at 1.35.1ff. ('uersus scribere me parum seueros / nec quos praelegat in schola magister, / Corneli, quereris'), a remark which looks back to the last word of the preceding epigram (*futui*). Cicero did not use *futuo* openly in *Fam.* 9.22 (see § 1 *alterum*, an allusion to it). The etymology of *futuo* is obscure, but it may be related to **futo* ('hit, beat'?), which apparently provided the base of *refuto* and *confuto*.[1] Verbs of striking and the like are often applied metaphorically to the act of the male in intercourse.

Like *mentula*, *cunnus* and *culus*, *futuo* (and its derivatives) are found mainly in epigram (and in those short poems of Catullus which are in metres other than the elegiac) and graf-

---

[1] See Ernout and Meillet, *s.vv.* Cf. Pokorny, I, p. 112 (root **bhău-*, **bhŭ-*, 'schlagen, stossen'?; cf. *fustis*).

fiti. There are 63 examples in *CIL* IV (15 of which are in the recent supplements), and 2 in the *Graffiti del Palatino*. In Catullus there are 7 examples of *futuo* and its derivatives, of which 5 are in iambics and hendecasyllables (6.13, 29.13, 32.8, 37.5, 41.1, 71.5, 97.9).[1] Martial has *futuo* 49 times (cf. 11.20.3, an epigram of Augustus).[2] Other epigrammatists who used the word are the author of the *Priapea* (13.1, 26.7, 57.6, 58.4, 63.16) and Luxorius (*Anth. Lat.* 297.1, 5, 7, 317.3). Ausonius avoided it in his epigrams. Horace used *futuo* (like *cunnus*) early in the first book of the *Sermones* (1.2.127), but he later turned away from the direct style. *Futuo* and the other obscenities do not appear in the *Epodes*, despite the precedent of Archilochus and Hipponax.

Futuo survives all over the Romania. In France and Italy it took on a wide range of derived senses, in which its sexual force was weakened or lost.[3] In extant Vulgar Latin it shows no tendency to weakening, but the example of the compound *effutuo* in a popular verse quoted by Suet. *Iul.* 51 ('urbani, seruate uxores: moechum caluom adducimus. / aurum in Gallia effutuisti, hic sumpsisti mutuum') is transitional. Here one has an extension of the use of the compounds seen at Catull. 6.13 (*latera ecfututa*), 29.13 (*diffututa mentula*) and 41.1 (*puella defututa*), all of which mean 'exhaust (a person or body part) *futuendo*' (cf. *Priap.* 26.7). In the verse quoted the verb means 'exhaust, squander *money futuendo*' (i.e. *scortando*), and is thus halfway to the sense 'throw away' (*sine fututione*), which the reflexes of *futuo* can have: e.g. Como *fotà*, 'wegwerfen, schlagen'.[4] The object 'exhausted' is no longer a person or part of the body, but the means by which the squandering is effected are still sexual.

Futuo is occasionally used of an act which could be described as insulting or aggressive (e.g. *CIL* IV.4977 'Quintio hic futuit ceuentes et uidit qui doluit'; this example is, however, exceptional, in that the act referred to is *pedicatio*: see below), but its tone is by no means primarily or predominantly aggres-

---

[1] With the example at 97.9 ('hic futuit multas'), compare *CIL* IV.2175 'hic ego puellas multas futui'.

[2] The type of expression in Augustus ('futuit Glaphyran Antonius') was almost formulaic in graffiti; e.g. *CIL* IV.2288 'Synethus Faustillam futuit'.

[3] *FEW* III, p. 928.

[4] *FEW*, loc. cit.

sive.[1] It is often used neutrally or even affectionately when the circumstances or addressee are such that euphemism was not called for (as in exchanges between whores and their clients). *CIL* IV.4239 (= *CE* 41) appears to be an affectionate address: 'Fortunate, animula dulcis, perfututor, scribit qui nouit' (the last clause may have been written by someone else). A number of Pompeian graffiti seem to be the work of prostitutes praising the sexual capacities of their clients: e.g. *CIL* IV.2176 'Felix bene futuis', 2274 'Victor (?) bene ualeas qui bene futuis' (cf. 2184-88, 2219, 2260). 2217 ('fututa sum hic') was obviously written by a woman; it is not the sort of remark one would expect from a person who considered that she had been the victim of a humiliating act. Another neutral use of the word appears at *CIL* IV.1751 'siqui futuere uolet, Atticen quaerat a. XVI', which reads like a whore's advertisement.

Conversely the client (using *futuo*) might praise (by implication) the services provided by the whore. Catullus' *fututiones* (32.7f. 'sed domi maneas paresque nobis / nouem continuas fututiones') occurs in an affectionate address of a prostitute (note lines 1–2). An inscriptional context in which *futuo* commonly appears is in records of enjoyable diversions with unnamed women: e.g. *CIL* IV.10677 'pranderunt hic iucundissime et futuere simul' (two friends record a pleasant time together), 10678 'amabiliter futuimus bis bina' (cf. 10675). In these contexts the word is empty of offensive intent.

In male boasts, *futuo* is chosen merely as the proper designation of an act or acts indicative of the subject's virility. The writer scarcely sees himself as humiliating his partner, whose identity is of no consequence: e.g. *CIL* IV.2175 'hic ego puellas multas futui', 2145 (a soldier's boast), 2248 ('Phoebus bonus futor'), 4029. The egotist of this kind usually regards himself as desirable, not as an aggressor: note Catull. 97.9 'hic futuit multas et se facit esse uenustum'.

It seems certain that *futuo* was freely used as an unemotive technical term in brothels by both clients and prostitutes (cf. Mart. 1.94.1).[2] Whether it was used neutrally by, or in direct

---

[1] Compare the recent controversy in *LCM* on the tone of βινέω: A. H. Sommerstein, 5.2 (Feb. 1980), p. 47, Jocelyn, 5.3 (Mar. 1980), pp. 67ff., 6.2 (Feb. 1981), pp. 45f., J. Henderson, 5.10 (Dec. 1980), p. 243, D. M. Bain, 6.2 (Feb. 1981), pp. 43f.

[2] For βινέω used by a low-class woman in Greek, see the mime at *POxy.* 413 (line 108), where a woman summons a slave ἵνα με βεινήσῃ.

address of, *matronae* (see below, p. 217), one cannot tell. The example at Mart. 11.23.5 is by no means neutral. Fulvia's words (Augustus *ap.* Mart. 11.20.7) 'aut futue aut pugnemus' are of no significance, since they were put into her mouth by a man. For the same reason the expression of female desire found at (e.g.) Mart. 11.71.2 'queritur futui ... necesse sibi' provides no evidence for the way in which women spoke. But it is a fair guess that *futuo* would have had some place in the private amatory language. Sexual taboo words may shed their taboo character in converse between intimates. It was recognised that there were certain *nupta uerba* which a bride would learn to use: Plaut. frg. 68 Lindsay 'uirgo sum: nondum didici nupta uerba dicere' (cf. Fest. p. 174). But one cannot generalise about what is a secret register in any language.

Occasionally *futuo* is used as a substitute for *pedico* (cf. OFr. *fot-en-cul*, <*futuo*, = 'pederast'),[1] just as βινέω could be used for πυγίζω (e.g. Aristoph. *Lys.* 1092): CIL IV.1261 'futebatur inquam futuebatur ciuium Romanorum atractis pedibus cunus' (*cunnus* seems to be used here as an equivalent of *culus*, but the interpretation of the inscription is not absolutely certain), 4977 (a clear-cut example, quoted above, p. 119), 8897 'Nymphe fututa, Amomus fututa, Perennis fututu<s>' (so the editor, but *u* may have been misread for *a*). Some other alleged examples[2] of the phenomenon are open to doubt. CIL IV.2188 ('Scordopordonicus hic bene fuit [= *futuit*] quem uoluit') may display the encroachment of the masculine forms of the relative on the feminine. CIL IV.2258 ('Victor cum Attine [= *Attide*] hic fuit') is of the same type as 2192 'Hermeros cum Philetero et Caphiso hic futuerunt' (groups of men record diversions with unnamed prostitutes). Nevertheless the usage certainly existed; it is analogous to the employment of *cunnus* = *culus* (of a male pathic) (see p. 116).

Except in the passive, *futuo* was not as a rule used of the female role.[3] The woman in Mart. 7.70 ('ipsarum tribadum tribas, Philaeni, / recte, quam futuis, uocas amicam') is a *tri-*

---

[1] See *FEW* III, p. 925.
[2] See J. Mussehl, *Hermes* 54 (1919), p. 405.
[3] At *GL* III.473.14ff. ('nemo enim dicit "haec futuens", nisi in epicenis nominibus animalium, ut "haec aquila futuens", in quo, quamuis femininum proferamus, tamen marem intelligimus') Priscian means that *aquila*, though strictly feminine in form, could behave as a masculine because there was no distinctive masculine form.

bas who behaves like a man (cf. Sen. *Epist.* 95.21, where *ineo* is applied to the activities of similarly abnormal women); compare *fututor* at Mart. 1.90.6 ('at tu, pro facinus, Bassa, fututor eras'). But at Mart. 11.7.13 *futuo* (act.) is definitely used of the female part in normal sexual intercourse: 'quanto tu melius, quotiens placet ire fututum, / quae uerum mauis dicere, Paula, uiro'. There is no evidence that the supine was treated as indifferent in respect of voice. This example anticipates the intransitive use of *fotre* in Old French, of the woman.[1] It is typically in the intransitive that verbs of this sense are transferred to the female role (cf. Eng. *she fucks*).

There is also some evidence that *fututrix* had acquired a corresponding use (= 'ea quae futuitur'): Audollent[2] 191 'C. Babullium et fotr(icem) eius Tertia Saluia'.[3] Note too *CIL* IV.2204 ΜΟΛΑ ΦΟΥΤΟΥΤΡΙΣ. It is suggested at *TLL* VI.1.1664.61f. that the reference here may be to a *tribas*, but that is unlikely: note *CIL* IV.2203 'futui Mula hic', and for *Mula* see also 8185. *CIL* IV.4196 ('Miduse fututrix') and 4381 are impossible to interpret.

Some humorous metaphorical uses of *fututrix* are found in Martial: 11.22.4 'inguina saltem / parce fututrici sollicitare manu' (of fondling of a *puer*; since the *puer* is *pathicus*, the 'female' in the relationship, he can be described as suffering *fututio* (cf. *futuo* = *pedico* above); in this case, however, the language is incongruous, since it is not the *mentula quae fututit*, nor is it the *culus qui futuitur*); 11.61.10 'arrigere linguam non potest fututricem' (a more obvious metaphor, of a *cunnilingus*' tongue). Cf. Mart. 11.40.3–6 'quam toto sibi mense non fututam / cum tristis quereretur et roganti / causam reddere uellet Aeliano, / respondit Glycerae dolere dentes', where the implication may be that Glycera was *fututam ore*.

---

[1] See A. Tobler and E. Lommatzsch, *Altfranzösisches Wörterbuch* III (Wiesbaden, 1954), 2174.

[2] The text of the *defixio* is doubtful: see Audollent, p. 253 for various suggestions.

[3] See *TLL* VI.1.1215.70 (s.v. *fotrix*), offering *fututrix* as one equivalence of *fotr*; cf. *futor* = *fututor* at *CIL* IV.2248.

(ii) *Pedico*

If *pedico* was genuinely derived from παιδικός, τὰ παιδικά,[1] it illustrates the tendency of Latin to take terms related to homosexuality from Greek (cf. *cinaedus, catamitus, pathicus*). The character of the word (= 'bugger', with object usually male, but sometimes female: Mart. 11.104.17; cf. 11.99.2) receives comment at *Priap.* 3.9f. ('simplicius multo est "da pedicare" Latine / dicere'). To use *pedico* was to speak *Latine*, to employ direct and basic Latin of a type which one might feel motivated to avoid. See also *Priap.* 38.1–3 'simpliciter tibi me, quodcumque est, dicere oportet, / . . . pedicare uolo', Mart. 11.63.4f. 'dicam simpliciter tibi roganti: / pedicant, Philomuse, curiosos'. One might compare Martial's remark (11.20.10) on the epigram of Augustus which contains *futuo, pedico* and *mentula*. Augustus, we are told, knew how to call a spade a spade ('qui scis Romana simplicitate loqui').

The distribution of *pedico* shows a familiar pattern. There are 13 definite examples in the Pompeian inscriptions,[2] and a few additional possibilities. In the *Graffiti del Palatino* an unambiguous example is found at I.364; at I.121, 232 *pedico* is probably a noun (on which see below). In literature the verb occurs in farce and mime (Pompon. 148, Laber. 21), in Catullus (3 times in hendecasyllables: 16.1, 14, 21.4) and epigram: Augustus *ap.* Mart. 11.20.6, Lucan *ap.* Mart. 10.64.6, 16 times in Martial, and at *Priap.* 3.9, 28.3, 35.5, 38.3 (cf. 7 and 67, letter puzzles of which *pedico* is the solution).

The nominal correspondents to *pedicare* were *pedico* and *pedicator*, both with suffixes productive in the popular language. *Pedico* was perhaps the predominating form in the first century (*CIL* IV.2194, 2389, 2442*b*, 2447 (the interpretation of the last three examples is not completely certain), 5 times in Martial, at *Priap.* 68.8; cf. *CIL* XII.5695.3 = *CE* 358, and the examples from the *Graffiti del Palatino* cited above), but it was rivalled by *pedicator*, which was used by Calvus in an epigram (*ap.* Suet. *Iul.* 49.1) and appears at *CIL* IV.4008. From the sexual and excretory spheres various such forma-

---

[1] See Ernout and Meillet, s.v. *paedico*.
[2] *CIL* IV.1691 add. p. 211, 1882, 2048, 2210, 2254 add. p. 216, 2319*b* add. p. 216, 2360, 2375, 3932, 4008, 4523, 8805, 10693.

tions are attested at Pompeii (*cacator, destillator, fellator, fututor, irrumator* and *perfututor*).[1]

Pedico (unlike *futuo*) is sometimes used in threats. It is familiar to anthropologists and zoologists that punishment or humiliation may be inflicted on an enemy or malefactor, or one's rank asserted, by a sexual violation, particularly *pedicatio*.[2] Such acts, real or fictitious, are sometimes mentioned by Latin writers (e.g. Val. Max. 6.1.13 'Cn. etiam Furium Brocchum qui deprehenderat familiae stuprandum obiecit'). But sexual violations genuinely perpetrated are no doubt less common than substitute forms of linguistic aggression. Instead of carrying out a violation, an aggressor may threaten to carry it out. The intention of the threat, at least in origin, is much the same as that of the violation: the hearer is meant to imagine himself as the victim of a sexual attack. Such threats tend to deteriorate into empty verbiage. Catullus' 'pedicabo ego uos et irrumabo' (16.1, 14) scarcely indicates a real intention on Catullus' part, but is verbal aggression.[3] That aggression manifested itself in this way in popular speech is clear from *CIL* IV.2254 add. p. 216 'Batacare, te pidicaro' (*sic*); note too the following inscription from Ostia, directed at those who scribble on walls: πάντες διαγράφουσι, ἐγὼ μόνος οὐδὲν ἔγραψα, πυγίζο πάντες τούτ[ους οἳ] ἐπὶ τοίχο γράφουσι.[4]

Pedico shows signs of a weakening of sense. There is a type of joke in Pompeian graffiti whereby the reader of the inscription ('he who reads', or 'I who read') is said to 'be *X*', or to 'do *X*', where *X* represents a sexual term: *CIL* IV.2360 (= *CE* 45) 'pedicatur qui leget ... paticus est qui praeterit ... ursi me comedant, et ego uerpa qui lego', 4008 'pedic[a]t[u]r qui leg[et]', 8617 'uerpes [= *uerpa es*] qui istuc leges' (see also below, p. 131). There is a difference between an accusation of perversion directed against a specific referent, and that directed against any passer-by. In the second case the sexual term is used as generalised abuse. Weakening is particularly

[1] Examples in V. Väänänen, *Le latin vulgaire des inscriptions pompéiennes*[3] (Berlin, 1966), pp. 89f.
[2] See Fehling, pp. 18ff., Dover, pp. 104ff., 204.
[3] The interpretation of *c.*16 is not completely clear. For bibliography, see Fehling, *RhM* 117 (1974), p. 103 n. 1; add C. W. MacLeod, *CQ* N.S. 23 (1973), pp. 300f., Buchheit, *Hermes* 104 (1976), pp. 331ff., J. Griffin, *JRS* 66 (1976), p. 97.
[4] See H. Solin, *Arctos* 7 (1972), p. 195; cf. Fehling, *RhM* 117 (1974), p. 106.

clear in the graffiti which contain the expression 'pedicatur qui leget', if it means 'he who shall read [or 'reads'] this is suffering *pedicatio*'. There is no question of a real act in progress: the passer-by's folly in stopping to read the graffito is tantamount to a metaphorical submission to *pedicatio*. One could alternatively take the expression to mean 'he who shall read this is in the habit of suffering *pedicatio*' (i.e. 'he is a *pathicus*'). If so the writer has accused someone unknown to him, and the word would not be taken seriously by readers. Such jokes show that various sexual terms were thrown around with little or no thought for their cognitive force. That does not mean that in other contexts they could not be used with their proper sense. I shall return to this subject below.

In epigram *pedico* sometimes occurs in collocations found in graffiti, though the contexts may differ. With *CIL* IV.2048 'Secundus pedicaud pueros' (note the word order), cf. Mart. 7.67.1 'pedicat pueros' and 11.94.6 'pedicas puerum'; with *CIL* IV.2210 'pedicare uolo', cf. *Priap.* 38.3 (same phrase and word order) and also Catull. 21.4 'pedicare cupis'; and with *CIL* IV.8805 'Q. Postumius rogauit A. Attium pedicarim', cf. Aug. *ap.* Mart. 11.20.5 f. 'quid si me Manius oret / pedicem, faciam?'.

(iii) *Irrumo*

Irrumo is by implication classed as obscene by Seneca, *Ben.* 4.31.4 '(Mamercus Scaurus) Pollioni Annio iacenti *obsceno uerbo* usus dixerat se facturum id, quod pati malebat; et cum Pollionis adtractiorem uidisset frontem "quidquid" inquit "mali dixi, mihi et capiti meo" ' (see below), and its distribution suggests that its status was much the same as that of *futuo* and *pedico*. There are 6 instances of the verb in the Pompeian graffiti,[1] and one each of its derivatives *irrumabiliter* (*CIL* IV.1931)[2] and *irrumator* (1529). For an important inscriptional example from Ostia, see below, p. 130. In literature *irrumo* occurs 6 times in Catullus (16.1, 14, 21.13, 28.10, 37.8, 74.5; cf. *irrumator* at 10.12 and *irrumatio* at 21.8), 5 times in

---

[1] Two of them indexed; see further *CIL* IV.8790 (?), 10030, 10197, 10232.

[2] *Arrurabiliter* at 4126 is conceivably a misspelling of *irrumabiliter*, with both vocalic ($i > a$) and consonantal assimilation ($m > r$). The translation offered by A. Richlin, *CP* 76 (1981), p. 43, n. 6 ('plow - ably') does nothing to elucidate the problem. The second syllable is not consistent with a derivation from *aro*.

126   *The Latin Sexual Vocabulary*

Martial,[1] and 4 times in the *Priapea* (35.2, 5, 44.4, 70.13). There is an isolated example in prose at Schol. Juv. 6.51.

Irrumo in etymology reflects the popular obsession among Latin speakers with a similarity felt between feeding and certain sexual practices (see pp. 138ff.). It is a denominative of *ruma* / *rumis*, 'teat',[2] and would originally have meant 'put in the teat'. For an analogy between 'putting in the teat' and an oral sexual practice, one might consult the anecdote told of Tiberius by Suetonius, *Tib.* 44.1. *Irrumo* and *fello* describe the same type of sexual act, but from different points of view: *irrumo* from the viewpoint of the active violator (= *mentulam in os inserere*), *fello* from that of the passive participant. Languages do not necessarily make such a lexical distinction. While *fellatio* is a widely recognised form of sexual behaviour, *irrumatio* is not universally seen as a positive sexual act. But the distinction was important to Latin speakers, and it gives rise to a few subtle jokes in the literature. At 3.82.33 Martial contemplates *irrumatio* as a punishment for Zoilus, but the act, he says, would be futile, because Zoilus *fellat*. *Irrumatio* holds no terrors for the *fellator*: he regards it not as *irrumatio*, but as *fellatio*, which he enjoys. The lexicon of standard English possesses no straightforward way of expressing the difference of attitude and role inherent in the joke '*irrumabo te*'. '*fello*'. A joke at Plaut. *Amph.* 348f. appears to be similar: 'ego tibi istam hodie, sceleste, comprimam linguam. SO. hau potes: bene pudiceque adseruatur'. The first speaker threatens to 'check the tongue', i.e. 'silence' the other. The second seems to take this as a threat to 'silence' him by *irrumatio*, and replies (in effect) that he does not *fellat*. In plain Latin the conversation could be rewritten in the form '*irrumabo te*'. '*non fello*'. *Comprimo* had a well-established sexual sense in Plautus (= *futuo*: see p. 182), which is elsewhere exploited in a double entendre (*Truc.* 262). One who *futuit* the *linguam* of another presumably *irrumat* (see Mart. 11.40.3 for *futuo*, with *dentes* as implied object, applied to *irrumatio*).[3] It was a standard joke

---

[1] Always in two early books (2 and 4): see Krenkel, p. 85a. Thereafter Martial preferred euphemisms.

[2] See Ernout and Meillet, s.v. *ruma, rumis*.

[3] Some doubt remains about the interpretation of the passage. It is possible that Plautus simply personified *lingua* as a woman, and used *comprimo* in the secondary sense '*futuo*'. Cf. *Asin.* 292, and see Fraenkel, *Elementi Plautini*, pp. 31f.

to speak of *irrumatio* as a means of silencing someone. An obvious case is at Mart. 3.96.3 'garris quasi moechus et futu- tor. / si te prendero, Gargili, tacebis'. Catull. 74.5f. is of the same type: 'quod uoluit fecit: nam, quamuis inrumet ipsum / nunc patruom, uerbum non faciet patruos'. Gellius has put a stop to his uncle's moralising about illicit affairs by commit- ting adultery with the man's own wife; the uncle's shame is such that he dare not speak. Now, even if he suffer the greater humiliation of *irrumatio*, he will say nothing. The conclusion is paradoxical: if he suffers *irrumatio*, he will not be able to say anything in any case. Mart. 14.74 presents a variation on the theme: 'corue salutator, quare fellator haberis? / in caput intrauit mentula nulla tuum'. The crow was popularly believed to *ore coire* (Plin. *Nat.* 10.32 'ore eos (coruos) parere aut coire uulgus arbitratur'). But he cannot be a *fellator* (i.e. *irrumatus*), because he is so noisy. There is perhaps a further hint of the joke at Mart. 12.35.4 'dicere percisum te mihi saepe soles. / . . . nam quisquis narrat talia plura *tacet*' (Callistratus is a *fellator*).

Irrumatio was in general regarded as a hostile and humili- ating act, of the sort which one's enemies might wish to inflict on one: see *CIL* IV.10030 'malim me amici fellent quam inimici irrument'. In Catullus 74 the possible *irrumatio* of the husband is viewed as the ultimate humiliation which might befall him. And at *CIL* IV.10232 ('L. Habonius sauciat irrumat Caesum Felic(e)m') the juxtaposition of *irrumat* with *sauciat* indicates its aggressive tone. For the most part the object of the verb is masculine. At Mart. 4.50.2 ('nemo est, Thai, senex ad irru- mandum') the poet is in effect threatening the woman. At 4.17.3 ('facere in Lyciscam, Paule, me iubes uersus / quibus illa lectis rubeat et sit irata. / o Paule, malus es; irrumare uis solus') he is addressing another male, and hence can be indif- ferent to the impact of the word on the woman. But at *CIL* IV.10197 (if the inscription has been correctly read) *irrumo* is apparently used as a neutral term for the active role in the act (complementing *elingo*, of the passive role): 'elige, [p]uela. iruman[ti] . . . nuli negant'.[1] For another neutral example, of the passive (female) role, see Schol. Juv. 6.51 'quia et irru- mantur mulieres'. Like other obscenities, *irrumo* would have

---

[1] The editor fills the gap with *manu polluenti*, but in the illustration given I can find little justification for this reading.

derived its tone from the circumstances of utterance. Directed at a man in public, it would be very offensive indeed. Spoken to a female in private, when linguistic taboos need not operate, it might be emptied of its emotive content.

Irrumatio, like *pedicatio*, was regarded as a means of asserting one's rank or punishing a malefactor. At Mart. 2.47.4, for example, it is envisaged as a punishment for adultery; similarly *pedicatio* was often threatened against or inflicted on adulterers, as at Hor. *Serm.* 1.2.44 (see p. 142), Val. Max. 6.1.13, Mart. 2.60.2; cf. the symbolic act at Catull. 15.19.[1] In Catullus' threat at 16.1, 14 *irrumabo* is coupled with *pedicabo*. It is clear from the inscription published by H. Comfort at *AJA* 52 (1948), pp. 321 f. ('irumo te, Sex(te)', with present for future) that threats of *irrumatio* would have been heard in vulgar speech. The hyperbolical character of Catull. 37.7 f. ('non putatis ausurum / me una ducentos inrumare sessores?') implies that the threat was a substitute for action, though none the less aggressive for that. Exaggeration is part and parcel of linguistic aggression. An anonymous senator was able to take up Caesar's innocent remark, made in the senate, 'proinde ex eo insultaturum omnium capitibus' (Suet. *Iul.* 22.2), and interpret it as a threat to inflict *irrumatio* on all his opponents: 'ac negante quodam per contumeliam facile hoc ulli feminae fore'.

For other examples of the threat, see Catull. 21.7f. 'nam insidias mihi instruentem / tangam te prior inrumatione' (cf. 21.13 'quare desine, dum licet pudico, / ne finem facias, sed inrumatus'), *Priap.* 35.5 'pedicaberis irrumaberisque', 44.3f. 'deprensos ego ter quaterque fures / omnes, ne dubitetis, irrumabo'. It is often phrased differently: e.g. *CIL* IV.1854 'Caliste, deuora', 5396 'Ccossuti [*sic*], fela ima', Mart. 3.83.2 'fac mihi quod Chione', *Priap.* 13.2 'percidere puer, moneo: futuere puella: / barbatum furem *tertia poena manet*' (compare the terminology at *CIL* XI.7263 'inuide, qui spectas, hec tibi poena manet'; the illustration is missing), 22.2 'caput hic praebeat', 28.5 'altiora tangam', 59.2 'si fur ueneris, impudicus exis' (cf. Catull. 21.12f. above); cf. Mart. 3.96.3 above.

Aggressive though the threat might have been in the appropriate context (as in the passages of Catullus above), one cannot but notice that it was deteriorating into a joke. It is

---

[1] See Fehling, pp. 21f.

sometimes motivated by the mildest of offences of a non-sexual kind, as at Mart. 3.83.2 (cf. 3.82.33, not strictly a threat but a contemplated *irrumatio*, which can be treated as an implied threat). The threat, implied rather than openly expressed, provides a source of humour at Plaut. *Amph.* 348f., Mart. 3.82.33, 3.96.3 and Suet. *Iul.* 22.2 (cf. Catull. 74.5f. and *CIL* IV.2360, discussed below, for joking allusions of different types to the practice).[1] Annius Pollio's shocked response to such aggression is presented at Sen. *Ben.* 4.31.4 as an abnormality.[2] These passages, along with the manifest exaggeration at Catull. 37.7f., indicate that speakers tended not to take *irrumatio* seriously. Even if there were no other evidence on the matter, one could say that conditions were ideal for a weakening of sense to occur. The repetition of a threat which is never carried out, and which is uttered on the flimsiest of excuses, will in due course cause it to be treated as no worse than non-specific aggression, and some speakers may become unaware of its original meaning. One can never be sure, even in a modern language, that all speakers are ignorant of the etymology of a threatening sexual term. But if they throw it around in contexts in which its cognitive force is not an issue, one can legitimately speak of a form of deterioration of sense.

A vacuous curse at *CIL* IV.2360 = *CE* 45 ('ursi me comedant et ego uerpa(m) qui lego') further demonstrates that *irrumatio* had degenerated into a source of jest. On Housman's interpretation (sc. *comedam*),[3] the reader is made to wish *irrumatio* on himself. In effect the only *irrumatio* which he is in danger of suffering is that constituted by his stupidity in reading the whole of the inscription. I should not wish to maintain that a reader would be ignorant of the meaning of *uerpam comedam*; but in the context he would surely have treated the imprecation as equivalent to 'I have been fooled'.

The metaphorical use of *irrumo* can be illustrated from Catullus. Despite the graphic detail at 28.9f. ('O Memmi, bene me ac diu supinum / tota ista trabe lentus inrumasti'), Catullus does not mean that a sexual act took place. While on the

[1] Richlin's generalisation, *CP* 76 (1981), p. 43, 'the general threat is made by an irrumator who is claiming to be enormously virile; he sneers at his irrumated victim as effeminate, or at best emasculate', is something of an exaggeration.

[2] See Housman, *Classical Papers*, p. 733.

[3] *Classical Papers*, p. 1179.

staff of Memmius he was treated with contempt (he was unable to enrich himself in the usual way), and he describes this ill treatment metaphorically as *irrumatio* (cf. 28.12f. 'nam nihilo minore uerpa / farti estis': Veranius and Fabullus were also badly treated on the staff of Piso).[1] So at 10.12 Catullus calls Memmius an *irrumator* for the same reason (note line 13 'nec faceret pili cohortem', which indicates the force of *irrumator*). When someone threatens *irrumatio* against another he is not speaking metaphorically, because, although he may have no intention of carrying out the threat, the act can be envisaged by both hearer and speaker as a possibility (at least up to the point when the threat becomes totally banal). But if he describes as *irrumatio* a non-sexual action which has already occurred, that action is by implication likened to *irrumatio*, and a metaphor has been used. The violence of the language is meant to convey only the strong disgust or resentment of the speaker; the sexual term has certainly been emptied of its full force.[2]

If further evidence were needed that *irrumo* was capable of losing its proper sense, it is provided by an inscription on a wall of the room of the Seven Sages at Ostia: 'amice fugit te prouerbium bene caca et irrima medicos'.[3] The hearer is not being instructed literally to *irrumare* the doctors. He is told to *bene caca*, which act will in effect constitute an *irrumatio*. *Irruma* is a non-sexual (metaphorical) expression of contempt; its equivalent in English would be *fuck the doctors*.

(iv) *Fello*

Fello was in origin not inherently sexual, and there are occasional neutral examples attested (Varro *Men.* 261, 476, Macrob. *Sat.* 7.16.25, Cael. Aurel. *Acut.* 2.21). The one Romance reflex (Abruzz. *fellate* 'young sheep') suggests that the verb had a lingering tendency to be used in an innocent sense. But in extant Latin it is largely specialised in the sexual meaning, in which its distribution is much the same as that of the other basic obscenities. *Fello* = 'commit *fellatio*' would originally

---

[1] These passages are discussed by Housman, *Classical Papers*, p. 1180.
[2] The remarks of Richlin, *CP* 76 (1981), p. 42, on the alleged absence of weakening of the Latin primary obscenities, can be disregarded.
[3] See G. Calza, *Die Antike* 15 (1939), p. 103 for the inscription.

have been a metaphor, since the primary sense of the verb was not 'suck' in general, but 'suck the teat'.[1] The image is exactly the same as that in *irrumo*. In the historical period users of *fello* as a sexual term are unlikely to have interpreted it as metaphorical.

The sexual use of *fello* is common in graffiti. In the Index to *CIL* IV it appears 37 times, and in the Supplements I have noted another 18 examples. *Fellator* is cited 17 times in the Index to *CIL* IV, and *fellatrix* 4 or 5 times. In literature *fello* is found in epigram (Catullus, Martial), but excluded from satire. The one example in Catullus (59.1 'Rufa Rufulum fellat') illustrates Catullus' habit of taking up formulae from the low sexual language: cf. *CIL* IV.1427 'Saluia felat Antiocu luscu'. Martial has *fello* 11 times, and *fellator* 5 times. The example at 9.4.4 ('non fellat tanti Galla') is reminiscent of graffiti in which the price of *fellatio* is given (e.g. *CIL* IV.1969 'Lahis felat a(ssibus) II'; cf. 5408). There are also single examples of *fello* and *fellator* in Ausonius (*Epigr.* 79.7, p. 341 P., 78.3, p. 341).

Like other obscenities, *fello* could, at least in the world of prostitution, be used as a neutral technical term. Various graffiti record praise of female practitioners of the art: *CIL* IV. 2273 'Murtis bene felas', 2421 'Rufa ita uale, quare bene felas'. The practice was particularly degrading for a man (note Mart. 7.67.14, of a *tribas*: 'non fellat – putat hoc parum uirile –, / sed plane medias uorat puellas'), and there is no doubt that *fellator* directed at a man, or *fellat*, could be an emotive term of abuse.[2]

Fello, like *pedico*, is found in jokes of the type, 'he who reads this, *X*', in which it sheds its proper force to some extent. See *CIL* IV.8230 'quisquis in catedra sederit, dabit uini)II. qui lego felo, sugat qui legit' ('I who read this commit *fellatio*, and let anyone who reads it suck', or 'I who read this am a *fellator*'). On the first interpretation the implication of 'qui lego felo' would be roughly 'I who read this am taken in, fooled'. On the second, the charge which the reader makes against himself would not be taken literally. The inscription is also notable for the use of *sugo* = *fello*. *Fello* leaves little trace in the Romance

---

[1] See Ernout and Meillet, s.v. *fecundus*. The non-sexual examples cited above have this meaning.

[2] Various relevant examples can be found in the collection of graffiti given by Krenkel, pp. 85ff.

languages (see above); it was replaced by *sugere*, *suctiare and
*suculare. Another inscription of much the same type is *CIL*
IV.1623 (with add. p. 209) 'et qui scripit felat' ('he who writes
(on this wall?) commits *fellatio*'). *CIL* IV.8400 'moue te, fellator' ('shift yourself, *fellator*') was presumably aimed at any
bystander, and is likely to have been intended as empty abuse.

By the time that *laecasin* (< λαικάζειν, = *fellare*) entered
Latin, it had become a generalised expression of contempt (see
below, p. 134).[1]

The phenomenon of weakening, which has been referred to
often in the preceding pages, requires further comment. Sexual
terms may have cognitive (literal) or connotative (emotive)
force. The two qualities are not mutually exclusive. Sometimes
a word may lose its cognitive sense entirely, and develop into
an empty abusive term (Fr. *con*, Eng. *sucker*). But it is more
common for the cognitive and connotative uses to coexist, with
the implication of the word determined by the context. In
English both *bugger* and *bastard* can retain their literal senses, but as terms of abuse they are purely emotive. In extant
Latin sexual words are often weakened into connotative terms,
but they kept (in the appropriate context) their cognitive force.
There is no evidence that the meaning of any sexual word was
forgotten entirely, if one excludes the loan-word *laecasin*.

The extent to which a sexual term aimed abusively at a
person retains its cognitive force depends partly on the pro-
clivities of the referent. The use of *impudicus* at Catull. 29.2
('quis hoc potest uidere, quis potest pati, / nisi impudicus et
uorax et aleo, / Mamurram habere quod Comata Gallia / habebat ante et ultima Britannia') had some applicability to
Caesar, in view of certain charges which were made against
him (Suet. *Iul*. 49). The word has some cognitive force.

But if a sexual term is applied to a person in a context in
which a sexual act is not at issue, and if there is no reason to
associate the referent with any such act, the connotative force
will come to the fore. At Catull. 10.24 ('hic illa, ut decuit
cinaediorem, / "quaeso" inquit mihi "mi Catulle, paulum / is-
tos commoda" ') *cinaediorem* is used in reference to a woman
in a non-sexual context, in which it certainly cannot be given
its proper force. It means no more than 'shameless'. καταπύγων

---

[1] On λαικάζω, see Shipp, *Antichthon* 11 (1977), pp. 1f., Jocelyn, *PCPhS* 206
(1980), pp. 12ff.

was also so weakened (note παγκατάπυγον at Aristoph. *Lys.* 137, of women).[1] An expression in the *flagitatio* at Catull. 42 is more difficult to interpret. The woman who has refused to return Catullus' *pugillaria* (5) is addressed in the refrain as *moecha putida*. Catullus has made a specific charge of a non-sexual kind, and for extra effect thrown in a sexual term which has nothing to do with the original accusation. Only if the subject of the poem was known to Catullus' readers as a *moecha* could the word have any cognitive force. But she is not named. One cannot be sure that the arrangement of the poems would not have made her identity clear. Nevertheless when a sexual word is irrelevant to its context, as here, it will tend to take on some connotative force, whatever the reputation of the referent.

It is particularly obvious that a sexual term is not literally applicable to its referent if it is directed at a person unknown to the writer. When a graffitist calls the reader of his scribble a *uerpa* (*CIL* IV.8617 'uerpes qui istuc leges'), he is simply displaying a humorous aggression towards passers-by, some of whom will be female. Cf. *CIL* IV. 2360 'paticus est qui prae-terit', 7089 'imanis metula es'.

Slightly different again are the expressions 'pedicatur qui leget' (*CIL* IV.2360, 4008), 'bene caca et irrima medicos' (see above), 'qui lego felo' (*CIL* IV.8230), and certain examples of *irrumo* and its derivatives in Catullus. The metaphorical use of obscenities (cf. Catull. 36.1, 20 'Annales Volusi, *cacata* car-ta') can be treated as a form of weakening. It is significant that *futuo* is not used in this way. An act of *fututio* was not as a rule spoken of as a humiliation to its victim, and hence a non-sexual humiliation was not readily likened to *fututio*. It is presumably because *futuo* retained its full cognitive force that it lived on into the Romance languages. *Irrumo*, *pedico* and *fello* disappeared (if one excludes the single reflex of *fello*, based on the literal sense). One may conjecture that in Vulgar Latin they were eventually emptied of proper force to such an extent that they had to be replaced. Languages need a word meaning the same as *pedico* (if not *irrumo*).

The weakening of sexual verbs caused by their appearance in threats deserves special mention. A threat to inflict a sexual violation is more likely to be taken seriously by an intimate

[1] On the weakening of καταπύγων, see Dover, pp. 113f., 143.

of the speaker than by an enemy or a stranger. A man might be regarded as having the opportunity to *pedicare* his own wife; the hearer of such a threat might assign to it more cognitive force than he would to a threat aimed at a passer-by. When Mamercus Scaurus threatened to *irrumare* Annius Pollio (Sen. *Ben.* 4.31.4), the offence he caused was no doubt due to friendship between the two men. On the other hand the same threat seems to have been thrown around against enemies, real or imagined, without being taken seriously. I would suggest that the more often a threat is made against enemies or strangers, without the intention or hope of fulfilment, the less will be its cognitive force. It would also seem to me to be a good sign of its deterioration into a vacuous manner of speaking, if it tends to be motivated even by trifling offences, which the speaker would not seriously think of avenging by a gross sexual violation. The total loss of cognitive force by a sexual term in a threat is exemplified by *laecasin* at Petron. 42.2 ('frigori laecasin dico') and Mart. 11.58.12 ('sed lota mentula lana / λαικάζειν cupidae dicet auaritiae'), where it is directed at abstractions. In this syntagm, the syntax of which is Greek, the verb is obviously a popular borrowing. The weakening would already have taken place in Greek.

It has to be conceded that it is difficult to analyse the various types of 'weakening' in sexual words. It is often impossible to tell how important the cognitive element in a sexual term of abuse is to its user. Inscriptional contexts are frequently uninformative.

(v) *Lingo*

Lingo was not inherently obscene. It is common in the historical period in non-sexual applications. But it had a well-established use in reference to oral stimulation of the sexual organs (*mentula*, *cunnus* and *culus* are all recorded as objects of the verb), and in this sense it had no doubt acquired an offensive tone. It was the *vox propria* for the practice of cunnilinctio. As a sexual term *lingo* has much the same distribution as *fello*, etc.: it is found in graffiti and epigram, but avoided in satire and other literary genres.

The index to *CIL* IV gives 25 examples of the verb. Catullus has it twice (in the elegiac epigrams), with *culus* as object (97.12, 98.4). For this expression in graffiti, see *CIL* IV.4954.

Martial uses it 13 times (note the formula *cunnum lingere*, e.g. 1.77.6, 2.84.3: see below), and there is an example in the epigrams of Ausonius (78.4, p. 341). It is possible that it was not as obscene as other primary obscenities. Ausonius never uses *mentula, cunnus, futuo, pedico* or *culus*, but he does have *fello* and *fellator* once (and also *podex*). The impact of *lingo* in particular and *fello* may have been softened by their continued possession of more general senses. But the tendency of *fello* to be specialised to the sexual sphere is far more marked than that of *lingo*.

The uses of *lingo* are illustrated at *CIL* IV.2400: 'Satur noli cunnum lingere extra porta set intra porta, rogat te Artocra ut sebi lingeas mentulam'. *Cunnum* comes before *lingere*, but *mentulam* comes after the verb. In graffiti *cunnum* regularly has this position in relation to *lingo*, as at *CIL* IV.763, 2081, 3925, 4264, 4995, 8698, 8898, 8939, 8940; for the reverse order, see 1578, where the verb is imperative. *Mentulam*, on the other hand, also comes after the verb at 8512 (and after *oblingo* at 760). *Mentulam* is much rarer as object of *lingo* than is *cunnum*. The difference of word order, and the differing frequency of the two phrases, show that *cunnum lingere* was the older phrase. It had obviously come into use at the time when the order object + verb was regular, whereas *lingere mentulam* must belong to a later period when the basic order was changing. The compound *cunnilingus* (*CIL* IV.4304, 5365, Mart. 4.43.11) reflects the long-standing currency of the phrase *cunnum lingo*.

Lingo mentulam is not an otiose synonym of *fellare*. *Fellare* is not as a rule used with an anatomical term as object; *lingo mentulam* on the other hand is used when the writer needs to specify the nominal object of the action, as at *CIL* IV.2400, where there is a contrast between *cunnum* and *mentulam* + *lingere*. For *mentulam* (or an equivalent) + *lingere* in literature, see Mart. 7.55.6, 9.40.4.

Two compounds of *lingo* are used in a sexual sense at *CIL* IV.760 'oblige mea, fela . . . mentlam elinges . . . destillatio me tenet'. The most usual meaning of the compounds later is 'eat by licking up'.[1] It is possible that the graffito displays the metaphor of 'eating' the genitalia (see below, p. 140).

---

[1] See *TLL* V.2.390.41ff., IX.2.96.36ff.

(vi) *Lambo*

Lambo was not an obscenity, but I include it here because it was synonymous with *lingo*. Its association with sexual behaviour was weak. The index to *CIL* IV gives no examples of the verb. The vast majority of cases quoted in the *TLL* are nonsexual, and those which do have a sexual meaning are in writers prone to euphemism (but note Mart. 2.61.2, 3.81.2).[1] Juvenal, who avoids *lingo*, uses *lambo* (2.49 'Tedia non lambit Cluuiam nec Flora Catullam'). Ausonius, who uses *lingo* only once in the epigrams, has *lambo* at 78.1, p. 341 P., 82.2, p. 343, 83.1, p. 343, 86.1, p. 344. Both examples of *lambo* in Martial are used in conjunction with *lingua*; he was presumably avoiding the jingle *lingo* + *lingua*. It is an indication that *lambo* had no well-established sexual use that it was not specialised but applied indifferently to stimulation of the *cunnus* (Juv. 2.49, Auson. *Epigr.* 82.2, p. 343 P., Claud. *Carm. Min.* 43.7, 44.8) or *mentula* (Mart. 2.61.2, 3.81.2, Auson. *Epigr.* 78.1, p. 341 P.).

On the use of *lambo* at Juv. 9.5, see p. 140.

(vii) *Criso* and *ceueo*

Latin possessed two technical terms for types of sexual motion (in both cases that of the passive partner), *criso* and *ceueo*.[2] *Criso* indicated the motions of the female in intercourse: note ps.-Acron Hor. *Serm.* 2.7.50 'idest dum ego iaceo supinus et ipsa supra me crisat', and cf. Juv. 6.322 'ipsa Medullinae fluctum crisantis adorat', *Priap.* 19.4 'crisabit tibi fluctuante lumbo' (cf. Mart. 10.68.10, 14.203.1).[3] The passage in ps.-Acron should not be taken as implying that *criso* was appropriate only to the *schema* with the woman astride.

Ceueo was used of the corresponding movements of the male pathic (cf. *ceuulus* = 'pathic', *CGL* II.357.20): *Schol. Pers.* 1.87

---

[1] See *TLL* VII.2.899.35ff.

[2] On *ceueo*, see Mussehl, *Hermes* 54 (1919), pp. 387ff.; cf. Fraenkel, *Kleine Beiträge zur klassischen Philologie*, II, pp. 45ff.

[3] The comparison of lascivious movements with the motions of the waves which is implicit in two of these passages was conventional: cf. Apul. *Met.* 2.7 'decenter undabat', Arnob. *Nat.* 2.42 'clunibus et coxendicibus subleuatis lumborum crispitudine fluctuaret', 5.44 'illis fluctibus, quos super aggerem tumuli Semeleiae subolis urigo contorsit', 7.33 'clunibus fluctuare crispatis'. Cf. Lucr. 4.1077.

'molles et obscaenos clunium motus significat'. Note too the equivalence at Juv. 2.21 'de uirtute locuti / *clunem agitant.* "ego te ceuentem, Sexte, uerebor?" ', and cf. Mart. 3.95.13 'sed *pedicaris*, sed pulchre, Naeuole, ceues'. Cf. *CIL* IV.4977, Pers. 1.87, Juv. 9.40.

Ceuentinabiliter at *CIL* IV.4126 ('Trebonius Eucini ceuentinabiliter arrurabiliter') and 5406 ('inclinabiliter ceuentinabiliter') is presumably equivalent to the present participle *ceuens*. Strictly it would appear to be formed on an extended **ceuentinare*, but the ending *-inabiliter* may simply have been taken from the associated *inclinabiliter* and attached to the participial stem *ceuent-*.[1]

Criso and *ceueo*, like the primary obscenities *mentula, cunnus, futuo*, etc., had no more basic meaning in recorded Latin. But their presence in Persius and Juvenal, who excluded the other obscenities, implies that they were not as offensive as *mentula* etc. *Criso* is even used by Donatus (Ter. *Eun.* 424), who would not have admitted a word of the status of *futuo*. A common type of euphemism is that which refers to a concomitant action, such as the movements of copulation (see p. 193), rather than to sexual penetration itself. Though *criso* and *ceueo* were not used of movements other than sexual, it may have been less offensive to speak in direct terms of such movements than of the active partner's role in the act (*futuo, pedico*).

Arnobius uses *crispo* ('wave, brandish') and *crispitudo* in contexts describing lascivious movements (*Nat.* 2.42, 7.33, quoted at p. 136 n. 3). The phonetic similarity of *crispo* to *criso* would surely have caused the reader to think of *criso*. Phonetic suggestiveness of this kind is typical of sexual innuendo. At frg. 168 Lindsay ('ipsa sibi auis mortem creat'), in an allusion to a proverb which contained *caco* (Isid. *Etym.* 12.7.71 'unde et

---

[1] There is a remarkable group of *-biliter* adverbs in graffiti, in which the adverbial termination seems in some cases to have been weakened into the equivalent of a present participle or ablative of the gerund: see G. N. Olcott, *Studies in the Word Formation of the Latin Inscriptions* (Rome, 1898), p. 209. Note *festinabiliter* (*CIL* IV.4758), *fratrabiliter* (659), and in sexual slang *irrumabiliter* (1931) and *inclinabiliter* (above at 5406, and also 1322 (1332*a*) = 3034*c*, add. p. 466; for *inclino* in a sexual sense, see p. 192). *Amabiliter* (2032; cf. 2374, and Petron. 113.1 'uultumque suum super ceruicem Gitonis amabiliter ponente') may have provided the analogy for the sexual coinages in the vulgar language.

prouerbium apud antiquos erat, "malum sibi auem cacare" '),[1]
Plautus avoided the offensive *caco*, but selected a word with
the same initial sound and the same number of syllables.[2]
Macrobius quotes a joke by the painter L. Mallius in which
fingo implies *futuo* partly because of its initial *f*: *Sat.* 2.2.10
'apud L. Mallium, qui optimus pictor Romae habebatur, Ser-
uilius Geminus forte cenabat, cumque filios eius deformes uidisset, "non similiter", inquit, "Malli, fingis et pingis". et
Mallius "in tenebris enim fingo", inquit, "luce pingo" '.

2. Metaphors

There is an almost complete overlap between metaphors for
fututio and *pedicatio* in Latin, just as non-metaphorical euphemisms for the two acts overlap. Even the obscenities *futuo*
and *pedico* are not rigidly distinguished. I have made no consistent attempt to distinguish metaphors equivalent to *futuo*
from those equivalent to *pedico*. The one remarkable metaphor
for oral activities in Latin (that of eating) is included along
with those for *fututio* and *pedicatio*. I begin at the lower end
of the stylistic scale.

(i) 'Eat'

The metaphor of 'eating' has surprising ramifications in the
sexual sphere in Latin. It occurs in graffiti, and must have had
a place in low slang. From slang it was taken over into literary
genres which had a vulgar or coarse element (notably epigram). A few parallels can be quoted from Greek, but the
metaphor was not literary in Latin. It had two main applications, the first relatively unimportant.

The *culus* or *cunnus* is sometimes personified and described
as 'eating' or 'devouring' the *mentula*. The verb *uoro* seems to
have been the appropriate term in this sense: Catull. 33.4 'culo
... uoraciore', Mart. 2.51.6 'infelix uenter spectat conuiuia
culi, / et semper miser hic esurit, ille uorat', 12.75.3 'pastas
glande natis habet Secundus' (*glans* is ambiguous: see p. 72).
There is an extension of this type of imagery at Auson. *Cent.*

[1] See Otto, p. 52.
[2] See Fraenkel, *Elementi Plautini*, p. 440.

Nupt. 118, p. 217 P., where the *mentula* 'drinks': 'haesit uir-gineumque alte bibit acta cruorem'. *Bibit* was probably an *ad hoc* metaphor, facilitated by the tendency for the *mentula* to be personified. For Greek note the jokes at Aristoph. *Ach.* 801f., where Dicaeopolis asks if the pig (= κύσθος) eats chick peas and figs (= πέος): τρώγοιτ᾽ ἂν ἐρεβίνθους; ... τί δαί; φιβάλεως ἰσχάδας.

But usually the metaphor is applied to oral acts: the sexual organ of either sex is said to be 'eaten'. The usage is found in graffiti: *CIL* IV.1854 'Caliste, deuora',[1] IV.1884 'qui uerpam uissit, quid cenasse illum putes?' ('he who went to visit the *uerpa*, what would you think he had for dinner?'),[2] IV.2360 'ursi me comedant et ego uerpa qui lego';[3] cf. *esurio* ('want to eat') in the context of *fellatio* at *CIL* IV.1825 'Cosmus equitaes magnus cinaedus et fellator esuris apertis mari(bus)', XI.6721.34 'esureis et me felas'.[4] See further Catull. 28.12f. 'nam nihilo minore uerpa / farti estis' (*farcio* is typically ap-plied to stuffing with food),[5] 80.6 'grandia te medii tenta uorare uiri', 88.8 'demisso se ipse uoret capite', Mart. 7.67.15 'sed plane medias uorat puellas' (= *cunnum lingere*), 14.70.2 'si uis esse satur, nostrum potes esse Priapum; / ipsa licet rodas in-guina, purus eris'. In three of the above passages it is a *uerpa* which is 'eaten'; to 'eat the *uerpa*' was obviously a slang expression.

There may be an allusion to the metaphor in Mart. 3.77. Baeticus, the *cunnilingus* (see 3.81), is described as rejecting delicious and eating foul food. In the final line (10) he is asked why he eats what is putrid ('ut quid enim, Baetice, sapro-phagis?'). There may be a double entendre in the last word: Baeticus 'eats' the *cunnus* (cf. Auson. *Epigr.* 86.1, p. 344 P. 'uxoris grauidae *putria* inguina'), and hence has a need of foul and pungent foods to conceal his bad breath.

The verb which Juvenal uses at 10.223 is unusual, perhaps because he wanted to avoid the slang terms associated with the image (notably *uoro* and *uerpa*): 'quot longa uiros exorbeat

---

[1] For this inscription, see Svennung, in *Studi in onore di Luigi Castiglioni* (cited above, p. 65, n. 5), II, p. 978 n. 13.

[2] For *uerpa* used *pars pro toto*, see p. 13.

[3] On the interpretation of the inscription, see above, p. 129, and n. 3.

[4] On these inscriptions, see Krenkel, p. 83; see also *esurit* at Mart. 2.51.6 above, p. 138.

[5] See *TLL* VI.1.280.31ff.

uno / Maura die'.[1] Cf. 6.126 'ac resupina iacens cunctorum absorbuit ictus' (or is it the *cunnus* which *absorbuit* here?: cf. Hor. *Serm.* 2.7.49 'quaecumque *excepit* turgentis *uerbera* caudae'). Note too the double entendre at Juv. 9.5 'nos colaphum incutimus lambenti crustula seruo'.[2] A protracted example of the metaphor is provided by Tertullian, *Apol.* 9.12 'minus autem et illi faciunt, qui libidine fera humanis membris inhiant, quia uiuos uorant? minus humano sanguine ad spurcitiam consecrantur, quia futurum sanguinem lambunt? non edunt infantes plane, sed magis puberes'. Tertullian permitted himself drastic phraseology here.

The note 'siue membrum uirile' on *colyphium* at Juv. 2.53 ('luctantur paucae, comedunt coloephia paucae') may be based on a belief that *comedunt* has a sexual sense.

Krenkel (p. 84) draws attention to a few passages in which voyeurs are said to 'devour boys with their eyes': Mart. 1.96.12 'sed spectat oculis deuorantibus draucos', 9.59.3 'inspexit molles pueros oculisque comedit'. Given the established sexual sense of the verbs, these passages might have implied to some readers that the subjects were doing the next best thing to devouring with their mouths. For lascivious eyes described as doing what is normally done by the sexual organs, see p. 143 on Pers. 1.18 '*patranti* fractus ocello'.

The predominating sense of *ligurio* (like that of *elingo* and *oblingo*: see p. 135) was 'eat by licking up' (Hor. *Serm.* 1.3.81, 2.4.79) rather than 'lick' in general (*lingo*). When the verb is applied to a sexual act, it may be akin to, if not identical with, the above usages: see *Atell. inc. nom. rel.* 4 Ribbeck 'hircus uetulus capreis naturam ligurrit', Suet. *Gramm.* 23.6 'uis tu, inquit, magister, quotiens festinantem aliquem uides abligurire'. Note too Cic. *Dom.* 47 'hanc tibi legem Cloelius scripsit spurciorem lingua sua, ut interdictum sit cui non sit interdictum? Sexte noster, bona uenia, quoniam iam dialecticus es et haec quoque liguris . . .'. Whether or not the text is right,[3] the context (note 'spurciorem lingua sua') and the presence of *quoque* (which shows that the referent was a 'licker up' of some-

---

[1] For Maura the *fellatrix*, see Courtney, p. 297 (on 6.307-8).

[2] See Courtney, p. 428 '*Lambere* is wittily used both of slaves who lick the morsels . . . and in the obscene sense'. In that obscene sense there is present a notion of 'eating', or 'eating by licking'.

[3] See R. G. Nisbet, *M. Tulli Ciceronis De domo sua ad pontifices oratio* (Oxford, 1939), *ad loc.*

thing else apart from what is implied in *dialecticus*) make it likely that the verb is intended to have a sexual implication. Cf. *ligurritor* (Auson. *Epigr.* 87.1, p. 344 P.). Catull. frg. 2 ('de meo ligurrire libido est') may also be obscene.

At Pompon. 151 ('ego quaero quod comedim, has [= *hae*?] quaerunt quod cacent: contrariumst') and Novius 6 ('quod editis, nihil est: si uultis quod cacetis, copia est') *comedim* and *editis* may be metaphorical (see p. 172). And at *Priap.* 70.10–14 and 78, though the metaphor is not explicit, there is an association on the one hand between hunger and *irrumatio* (hungry dogs will suffer *irrumatio*) and on the other between eating food (78.1 *escam*) and cunnilinctio.

A few other examples of the metaphor given by Krenkel are unconvincing. At Mart. 9.63 ('ad cenam inuitant omnes te, Phoebe, cinaedi. / mentula quem pascit, non, puto, purus homo est') Phoebus is not a *fellator*,[1] but a professional *pedicator* (see 1.58). The use to which he puts the *mentula* (with *cinaedi*) provides him with money (1.58.5) or a meal. For the idea, see Juv. 9.136. And the manner in which Novius 80 ('quid ego facerem? otiosi [*otiose*?] rodebam rutabulum') is cited by Festus, p. 318 does not favour a sexual interpretation of *rodebam* and *rutabulum*.[2] The quotation comes after a definition of *rutabulum* as an implement used 'in proruendo igne, panis coquendi gratia'. Festus then says that Naevius (*Nauius* cod.) used the word to mean 'obscenam uiri partem', and gives a quotation.

For the metaphor in Greek, see Archil. spur. 328.9 West ἐκροφοῦντες ἥδονται πέος. At Aristoph. *Pax* 885 τὸν ζωμὸν αὐτῆς προσπεσὼν ἐκλάψεται the idea is of licking up vaginal secretions rather than 'devouring' a sexual organ.

The above expressions in Latin should be compared with *fello* and *irrumo*, which, we have seen, were originally metaphors from suckling. There was obviously a long-standing popular association between oral sexual acts and feeding. To judge by its use and distribution, the metaphor had a coarse or vulgar flavour, at least when the verb meant explicitly 'eat, devour' (as distinct from 'lick up').

---

[1] Despite Krenkel, p. 83.
[2] Despite Krenkel, p. 79.

(ii) 'Urinate' and expressions for 'ejaculate'

Verbs meaning 'urinate' are often used of ejaculation in Latin: Catull. 67.30 'qui ipse sui gnati minxerit in gremium', Hor. *Serm.* 1.2.44 'hunc perminxerunt calones' (presumably of *pedicatio*; the passage deals with the punishment of adulterers, and anal penetration in various forms is a common punishment for adultery: see p. 128), *Serm.* 2.7.52 'ne / ditior aut formae melioris meiat eodem', Pers. 6.73 'patriciae inmeiat uoluae', Mart. 11.46.2 'incipit in medios meiere uerpa pedes', *Anth. Lat.* 374 tit. 'De Diogene picto, ubi lasciuienti menetrix barbam euellit et Cupido mingit in podice eius', *ibid.* 6 'mingitur archisophus'. Note too the marginal gloss 'frequenter mingebam' (φ) on the *spurcum additamentum* at Apul. *Met.* 10.21.[1] With these verbal usages should be compared *urina* = *semen* at Juv. 11.170. In Greek μοιχός ('adulterer') is the agent noun corresponding to ὀμείχω 'urinate'.[2] Also worth noting is the popular etymology of the name Orion: Schol. *HPQ* to Hom. *Od.* 5.121 οἱ θεοὶ εἶδον τὴν βύρσαν τοῦ σφαγέντος βοὸς κειμένην κάτω, καὶ οὐρήσαντες εἰς αὐτὴν ἐξ αὐτοῦ τοῦ οὔρου καὶ τῆς βύρσης ἐποίησαν τὸν Ὠρίωνα.[3] There is probably a similar idea behind Juv. 6.64 (see p. 92).

The distribution of the above usages (satire and epigram in the earlier period) suggests that they had a vulgar ring. They seem to have been applied particularly to squalid or humiliating sexual acts. It is not plausible to suggest that they reflect a 'primitive' failure to distinguish sharply between urine and sexual secretions.[4] In Latin at least it is more likely that they would have been interpreted as crudely figurative, or as infantilisms deliberately maintained in vulgar speech. Semen is sometimes likened to other bodily secretions (e.g. mucus, *CIL* IV.1391, tears, Lucil. 307).

It will be convenient at this point to collect other expressions in Latin used of ejaculation or reaching orgasm, though not all are metaphorical.

Patro was used elliptically from at least as early as the first century, = 'accomplish (it)'. There is a particularly clear ex-

---

[1] See Mariotti, p. 240 = p. 59.

[2] See J. Wackernagel, *Sprachliche Untersuchungen zu Homer* (Göttingen, 1916), p. 225, n. 1.

[3] See R. Muth, 'Urin', *RE*, *Suppl.* XI, 1292ff., especially 1301, S. Laser, *Gnomon* 28 (1956), pp. 613f., Herter, 'Genitalien', 20f. See also Pokorny, I, p. 81.

[4] See Muth, 1303.

ample at Porph. Hor. *Serm.* 1.5.84 'deinde per somnium ima-
ginantem se, cum eandem puellam uidisset, concumbere super
se ipsum patrasse' (of a nocturnal emission, not copulation).
Cf. Pers. 1.18 'patranti fractus ocello',[1] and perhaps Catull.
29.16 'parum expatrauit an parum helluatus est'. The sense of
the verb is illuminated by the use of *patratio* ('orgasm') in
Theodorus Priscianus: *Eup.* 2.32, p. 130.15 Rose 'satyriasis
. . . tensionem particulae cum assidua patratione auidissimam
facit' (it is a question of ejaculation, not copulation: cf.
p. 130.8). Isidore (*Etym.* 9.5.3 'pater autem dictus eo quod patratione peracta filium procreet. patratio enim est rei ueneriae
consummatio') was right to say that *patratio* indicated consum-
mation, but if *res ueneria* means 'sexual intercourse' it has no
place in the definition. Isidore was bound to offer a false definition of *patro*, given his etymology of *pater*.

The verb is complemented at *Anth. Lat.* 358.5 'nec die
quaeris coitum patrare', but *coitum patrare* looks like a ra-
tionalisation of the elliptical idiom. An elliptical euphemism
need not have its origin in the abbreviation of a longer, more
explicit expression. *Facio*, for example ('do (it)'), scarcely stems
from an expression such as *fututionem facio*. The hearer had
no doubt been expected to supply his own complement as long
as the usage existed. Quintilian's remark (8.3.44) that by his
day the Sallustian expression *patrare bella* had acquired an
obscene implication must mean either that *patro* had become
so suggestive that it was unusable in polite society in any
collocation, or that, since *bella* could be used metaphorically
of intercourse, the phrase might be taken to mean 'consum-
mate sexual wars'.[2]

The elliptical use of *patro* has an exact parallel in that of

[1] Here a term strictly appropriate to the *mentula* has been transferred to the
eye, partly because of the belief that the effects of orgasm or sexual desire
could be seen in the eye: see Juv. 7.241 'non est leue tot puerorum / obseruare
manus oculosque in fine trementis' (note *in fine*, of orgasm: Courtney compares
Mart. 9.69.1 'cum futuis, Polycharme, soles in fine cacare'; cf. Auson. *Cent.
Nupt.* 129, p. 217 P., *Epigr.* 106.16, p. 351). The present participle seems to
have an inceptive or desiderative force, = 'worn out with his eye attempting
to make it', i.e. dreaming of the pleasures of orgasm or intercourse. For the
eye and sexual desire, see J. C. Bramble, *Persius and the Programmatic Satire*
(Cambridge, 1974), p. 77, n. 3. Persius was imitated at *Anth. Lat.* 902.3 'sunt
lusci oculi atque patrantes'.

[2] Bramble, pp. 76f. mentions with approval the definition of the Delphin
edition of Persius, 'patrare proprie est παιδοποιεῖν', and then misquotes the
Sallustian expression in the form *patrare bellum*. If Quintilian had seen *bellus*
in the expression, he would have written *bellum*, not *bella*.

perficio at *H.A.*, *Maxim.* 4.7 'diceris, Maximine, sedecim et
uiginti et triginta milites aliquando lassasse: potes tricies cum
muliere perficere?' ('can you make it thirty times with a
woman?'). *Perficio* perhaps had a place in ordinary speech (note
that it is here used in direct speech). Cf. Mart. 3.79.2 'hunc
ego, cum futuit, non puto perficere'. There was also said to
exist a goddess *Perfica*, 'quae obscenas illas et luteas uoluptates *ad exitum perficit* dulcedine inoffensa procedere' (Arnob.
Nat. 4.7). With *exitus* here, compare *finis* (see p. 143 n. 1), and
Mart. 11.81.4 '*sine effectu* prurit utrique labor'. Similar to the
above use of *perficio* is *perago (rem)* at Marc. Emp. 33.73; cf.
Isid. *Etym.* 9.5.3 above.

The metaphor of 'reaching a goal' was used of achieving
orgasm: see Lucr. 4.1195f. 'communia quaerens / gaudia sollicitat *spatium decurrere amoris*', Ovid *Ars* 2.727 'nec cursus
anteeat illa tuos; / *ad metam properate* simul', Auson. *Cent.*
Nupt. 128f., p. 217 P. 'iamque fere spatio extremo fessique *sub*
ipsam / *finem aduentabant*' (note *finem*, and see p. 143 n. 1).
Propero (see Ovid *Ars* 2.727) seems to have been idiomatic in
much the same sense as Eng. *come*: see Mart. 1.46.1 'cum dicis
"propero, fac si facis", Hedyle, languet / . . . Venus'; cf. *festino*
at Suet. *Gramm.* 23.6 'uis tu, inquit, magister, quotiens festinantem aliquem uides abligurire?'.[1] There is remarkably similar
phraseology to that of Martial on a wall of the room of the
Seven Sages at Ostia.[2] It is impossible to tell what some partially obliterated figures are doing, but between them they say
'mulione sedes', 'agita te, celerius peruenies', 'propero' and
'amice fugit te prouerbium bene caca et irrima medicos'. The
last remark makes it natural to think that the figures were
pictured in a latrine relieving themselves. But the terminology
has a distinctly sexual appearance. For *sedeo* used of a sexual
schema, see p. 165. For 'arriving' (*peruenies*), of orgasm, see in
particular *aduentabant* above. *Celerius* is reminiscent of *uel-*
ocius at Mart. 1.46.3 'expectare iube: uelocius ibo retentus'
(*ibo* here, like *propero*, is roughly equivalent to Eng. *come*).
Agito had various sexual uses. With *clunes* and the like as
object it could be used of the motions of the passive partner in
intercourse (p. 194); and for the meaning 'masturbate', note
the obscene interpretation of the Virgilian 'incipiunt agitata

[1] See Housman, *Classical Papers*, p. 1184.
[2] See Calza, *Die Antike* 15 (1939), p. 103.

tumescere' (*Georg.* 1.357) attributed to Celsus at Quint. 8.3.47. It is possible that one man was about to commit *pedicatio* with another, and that he was urged to employ masturbation to speed up the act. On this interpretation *propero* would be a parallel for Mart. 1.46.1. Even *bene caca* could have a sexual implication: cf. *CIL* X.4483 'caca, ut possimus bene dormire . . . et pedicare natis candidas'. If the reference throughout is to *cacatio*, *propero* would still be a similar metaphor to that in Martial (of hurrying to a different type of goal).

(iii) 'Strike' and the like

One of the largest semantic fields from which metaphors for sexual acts were taken in Latin is that of striking, beating and the like (cf., e.g. κρούματα at Aristoph. *Eccl.* 257, κρούω at 990, and προκρούω at 1017). Metaphors from this semantic area could be freely coined, but it cannot be doubted that certain words were in current use.

Caedo was one such metaphor. Used literally it possessed the senses 'cut' and 'beat', either of which might have served as the basis for a sexual metaphor. The *mentula* is often described metaphorically as a sharp instrument, and hence its function might be seen as cutting. But *caedo* is more commonly used = 'beat', and this is the meaning which probably lay behind the metaphor (although it will be suggested below that one and the same word can provide different types of sexual metaphors: see p. 155). *Caedo* sometimes implies a sexual act seen as a punishment. In its literal sense 'beat' the verb indicated a form of punishment. For a sexual act described in terms appropriate to a punishment see Mart. 2.60.2 'supplicium tantum dum puerile times'.

At Lucil. 283 ('uxorem caedam potius quam castrem egomet me') *caedo* is a substitute for *futuo*, but usually it refers to *pedicatio*. This partial restriction probably reflects the fact that *pedicatio* is more often considered a punishment or humiliation than is *fututio*. For *pedicatio* (expressed by *caedo*) inflicted to punish someone, see Catull. 56.7 'deprendi modo pupulum puellae / trusantem: hunc ego, si placet Dionae, / protelo rigida mea cecidi'. Catullus had caught a youth masturbating.[1] The opportunity for *pedicatio* was conveniently presented, but there was an element of punishment in the act.[2] So at *Priap.* 26.10 ('solebam / fures caedere') *caedo* refers to Priapus' punishment of thieves. And at Petron. 21.2 it is used of the humiliation inflicted on Encolpius and Ascyltos by a homosexual: 'cinaedus . . . modo extortis nos clunibus cecidit, modo basiis olidissimis inquinauit'. For further examples, see Laber. 23 'numne aliter hunce pedicabis? – quo modo? / – uideo, adulescenti nostro caedis hirulam', Tert. *Pall.* 4.4 'sed et qui ante Tirynthium accesserat, pugil Cleomachus, post Olympiae cum incredibili mutatu de masculo fluxisset, intra cutem caesus'.[3]

Percido (lit. usually of hitting rather than cutting) would also have had some currency, to judge by its attestation in inscriptions as well as literary sources: see *CIL* IV.2319 *l* 'Tyria percisa, . . . περκισα', and cf. 2319 *e* add. p. 217, 2319 *p*. These inscriptions, in all of which the referent is a certain Tyria, show that the word was not used exclusively of *pedicatio*. But that is its predominating application in literature: see Mart. 4.48.1 twice, 4, 6.39.14, 7.62.1, 12.35.2, *Priap.* 13.1, 15.6, and note *CGL* II.148.52 'percisus pedicatus [*perd.* cod.]

---

[1] On the sense of *trusantem*, see Kroll *ad loc.*, comparing Mart. 11.46.3 'truditur et digitis pannucea mentula lassis', Housman, *Classical Papers*, p. 1175 and Fehling, p. 23 n. 98. Fehling notes that it is impossible to construe *puellae* as a dative. *Mentulam* is understood with *trusantem*, as with *frica* at Mart. 11.29.8 and *deglubit* at Auson. *Epigr.* 79.7, p. 341 P. It is worth mentioning here that Shackleton Bailey (*CP* 71 (1976), p. 348) has recently attempted to revive a conjecture of E. Baehrens, *crusantem = crisantem*. Shackleton Bailey also changes *hunc* to *hanc*, on the grounds that 'logic . . . suggests that the object of Catullus' intervention . . . should be, not the boy, but his playmate'. Baehrens (*Catulli Veronensis Liber*, rev. by K. P. Schulze (Leipzig, 1893), p. 281) argued that the boy and girl were playing at being man and wife, but, being ignorant of sexual matters, had adopted the wrong positions: the girl was on top and the boy was *crisantem* in the manner of women (*puellae* would then be a dative of advantage, like *tibi* at *Priap.* 19.4). There are various objections to this notion: (*a*) Mart. 11.46.3, a passage apparently not known by Baehrens, provides a good parallel for the use of *trusantem* required here; (*b*) it was a recognised *schema* for the female to be astride, and not one which would suggest a reversal of roles and hence prompt a bizarre and unparalleled use of *criso*, of the male; (*c*) there is no evidence that *cruso* was an old form of *criso*. *Hanc* is also unsatisfactory. *Caedo*, we have suggested, tends to imply a sexual act perpetrated as a punishment. Even if there is a girl present here, it is the boy who has been caught at some punishable offence, and the boy who must be punished.

[2] See Fehling, p. 24.

[3] The phrase *intra cutem caesus = intercutitus* (see below, p. 147).

πεπυγισμένος'. The misspelling in another gloss (*CGL* V.575.43 'pertisis uiolatis') perhaps has a parallel at *CIL* IV.3120 περτισ (*pertis*(-*a*, -*us*)?). The example at Mart. 2.72.3 (with *os* as object) may refer to *irrumatio* (see below, p. 212).

Concido can mean 'beat' (Cic. *Verr.* 3.56, Juv. 3.300), but the sense 'cut' lies behind the metaphorical use = *pedico* at *H.A.*, *Hel.* 10.5 'nubsit et coit <cum illo it>a, ut et pronubam haberet clamaretque "concide Magire" '. Zoticus, with whom the emperor submitted to a homosexual marriage, was nick-named *Magirus* (μάγειρος, 'cook, butcher'), and the double entendre here is from the language of butchering. The other sexual example of the verb (Pompon. 83 'dolasti uxorem: nunc eapropter me cupis / concidere') could be based on either literal meaning, but the presence of *dolo* suggests that here too the metaphor was one of cutting.

One metaphor of beating for the currency of which we have Cicero's testimony is *battuo*: *Fam.* 9.22.4 ' "battuit" inquit impudenter, "depsit" multo impudentius'; cf. Petron. 69.3 'ut ego sic solebam ipsumam meam debattuere', in a speech of Trimalchio. This second example, like various other graphic metaphors which will be discussed in the following pages, is applied to an illicit liaison: the speaker uses the word with a contemptuous tone in a boast (cf. Eng. *bang someone else's wife*).

Certain other verbs of beating or striking were probably occasionally used off-the-cuff, but evidence for them is more fleeting. *Percutio* is nowhere found with the sense in question. *Percussor* is perhaps used in a double entendre in a speech at Petron. 9.9 'non taces, nocturne percussor, qui ne tum quidem, cum fortiter faceres, cum pura muliere pugnasti'. The context is sexual (note *pugnasti*), but *percussor* could be an unconnected term of abuse. The word certainly has a sexual implication at Maxim. *Eleg.* 5.134 'fert tacitum ridetque suum laniata dolorem / et percussori plaudit amica suo'. Paulus' (Festus') remark, p. 100 'intercutitus uehementer cutitus, hoc est ualde stupratus' suggests that he derived *intercutitus* from a verb *cutio* (with prefix *inter-*) rather than (correctly) *intercus* (for which in a sexual sense see Gell. 13.8.5, Cato *Orat.* frg. 60; cf. Paul. Fest. p. 98 *inter cutem*, Tert. *Pall.* 4.4 quoted above; for the formation see *recutitus*). *Cutio* he would presumably have regarded as the simplex of *percutio* (despite the inconsistency between the participial forms). Behind this derivation is the assumption that *percutio* might appropriately be applied to a sexual act. In the *Cento Nuptialis* Ausonius uses another compound, *recutio*, in a sexual sense: 126, p. 217 P. 'itque reditque uiam totiens uteroque recusso / transadigit costas' ('striking the womb' indicates depth of penetration). *Percussorium* is given the meaning 'penis' at *CGL* V.252.28, but the metaphor is from music (*percussorium* = 'plectrum': see p. 25).

Tundo and *pertundo* are not certainly attested as substitutes for *futuo* or *pedico*,[1] but there are indications that they would have been capable of sexual undertones in a suggestive context. A goddess *Pertunda* allegedly played a part in the deflowering of the bride (Tert. *Nat.* 2.11.12, Arnob. *Nat.* 4.7, Aug. *Ciu.* 6.9). The name must be based on a sexual use of *pertundo*. The verb appears in a sexual context at Catull. 32.11 ('pertundo tunicamque palliumque'), but it expresses the striking of the *mentula* against the writer's clothing rather than against the victim of a sexual act. It is a small step from such a usage to the sense '*futuo*'. Hence *pulso* is used in the same way as *pertundo* in Catullus by both Martial (11.16.5 'rigida pulsabis pallia uena') and the author of the *Priapea* (23.5f. 'mentulaque / nequiquam sibi pulset umbilicum'), whereas Ausonius was able to apply the verb to an act of *fututio*: *Cent. Nupt.* 127, p. 217 P. 'transadigit costas et pectine pulsat eburno'.

The simplex *tundo* is possibly synonymous with *futuo* at Catull. 59.5 ('ab semiraso tunderetur ustore'), but it is more likely that it means 'hit'. *Pertunsorium*, like *percussorium*, is equated with *mentula* in glosses. If the usage is genuine, it too was probably a musical metaphor (see p. 25).

For *ferio*, see Maxim. *Eleg.* 5.97 (addressed to a *mentula*) 'quo tibi feruor abit, per quem feritura placebas, / quo tibi cristatum uulnificumque caput?'. The verb survived with this sense in Old French.[2] The view that it is also used thus at Plaut. *Bacch.* 1174[3] is unconvincing. Cf. *icta* at Maxim. *Eleg.* 5.131 'sternitur *icta* tuo uotiuo uulnere uirgo / et perfusa nouo laeta cruore iacet'. The noun *ictus* is used of the male sexual

---

[1] *Pertundo* at Lucil. 1071 ('nemo istum uentrem pertundet') could mean 'punch in the belly'. For a sexual interpretation of the verb, see Goldberger (1932), p. 103, Buchheit, *Hermes* 90 (1962), p. 253 n. 9.

[2] *FEW* III, p. 465.

[3] See Preston, p. 43.

act at Juv. 6.126 'iacens cunctorum absorbuit ictus', *Anth. Lat.*
712.19 'dent crebros ictus', and in Medieval Latin: William of
Blois, *Alda* 505 'post crebros igitur ictus sudataque multum /
proelia presudat hausta labore suo', anon., *Baucis et Traso* 275
'non noui quid amor, quid amoris sentiat ictus' (perhaps a
double entendre).[1] Similarly Lucretius uses *ictus* of the 'blow'
of semen: 4.1245 'aut non tam prolixo prouolat ictu (semen)',
1273 'atque locis auertit seminis ictum'. Note finally *uerbera*
at Hor. *Serm.* 2.7.49 'quaecumque excepit turgentis uerbera
caudae'.

(iv) 'Cut, split, penetrate' and the like

The *podex* of Charinus at Mart. 6.37 is so cut that it is unre-
cognisable: lf. 'secti podicis usque ad umbilicum / nullas rel-
liquias habet Charinus'. The joke was possible because a
sexual act is readily likened to cutting (see above, p. 147 on
concido). For Greek see, for example, the punning use of τέμνω
at *A.P.* 11.262.2 (anon.).

Dolo (lit. 'chip, hew' with a sharp instrument, usually in
wood), like other verbs of cutting (e.g. *caedo*, *seco*), tended to
be weakened into the sense 'beat' (Hor. *Serm.* 1.5.23), but the
literal sense, which predominates, probably gave rise to the
following metaphorical use: Pompon. 82 'dolasti uxorem',
Mart. 7.67.3 'et tentigine saeuior mariti / undenas dolat in die
puellas', Apul. *Met.* 9.7 'inclinatam dolio pronam uxorem fabri
superincuruatus secure dedolabat'.

Scalpo (lit. 'chisel, cut away (stone), sculpt', also 'scratch')
may refer to *pedicatio* at Pompon. 76 'praeteriens uidit Dos-
sennum in ludo reuerecunditer / non docentem condiscipulum,
uerum scalpentem nates'.[2] For *nates* used loosely (= *culus*) of
the site of *pedicatio*, see *CIL* X.4483 (quoted above, p. 115).
But the inadequate context does not rule out the meaning
'scratch' (for which, see, e.g. Juv. 9.133), of a homosexual act
perhaps the same as that at Mart. 1.92.2 'tangi se digito,
Mamuriane, tuo', though the interpretation of the epigram is
problematical. I am inclined to take 11–12 ('non culum, neque

---

[1] Both of these texts are in Cohen. There is a new edition of the *Baucis et
Traso* by G. Orlandi, *Commedie latine del xii e xiii secolo* III (Università di
Genova, Pubblicazioni dell' Istituto di Filologia Classica e Medievale, 1980).
Orlandi prefers *ictum* (B) to *ictus*.
[2] So Frassinetti, p. 104.

enim est culus, qui non cacat olim, / sed fodiam digito qui superest oculum') as looking back to 2, and the whole phrase *fodiam digito* (rather than *fodiam* alone) as understood with *culum* in 11. Hence Mamurianus would have touched the *culus*, not the *mentula*, of the boy.

For *scindo* = *futuo*, *pedico*, see Laber. 25 'an concupiuisti eugium scindere', *Priap.* 54.2 'qui medium uult te scindere', 77.9 'furum scindere podices solebam'. There are various such metaphors in the sparse fragments of mime and farce. Both genres must reflect low sexual slang and crude popular humour. Some similar metaphors, as we shall see, are found in Plautus.

There is a pun on a sexual meaning of *inforare* (cf. τρυπάω at Theocr. 5.42, Antistius, *A.Plan.* 243.6) at Plaut. *Curc.* 401f.: 'licetne inforare, si incomitiare non licet? / CV. non inforabis me quidem, nec mihi placet / tuom profecto nec forum nec comitium'. Similarly *perforo* was given a sexual meaning by the author of the *Priapea*: 76.3 'deprensos ego perforare possum / Tithonum Priamumque Nestoremque'. Note the medieval expression, Lehmann no. 17, p. 242 'proforasti uxorem meum' (*sic*) (for *perforasti*).

Traicio (which often denoted piercing or penetrating by means of a sharp instrument) is used as an *ad hoc* metaphor at *Priap.* 11.3 'traiectus conto sic extendere pedali'. The extending of the image into a second word (*contus*) shows that the writer was not using banal terminology.

Dirumpo was capable of various sexual senses. At Plaut. *Cas.* 326 ('ego edepol illam mediam dirruptam uelim') the participle is taken as equivalent to *fututam* by the next speaker; for *mediam* in such a context (= 'split up the middle'), see *Priap.* 54.2, above. A formulaic and usually innocent expression has here been forced to bear a sexual sense (for the phrase used in its literal meaning, of bursting, see Plaut. *Bacch.* 603 'sufflatus ille huc ueniet. PI. dirruptum uelim'). It was a common form of humour to give proverbs and set phrases a sexual implication (see p. 34). *Dirumpo* is used rather more literally of the effects of an act of *fututio* on the woman at Apul. *Met.* 7.21 ('misera illa compauita atque dirupta ipsa quidem cruciabilem cladem sustinuisset') and 10.22. On the other hand at Plaut. *Cas.* 810 ('illo morbo quo dirrumpi cupio, non est copiae') the metaphor of bursting is applied to the effects of sexual desire or activity on the male: for this meta-

phor in various connections, cf. Prop. 2.16.14 'rumpat ut assi-
duis membra libidinibus', Hor. *Serm.* 1.2.118 'malis tentigine
rumpi', *Priap.* 23.5 'hac tentigine, quam uidetis in me, / rum-
patur', 33.5 'sed ne tentigine rumpar'; cf. Catull. 11.20 'sed
identidem omnium / ilia rumpens', 80.7 'clamant Victoris
rupta miselli / ilia'. Such terminology used of a rupture caused
by sexual excess is not metaphorical (see Varro *Men.* 192).

At Plaut. *Aul.* 285f. ('bellum et pudicum uero prostibulum
popli. / post si quis uellet, te hau non uelles diuidi') Congrio
takes Anthrax's remark (284 'si quo tu totum me ire uis,
operam dabo') as sexually significant, and hence gives *diuidi*
the same meaning as *pedicari*. Some of Anthrax's phraseology
was capable of a sexual misinterpretation. For *totum*, see Mart.
1.92.3 'totum tibi Ceston habeto' (cf. Apul. *Met.* 10.22, a different application), and for *operam dare*, see p. 157. I do not
accept[1] that Petronius has the same metaphorical use of *diuido*
at 79.12.

Penetrare does not occur in a sexual sense in the Classical
period, but note *Leg. Liutprandi* 76, p. 138 'uoluntariae adulterium penetrauerit' (cf. 121, p. 158). Here *penetrare* has been
conflated with *perpetrare* (for *patrare* see p. 142). The contamination is of no wider significance.

The metaphors seen in this section were for the most part
ad hoc coinages, used particularly in mime, farce and Plautine
comedy. They were clearly part of the stock-in-trade of popular
humour.

(v) 'Dig'

For this metaphor (for Greek see ὀρύττειν at Aristoph. *Pax*
898), see Juv. 9.45 'seruus erit minus ille miser qui foderit
agrum / quam dominum', *Priap.* 52.8 'cum te male foderint
iacentem', Arnob. *Nat.* 4.7 'uirginalem scrobem effodientibus
maritis'; cf. Auson. *Epigr.* 77.7, p. 341 P. 'peruersae ueneris
postico uulnere fossor'. At Mart. 1.92.11 (see above, p. 150) the
whole verb-phrase *fodiam digito*, rather than *fodiam* alone,
should perhaps be taken with *culum* in 11.[2] The metaphor was
in vogue in Medieval Latin: *Babio* 272 'iuro sacras per aras,
non fodit hanc Fodius', 278 'non fodit hanc Fodius, fodit eam

---

[1] With Pierrugues, *s.v.*, Goldberger, (1932), p. 104.
[2] See, however, Citroni, *ad loc.*

Fodius', Matthew of Vendôme, *Milo* 68*d* 'quo fodiatur ager non habet, uxor habet'. The presence of nominal metaphors of an agricultural kind alongside *fodio* in a number of the above passages suggests that *fodio* retained its metaphorical character. *Excauo* (*Priap.* 51.4 'usque curuos excauetur ad lumbos') is an *ad hoc* variation on the usual word.

(vi) 'Wound'

This metaphor (usually in a nominal form) is often associated with the deflowering of a bride (cf. τρώσεις at Heliod. 1.18.5): Mart. 11.78.6 'dum metuit teli uulnera prima noui', *Priap.* 3.8 'quod uirgo prima cupido dat nocte marito, / dum timet alterius uulnus inepta loci', Auson. *Cent. Nupt.* 121, p. 217 P. 'altius ad uiuum persedit uulnere mucro' (here *uulnus* comes close to the sense '*cunnus*'), Maxim. *Eleg.* 5.131 'sternitur icta tuo uotiuo uulnere uirgo / et perfusa nouo laeta cruore iacet'. But it is not always thus restricted: cf. *CIL* IV.10232 'L. Habonius sauciat irrumat Caesum Felic(e)m', Auson. *Epigr.* 77.7, p. 341 P. 'peruersae ueneris postico uulnere fossor', Maxim. *Eleg.* 5.98 'quo tibi cristatum uulnificumque caput?'.

Trades and other manual occupations are a constant inspiration of metaphors for the sexual act in Latin. An example from the language of butchers has already been given (*concido* at *H.A.*, *Hel.* 10.5), and digging could also be classed as a manual activity. Rural activities are a particularly common source of sexual metaphors in Latin (see p. 24), partly because the Latin vocabulary in general is rich in rustic metaphors, and partly because the fertility of the field and the working of the land have a sexual symbolism which may be universally recognised. There follow some metaphors which are based on occupations of one kind or another. Not all had the same tone.

(vii) 'Grind'

Molo (lit. 'grind wheat into flour in a mill') had already acquired a sexual use in Republican Latin (cf. μύλλω at Theocr. 4.58).[1] The protracted metaphor at Pompon. 99f. has the woman explicitly likened to the millstone (*mola*) moved by the *asinus*:

---

[1] Med. Fr. *moudre à* (*FEW* VI.3, p. 30) is probably independent of the Latin metaphor.

'nescio quis molam quasi asinus urget uxorem tuam, / ita op-
ertis oculis simitu manducatur ac molit'. Similarly at Lucil.
278 ('hunc molere, illam autem ut frumentum uannere lumbis') the female as well as the male role is expressed by a rustic
metaphor (*uannere* = 'winnow', of the grain: cf. Lucil. 330
'crisabit ut si frumentum clunibus uannat'). If the context was
sexual at Varro *Men.* 331 ('sed tibi fortasse alius molit et
depsit'), the metaphorical character of *molo* would no doubt
have been felt in the presence of *depso* (see below), but in other
places the metaphor seems to have been banalised: Hor. *Serm.*
1.2.35 'huc iuuenes aequom est descendere, non alienas / permolere uxores', Auson. *Epigr.* 79.7, p. 341 P. 'deglubit, fellat,
molitur per utramque cauernam' (a mixture of metaphors),
82.2, p. 343 'diceris hanc mediam lambere, non molere'; cf.
94.3, p. 347 P. 'cum dabit uxori molitor tuus et tibi adulter'.
At Pompon. 100 and Hor. *Serm.* 1.2.35 the metaphor is unambiguously applied to the activities of an adulterer with
someone else's wife. At Varro *Men.* 331 *alius* should be noted
alongside *alienas* in Horace; and at Lucil. 278 also an act of
adultery may be at issue (see Marx *ad loc.*). Given this tendency of the verb to be restricted to the male role in adulterous
liaisons (cf. *debattuo* at Petron. 69.3 above), it probably had
an offensive tone.

At Petron. 23.5 the sense of *molo* is different: 'super inguina
mea diu multumque frustra moluit' (of the activities of a *cinaedus*). It may be a graphic metaphor for masturbation, or
for the motions of the *cinaedus* astride Encolpius. At 24.4
distero, which one might have expected to mean the same as
futuo or *pedico* (see p. 183), has the second sense; on this
analogy one may also take *molo* thus. There are various metaphorical and other sexual verbs which are not restricted to the
designation of just one type of sexual act (see pp. 185, 187).

I have elsewhere argued[1] that the expression *reliquiae ali-
cariae* at Plaut. *Poen.* 266 implies a sexual metaphor based on
the grinding of *alica*.

(viii) 'Knead'

The offensive tone of *depso* is noted by Cicero at *Fam.* 9.22.4
' "battuit" inquit impudenter; "depsit" multo impudentius'.
The intensive *perdepso* at Catull. 74.3 ('patrui perdepsuit

---

[1] 'Words for "prostitute" in Latin', forthcoming in *RhM*.

ipsam / uxorem') is found in the same type of context as the
intensive *permolo* at Hor. *Serm.* 1.2.35 above (of intercourse
with another man's wife). Catullus and Horace were no doubt
drawing on the current vulgar language (cf. *perfututor* at *CIL*
IV.4239). It has been noted above that *depso* may be metaphorical at Varro *Men.* 331.

Another intensive compound at Pompon. 86 ('partem insipui
conclusi condepsui') perhaps has a sexual force.

(ix) 'Plough' and 'sow'

The metaphor of ploughing, in both its nominal and verbal
manifestations,[1] is quite widespread from Plautus onwards (for
Greek, see Soph. *Ant.* 569 ἀρώσιμοι γὰρ χἀτέρων εἰσὶν γύαι).[2]
There is no evidence from its use or distribution that it was
vulgar or offensive in tone.[3] In Plautus note *Asin.* 874 'fundum
alienum arat, incultum familiarem deserit', *Truc.* 149f. 'si ar-
ationes / habituris, qui arari solent, ad pueros ire meliust'. If
one introduces *arat* for *amat* at Mart. 9.21.4,[4] the metaphor is
the same:

> Artemidorus habet puerum sed uendidit agrum;
> agrum pro puero Calliodorus habet.
> dic uter ex istis melius rem gesserit, Aucte:
> Artemidorus arat [*amat* codd.], Calliodorus arat.

A paradox would be introduced, in that Artemidorus still
ploughs (the boy's *ager*). There are very similar paradoxes in
12.16 and 12.33. *Opus* is a double entendre from agriculture
at Plaut. *Asin.* 873 (see p. 157). For *aro* in late Latin, see *Anth.
Lat.* 712.17 'arentque sulcos molles'.

'Sowing' was a literary metaphor (cf. σπείρω at, e.g. Soph.
Aj. 1293): Lucr. 4.1107 'muliebria conserat arua', Tib. 1.8.36
'teneros conserit usque sinus', Aug. *Ciu.* 14.23 'genitale aruum
uas ... seminaret'. Note too the double entendre in *superseminauit* at Lehmann no. 14, p. 228 'inimicus homo qui ...
superseminauit zizania et cubile meum multa maculauit
perfidia'.

[1] For nominal metaphors, see above, pp. 82ff.
[2] For verbal metaphors of an agricultural kind in Greek, see Taillardat,
pp. 100f.
[3] See Herter, *Gnomon* 17 (1941), p. 328 on the tone of the corresponding
Greek metaphors.
[4] See S. Gaselee, *CR* 35 (1921), pp. 104f.

An agricultural metaphor found in twelfth century comedy
from France was that of reaping (*meto*): see Matthew of Vendôme, *Milo* 184 'cultoris uacat egra manu qui uimina nulla /
falce metit'; cf. *uindemio* at Lehmann no. 14, p. 229 'uinde-
miant te omnes qui pretergrediuntur uiam', and the use of
messis = *cunnus*, ibid.

(x) *Subigo, subigito*

I mention *subigo* here because in part its sexual use can be
classed as a metaphor based on a manual activity. But it is
open to different interpretations in different passages. A distinction must be made between *subigo* and *subigito*. *Subigo*
was used of the active role in homosexual or heterosexual
intercourse, in which sense it was probably established in
ordinary speech. *Subigito* (in comedy) had a weaker sense.
    Subigo is found in a soldiers' song quoted by Suetonius, *Iul.*
49.4 ('Gallias Caesar subegit, Nicomedes Caesarem: / . . . Nicomedes non triumphat qui subegit Caesarem'), at *Epigr. Bob.*
24.2 ('deformis uxor cui sit, ancilla elegans, / uxorem habere,
subigere ancillam uelit'), at Cael. Aurel. *Chron.* 4.131 ('molles
siue subactos Graeci malthacos uocauerunt'; cf. 134), and also
in Macrobius and Festus (see below). Two nominal derivatives
are *subactor* = *pedicator* (cf. *subactus* = *mollis* in Caelius
above) in the *H.A.* (e.g. *Hel.* 5.4 'posterioribus eminentibus in
subactorem reiectis et oppositis'; in the same chapter, §1, *su-
baret* rather than *subigeret* is probably the correct reading),
and the name of the marital god *Subigus* (Aug. *Ciu.* 6.9 'si
adest deus Subigus, ut uiro subigatur').
    Ernout and Meillet (p. 18) state that *subigo* meant 'bring
the female to the male', but I have not tracked down such a
technical use of the verb. Nisbet and Hubbard (II, p. 80) point
out that *subigo* could be applied to the breaking in of animals,
and that such is the metaphor at Hor. *Carm.* 2.5.1 ('nondum
subacta ferre iugum ualet / ceruice, nondum munia conparis /
aequare').[1] But the metaphor was interpreted in different ways
by different speakers. In the soldiers' song in Suetonius it is
clear from the context (note *triumphat* in the same line) that

[1] Nisbet and Hubbard II find the same pun at Lucil. 1041ff. The notion that
ceruice has a gynaecological sense here (*ceruix* did have such a use in the
medical language, where it was a calque: see p. 108) is fanciful.

the metaphor is military, = 'master, subdue'.[1] On the other hand an anonymous *sutor*, in a joke quoted by Macrobius, and Festus associated the sexual use of *subigo* with the working of leather (for *subigo* used of the working or kneading of materials, see, e.g. Cato *Agr.* 74): Macrob. *Sat.* 2.2.6 'Plancus in iudicio forte amici, cum molestum testem destruere uellet, interrogauit, quia sutorem sciebat, quo artificio se tueretur. ille urbane respondit: "gallam subigo". sutorium hoc habetur instrumentum, quod non infacete in adulterii exprobrationem ambiguitate conuertit. nam Plancus in Maeuia Galla nupta male audiebat', Paul. Fest. p. 443 'scorta appellantur meretrices, quia ut pelliculae subiguntur'. On this interpretation *subigo* is a similar metaphor to *depso*.

In comedy *subigito* means no more than 'fondle, lay hands on', as can be deduced from Plaut. *Merc.* 203, Ter. *Heaut.* 566, and from the use of *subigitatrix* at Plaut. *Pers.* 227 (following 'ne me attrecta', a verb which could be used of fondling). It is not possible to determine what literal meaning of *subigito* produced the metaphor in comedy.

Ps.-Acron on Hor. *Serm.* 1.2.35 glosses *permolere* with the words 'subigitare, ut habemus in Terentio de ipso actu turpi'. He has given to *subigito* the meaning which *subigo* had later.[2]

(xi) 'Work'

The *pedicator* Naevolus in Juv. IX, who is a prostitute, looks upon his activities as work or labour (e.g. 28 'utile et hoc multis uitae genus, at mihi nullum / inde *operae* pretium', 42 'numerentur deinde *labores*'), and he compares them with other forms of toil (45f.).[3] Sexual activity can in the strict sense be regarded as 'work' if it is performed for money; hence, for example, the use of *quaestus* of the prostitute's employment.[4]

---

[1] See A. Spies, *Militat omnis amans. Ein Beitrag zur Bildersprache der antiken Erotik* (Tübingen, 1930), p. 51. Among the comparable metaphors which Spies quotes note Lucil. 1323 'uicimus, o socii, et magnam pugnauimus pugnam', which (as is clear from Don. Ter. *Eun.* 899) has an amatory sense (cf. Ovid *Ars* 2.728). On military metaphors, see p. 158.

[2] Preston, p. 29 points out that *tempto* is used in the same way at Prop. 1.3.15 ('subiecto leuiter positam temptare lacerto') as *subigito* in comedy. Cf. Col. 8.11.8.

[3] See Courtney, p. 425.

[4] For commercial terminology applied to prostitution, see Preston, pp. 15f. See also p. 203 on *commercium*.

But various words for 'work' and the like are used of sexual acts even when there is no question of payment. The act is by implication likened to gainful labour, just as it is often more specifically compared to particular trades or occupations.

Opus (cf. ἔργον at, e.g. Strato, *AP*. 12.209.3, Ach. Tat. 1.10.2)[1] is often used of the male part in the act. At Plaut. *Asin.* 873 'ille operi foris faciendo lassus noctu <ad me> aduenit; / fundum alienum arat, incultum familiarem deserit' *opus* is an agricultural metaphor, as the next line shows. But it is usually not so explicit, though sometimes the act is mentioned along with varieties of real work. See Ovid *Am.* 2.10.36 'cum moriar, medium soluar et inter opus', Mart. 7.18.5 'accessi quotiens ad opus' (of 'going to work'), 11.81.3 'uiribus hic, operi non est hic utilis annis: / ergo sine effectu prurit utrique labor' (note too *labor*),[2] Apul. *Met.* 9.7 'utroque opere perfecto' (of intercourse with the woman, and the job of inspecting the *dolium*). Cf. Caecil. 167, Hor. *Epod.* 12.16, Mart. 11.60.7, 11.78.2, 11.104.11, Arnob. *Nat.* 5.14, Aug. *Ciu.* 6.9, Ambr. *Exp. Luc.* 1.43, Maxim. *Eleg.* 5.56.[3]

Opera was used in much the same way as *opus*.[4] Note Plaut. *Trin.* 651 'in foro operam amicis da, ne in lecto amicae, ut solitus es', Cic. *Fam.* 9.22.3 'eius operae nomen non audent dicere', Ovid *Ars* 2.673 'aut latus et uires operamque adferte puellis' (this 'labour' is listed with various others, 669ff.: note 669 'dum uires annique sinunt, tolerate *labores*'; the passage may be an interpolation). Cf. Apul. *Met.* 2.26. The formula *operam dare* (and equivalents) is sometimes given a sexual twist (see above, p. 151, on Plaut. *Aul.* 284).

Compare the adjective at Apul. *Met.* 10.22 ('operosa ... nocte').

(xii) 'Wrestle, fight'

Luctor has reflexes in the Romance languages used of sexual intercourse (OFr. *luitier*, 'couvrir la brebis', OSp. *luchar* = *coire*).[5] The metaphor was a familiar one both in Greek (Aris-

[1] See further Opelt, 950 for ἔργον in various combinations.
[2] For *labor* (used mainly of animals), see *TLL* VII.2.793.7ff. (cf. Hor. *Carm.* 3.15.3).
[3] See further *TLL* IX.2.851.8ff., Brandt, *Am.* 2.10.36, Grassmann, p. 83.
[4] See *TLL* IX.2.662.25ff.
[5] See *FEW* V, p. 440a; cf. M. Bambeck, *Lateinisch-Romanische Wortstudien* I (Wiesbaden, 1959), p. 36.

toph. *Pax* 894ff., Strato, *A.P.* 12.206, ps.-Luc. *Asinus* 9f., Ach. Tat. 5.3.5) and Latin. For Latin, see Prop. 2.1.13, 2.15.5 (*luctor*), Sen. *Contr.* 1.2.6, Arnob. *Nat.* 5.9 (*conluctor*), Apul. *Met.* 2.17, 9.5 (*colluctatio*), Claud. *Carm. Min. App.* 5.76 (*luctamen*). The emperor Domitian called intercourse 'bed wrestling', using a Greek word: Suet. *Dom.* 22 'assiduitatem concubitus uelut exercitationis genus clinopalen uocabat' (κλινοπάλη).[1] Cf. Mart. 10.55.4 'idem post opus et suas palaestras / loro cum similis iacet remisso' (note also Ter. *Phorm.* 484, and cf. παλαίστρα at Theocr. 7.125 and Paulus Silentiarius, *A.P.* 5.259.5), 14.201.2 'non amo quod uincat, sed quod succumbere nouit / et didicit melius τὴν ἐπικλινοπάλην'. The use of (ἐπι)κλινοπάλη twice in sexual puns in the early Empire would suggest that the term was current in wrestling.

The most remarkable ancient example of the metaphor is that at ps.-Luc. *Asinus* 9f. The encounter between Palaestra and Lucius is described in great detail, with Palaestra, using imperatives, acting as διδάσκαλος. For the technical terminology used literally, see *POxy.* 466 (directions for wrestling). Apuleius made a drastic departure from the original at this point (if the *Asinus* preserves the extended metaphor of the original). At *Met.* 2.16 the encounter is called a *proelium*. In chapter 17 Photis orders Lucius to fight. Like Palaestra, she uses a series of imperatives, but there is scarcely any other similarity between the two passages: ' "proeliare" inquit "et fortiter proeliare; nec enim tibi cedam nec terga uortam. cominus in aspectum, si uir es, derige et grassare nauiter et occide moriturus. hodierna pugna non habet missionem'. There follows a euphemistic account of intercourse, in which the *schema* and movements are briefly alluded to. Apuleius clearly set out to remove the physical explicitness of the original.

The metaphor of fighting seen here is so widespread as to need no extensive illustration.[2] See, for example, Prop. 2.15.4 (*rixa*),[3] Tib. 1.10.53 (*bella*),[4] Petron. 9.10 (*pugno*),[5] Apul. *Met.*

---

[1] For intercourse as a kind of 'exercise' (*exercitatio*), see *exerceo* at Plaut. *Amph.* 288, *Bacch.* 429, Claud. *Carm. Min. App.* 5.76; cf. Preston, p. 52.

[2] The dissertation of Spies (cited above, p. 156 n. 1) is worth consulting. On elegy see also A. La Penna, *Maia* 4 (1951), pp. 193f. See further Preston, p. 50 for examples both from Greek and Latin.

[3] Cf. Spies, pp. 52f.

[4] Cf. Ovid *Am.* 1.9.45 and Brandt *ad loc.* Cf. Spies, *loc. cit.*

[5] Numerous examples are collected by Spies, p. 52 (with πολεμεῖν).

5.21 (*proelium*).[1] The image of 'taking by storm' (used of deflowering, and apparently current in oratory) occurs at Cic.
Verr. 5.34, Sen. *Contr.* 2.3.1, 2.7.7 (see p. 195). For the metaphor of 'attacking', see Hor. *Serm.* 1.2.116ff. 'tument tibi cum
inguina, num, si / ancilla aut uerna est praesto puer, *impetus
in quem / continuo fiat*' (for *peto* in another sexual sense, see
further p. 212, n. 1), Apul. *Met.* 7.21 'uisa quadam honesta
iuuene . . . in eam furiosos direxit impetus' (perhaps not metaphorical), Arnob. *Nat.* 5.9 'ui matrem adgressus est'. See further above, p. 156 on *subigo*.

(xiii) 'Kill, die'

Akin to the metaphor of fighting is that of 'killing' applied to
the male role: Apul. *Met.* 2.17 'derige et grassare nauiter et
occide moriturus'. *Conficio* ('finish off') is ambiguous in its
literal use between the senses 'kill' and 'exhaust'. Either could
lie behind the metaphor at Suet. *Nero* 29 'cum affatim de-
saeuisset, conficeretur a Doryphoro liberto'; at *Priap.* 26.8,
however, *confectus* means 'exhausted'. The other side of the
coin is the metaphor of 'dying', used of either or both partners
in intercourse (cf. *moriturus* in the passage of Apuleius above):
Prop. 1.10.5 'cum te complexa morientem, Galle, puella / uidi-
mus' (cf. 1.4.12), Petron. 79.8 *v.* 5 'ego sic perire coepi', Apul.
Met. 2.17 'inter mutuos amplexus animas anhelantes', Auson.
Cent. Nupt. 120, p. 217 P. 'illa manu moriens telum trahit' (of
the female), 131 'labitur exanguis' (of the male). For 'killing'
in Greek, see the double entendre in φονεύσεις at Heliod.
1.18.4–5.

(xiv) 'Marry'

At Apul. *Met.* 7.21 (' . . . auersa Venere inuitat ad nuptias'),
where *nuptiae* is used not of marriage but of intercourse, Apuleius was following the Greek version: cf. ps.-Luc. *Asinus* 32
τὴν δὲ γυναῖκα . . . γαμεῖν ἐβούλετο. On the other hand Jul.
Val. p. 6.7 ('at ille sceptro deposito conscensoque lectulo nuptias agit eximque utero eius superiecta manu . . .') is an elab-
oration of ps.-Callisthenes 1.7, p. 7.17f. Kroll ὁ δὲ πάλιν
ἀνιστάμενος ἀπ' αὐτῆς, τύψας αὐτῆς τὴν γαστέρα εἶπε . . . .

[1] See Spies, p. 53.

160   *The Latin Sexual Vocabulary*

Gk. γαμέω was often used of intercourse (cf. γαμητιάω of the
male at *Vita Aesopi* W 103), and it survives in the sense 'βινέω'
in Mod. Gk.[1] But Latin had the same euphemism independently. The term 'marriage' dignifies a purely sexual liaison,
as is recognised at Virg. *Aen.* 4.172 'nec iam furtiuum Dido
meditatur amorem: / coniugium uocat, hoc praetexit nomine
culpam' (see further *Rhet. Her.* 4.45, quoted below).[2] For Latin
see Plaut. *Cist.* 43f. 'haec quidem ecastor cottidie uiro nubit,
nupsitque hodie, / nubet mox noctu: numquam ego hanc ui-
duam cubare siui' (of a prostitute;[3] the adverbs *cottidie, hodie*
and *noctu* show that the verb expresses individual acts of
intercourse), *Rhet. Her.* 4.45 ' "cuius mater cotidianis nuptiis
delectetur" ' (the author comments that the *translatio* was
'obscenitatis uitandae causa'; compare *cotidianis* with *cottidie*
above), Petron. 112.3 'iacuerunt ergo una non tantum illa
nocte qua nuptias fecerunt, sed postero etiam ac tertio die'
(this passage is slightly different from the preceding two, in
that the phrase refers only to the first occasion on which intercourse took place). At Mart. 1.24.4 'nolito fronti credere:
nupsit heri' the meaning is presumably 'he had (homosexual)
intercourse yesterday'; *heri* should be compared with *hodie* etc.
in the passages above. But it is possible that Martial is thinking of a mock marriage ceremony of the type submitted to by
homosexuals (see Mart. 12.42.1, Tac. *Ann.* 15.37, Juv. 2.117ff.
(note 137 *nubentibus*), Suet. *Nero* 29, *H.A., Hel.* 10.5.[4]

Matrimonium comes close to the meaning '*concubitus*' at
Firm. Mat. *Math.* 6.29.22 'incesto furoris ardore et nefariae
cupiditatis instinctu filias patribus inlicitis matrimoniorum
uinculis copulari' (cf. 6.29.21 'illicitos filiarum concubitus').[5]
Note too Apul. *Met.* 5.4 'uxorem sibi Psychen fecerat', *hymenaei*
used of mating at Virg. *Georg.* 3.60 ('aetas Lucinam iustosque

---

[1] See L. Robert, *RPh* 41 (1967), pp. 78f., Shipp, pp. 187f. Another Greek
parallel for this semantic change is seen in ὀπυίω: see Wackernagel (cited
above, p. 142 n. 2), p. 228 n. 1. Dr D. M. Bain drew my attention to Robert's
article.
[2] Compare Servius' note on Virg. *Aen.* 4.23 ('ueteris uestigia flammae'): 'bene
inhonestam rem sub honesta specie confitetur, dicens se agnoscere maritalis
coniugii ardorem: hoc est, quo mariti diligi solent; nam erat meretricium
dicere: in amorem Aeneae incidi'.
[3] Shipp, p. 187 compares Dem. 18.129.
[4] Neither Citroni nor Howell (cited above, p. 33, n. 1) *ad loc.* distinguishes
between the two possible uses of *nubo*.
[5] See *TLL* VIII.476.51ff. for similar examples in Maternus.

pati hymenaeos / desinit ante decem, post quattuor incipit annos'), and *conubium* of sexual union at, e.g. Lucr. 3.776, Ovid
Am. 2.7.21, Arnob. *Nat.* 3.8. *Contubernium*, which could denote the equivalent of a marital relationship between partners
of whom at least one was a slave, is perhaps used of intercourse
at Petron. 53.10 'liberta in balneatoris contubernio deprehen-
sa' and Suet. *Cal.* 36.1 'Valerius Catullus ... stupratum a se
ac latera sibi contubernio eius defessa etiam uociferatus est'.
Legitima seems to indicate copulation at *Mul. Chir.* 15 'equos
admissarios ... ne in legitima mittantur'.[1] *Legitimus* was
habitually applied to *nuptiae* (e.g. Cic. *Inu.* 1.2), *coetus* (Auson.
Epigr. 79.1, p. 341 P.), *amor* and the like,[2] and it is obviously
from this use that the substantival neuter developed: cf. Ovid
Trist. 2.249 'nil nisi legitimum concessaque furta canemus'.
Legitima is a similar type of euphemism to *nuptiae*, *nubo*, etc.,
if applied to copulation when there is no question of marriage.

For further overlap between terms applicable to marriage
and intercourse, see below pp. 178 (on *coeo*) and p. 179 (verbs
of joining). Note also Mart. 12.95.5f. 'ne thalassionem / indicas
manibus libidinosis' (of masturbation); with this passage compare Agathias, *A.P.* 5.302.19f. πάντ' ἄρα Διογένης ἔφυγεν
τάδε, τὸν δ' Ὑμέναιον ἤειδεν παλάμῃ, Λαΐδος οὐ χατέων.

(xv) 'Joke, play'

Iocari went into Old French (*joer*) and Spanish (*yogar*) with
the sense '*coire*'.[3] Both *iocari* and *iocus* are sometimes found in
amatory contexts in which it would be going too far to inflict
on them a specifically physical sense (e.g. Hor. *Epist.* 1.6.65f.,
Petron. 26.2, Justin 7.3.4), but there are also places where the
writer seems to have had sexual acts in mind: Ovid *Ars* 2.724
'accedent questus, accedet amabile murmur / et dulces gemitus
aptaque uerba ioco' (*ioco* could surely not refer to a verbal jest
here), 3.787 'mille ioci Veneris' (most *codd.* have *modi*, and
sexual *schemata* are at issue), 3.796 'nec blandae uoces iucun-
daque murmura cessent / nec taceant mediis improba uerba
iocis' (or is Ovid referring to verbal jests containing obsceni-

[1] See the index in Oder, *s.v. Legitimarius* similarly may = *admissarius* at
Mul. Chir. 773 (see the index, *s.v.*).
[2] See *TLL* VII.2.1111.33ff.
[3] See *FEW* V, p. 37*a*, Bambeck (see above, p. 157 n. 5), pp. 100ff. Bambeck's
Latin evidence is not completely satisfactory.

ties?), Plin. *Nat.* 8.144 'memoratur et Nicomedis Bithyniae regis, uxore eius Cosingi lacerata propter lasciuiorem cum marito iocum', Vulg. *Gen.* 26.8 'rex ... uidit eum iocantem cum Rebecca uxore sua' (the LXX has παίζοντα, a verb which was also in use as a sexual euphemism (see Asclepiades, *A.P.* 5.7.4, and also 5.158.1 for the compound συμπαίζω),[1] and the *Vetus Latina* is split between *ludentem* and *iocantem*), *Anth. Lat.* 22.2 'ite, uerecundo coniungite foedera lecto / atque cupidineos discite ferre iocos', *CIL* XIV.3565 (= *CE* 1504.5) 'da mihi ut pueris et ut puellis / fascino placeam bonis procaci / lusibusque frequentibus iocisque / dissipem curas . . .'. Cf. Catull. 8.6 'ibi *illa multa* cum *iocosa* fiebant, / quae tu uolebas nec puella nolebat', where in the vicinity of the sexual use of *uolo* and *nolo*, *iocosa* must refer to sexual acts.

Ludo and *lusus* take their implication from the context. At Ter. *Eun.* 373 'cibum una capias, adsis, tangas, ludas, propter dormias' there is an ascending sequence, with *ludas* indicating unspecified physical play which falls short of intercourse. On the other hand the declaimer quoted at Sen. *Contr.* 1.2.22 ('nouimus, inquit, istam maritorum abstinentiam qui, etiamsi primam uirginibus timidis remisere noctem, *uicinis tamen locis ludunt*') was thinking of *pedicatio*, or at least his words were given this sense by a member of the audience (see the whole anecdote). Catullus uses the verb of heterosexual intercourse at 61.204 'ludite ut lubet, et breui / liberos date', Petronius of homosexual activities at 11.2 'inuenit me cum fratre ludentem'.

Ludo could indicate the activities of both sexes in sexual behaviour viewed as mutually pleasurable; hence either the male or the female may be subject of the verb. For the male as subject, see, e.g. Sen. *Contr.* 1.2.22 above, for the female, Catull. 17.17, Prop. 2.15.21, Ovid *Am.* 1.8.43, and for both, *CIL* IV.1781. Both the noun and the verb are often used of the amatory indulgence granted to youth: e.g. Cic. *Cael.* 28 'datur enim concessu omnium huic aliqui ludus aetati' (cf. 42).[2] But

---

[1] For the usage in Greek, see A. S. F. Gow and D. L. Page, *The Greek Anthology: Hellenistic Epigrams* (Cambridge, 1965), on line 824.

[2] See the parallels collected by R. G. Austin, *M. Tulli Ciceronis pro M. Caelio oratio*[3] (Oxford, 1960), *ad loc.* For further examples of the two words applied to the sexual behaviour of the young, see Ovid *Am.* 2.3.13 'est etiam facies, sunt apti lusibus anni', *Ars* 3.62 'dum licet et ueros etiam nunc editis annos, / ludite: eunt anni more fluentis aquae'; cf. Catull. 17.17, Prop. 2.15.21.

this is by no means their exclusive use (cf., e.g. Mart. 2.60.3, 11.104.5).

(xvi) 'Duty, service', etc.

Words of the semantic field 'serve, do one's duty' are frequently used metaphorically of different forms of sexual activity. For Greek, see ὑπουργέω at, e.g. Plat. *Symp.* 184d (of the services provided by a boy in a homosexual liaison), Anaxil. frg. 21.2 Kock (of the woman's services).[1]

For *seruio* of homosexual *patientia*, see Cic. *Cat.* 2.8 'alios ipse amabat turpissime, aliorum amori flagitiosissime seruiebat', *Phil.* 2.86 'ut omnia paterere, ut facile seruires'.

Officium could express the services provided by either partner (active: Prop. 2.22A.24 'saepe est experta puella / officium tota nocte ualere meum', Ovid *Am.* 3.7.24 'ter Libas officio continuata meo est'; passive: Plaut. *Cist.* 657 'faciundum est puerile officium: conquiniscam ad cistulam', Ovid *Ars* 2.688 'officium faciat nulla puella mihi').[2] It is worth stressing that it was not only the female / pathic role which could be seen as a service. Romans were capable of speaking of the female as the dominant partner in a sexual relationship (particularly in elegy), and the lexicon of the language did not exclusively assign to females a subordinate role. Nevertheless words or expressions which were strongly redolent of servility or obedience were restricted to the female or pathic side of the act (see below).

According to Seneca (*Contr.* 4 *praef.* 10), the declaimer Haterius had once made the remark that a freedman had a duty to be his patron's lover if required: 'impudicitia in ingenuo crimen est, in seruo necessitas, in liberto officium'. Because of the existing sexual use of *officium*, Haterius' remark was deliberately misconstrued, as if he were equating lexically *impudicitia* (i.e. pathic behaviour) and *officium*. His unintentional double entendre gave rise in the rhetorical schools to a spate of puns, in which *officium* at one level meant 'duty', but on another 'homosexual *patientia*': 'non facis mihi officium', 'multum ille huic in officiis uersatur'. Pathics were modishly called *officiosi*. The point of the anecdote lies not in any claim

---

[1] See further Dover, pp. 44f.
[2] See further *TLL* IX.2.520.30ff., Tränkle, p. 164.

that a new usage had emerged: *officium* had possessed a sexual sense since Plautus.[1] Because of Haterius' slip *officium* was pinned down in the schools to just one of the sexual 'services' which it might previously have indicated, and any use of the word was prone to be taken in this sense. This anecdote illustrates the frivolous atmosphere of the schools. Audiences were obviously on the lookout for unintentional sexual innuendo.

Munus could also be used of the services of either partner. At Petron. 87.8 ('et non plane iam molestum erat munus') it indicates those of a pathic youth. Contrast Catull. 61.227 'at boni / coniuges, bene uiuite et / munere assiduo ualentem / exercete iuuentam'. Cf. Plaut. *Asin.* 812, Hor. *Carm.* 2.5.2 (*munia*),[2] Mart. 9.67.8, Claud. *Carm. Min.* 25.130, ps.-Acron Hor. *Epist.* 1.18.75.[3]

Obsequium sometimes indicates wifely obedience in a non-sexual sense.[4] It was transferred euphemistically to the female and passive role in intercourse,[5] as at Livy 39.42.9 'eum puerum ... exprobrare consuli ... solitum, quod sub ipsum spectaculum gladiatorium abductus ab Roma esset, ut obsequium amatori uenditaret' and Col. 6.37.9 'asellus admouetur, qui sollicitet obsequia feminae' (cf. 6.27.10). The semantic development of *morem gero*, which was perhaps in origin a ritual term, was much the same. It was early (in Plautus) used to express 'the ideal married relationship of wife to husband',[6] but later tended to be narrowed down to female sexual behaviour of various types (Suet. *Tib.* 44.2,[7] Apul. *Met.* 2.16).[8]

---

[1] D. R. Shackleton Bailey, *Propertiana* (Cambridge, 1956), p. 289 states that 'the use [of *officium*] seems to have been exceptional in the Augustan period to judge from the anecdote in Sen. *Contr.* 4. *praef.* 10, but attained respectability in post-classical writing'. This conclusion is not justified. See further Tränkle, p. 164 n. 2.

[2] See Nisbet and Hubbard II, *ad loc.*

[3] See further *TLL* VIII.1667.11ff.

[4] *TLL* IX.2.181.68ff. By a neat reversal of the normal phraseology, Ovid *Ars* 2.179ff. by implication employs *obsequium* of male subservience to a woman.

[5] See Hey, p. 532.

[6] Gordon Williams, *JRS* 48 (1958), p. 20.

[7] The compound *morigeror*, applied to *fellatio*.

[8] See Williams, *loc. cit.* For Plautine examples in the weaker sense, see also Preston, p. 33. Cf. *morigerus* at Apul. *Apol.* 74.

(xvii) 'Ride'

In this metaphor the man is seen as the horse (κέλης), with the woman as rider; the image is applied specifically to one *schema*, that with the woman (or effeminate male) astride. The position was regarded as slightly abnormal, and one which a woman would concede only as a special favour.[1] For examples of the metaphor in Greek, see Aristoph. *Vesp.* 501, *Lys.* 677f., Asclepiades or Posidippus, *A.P.* 5.202, Asclepiades, *A.P.* 5.203.[2]

The verb describing the position of the female in Latin might be *sedeo*, as at Mart. 11.104.14 'Hectoreo quotiens sederat uxor equo' (cf. Ovid *Ars* 3.778 below). When this verb is applied to the female role it would seem reasonable to treat the metaphor as one of riding, even if no mention is made of the horse, as at Apul. *Met.* 2.17 'super me sessim residens'; cf. (perhaps) *CIL* IV.8767 'neque mulieres scierunt nisi paucae et seserunt' (= *sederunt*?).[3]

For examples of the image in Latin, see Pompon. 40 'et ubi insilui in coleatum eculeum, ibi tolutim tortor' (doubtful), Hor. *Serm.* 2.7.47ff. 'acris ubi me / natura intendit, sub clara nuda lucerna / quaecumque excepit turgentis uerbera caudae / clunibus aut agitauit equum lasciua supinum', Ovid *Ars* 2.732 'cum mora non tuta est, totis incumbere remis / utile et admisso subdere calcar equo', 3.777f. 'parua uehatur equo: quod erat longissima, numquam / Thebais Hectoreo nupta resedit equo', *CIL* IV.1781 'hunc lectum campum, me tibei equum esse putamus',[4] Petron. 140.7 'puellam quidem exorauit ut sederet super commendatam bonitatem',[5] Arnob. *Nat.* 4.7 'Tutunus, cuius inmanibus pudendis horrentique fascino uestras inequitare matronas'.

In these places the rider is a woman. There is no great difference between this *schema*, and that at Petron. 24.4, where the rider is a *cinaedus*: 'equum cinaedus mutauit transituque ad comitem meum facto clunibus eum basiisque distriuit'. The same imagery seems to be applied to a *cinaedus* in

---

[1] See D. M. MacDowell, *Aristophanes Wasps* (Oxford, 1971), on 501.

[2] See further Taillardat, p. 105.

[3] The interpretation of this inscription is not absolutely certain: for the possible sexual force, see N. J. Herescu, *Glotta* 38 (1960), pp. 125ff.

[4] On the text of the inscription, see W. D. Lebek, *ZPE* 32 (1978), pp. 215ff.

[5] There may also be a play on words at Petron. 126.10 'ego etiam si ancilla sum, numquam tamen nisi in equestribus sedeo': see Herescu (cited above, n. 3), pp. 129ff.

a graffito, *CIL* IV.1825 'Cosmus equitaes magnus cinaedus et fellator: esuris apertis mari(bus)'. Here *equitaes* = *eques;*[1] if the allusion were to a Roman knight rather than a 'rider', *Romanus* would almost certainly have been used. This graffito demonstrates that, though the metaphor of horse riding had Greek associations (and hence may sometimes have been used by a Latin writer with Greek idiom in mind), it had passed beyond the literary sphere and entered ordinary Latin parlance. Another slightly different example is at Juv. 6.311 ('inque uices equitant ac Luna teste mouentur').[2] The riders are females, but the act is between lesbians. It was not usual to apply the image to the more normal *schema*, with the man *pronus*. Nevertheless, according to Artemidorus (1.56, p. 64.13f. Pack; cf. 4.46), a horse symbolised a woman: ἵππος γὰρ γυναικὶ μὲν καὶ ἐρωμένῃ τὸν αὐτὸν ἔχει λόγον, ὅτι καὶ ἐπὶ κάλλει μέγα φρονεῖ καὶ τὸν ἐλατῆρα βαστάζει.[3]

The metaphor of the race is related to that of horse riding: see Ovid *Rem.* 429f. 'ille quod obscenas in aperto corpore partes / uiderat, in cursu qui fuit, haesit amor', and compare Lucr. 4.1195f., Ovid *Ars* 2.726, Auson. *Cent. Nupt.* 128f., p. 217 P., quoted above, p. 144 (of 'reaching the goal').[4] More general metaphors of travel are not suggestive of any particular *schema*: see Prop. 2.33A.22 'noctibus his uacui, ter faciamus iter' (for Greek, see Dioscorides, *A.P.* 5.55.3).

---

[1] See Krenkel, p. 83 (with n. 41), comparing *municipes* = *municeps*.

[2] The use of *in uices* seen in this passage is sometimes found in sexual contexts, in the sense 'taking turns', of changes of role in sexual activity. Here the women take it in turns to be 'rider' and 'horse' in sexual acts. At *Nat.* 7.15 Pliny talks of *androgyni* who alternate between the active and passive roles in intercourse: 'supra Nasamonas confinesque illis Machlyas androgynos esse utriusque naturae, inter se *uicibus* coeuntes'. Cf. Juv. 7.240 'exigite ut sit / et pater ipsius coetus, ne turpia ludant, / ne faciant *uicibus*'. Presumably the boys might take it in turns to be *pedicator*.

[3] It is possible that at Mart. 7.57 ('Castora de Polluce Gabinia fecit Achillan: / πὺξ ἀγαθός fuerat, nunc erit ἱππόδαμος') ἱππόδαμος is applied to the active male. Achillas is perhaps converted from a passive to an active (heterosexual) lover, as a result of the attractions of Gabinia. πὺξ may be meant to suggest πυγή, πυγίζειν and the former pathic tendencies of Achillas. See V. Buchheit, *Studien zum Corpus Priapeorum* (Munich, 1962), p. 104.

[4] See further A. La Penna, *Maia* 4 (1951), pp. 208f., Citroni, p. 151.

(xviii) 'Row, sail'

The symbolism of rowing, seafaring and boats was often put to use in Greek (the male usually being the 'rower' or 'passenger'): Dioscorides, *A.P.* 5.54.3f., Hedylus or Asclepiades, *A.P.* 5.161, Meleager, *A.P.* 5.204, Antiphilus, *A.P.* 9.415, Philip, *A.P.* 9.416, Automedon, *A.P.* 11.29.5f., Rufinus, *A.P* 5.44.[1] A ναῦς could symbolise a woman, and the κύσθος could also be seen to resemble the sea (anon., *A.P.* 11.220.2, Nicarchus, *A.P.* 11.328.3; according to Artemidorus, 3.16, p. 210.23f., Pack, 4 prooem. p. 240.7 the sea resembles a woman because it is moist).

For the metaphor of rowing in Latin, see Ovid *Ars* 2.731f. 'cum mora non tuta est, totis incumbere remis / utile et admisso subdere calcar equo'; cf. 725 'sed neque tu dominam uelis maioribus usus / defice'. Ovid may have regarded the imagery here as Grecising, but that the language of seafaring could be used in sexual double entendre in Latin is shown by the joke of Julia, quoted by Macrobius, *Sat.* 2.5.9 ('numquam enim nisi naui plena tollo uectorem'), where the *nauis* represents the womb, and the passenger (*uectorem*, = *is qui uehitur*) the man. For the woman 'taking up, bearing' (*tollo*) the man, compare the similar nautical images in Philip, *A.P.* 9.416.6 ἐλθόντα δέχομαι πάντα, βαστάζω ξένον (for βαστάζω in a different context, see Artem. 1.56, quoted above), and Antiphilus, *A.P.* 9.415.8 πολλοὺς οἶδα φέρειν ἐρέτας. For *tollo*, see Petron. 25.6 'hinc etiam puto prouerbium natum illud, [ut dicatur] posse taurum tollere, qui uitulum sustulerit'. There is some overlap between the phraseology applicable to animals mating, and nautical terminology. Just as the passenger 'goes aboard', so the male animal 'mounts'. Animal terminology and the metaphor of 'climbing, mounting' are dealt with below, p. 205.

(xix) 'Theft'

Furtum indicates illicit sexual intercourse, such as adultery (Serv. *Aen.* 10.91 'furtum est adulterium').[2] It is found mainly in poetry (particularly elegy), starting with Catull. 68.136; for

---

[1] See further Taillardat, pp. 101f.
[2] See *TLL* VI.1.1649.68ff.

prose, see Arnob. *Nat.* 5.9. Martial probably took the phrase *furta tegis* at 1.34.2 from Ovid (*Met.* 9.558, *Ars* 2.555). Its juxtaposition with *peccas* shows the implication of the word. For the metaphor in Greek, see Rufinus, *A.P.* 5.18.2 οἱ μὴ τοῖς σπατάλοις κλέμμασι τερπόμενοι.[1]

(xx) *Glubo, rado*

Given the variable application in sexual contexts of certain vague verbs (see below, pp. 185, 187), one is led to suggest that the controversy over the exact implication of *glubo* at Catull. 58.5 is misguided.[2] The metaphor of the stripping of the bark (= 'foreskin': for *cortex* given this meaning by Ausonius, see p. 74) might in principle have been applied to the 'stripping' of the *mentula* by whatever means, whether by manual, oral or vaginal stimulation. At *Epigr.* 79.7, p. 341 P. Ausonius certainly had in mind masturbation when he used *deglubo*,[3] but Catullus provides no clue what form of stimulation he intended. The verb may be deliberately ambiguous (cf., e.g. *sollicito* at Lucr. 4.1196, below, p. 184). Alternatively it may have had a well-established slang sense which Catullus' readers would have recognised without contextual pointers. If so it is pointless to argue from probabilities or from the uninformative poem itself. If *glubo* was a slang term, the only evidence which we have for its meaning is that provided by Ausonius.

Rado at Mart. 2.17.5 ('non tondet, inquam. quid igitur facit? radit') is similarly vague. It is taken to mean 'masturbate' by H. Jordan.[4]

Of the metaphors discussed above those of 'eating' and 'urinating' are shown by their distribution to have been in common use. Other coarse metaphors were *caedo, percido, molo, battuo, depso* and perhaps (at least in the later period) *iocor* and *luctor*. The semantic fields 'cut, strike, split, burst' *et sim.* were a fertile source of metaphors in risqué humour, even if

[1] On κλέμμα, see D. L. Page, *The Epigrams of Rufinus* (Cambridge, 1978), pp. 75f.
[2] See most recently Jocelyn, *LCM* 4.5 (May 1979), pp. 87ff., O. Skutsch, *LCM* 5.1 (Jan. 1980), p. 21. In Greek δέρω at Aristoph. *Lys.* 158 is roughly comparable.
[3] See R. Penella, *Hermes* 104 (1976), pp. 118ff.
[4] *Hermes* 4 (1870), p. 231 n. 1.

not all manifestations of these metaphors in the remains of the language were in banal use. More urbane or literary were the metaphors of 'playing', 'fighting', 'marrying', 'rowing' ('sailing'), 'stealing' (*furtum*), 'ploughing' and 'sowing'. *Officium*, we have seen, had something of a vogue among the educated in the first century A.D. Most of the metaphors listed above as coarse were probably felt to be less euphemistic than those classed as literary. A desire for euphemism is a common motivator of metaphors, but metaphors can also be coarse. The nature of the activity which generates the image probably determines its tone. Activities which require the use of an instrument suggestive of the penis seem generally to have produced metaphors coarse in tone; I use the word 'coarse' not as an impressionistic term, but with the distribution of various metaphors in mind. Of metaphors with specialised implications I mention those of riding (indicating a particular *schema*), wounding (usually of deflowering), urinating (of ejaculation) and reaching a goal (of ejaculation); note too the remarks above on *caedo, molo, battuo, depso* and their compounds.

Greek parallels to many of the metaphors discussed here have been quoted, but I should not wish to imply that most metaphors attested in Latin were Greek in inspiration. Latin shared many metaphors with Greek simply because the two societies were similar and contemporaneous (see further below, p. 229). One would expect ancient trades, occupations and sports (wrestling, racing)[1] to generate metaphors in both languages, just as modern languages share metaphors of an industrial or mechanical origin. The productivity of the cutting instrument as a source both of nominal and verbal sexual metaphors in both languages is due to its importance in ancient society. In the modern world the gun has replaced the sword as a sexual symbol. The more Grecising a literary genre, the more likely it is that a Latin writer would have had in mind Greek idiom, but that is not to say that the metaphors he used were not independently current in Latin. It is likely that Ovid had Greek usage before him when he employed the

---

[1] In early Latin the use of *datatim* in sexual contexts (see Pompon. 1, and perhaps Naev. com. frg. 75, Afran. 222) seems to have been a metaphor from a game played with *pilae* (see Plaut. *Curc.* 296, Novius 22). The force of *datatim* in both its literal and metaphorical uses is unclear.

metaphor of sailing and rowing in the *Ars Amatoria*, but it would be rash to say that Julia's seafaring joke was Grecising. The problem of determining the relation of Latin sexual metaphors to Greek is in no case clearer than in that of the image of horse riding. One suspects, but cannot prove, that the metaphor in Latin derives from Greek, and that Latin writers were sometimes conscious of the derivation. But it seems to have passed into ordinary use.

3. Metonymy

The majority of euphemisms for sexual acts refer to an event or activity which is concomitant or associated in some way with the sexual penetration (metonymy). The associated event may precede intercourse, occur at the same time, or follow it. Not that metonymy is necessarily euphemistic. The associated event may itself be quite gross, as in the expression *mentulam caco* (= *pedicor*). Anatomically explicit metaphors and metonymies seem to have been characteristic of slang (cf. *mingo*, etc. = 'ejaculate', *uerpam comedo* and the like). Sometimes one indecency is simply substituted for another (in the expression *uerpam comedo*, *uerpa* is just as obscene as *fello*).

Metonymy results usually in a narrowing of meaning. If intercourse is called a 'disgrace', the generic term 'disgrace' is narrowed down to just one of the acts in which the general quality may be manifested. If the specialised meaning prevails over the general, the desire for euphemism has motivated a semantic change (see below, p. 199 on *stuprum*). But metonymic transfers are often adopted *ad hoc*. A word may be given a specialised sense in a particular context, without losing its general meaning.

Metonymies, like metaphors, display a wide range of tones and implications. They often reflect the attitude of the speaker to a particular sexual act. A person who disapproves of an act may call it a 'disgrace, violation, injury', etc., depending on the circumstances. One who seeks approval for his activities may employ a different type of 'persuasive' designation, such as 'fun, pleasure' or the like. A persuasive designation implies a judgement on the part of the user, and an attempt to impose that judgement on the listener.

It is in the nature of euphemisms that, if used often enough, they become so associated with the unpleasant act or object referred to that they deteriorate in tone, whatever the attitude they expressed initially. It was fashionable in the late first century B.C. to call illicit sex a 'diversion, pleasure' (*deliciae*). But what was a mild word to the smart youth such as Caelius, could be turned into a term of disapproval in the mouths of contemporary moralisers. The stern uncle of Gellius in Catull. 74 spoke against *deliciae*. At this time the word no doubt took its tone from the tone of voice of its user. On the other hand a word which in origin had a strongly pejorative flavour could undergo an amelioration of tone. It is common for intercourse to be called 'violence, violation' or the like by those who wish to imply that an act was inflicted against the will of the victim. The excessive use of a condemnatory term in contexts in which it is not justified may cause it to weaken into a fairly neutral designation for the male role. Words and expressions of this type in Latin are sometimes used when there is no question of violence.

I begin as in the preceding section with some manifest vulgarisms (i–ii). The examples of metonymy which then follow are arranged according as the associated act precedes, is concomitant with, or follows the sexual penetration (iii–xxiv). I then deal with persuasive designations.

(i) *Mentulam caco*

The obvious interpretation of this expression (see *CIL* X.8145 'hanc (mentulam supra pictam) ego cacaui') is that a *pedicatus cacauit* on someone's *mentula*, i.e. suffered *pedicatio* from the *mentula* illustrated. For this use of *caco* (= 'defile *cacando*') see Catull. 36.1 'annales Volusi, cacata carta' (metaphorical). In the graffito an associated event has been described rather than the sexual act itself, but the event suggesting *pedicatio* is itself indecent. *Mentulam caco* may have been a slang expression, = *pedicor*.

Housman's interpretation of the inscription and of some similar passages is far-fetched.[1] On *Priap.* 69.3f. ('ad me respice, fur, et aestimato / quot pondo est tibi mentulam cacandum') he writes: 'cacat, hoc est merdae modo emittit, mentulam cui

---

[1]*Classical Papers*, p. 1177; against, Buchheit, (cited above, p. 166 n. 3), pp. 144ff., with a useful (but incomplete) collection of passages.

eam finito opere extrahit pedicator'. The alleged parallels for such a use of *caco* mean not 'force out *cacando*', but 'produce *cacando*', or 'produce in one's *stercus*' (e.g. Pelagon. 308 'sanguinem ... cacat'). The insertion of *mentulam* into such a syntagm creates an absurdity. Housman makes no mention of *cacata* at Catull. 36.1, but contents himself with the remark that *concaco* is applied to the excretion of little birds.

There is abundant evidence that the *pedicatus* was considered to *cacare*, or to defile the *mentula* of the *pedicator*: Mart. 9.69 'cum futuis, Polycharme, soles in fine cacare. / cum pedicaris, quid, Polycharme, facis?', Juv. 9.43f. 'an facile et pronum est agere intra uiscera penem / legitimum atque illic hesternae occurrere cenae?', *Priap.* 68.8 'pediconum mentula smerdalea est', *CIL* X.4483 'caca, ut possimus bene dormire ... et pedicare natis candidas'. At Auson. *Epigr.* 77.10, p. 341 P. it is predicted that a *pedicator* in his next incarnation will be a dung beetle (cf. Lucil. 967 with Marx *ad loc.*). Other passages which definitely or possibly have the same point are Lucil. 1186 'haec inbubinat, at contra te inbulbitat <ille>' (Paul. Fest. p. 29 'inbulbitare est puerili stercore inquinare'), Pompon. 64 'conforisti me, Diomedes'. Courtney (on Juv. 9.44) draws attention to Mart. 11.88, 13.26 and Arnob. *Nat.* 4.7 ('luteas uoluptates'); the last example is not a parallel, but compare Auson. *Epigr.* 106.9, p. 351 P. 'luteae Symplegadis antrum'. At Pompon. 151 ('ego quaero quod comedim, has [= *hae*?] quaerunt quod cacent: contrariumst') and Novius 6 ('quod editis nihil est; si uultis quod cacetis, copia est') it is possible that, if *cacare* alludes to a sexual act, *comedim* and *editis* also have a sexual implication. The speaker in Pomponius might be expressing the desire to *fellare*, in contrast with certain *cinaedi* who want to be *pedicari*. The two acts are at opposite ends of the body (*contrariumst*).

(ii) *Calare*

Calare entered Latin as a loan-word (< χαλάω, 'loosen, slacken'), and it eventually became influential in the Romance languages. The meaning ('lower') which it has at Veg. *Mil.* 4.23 ('aduersum arietes etiam uel falces sunt plura remedia. aliquanti centones et culcitas funibus calant'; of the lowering of blankets over the side of a wall to soften the blow of the ram and weapons) is basically that which it handed on to its

Romance reflexes,[1] though in Romance it tends to be specialised in certain nautical applications: note Isid. *Etym.* 6.14.5 'apud nautas "calare" ponere dicitur'. So χαλάω was used in later Greek as a nautical and shipping term.[2] There is no evidence that when *calare* first came into Latin it was a nautical term. The examples at Vitr. 10.8.1, 10.8.5 are not nautical. The nautical use seems to have emerged later, perhaps under the influence of the Greek development.

In graffiti *calo* is virtually a substitute for *futuo*: CIL IV.2021 add. p. 214 'Dionysius qua hora uolt, <l>icet chalare', 8715 'Iucudus male cala' (= *calat*), XII.5687.38 'uides quam bene chalas', *Rev. Épigr.* V, p. 141 'uides quam bene calas'. It is not possible to relate this sexual use to the later nautical senses. The implication must be much the same as that of *laxo* at *Priap.* 31.3 'haec mei te uentris arma laxabunt' (= 'make *laxus*', of *pedicatio*; for *laxus, -a* used thus, see, e.g. CIL XI.6721.11 'laxe Octaui sede', IV.10004 'Eupla laxa landicosa', *Priap.* 17.3 'laxior redibit', 18.2 'laxa ... femina' (cf. 46.5, Mart. 11.21.1)). *Calo* would strictly have expressed the 'loosening' of the female by or for entry. One of the above inscriptions (XII.5687.38) is spoken by a woman pictured on a medallion astride a man, and obviously *laxa*.[3] But the verb need not have been applicable just to this one *schema*. For χαλάω used of the same act as that expressed by *calo*, but in a metaphorical double entendre, see anon., *A.P.* 5.99.2 ἤθελον, ὦ κιθαρῳδέ, παραστάς, ὡς κιθαρίζεις, / τὴν ὑπάτην κροῦσαι, τήν τε μέσην χαλάσαι (musical terminology).

Like a few other Greek loan-words in the Latin sexual language (*eugium, strutheum*), *calare* may have been introduced by Greek prostitutes. In some of the graffiti prostitutes seem to be praising (or condemning) the performance of their clients (for this type of graffito, see, e.g. CIL IV.2176 'Felix bene futuis', and above, p. 120). Greek must often have been heard in brothels, and it is possible that in the Greek words mentioned in this paragraph one has some examples of brothel slang. The use of Greek in the bedroom by non-Greek women is castigated by Martial (10.68) and Juvenal (6.191ff.). The

---

[1] See *FEW* II.1, pp. 60f. for a discussion of the meanings of the Romance reflexes of *calare*.

[2] See Shipp, pp. 564f.

[3] For an illustration see P. Wuilleumier and A. Audin, *Annales de l'Université de Lyon* 22 (1952), p. 56.

restriction of *calo* to graffiti in a sexual sense shows that it was a vulgarism.

I move on to a few suggestive words and expressions which strictly denoted events prior to copulation. One could often interpret these expressions as elliptical euphemisms, since a complement might be implied or deleted ('go to', for example, implies 'go to *coeundi causa*': see below, (v)).

(iii) *Duco* and its derivatives

'To take (*ducere*) a whore, woman' was a euphemism for engaging in paid intercourse. Much the same terminology is used in comedy (notably that of Plautus) for taking a wife and a prostitute. In reference to marriage there are four common Plautine expressions, *ducere uxorem domum*, *ducere uxorem*, *ducere domum*, *ducere*.[1] If *domum* is not expressed, it was presumably often understood. When the reference is to prostitution, however, *domum* is an abnormal complement (but see Plaut. *Poen.* 269 'quas adeo hau quisquam umquam liber tetigit neque duxit domum, / seruolorum sordidulorum scorta diobolaria'), and it was probably not as a rule understood, because it would not have been usual to bring prostitutes to one's house.[2] Occasionally *duco* is complemented, as in the mock-official graffito *CIL* IV.2450 'a.d. XI k. Decembr. Epapra Acutus Auctus ad locum duxserunt mulierem Tychen; pretium in singulos a(sses) V f(uit). M. Mesalla, L. Lentulo cos.', but it is more often absolute; presumably the verb would originally have indicated the taking of the whore from the place where she was soliciting to an unspecified destination. But *scortum ducere* (without a complement) was so banal, at least at the time of Plautus,[3] that *ducere* need not necessarily have implied motion from one place to another (= 'acquire, get'?).

Various derivatives of *duco* are used in the same sense: for *ducto*, see Plaut. *Asin.* 189, *Poen.* 868 (as a result of this usage

[1] A large collection of examples, classified according to these categories, can be found in J. Köhm, *Altlateinische Forschungen* (Leipzig, 1905), pp. 55ff.

[2] But see Plaut. *Merc.* 813, C. Gracchus, *Orat.* frg. 27 'si ulla meretrix domum meam introiuit'; at Ter. *Heaut.* 819 'mihi / amicam adduxti quam non licitumst tangere' *domum* may be implied: so P. McGlynn, *Lexicon Terentianum* (London and Glasgow, 1963–7), I, p. 13a.

[3] G. Lodge, *Lexicon Plautinum* (Leipzig, 1924–33), I, p. 434b quotes 9 examples.

the verb became indelicate: Quint. 8.3.44),[1] and for *ductito*, see
Plaut. *Poen.* 272. *Adduco* is found in Plautus (*Merc.* 813, 924)
and Terence (*Heaut.* 819, 1041, *Adelph.* 965), and it was in use
in Atellane farce: see Varro *Ling.* 7.84 'in Atellanis licet ani-
maduertere rusticos dicere se adduxisse pro scorto pelliculam'
(or is Varro quoting only the last word?).

There are various indications in the above material that the
idiom was established in ordinary speech in the Republic and
early Empire (note the graffito, and the comments of Varro
and Quintilian). It does not seem to be so common later.

Such verbs rarely have the *meretrix* as subject (Plaut. *Mil.*
93?: text doubtful).

(iv) *Rapio*

The basic sense of *rapio* was 'drag off into captivity (sc. *coeundi
causa*)':[2] see, e.g. Livy 1.9.10, Ovid *Met.* 12.225; cf. *rapto* at *Met.*
12.223. It is possible that it tended to be weakened into a
synonym of *uim afferre*, *uitiare*, etc., expressing an act of sexual aggression without a concomitant 'capture'. In the declamation Sen. *Contr.* 7.8, where the verb occurs repeatedly, it is
a question of a single sexual violation which took place on one
night (7.8.4 *quadam nocte*). *Rapio* alternates in the declamation with *uitiare* and its derivatives (§§ 3, 4, 7; cf. Quint.
9.2.70). *Rapio* is a similar type of euphemism to *duco*: both
express the taking off of someone for unspecified purposes. But
rapio had a strong implication that the act was carried out
against the will of the victim.

Rapio was frequent in declamation (cf. ἁρπάζω at Sen. *Contr.*
2.3.23). For examples in prose, see Sall. *Cat.* 51.9, Quint. 7.7.3.
Raptor is also common; cf. *raptum* at Sen. *Contr.* 7.8.10.

(v) 'Go, come to'

The euphemism illustrated at Plaut. *Truc.* 150 'ad pueros ire
meliust' (*pedicationis causa*) was current at all periods, with
variations of verb. For *ire*, cf. Petron. 113.11, Tac. *Ann.* 13.46,
Anon. *Med.* ed. Piechotta LXXVIII.[3] For *accedo*, see Vulg. *Lev.*

---

[1] Preston, p. 18 points out that, unlike *duco*, *ducto* is not used of marriage,
and he plausibly relates this restriction to its frequentative force.

[2] See Nisbet and Hubbard II on Hor. *Carm.* 2.4.8.

[3] See further *TLL* V.2.639.32ff.

18.19 'ad mulierem, quae patitur menstrua, non accedes' (contrast the different complement at Mart. 7.18.5 'accessi quotiens ad opus'). *Accedo* is used rather differently, of approaching a prostitute in the street, at Sen. *Contr.* 2.7.4 'tantum non ultro blandientes ut quisquis uiderit non metuat accedere' (contrast Petron. 140.11).[1] With Mart. 12.75.1 'festinat Polytimus ad puellas', compare Juv. 6.331 'si nihil est, seruis incurritur' ('one hastens to slaves'). For *adeo*, see Catull. 8.16 'quis nunc te adibit?'. *Ad uirum pergunt* at Hippocr. *Aer.* 21, p. 41.13f. ('non enim prius ad uirum pergunt cum in utero habent') renders παρὰ ἄνδρα ἀφικνεύμεναι.

Sometimes verbs meaning 'go in' are used elliptically in the sense 'go in (to a room, *coeundi causa*)': Firm. Mat. *Math.* 1.10.10 'ad sororem frater . . . quasi maritus intraret',[2] Vulg. *Gen.* 6.4 'ingressi sunt filii . . . ad filias' (LXX εἰσεπορεύοντο . . . πρός).[3] These idioms are not always distinguished in the dictionaries from the use of the same group of verbs of physical penetration.

Venio often has the female as subject: e.g. Prop. 1.5.32 'non impune illa rogata uenit' (cf. 2.14.20), Mart. 1.71.4 'et quia nulla uenit, tu mihi, Somne, ueni' (cf. 11.73.1), Porph. Hor. *Serm.* 1.5.84 'illam promisisse quidem se uenturam, sed non uenisse' (cf. *Catalept.* 1.1, Ovid *Am.* 1.10.30). A female, viewing herself as the goal of motion, would have used *uenio* of a man coming to her, but most Latin writers were males writing from their own point of view. Nevertheless for *uenio* used of the man, see Ter. *Hec.* 67, Catull. 32.3, Sen. *Contr.* 1.2.1 (of clients coming to a brothel). Whores in Plautus sometimes talk of their clients as *aduentores*: *Truc.* 616 'si aequom facias, aduentores meos <non> incuses, quorum / mihi dona accepta et grata habeo' (cf. 96).

In Greek compare φοιτάω (e.g. Hdt. 4.1.3 and often), ἔρχομαι (with the man as subject, Philip, *A.P.* 9.416.6, and with the woman, Philodemus, *A.P.* 5.120.2, Automedon, *A.P.* 11.29.1, Macedonius, *A.P.* 5.235.1), and ἥκω, which occurs in a context identical to that of Mart. 11.73.1 and Porph. Hor. *Serm.* 1.5.84 at Asclepiades, *A.P.* 5.7.2, 150.1, Paulus Silentiarius, *A.P.* 5.279.5; cf. Philodemus, *A.P.* 5.46.7.

---

[1] *TLL* I.255.19ff. is inadequate on *accedo*.
[2] See *TLL* VII.2.61.35ff.
[3] See *TLL* VII.1.1569.29ff.

(vi) 'Be with'

The least specific of metonymies is seen in the expression *esse cum* (cf. σύνειμι at, e.g. Aristoph. *Pax* 863, συγγίγνομαι at Hdt. 2.121ε (listed by Pollux 5.92), γίγνομαι μετά at Luc. *Dial. Meretr.* 6.1; note too συνουσία, συνουσιάζω). It is found from early Latin onwards (e.g. Plaut. *Amph.* 817, 818, *Bacch.* 891, *Truc.* 688, Ter. *Hec.* 156).[1] The decency of the phrase is commented on by Varro *Ling.* 6.80 'aeque eadem modestia potius cum muliere fuisse quam concubuisse dicebant'. A particularly clear case is at Ovid *Am.* 2.8.27 ('quoque loco tecum fuerim quotiensque, Cypassi, / narrabo dominae quotque quibusque modis'), where it is combined with *modis* (indicating *schemata*; cf. Tibullus' use of *teneo*, p. 181). For a later example, see *Priap.* 14.3.

(vii) 'Sleep with, lie with'

On the currency of *dormio cum*, see Don. Ter. *Andr.* 430. Examples are numerous in (e.g.) Terence, Cicero, elegy, Petronius and Martial.[2] *Iaceo cum* is especially widespread, both in prose (e.g. in the narrative (26.4) and speeches (81.6, 112.3) of Petronius) and verse.[3] For *concumbere*, see *TLL* IV.102.27ff. (Cicero and elsewhere). *Cubo* (e.g. Plaut. *Merc.* 538, Ter. *Hec.* 138) and *cubito* (e.g. Plaut. *Curc.* 57, *Stich.* 547) could have the same implication; cf. *concubitus*, *cubitura* (Plaut. *Cist.* 379), *cubitus* (*Amph.* 1122). Expressions of this type are favoured in comedy[4] and elegy.

This euphemism may be universal. For Greek, see (e.g.) Hom. *Od.* 8.295 κοιμηθῆναι, Hdt. 2.181.2 συγκλίνοιτο, Aristoph. *Nub.* 49 συγκατεκλινόμην (cf. Pollux, 5.92), *Lys.* 904 κατακλίνηθι μετ' ἐμοῦ, Luc. *Dial. Meretr.* 6.2 συγκαθεύδουσα ἐπὶ μισθῷ. συναναπαύομαι is mentioned by Pollux, 5.92.

'Sleeping with', in the sense 'sharing the same bed with', someone is a mark of married status. In marital contexts the expression may indicate a conjugal right, without suggesting intercourse. Pomponia refused to 'sleep with' Quintus Cicero at a time of marital strife. She merely refused to share the

---

[1] Numerous examples from comedy are cited by Preston, p. 18 n.
[2] *TLL* V.1.2030.1ff.
[3] *TLL* VII.1.15.38ff.
[4] Preston, p. 32.

same bed: Cic. *Att.* 5.1.4 'mihique narrauit nec secum illam dormire uoluisse et . . .'.

(viii) 'Stay, spend the night with'

Maneo had a classical meaning 'spend the night',[1] which lives on with some of its reflexes in Romance (e.g. Engad. *manair*). From this idiom derives the euphemism *maneo (cum)*, = 'have intercourse with'.[2] The usage is common in Christian Latin,[3] but it was also established in early popular Latin. See now *CIL* IV.8792 'Antiochus hic mansit cum sua Cithera'; and on its popular currency, note Donatus' remark on Ter. *Andr.* 430 'quod uulgo dicitur "cum illa manere" '.

The more explicit phrase 'to spend the night with' was also suggestive of intercourse, and *nox* sometimes behaves as an equivalent of *stuprum*, as in such expressions as *noctem promittere, poscere, locare* (e.g. Tib. 2.6.49, Ovid *Am.* 1.8.67, 1.10.30, Mart. 1.106.4f.). These phrases were no doubt characteristic of the world of prostitution: note ps.-Acron on Hor. *Epist.* 1.17.36 'quae noctem talento uendebat'. See further Plaut. *Truc.* 278 ('cumque ea noctem in stramentis pernoctare perpetim'; cf. Aristoph. *Nub.* 1069 ἐν τοῖς στρώμασιν τὴν νύκτα παννυχίζειν),[4] Cic. *Att.* 1.16.5, Hor. *Epod.* 15.13, Ovid *Am.* 1.10.47, 1.11.13, Sen. *Contr.* 1.2.22, Tac. *Ann.* 13.44, Juv. 1.38.[5] For Greek see Theocr. 11.44 παρ' ἐμὶν τὰν νύκτα διαξεῖς, anon., *A.P.* 5.101.3 ζητεῖς δὲ τί; νύκτα.

Occasionally *moror* is used in much the same way as *maneo*: Virg. *Aen.* 5.766 'complexi inter se noctemque diemque morantur', *CIL* IV.2060 'Romula hic cum Staphylo moratur' (?).

(ix) *Coeo* and its variants

Coeo was often used of 'coming together' in matrimony (e.g. Gaius *Inst.* 1.59 'si tales personae inter se coierint, nefarias et

---

[1] *TLL* VIII.282.57ff.
[2] Note Nonius' etymology of *meretrix*, p. 684 L. 'menetrices a manendo dictae sunt, quod copiam sui tantummodo noctu facerent'.
[3] See *TLL* VIII.283.11ff., and also Rönsch, *Semasiologische Beiträge zum lateinischen Wörterbuch* (cited above, p. 55, n. 1), III, p. 58; cf. I, p. 42 (on *mansio = coitus*).
[4] See Preston, p. 46.
[5] See Courtney *ad loc.*

incestas nuptias contraxisse dicuntur'; cf. Quint. 5.11.32, Nerat. *Dig.* 12.4.8, Paul. *Dig.* 23.2.2). But as the verbal euphemism *par excellence* for copulation, heterosexual, homosexual or bestial (Vulg. *Exod.* 22.19), it was probably a metonymy rather than a metaphor like *nubo*, etc. *Coeo* is found first at Lucr. 4.1055 of sexual intercourse; it became common from the Augustan period.[1] The derivative noun was *coitus* (for which see further below, p. 189).[2] The form *coetus* is occasionally attested with the same sense,[3] usually in poetry, where it is metrically convenient (*coetus* was disyllabic, as at Auson. *Epigr.* 79.1, p. 341 P., whereas *coitus* was trisyllabic, as at Ovid *Met.* 7.709). Examples in prose (Arnob. *Nat.* 5.23) are difficult to evaluate (scribal slip, or due to the writer's taste for artificiality?). *Coitio* was a late recherché variant for *coitus* (e.g. Macrob. *Sat.* 7.16.6).[4]

Writers of late artificial prose cast around for replacements for *coitus*: *congressio, conuentio, conuentus* (cf. *conuenio* at, e.g. Plin. *Nat.* 11.85), *concilium* and *consortium* are all found (see *TLL* s.vv.). Arnobius had a taste for such words.

(x) 'Join', etc.

Iungo and *coniungo* were also common in reference to marriage,[5] but they were used as well of 'joining' in intercourse. For *iungo*, see Hor. *Carm.* 1.33.8 ('iungentur capreae lupis'),[6] and for *coniungo*, Lucr. 5.853. The derivative *coniugatio* (of copulation) turns up in later Latin: Tert. *Adu. Val.* 7.8 'ex coniugationibus masculorum et feminarum', Arnob. *Nat.* 2.16 'et nos corporum coniugationibus nascimur'. In a medieval parody *coniunctio* (like the juxtaposed *copula*) is a grammatical metaphor: Lehmann no. 13, pp. 223f. 'quid sit casus inflectere / cum famulabus Veneris; / quid copula, coniunctio: / quid signat interiectio, / dum miscet cruri crura'.[7] For the metaphorical use of grammatical terms, see Lucillius, *A.P.* 11.139.4 (πτώσεις, συνδέσμους, σχήματα, συζυγίας). The sexual misuse

---

[1] See *TLL* III.1418.7ff.
[2] *TLL* III.1567.48ff.
[3] *TLL* III.1444.43ff.
[4] See *TLL* III.1566.64ff.
[5] *TLL* VII.2.658.60ff., IV.333.17ff.
[6] See *TLL* VII.2.658.3ff., 60ff., 660.48ff., 661.58ff.
[7] For *copula*, see also Ambros. *Expos. Luc.* 1.43.

of such words is taken to its limit by the author of the medieval
Babio, 182, where the connective particle *-que* seems to stand
for intercourse: 'abdita iam tractat; pelle, nefanda, nefas! / uim
pateris, Viola: nunc, spero, facta uoluptas; / non procul est
etiam quod 'que' sit inter eos'.[1] On grammatical parody, see
further above, p. 39.

I mention here a mixed variety of expressions in which parts
of the body other than the sexual organs are said to join, come
into contact or the like, as for example the *latus* (Lucil. 305,
Ovid *Her.* 2.58), the *femur* (Tib. 1.8.26, Ovid *Am.* 3.14.22), the
head (note the comic formula *caput limare cum*, at Plaut. *Poen.*
292, Caecil. 140, Turpil. 112; cf. Prop. 2.14.22 'mecum habuit
positum lenta puella caput'), the lips (Plaut. *Pseud.* 1259), the
breast or chest (Plaut. *Pseud.* 1261, Lucil. 305), the legs (Lucil.
306) or even the feet (Auson. *Cent. Nupt.* 104, p. 216 P.). Or
the bodies (*corpora*) may be linked (Plaut. *Amph.* 833, Lucr.
4.1193, Ovid *Am.* 3.14.9). For Greek cf. Archil. 119 West,
Argentarius, *A.P.* 5.128. In such descriptions it was common
for an anatomical term or terms to be repeated in a different
case. This type of euphemism, in which the role of innocent
parts not intimately involved in the act is stressed, might be
compared with the distancing of allusions to oral acts by means
of the substitution for *os* or *lingua* of a vague noun (p. 212 n.
1).

(xi) *Misceo* and compounds

Misceo is used in the medio-passive, with a reflexive complement or accompanied by a nominal object such as *corpus* (see
below; for a different type of object, see Arnob. *Nat.* 5.31 'mis-
cuisse concubitus'), with either the male or female as subject.
The variety of constructions can be illustrated by comparing
Min. Fel. *Oct.* 25.10 ('quae . . . se uiris miscuissent') with Aug.
Ciu. 14.19 ('miscetur uxori'). Examples in poetry (e.g. Ovid
Met. 13.866 'sic se tibi misceat')[2] may owe something to the
frequent use of μίγνυμι in the same sense in Homer, Hesiod
and elsewhere (e.g. Hom. *Il.* 9.275 μή ποτε τῆς εὐνῆς ἐπιβή-
μεναι ἠδὲ μιγῆναι; cf. 21.143). Similarly the use of *misceo* and

---

[1] See Faral, *De Babione, poème comique du XIIᵉ siècle* (cited above, p. 15,
n. 3), *ad loc.*
[2] Cf. *TLL* VIII.1081.46ff.

the compounds *admisceo* and *commisceo* in medical and technical writers (e.g. Pliny the Elder) may sometimes have been influenced by the Greek medical use of μίγνυμι (e.g. Hipp. *Hom.* 3 μιχθείη and often).[1] Not that medical or veterinary examples in Latin can always be directly related to a Greek original. *Mul. Chir.* 459, for example ('qui cum conatur admiscere, continuo meiat'; absolute, of the male) does not correspond exactly to anything at *Hipp. Berol.* 33.10, *CHG* I, p. 170.7f., and *commisceatur* at Soran. Lat. (Mustio) p. 14.9f. was not determined by the Greek version (see Soran. *Gyn.* p. 201 Rose). For medical examples, see further Theod. Prisc. *Gyn.* 22, *Mul. Chir.* 756 (*mixtio*), 762, Cael. Aurel. *Gyn.* p. 16.390 ('corpora commiscentur'), *Chron.* 4.132.

But there are also signs that the idiom had been banalised in literary varieties of the language, on which Greek need not have been directly influential: e.g. Apul. *Met.* 9.24, Ampel. 9.9, Min. Fel. *Oct.* 31.3, Ulp. *Dig.* 23.2.43.2. At *Vet. Lat.*, *Lev.* 19.19, (Hesych. *in Lev.* 19.19, p. 2029 D.) *commisceri* corresponds to κατοχεύσεις in the LXX (Vulg. *coire*). The idiom had progressed beyond a mere calque, but sometimes Greek influence cannot be ruled out. Its distribution shows that it was learned in tone; in medical Latin it was a technical term.

(xii) 'Embrace, hold', etc.

An obvious concomitant of intercourse is holding or embracing, and verbs from these semantic fields are often used euphemistically. The euphemistic use of *teneo* is well illustrated at Tib. 2.6.52 'quisue meam teneat, quot teneatue modis', where the last word shows that Tibullus had in mind different *schemata*; cf. 1.5.39. For *complector*, *complexus*, see (e.g.) Prop. 1.13.19, and for *amplector*, Don. Ter. *Andr.* 430 '<amplecti> quod uulgo dicitur "cum illa manere, cum illa dormire" '. *Haereo* has a wide range of attested sexual uses: of copulation at Prop. 2.15.25 'atque utinam haerentis sic nos uincire catena / uelles', Petron. 79.8 'haesimus calentes' (cf. Lucr. 4.1113, 1205, and *cohaereo* at Plin. *Nat.* 10.173), of manual stimulation at Juv. 6.024 'saepius in teneris haerebit dextera lumbis', and of cunnilinctio at Mart. 11.61.11 'tumenti mersus haeret in uol-

---

[1] μιχθῆναι is mentioned as a designation of intercourse by Pollux, 5.92 (see also 5.93 for μῖξις).

ua'. Cf. Mart. 2.61.7 'haereat inguinibus potius tam noxia lingua', Sen. *N.Q.* 1.16.4 'inguinibusque alienis obhaeserat', Min. Fel. *Oct.* 28.10 'libidinoso ore inguinibus inhaerescunt', where the complements leave no doubt concerning the type of 'clinging' in question.[1]

(xiii) *Comprimo* and its synonyms

Verbs of pressing and the like are often used of the male role. *Premo* appears in direct speech at Suet. *Cal.* 25.1 'noli uxorem meam premere'. The goddess *Prema* allegedly had a part in the ceremony of the deflowering of a bride (Aug. *Ciu.* 6.9). *Pullipremo* (= *pedicator*) is printed by editors at Auson. *Epigr.* 77.8, p. 341 ('Lucili uatis subpilo pullipremo'; cf. Lucil. 967), but the text is doubtful (*pullo premor* Z, *pulo premor* T). Contrast Lucr. 4.1079 'quod petiere, premunt arte faciuntque dolorem / corporis', where *premunt* is genuinely used of a concomitant action and is not replaceable by *futuunt*.

   The chief representative of this root with a sexual sense was *comprimo*. It is the standard word for the indiscretions committed by the *adulescentes* in comedy, where it does not seem to have been determined by any term in Greek New Comedy.[2] *Comprimo* continued to be used in polite genres, both prose and verse. It is hardly ever used of animals (but see Col. 8.11.5), and is rarely employed of *pedicatio* (see Novius 95 (?), Apul. *Met.* 10.5). The nouns *compressus* and *compressio* are also attested (*TLL*, s.vv.). *Comprimo* was probably a native Latin euphemism of the educated language.

   Opprimo is an occasional variant of *comprimo* (found mainly in late and Christian Latin).[3] It also appears to have turned up in an early graffito: *CIL* IV.1879 'ea<m> Xamus amat <I>onicus: oppressit nam'.[4] If the inscription has been read correctly, the verb seems to be without any notion of forcible overwhelming. At Aug. *Ciu.* 1.18 ('femina ... uiolenter op-

---

[1] At Auson. *Cent. Nupt.* 118, p. 217 P. 'haesit uirgineumque alte bibit acta cruorem', it is the *mentula* which *haesit*.

[2] See *TLL* III.2157.70ff. for examples.

[3] *TLL* IX. 2.788.34ff.

[4] J. B. Hofmann and A. Szantyr, *Lateinische Syntax und Stilistik* (Munich, 1965), p. 506 do not mention this example of postponed *nam*. Postposition is said to be confined to poetry (first in Catullus) and late prose.

pressa et alieno compressa peccato') *oppressa* is simply a stylistic variant for *compressa*.

For *urgeo*, see Pompon. 99 'nescio quis molam quasi asinus urget uxorem tuam', Hor. *Carm.* 1.5.2 'quis multa gracilis te puer in rosa / perfusus liquidis urget odoribus'.

(xiv) 'Rub, stimulate' and the like

Verbs of this general semantic field are neither exclusively metonymies nor metaphors when applied to sexual acts. A verb meaning 'rub away' is metaphorical if used of sexual intercourse, but 'rubbing' can be interpreted as a concomitant of the sexual act. I have considered it convenient to lump together some different types of expressions in this section.

Tero had various agricultural uses ('grind, thresh'), but it was a more general word than *molo* (the basic sense was 'rub, wear away'), and its sexual use should be treated separately. See Plaut. *Capt.* 888 'Boius est, boiam terit', Prop. 3.11.30 'et famulos inter femina trita suos', Petron. 87.8 'utcumque igitur inter anhelitus sudoresque tritus, quod uoluerat accepit', *Priap.* 46.9 'erucarum opus est decem maniplis, / fossas inguinis ut teram dolemque / cunni uermiculos scaturrientis'. The vagueness of *tero* made it applicable (like some of its synonyms: see below) to sexual acts other than *fututio* and *pedicatio*. At *Priap.* 83.34 'licebit aeger angue lentior cubes, / tereris usque, donec . . .' it indicates masturbation (cf. τρίβω at Aristoph. *Vesp.* 1344, ἀνατρίβω at *Ach.* 1149).[1] For its use of cunnilinctio, see Juv. 9.4 'Rauola dum Rhodopes uda terit inguina barba'. At Mart. 1.66.7f. ('custodit ipse uirginis pater chartae, / quae trita duro non inhorruit mento') a book is compared to a locked-up virgin. *Trita mento* has the secondary implication 'kissed'. I see no grounds for finding an additional pun (of cunnilinctio).[2] For *tero* used of kissing, see Mart. 11.22.1 'mollia quod niuei duro teris ore Galaesi / basia'.

The intensive compound *distero* (= 'rub to pieces') at Petron. 24.4 ('equum cinaedus mutauit transituque ad comitem meum facto clunibus eum basiisque distriuit') must refer to the mo-

---

[1] Tränkle, p. 138 should not have included this example with those meaning '*futuo*', '*pedico*'.

[2] Citroni and Howell (see p. 33, n. 1) *ad loc.* do not make clear what secondary sense they see in *trita* here. Commentators discussing *tero* habitually lump together various distinct sexual uses.

tions of the *cinaedus* astride his victim. At *Anth. Lat.* 148.8 ('hanc fouet amplexu molli cunnumque caballae / adterit adsiduo pene fututor hebes') *attero* is applied to *fututio*. At Petron. 81.6 ('forsitan mutuis libidinibus attriti derident solitudinem meam') the participle seems primarily to mean 'worn out, exhausted'.

The predominating sexual meaning of *frico* is 'masturbate': see Schol. Juv. 6.238 'manu sua penem fricat sibi', *CIL* X.4483 'cunnu tibi fricabo' (arguably ambiguous; for *cunnum* as the object of *futuo*, see *CIL* IV.1830 add. p. 212, = *CE* 230 'futuitur cunnus . . .'), Petron. 92.11 'tanto magis expedit inguina quam ingenia fricare', Mart. 11.29.8 'nil opus est digitis: sic mihi, Phylli, frica' (cf. 1 'tractare uirilia'),[1] and perhaps Plaut. *Pseud.* 1189–90 'uncti hi sunt senes: fricari sese ex antiquo uolunt'. Note too *frictura* in the *spurcum additamentum* at Apul. *Met.* 10.21 'Priapo<n> frequenti frictura porrixabam'. *Frico* survived in Old French with the meaning '*futuo*' (*froier*),[2] and this may be its sense at *Anth. Lat.* 190.8 'te duce lasciuae nocte fricantur anus'. It is not certain what meaning of *frico* lies behind Tertullian's *frictrix* (*Resurr.* 16.6 'calicem . . . frictricis uel archigalli . . . spiritu infectum', *Pall.* 4.9 'aspice lupas, popularium libidinum nundinas, ipsas quoque frictrices, et si praestat oculos abducere ab eiusmodi propudiis occisae in publico castitatis'). The first passage implies that a *frictrix* was a *fellatrix*. If so it would have been an idiomatic use of *frico* applied to oral stimulation which produced the noun. In the second passage Tertullian uses the word as if it was familiar to his readers. There is nothing in either context to suggest that *frictrix* was a calque on τριβάς.

The interchange between the senses 'masturbate' and '*futuo*' is also illustrated by *sollicito*, which in Classical Latin could be applied to masturbation (Ovid *Am.* 3.7.74, Petron. 20.2, Mart. 11.22.4, Maxim. *Eleg.* 5.58), but in the Medieval comedy *Lidia* (514) refers to *fututio*: ' "parce, precor" Pirrus clamat, "dux, parce pudorem; / non honor est istis sollicitare locis" '. Slightly different again is the example at Lucr. 4.1196 ('nam facit ex animo saepe et communia quaerens / gaudia sollicitat

---

[1] The (possessive) dative *mihi* with *frica* was obviously idiomatic: it occurs in two of the other examples cited here, usually in conjunction with an anatomical term in the accusative (*penem*, *cunnum*). For the ellipse of *mentulam* at Mart. 11.29.8, see above, p. 146 n. 1.

[2] *FEW* III, p. 783.

spatium decurrere amoris'), used of unspecified acts (and words?) of stimulation employed by the female during intercourse.[1]

Tergeo ('rub, clean') may not have been an established metaphor = *futuo*, but it was used suggestively by Flaccus reported by Macrob. *Sat.* 1.15.21 (see p. 85).

We have now seen verbs of rubbing and the like used in a variety of senses which may be generally classified as sexual: (a) of *fututio* and *pedicatio* (*tero, attero, frico* (?), *sollicito*), (b) of masturbation (*tero, frico, sollicito*), (c) of oral acts (*tero, frico* (?)), (d) of the stimulation applied by a *cinaedus* by means of the *clunes* (*distero*), (e) of the stimulation employed by the woman in intercourse (*sollicito*), and (f) of kissing (*tero*). The imprecision of the verbs in question permits them to be used of any form of stimulation, the nature of which may or may not emerge from the context. If a writer wished to leave the details of an act unspoken, he could select one of the verbs without providing an additional pointer to its implication (note Lucr. 4.1196 above). See above, p. 168 on *glubo*.

The applicability of certain vague verbs to different forms of sexual stimulation can be further illustrated from the semantic field 'touch'.

(xv) 'Touch' and the like

Tango and its compounds and derivatives furnish a large class of euphemisms. Greek had the same euphemism: e.g. θιγγάνω (Eur. *Hipp.* 1044), ψαύω (Philodemus, *A.P.* 12.173.3), χροίζω (Theocr. 10.18), ἅπτω (ps.-Luc. *Asinus* 6).

At Ter. *Eun.* 373 *tango* means no more than 'touch, caress': 'cibum una capias, adsis, tangas, ludas, propter dormias'; cf. Donatus' five stages of *amor*, in which *tactus* comes before *osculum*: Ter. *Eun.* 640 'quinque lineae perfectae sunt ad amorem: prima uisus, secunda alloquii, tertia tactus, quarta osculi, quinta coitus'. For the verb implying intercourse, see, e.g. Plaut. *Poen.* 98, Ter. *Adelph.* 686, Catull. 89.5, Hor. *Serm.* 1.2.28, 54, Ovid *Ars* 2.692, Mart. 1.73.1 (cf. 4 *fututorum*), and in later Latin, *Mul. Chir.* 756 '. . . desiderare mixtionem masculi. qui cum tetigerit masculus, statim praegnantes fiunt' (*masculum* cod.; Oder retains the accusative and changes *qui*

---

[1] On *sollicito* at C. Gracchus *Orat.* frg. 27, see p. 200.

to *quae*, but since *tango* usually (but see below on *attingo*) describes the male role it is preferable to change *masculum*), Matthew of Vendôme, *Milo* 184 'cultoris uacat egra manu qui uimina nulla / falce metit, nullo uomere tangit humum' (I interpret this passage as containing a series of double entendres). For *tango* applied in circumlocutions to another type of sexual act, see Catull. 21.8 'tangam te prior irrumatione', *Priap.* 28.5 'altiora tangam'. At Ovid *Ars* 2.719f. it is used of masturbation: 'cum loca reppereris, quae tangi femina gaudet, / non obstet, tangas quominus illa, pudor' (cf. 713); cf. Mart. 1.92.2 'queritur . . . / tangi se digito, Mamuriane, tuo' (touching of the *mentula* or *culus*?). Various (non-verbal) derivatives of *tango* also have a sexual use: e.g. *integer* (e.g. Ter. *Hec.* 145, 150), *intactus* (Juv. 6.163, 7.87) (cf. ἄψαυστος, Paulus Silentiarius, *A.P.* 5.217.1), *tactus* (Petron. 81.5).

Attingo is used in the same sentence as *tango* at Catull. 89.5, and with the same meaning: 'qui ut nihil attingat, nisi quod fas tangere non est' (cf., e.g. 67.20, Ter. *Hec.* 136). At 97.11 the female is subject: 'quem siqua attingit'. *Contingo* is also well attested, particularly in late Latin (e.g. *Vet. Lat.*, I *Cor.* 7.1, *ap.* Tert. *Pud.* 16.13; Vulg. *tangere*, Gk. ἅπτεσθαι; cf. Eugraph. Ter. *Hec.* 153).

A range of uses attaches to *tracto* (< *traho*) and its compounds. *Tracto* itself was commonly used of masturbation: Naev. com. frg. 127, Varro *Men.* 368, Petron. 140.13, Mart. 11.29.1, *Priap.* 80.2; for Medieval examples, see *Babio* 180, *Pamphilus* 688 (of caressing, of an unspecified type). On the other hand the verbal noun *tractatio* at Petron. 139.1 ('torum frequenti tractatione uexaui, amoris mei quasi quandam imaginem') seems to express the actions typical of the male in intercourse (on *uexo*, see p. 200). *Contrecto* too could be employed of stroking or masturbation (e.g. Plaut. *Poen.* 1311, Sen. *Contr.* 1.2.3, 1.2.9, Suet. *Nero* 34.4, Arnob. *Nat.* 5.11 (of masturbation), Maxim. *Eleg.* 5.57 (of masturbation)). It was also applied to the active role in intercourse (e.g. Suet. *Dom.* 1.3 'contractatis multorum uxoribus'),[1] and even to oral practices (Aurel. Vict. *Caes.* 5.7 'utrique sexui genitalia uultu contrectabat'). At Sen. *Contr.* 1.2.13 it is used of kissing. A clear case of *attrecto* = *futuo* is at Cic. *Cael.* 20 'qui dicerent uxores suas a cena redeuntes attrectatas esse a Caelio' (cf. Suet. *Nero*

---

[1] Cf. *TLL* IV.774.47ff.

26.2). Other instances merely refer to fondling: e.g. Plaut. *Pers.* 227 'ne me attrecta', *Rud.* 420 'nimium familiariter / me attrectas'. *Pertracto* at Plaut. *Asin.* 224 ('si papillam pertractauit') also means 'fondle, caress'.

I mention finally a coinage in the *spurcum additamentum* at Apul. *Met.* 10.21: 'ipsoque pando et repando uentrem sepiuscule tactabam'.[1]

Various verbs seen in this section were used indifferently of manual stimulation, stimulation by means of the sexual organs or of oral stimulation.

(xvi) 'Have' and the like

Donatus registers the meaning 'have' = 'have intercourse with' (the female) for *habeo* in his note on Ter. *Adelph.* 389 'quia haberi uxor dicitur et haberi mulier, cum coit'. This meaning is illustrated at Mart. 12.20.2 'quare non habeat, Fabulle, quaeris / uxorem Themison? habet sororem' (a double entendre). 'Having a prostitute' was a particular application of the idiom: note Ter. *Andr.* 85 'heus puer, / dic sodes, quis heri Chrysidem habuit?' (cf. Plaut. *Bacch.* 1080 'habui scortum', and ps.-Acron on Hor. *Epist.* 1.17.36). See further Ovid *Met.* 9.497, Petron. 130.6.[2] Characteristically the female is object in Latin. The verb was also sometimes applied to homosexual relations: note Ovid *Ars* 1.524 'et si quis male uir quaerit habere uirum' (cf. Mart. 1.92.3). In Greek a prostitute could be subject of ἔχω, particularly in the expression ἔχω τινά, = 'have a client': Philodemus, *A.P.* 5.46.2 μή τιν' ἔχεις, Posidippus, *A.P.* 5.213.1 εἰ μὲν ἔχει τιν'; cf. Meleager, *A.P.* 5.191.5 ἢ τιν' ἔχει σύγκοιτον. The male too is sometimes subject (in reference to intercourse): e.g. Posidippus, *A.P.* 5.186.4 εἰ δ' ἕτερός σε / εἶχε (cf. Macedonius, *A.P.* 5.243.2). For the transfer to homosexual contexts, see Eratosthenes, *A.P.* 5.277.1 ἄρσενας ἄλλος ἔχοι. A rather different application is seen at Men. *Epitr.* frg. 1.2 ὁ νῦν ἔχων <τὴν> Ἀβρότονον τὴν ψάλτριαν (of 'having' a prostitute over a longer period); compare *teneo* at Mart. 11.40.2 'formosam Glyceran amat Lupercus / et solus tenet imperatque solus'.

---

[1] See Mariotti, p. 242 = p. 60.
[2] See Preston, p. 19 n. 36, Housman, *Classical Papers*, p. 735, *TLL* VI.3.2409.33ff.

Other verbs were occasionally used in the same way as *habeo*. For *possideo*, see Mart. 9.67.1 'lasciuam tota possedi nocte puellam'. *Potior* refers to the moment of orgasm at Lucr. 4.1076 'potiundi tempore in ipso / fluctuat ... ardor amantum'. Contrast Ovid *Met.* 9.753 'nec tamen est potienda tibi', Tert. *Apol.* 46.11 'mulieres sine concupiscentia aspicere non posset et doleret, si non esset potitus', Aug. *Ciu.* 1.19 'huius corpore cum uiolenter oppresso Tarquinii regis filius libidinose potitus esset'. To this category perhaps belongs *CGL* V.474.47 (510.51) 'poteri [= *potiri*?] fornicari'.

(xvii) *Amo, libido, uenus*

'Love', in an emotional sense, might be described as a concomitant of the sexual act. *Amo* was sometimes transferred euphemistically to the physical act. The verb has varying implications. At Plaut. *Poen.* 1230 'ego te antestabor, postea hanc amabo atque amplexabor' it refers to embracing, whereas at Cic. *Cat.* 2.8 the reference, both in *amabat* and *amori*, is to *pedicatio*: 'alios ipse amabat turpissime, aliorum amori flagitiosissime seruiebat'. Cf. *CIL* IV.1898 'quisquis amat calidis non debet fontibus uti. / nam nemo flammas [sic] ustus *amare* potest', Mart. 3.58.38 'alius (porrigit) coactos non amare capones' (= *futuere*).

Similarly *libido*, 'sexual lust, desire', tended to acquire the physical sense 'sexual act'. At Cic. *Phil.* 2.45 'nemo umquam puer emptus libidinis causa tam fuit in domini potestate' the word is ambiguous, whereas at Plin. *Nat.* 22.86 'mulieres libidinis auidissimas uirosque in coitum pigerrimos scripsere' it has the new sense (= *coitus*). With this meaning *libido* is quoted mainly from prose of the Empire,[1] but it is found occasionally earlier (Catull. 45.24 'uno in Septimio fidelis Acme / facit delicias libidinesque'). *Libido* is used quite neutrally by Pliny (above) and Catullus, but with a tone of disapproval by (e.g.) Suetonius at *Tib.* 11.4, *Cal.* 41.1.

The participants may simply 'feel desire' together: Catull. 88.1f. 'cum matre atque sorore / prurit', Mart. 9.73.6 'pruris domini cum Ganymede tui'.

Some of the above examples illuminate the semantic development of *uenus*, originally a neuter of root **wen-*, 'desire'.

[1] See *TLL* VII.2.1333.67ff.

The word became one of the standard neutral nouns of the educated language for sexual intercourse (contrast *stuprum*, the standard pejorative term: see p. 201).[1] The development of *uenus* was exactly the opposite of that of Ἀφροδίτη, which began as the name of a goddess and shifted to the senses 'sexual desire, intercourse'. But though *uenus* = 'intercourse' is not a calque on Ἀφροδίτη, late medical writers who used *uenus* may have been influenced by the presence of ἀφροδίσια (which is common in the Hippocratic corpus) in their sources (similarly, with *usus uenerius*, *usus ueneris* at, e.g. Cael. Aurel. *Gyn.* p. 11.253, Soran. Lat. (Mustio) pp. 9.3, 74.4f., compare ἡ τῶν ἀφροδισίων χρῆσις at, e.g., Plat. *Leg.* 841a). *Venus* was in rivalry with *coitus* as the neutral educated noun, but it was older and perhaps more common in most technical writers. *Coitus* is found first in the Augustan period (Ovid *Met.* 7.709);[2] *uenus* is common from Lucretius onwards, in writers who deal with sexual activity in a technical and neutral tone.[3] There can be no doubt that it was in use long before Lucretius took it up. It is no surprise that *uenus* in the sense in question is not found in Plautus or Terence, because characters in drama usually talk of intercourse in persuasive or emotive terms. *Venus* outnumbers *coitus* by 15:7 in Celsus, 11:5 in Columella, and 16:2 in Marcellus Empiricus. Pliny, however, seems to have preferred *coitus*. In the zoological book 8, for example, it occurs 22 times, whereas *uenus* is not used at all. *Venus* is employed of human intercourse at (e.g.) 10.172 twice, 11.131, and of that of animals at 10.100, 174, 182. Pliny may have felt *uenus* to be more applicable to humans than animals.

(xviii) *Patior*

Patior was the technical term of the passive role in intercourse. It does not occur in Plautus, but is found in Novius and the late Republic, and common from the Augustan period. The verb could be used absolutely, as at Sen. *Epist.* 95.21, of females ('(mulieres) pati natae . . . adeo peruersum commentae genus impudicitiae uiros ineunt'), or at Petron. 87.7, of a youth

---

[1] On *uenus*, see Ernout and Meillet, *s.v.*, and in particular Ernout, *RPh* 30 (1956), pp. 7ff., = id. *Philologica* II (Paris, 1957), pp. 87ff.

[2] See *TLL* III.1567.48ff.

[3] There is a rich collection of examples in Ernout's article, cited above; cf. Adams, 'Anatomical terminology', n. 17.

(cf. Novius 19). *Virum* or the like is a common complement: e.g. Col. 6.24.2 'sua sponte marem patiuntur (equae)' (cf. Sen. *N.Q.* 1.16.2, of a pathic). For various other complements, see Sall. *Cat.* 13.3 'uiri muliebria pati' (the same expression is at Tac. *Ann.* 11.36), Cic. *Phil.* 2.86 'ut omnia paterere' (*omnia* sometimes has a sexual implication: see Sen. *N.Q.* 1.16.5, Juv. 6.02).[1] *Patientia* was the abstract correspondent, as at Sen. *N.Q.* 1.16.6 and Petron. 9.6 (*muliebris patientiae*).

πάσχω is rare in a sexual sense in classical Greek (but note Aristoph. *Thesm.* 201 εὐρύπρωκτος εἶ / οὐ τοῖς λόγοισιν, ἀλλὰ τοῖς παθήμασιν).[2] παθικός is not quoted in Greek (but note Nicarchus, *A.P.* 11.73.7 παθικεύεται, of a woman); hence *pathicus* must have been a popular borrowing. It was in vulgar use (*CIL* IV.2360, XI.6721.39). *Pathicus* was applicable to males (Catull. 16.2, Juv. 2.99) and females (*Priap.* 25.3, 40.4, 73.1).

(xix) 'Know'

The familiar Biblical euphemism 'know' (of carnal knowledge) was well domiciled in Latin before it made an appearance in Bible translations:[3] e.g. Catull. 72.1 (*nosse*), 61.180 (*cognitae*), Caes. *Gall.* 6.21.5 (*notitiam habuisse*), Ovid *Her.* 6.133 (*cognouit*); cf. *CIL* VI. 12853.5 = *CE* 548 'dedita coniugi soli suo, *ignara* alienum'. Cf. Men. frg. 382.5 ἔπειτα φοιτῶν καὶ κολακεύων <ἐμέ τε καὶ> / τὴν μητέρ' ἔγνω μ'.[4]

(xx) 'Enter'

With hesitation I classify this usage as a metonymy. Certainly it involves specialisation of a general verb. *Ineo* was used of entry by men (e.g. Anton. *ap.* Suet. *Aug.* 69.2) and even women (*tribades?*) (Sen. *Epist.* 95.21), but its predominating use seems to have been of the male animal (see p. 206). For this verbal root, see also *Priap.* 74.1 'per medios ibit pueros mediasque

---

[1] Cf. Courtney *ad loc.* for Greek parallels.

[2] On πάσχω, see A. W. Gomme and F. H. Sandbach, *Menander, A Commentary* (Oxford, 1973), p. 270 (on *Dysc.* 892).

[3] See Opelt, 951 for the idiom in Christian Latin.

[4] For Greek see in particular W. Bauer – W. F. Arndt – F. W. Gingrich, *A Greek-English Lexicon of the New Testament* (Chicago, 1957), p. 160*b*, *s.v.* γιγνώσκω, (5).

puellas', 33.2 'Naidas antiqui Dryadasque habuere Priapi, / et
quo tenta dei uena subiret, erat'.

Only one late example of *ingredior* of entry in the sexual
sense is quoted at *TLL* VII.1.1569.83ff. For the verb used of
'going in to' (the *cubiculum*), see p. 176. *Intro* is not quoted
with our sense; see p. 176 ('go in to').

Various more vigorous verbs of similar meaning are used in
much the same way as *ineo*: *inruo* (Plaut. *Cas.* 889–90 'magis
iam lubet in Casinam inruere', ps.-Acron on Hor. *Serm.* 2.7.72
'putas te moechum non esse, si non palam in feminas irruis',
H.A., *Comm.* 5.11 'nec inruentium in se iuuenum carebat in-
famia'),[1] *incurro* (*Vit. Patr.* 5.5.26; *incurro* is rare in this sense;
Sen. *Contr.* 2.7.4 and Juv. 6.331 do not belong in this category,
despite *TLL* VII.1.1086.5f.), *incurso* (favoured by Tertullian:
Nat. 1.7.32, 1.16.11, *Pud.* 4.3). Verbs of rapid motion tend to
be weakened into synonyms of *ire*, and that development to
some extent accounts for the above usages. Sometimes there
may have been an idea of forcible violation present. Tertullian
uses *incurso* of illicit intercourse of various kinds; cf. *inruo* in
ps.-Acron above. *Ambulare in* at Sen. *Contr.* 1.5.9 ('ambulet in
masculos') seems to be a circumlocution for *ineo*; *in* has surely
not been used for *ad*, as M. Winterbottom's translation (Loeb)
implies.

(xxi) Positions and positioning

Allusions to sexual acts often take the form of descriptions of
the position or positioning of the participants (cf. on *sedeo* and
horse riding, p. 165). A verb of positioning may in effect be a
substitute for an offensive verb such as *futuo* or *pedico* (act. or
pass.), or it might suggest a particular *schema*. Sometimes
words or expressions suggestive of positions are used in conjunction with a verb = *futuo* or *pedico*, and are intended as
technical rather than euphemistic. I treat together here both
euphemistic substitutes for *futuo* or *pedico*, and a few other
recurring words and phrases used of various *schemata*.

Incuruo at Mart. 11.43.5 ('incuruabat Hylan') expresses the
positioning of the *pathicus* for *pedicatio*; it is virtually equivalent to *pedico*. Contrast Apul. *Met.* 9.7 'adulter, bellissimus
ille pusio, inclinatam dolio pronam uxorem fabri *superincur-*

[1] See further *TLL* VII.2.451.58ff.

uatus secure dedolabat', where the compound, applied to the posture of the male, is used along with rather than instead of a vivid verb (= *futuo* or *pedico*).

Inclino was in wider use for the positioning of the pathic (male or female): see Juv. 9.26 'ipsos etiam inclinare maritos', 10.224 'quot discipulos inclinet Hamillus', Schol. Juv. 2.21 (on *ceuentem*) 'inclinatum ad stuprum et sustinentem', and, of the female, Apul. *Met.* 9.7 above. On the inscriptional *inclinabiliter*, which establishes the currency of the sexual use of the verb, see p. 137 n. 1. The adverb seems to have been equivalent to the present participle, used intransitively in a middle sense ('bending over', sc. 'for *pedicatio*'); for the intransitive use of *inclino*, see, e.g. Lucr. 2.243, Juv. 3.316. Usages comparable to *inclino* are attested in Greek, but are without direct connection with the Latin.[1]

Pronus and *supinus* could take on a sexual significance (note *pronam* at Apul. *Met.* 9.7 above, and cf. Catull. 28.9 'bene me ac diu supinum / tota ista trabe lentus irrumasti', Juv. 6.126 'ac resupina iacens cunctorum absorbuit ictus',[2] Apul. *Met.* 8.29 'nudatum supinatumque iuuenem execrandis oribus flagitabant'). Hence Juvenal's *resupino*: 3.112 'auiam resupinat amici'; cf. 8.176 'resupinati cessantia tympana galli' (Schol. 'ebrii, turpia patientis').

Various phrases were suggestive of sexual acts or *schemata*. *Attractis pedibus* occurs not only at Catull. 15.18 but also at *CIL* IV. 1261 ('futebatur inquam futuebatur ciuium Romanorum atractis pedibus cunus'). *Capite demisso* (suggesting cunnilinctio or *fellatio*) is found at Cic. *Dom.* 83 and Catull. 88.8; cf. Sen. *N.Q.* 1.16.4 'cum caput merserat'. *Pedes tollere* (signifying the positioning of the female) is fairly common; it is in effect a suggestive euphemism = *futuo(r)*.[3] Note Cicero's joke, *Att.* 2.1.5 'noli, inquam, de uno pede sororis queri; licet etiam

---

[1] See, e.g. Dioscorides, *A.P.* 5.54.2, Scythinus, *A.P.* 12.232.3.

[2] See Courtney *ad loc.* on the text.

[3] I do not accept that, as Jocelyn, *AJP* 101 (1980), p. 433, nn. 64–5 implies, the phrase necessarily suggested the *schema* mentioned at Ovid *Ars* 3.775 'Milanion umeris Atalantes crura ferebat'. The act *tollendi pedes* could initiate intercourse, whatever the position ultimately adopted. See the lamp illustrations numbered Q 1407, Q 1408, Q 882, Q 979 in D. M. Bailey, *A Catalogue of the Lamps in the British Museum*, 2, *Roman Lamps made in Italy* (London, 1980), pp. 65f. for one or both feet of the woman raised but not on the shoulders of the man.

alterum tollas', and cf. Petron. 55.6, *v.* 11, Mart. 10.81.4,
11.71.8; cf. αἴρειν τὰ σκέλη (Aristoph. *Eccl.* 265, *Pax.* 889).

Arnob. *Nat.* 2.42 ('clunibus et coxendicibus subleuatis lumborum crispitudine fluctuaret') seems to refer to the female,
supina, with raised thighs or arched back.

Conquinisco and *ocquinisco* were popular terms of the Republic, signifying the act of squatting or bending over (i.e. the
position of the *pedicatus*). For *conquinisco*, see Plaut. *Cist.* 657
'faciundum est puerile officium: conquiniscam ad cistulam',
Pseud. 864 'si conquiniscet istic, conquiniscito' (not necessarily
sexual),[1] Pompon. 171 'in terram, ut cubabat, nudam ad eum
ut conquexi, interim / mulieres conspiciunt'. *Conquexit* at *Epit.*
Alex. 101 is a conjecture by Wölfflin; if it were accepted it
would be an archaism. For *ocquinisco*, see Pompon. 126, 149.
Apart from the Republican examples the two words are confined to grammarians and the like, by whom they are usually
equated with *inclino*: Prisc., *GL* II.508.28, Non. pp. 119, 213
L., *CGL* IV.129.34, V.636.12, V.645.1.

Coxim ('squatting, on one's haunches') was of the same root;[2]
the connection with *coxa* is a popular etymology. It too is a
Republican vulgarism (Pompon. 129, Varro *Men.* 471), with
an archaising example in Apuleius (*Met.* 3.1). The association
of *coxim* with defecation (Pompon. 129) and its use by Varro
(= 'stooping, limping') imply that the above verbs would not
originally have had a necessary connection with the position
adopted for *pedicatio* (see also Plaut. *Pseud.* 864 above). But
they were tending to be specialised in the period of recorded
Republican Latin.

(xxii) Movements

Verbs and expressions indicating movements not inherently
sexual form an important class of euphemisms for sexual acts.

Volutor ('have a roll'; cf. συγκυλίεσθαι at Athen. 588e) is
shown by its wide distribution to have been idiomatic: see Cic.
Har. Resp. 59 'quis umquam nepos tam *libere* est cum scortis
quam hic cum sororibus uolutatus' (cf. Petron. 79.9 'uolutat-
usque *liberius* cum fratre non suo'), Prop. 2.29B.36 'apparent

---

[1] Nonius, p. 119 L. has *ceueto simul:* see Fraenkel, *Kleine Beiträge zur
klassischen Philologie* II, pp. 45ff.
[2] See Ernout and Meillet, *s.v.*

non ulla toro uestigia presso, / signa uolutantis nec iacuisse duos'; cf. Sen. *Contr.* 1.2.13 (of an act which stops short of *stuprum*), 1.2.6 (*uolutatio*), Plin. *Nat.* 35.140, Apul. *Met.* 9.5. The similarity of Cic. *Har. Resp.* 59 to Petron. 79.9 suggests the possibility that *uolutor cum sorore* / *fratre* had originally been a non-sexual set phrase. If so its transfer to the sexual sphere would have constituted a metaphor akin to that of 'playing'. With *uolutor* can be compared *cado* ('tumble') at Plaut. *Pers.* 656 'libera eris actutum, si crebro cades'.[1]

Palpito super was no doubt Juvenal's own phrase: 3.134 'semel aut iterum super illam palpitet'.

Phrases containing *clunes* or *lumbi* as the object of a verb of movement were often used to suggest the sexual act. The movements were those of the pathic (male or female); hence the phrases could be substitutes for *criso* or (more often) *ceueo*. At Juv. 2.21, for example, *clunem agitant* suggests *ceuent* ('de uirtute locuti / clunem agitant. "ego te ceuentem, Sexte, uere-bor?" '). Movements in intercourse were employed by *scorta*, according to Lucretius (4.1274f.), as a means of avoiding conception and of being seductive. Wives had no need for such wiles (1268, 1277); for a complaint about a *uxor* who does not 'move', see Mart. 11.104.11. Sexual behaviour of this type clearly had a lascivious reputation. The same terminology was also used of dancing (note *Copa* 1f. 'Copa Syrisca, caput Graeca redimita mitella, / crispum sub crotalo docta mouere latus', Mart. 5.78.26ff. 'nec de Gadibus inprobis puellae / uibrabunt sine fine prurientes / lasciuos docili tremore lumbos'; cf. Ovid *Am.* 2.4.30, Petron. 23.3, Juv. 6.019, 11.164, *Priap.* 19.2f., 27.2).[2] There can be no doubt that a similarity was seen between the acts of *crisandi* and *ceuendi* on the one hand and dancing (note Don. Ter. *Eun.* 424). *Cinaedus* originally meant 'dancer' (note *CGL* V.654.7 'cynedi qui publicae clunem agitant id est saltatores uel pantomimi'; cf. Plaut. *Mil.* 668).[3] Musicians and dancers were often prostitutes.

For other examples of such phrases applied either to movements in the sexual act itself, or to seductive foreplay, see *Priap.* 83.23 'puer ... qui ... / iuuante uerset arte mobilem natem', and above, p. 48.

---

[1] See Preston, p. 42, *TLL* III.22.73ff. ('sensu obscaeno pro succumbere').

[2] See Courtney on Juv. 6.019. The dancers of Gades were particularly noted for lascivious dancing: see Juv. 11.164 and the passage of Martial cited.

[3] See W. Kroll, 'Kinaidos', *RE* XI.1.459f.; cf. Courtney, *loc. cit.*

Moueo itself (in the medio-passive) and some of its derivatives were applicable to sexual motions: Plaut. *Asin.* 788 'equi-
dem illam moueri gestio', Mart. 7.18.5f. 'mixtisque mouemur
/ inguinibus', Juv. 6.311 'inque uices equitant ac Luna teste
mouentur'. Cf. Ovid *Am.* 2.4.14 'spemque dat in molli mobilis
esse toro', 2.10.35 'at mihi contingat Veneris languescere motu', Lucr. 4.1268 'nec molles opus sunt motus uxoribus hilum',
Mart. 11.104.11 'nec motu dignaris opus nec uoce iuuare / nec
digitis'. It is pointless to compare *moueor* with κινέω, which is
usually equivalent to βινέω (and hence is not normal in the
middle: but see Aristoph. *Lys.* 227 προσκινήσομαι).

(xxiii) Some miscellaneous concomitant events

The bed might shake: Catull. 6.10f., Ovid *Am.* 3.14.26, Juv.
6.21f., 9.77f., Apul. *Met.* 2.7.[1]
Panting is an often mentioned accompaniment of intercourse: Juv. 6.37 'et lateri parcas nec quantum iussit anheles';
cf. Tib. 1.8.37, Petron. 87.8, and note *suspirat* at Lucr. 4.1192
and *suspiria* at *Anth. Lat.* 253.18.

(xxiv) Some miscellaneous consequences of the sexual act

Certain euphemisms allude to consequences effected by the
sexual act. The suggestive turn of phrase 'to make someone a
woman' was no doubt in use:[2] note *H.A.*, *Quad. Tyr.* 12.7 'omnes
tamen (uirgines), quod in me erat, mulieres intra dies quin-
decim reddidi'; cf. Cicero's joke, *ap.* Quint. 6.3.75 'ut Cicero
obiurgantibus, quod sexagenarius Publiliam uirginem duxis-
set: "cras mulier erit" inquit'.[3] Probably with this phrase in
mind, Varro coined the verb *muliero* to express an act of *pedicatio* perpetrated against a boy: *Men.* 205 'hic ephebum mu-
lierauit, hic ad moechada adulescentem cubiculum pudoris
primus polluit'.
'To deprive someone of virginity' is a common circumlocution
in polite prose. For *pudicitiam eripio*, see, e.g. Cic. *Mil.* 9 (of
pedicatio), and for *uirginitatem* as object of the same verb, see
Sen. *Contr.* 1.2.1. Cf. Cic. *Verr.* 1.9 'expugnatorem pudicitiae',

---

[1] See Courtney on Juv. 9.77.
[2] Cf. Luc. *Dial. Meretr.* 6.1 τὸ γυναῖκα γενέσθαι ἐκ παρθένου.
[3] For Christian Latin, see Opelt, 958.

Sen. *Contr.* 2.3.1 'expugnatam filiae pudicitiam' (military metaphors; see p. 159). The metaphor is akin to 'deflowering' at Sen. *Contr.* 1.2.12 'inlibatam uirginitatem decerpunt'. Laberius coined *depudico* as an equivalent of *pudicitiam eripio* (*inc. fab.* XVII Ribbeck, *ap.* Gell. 16.7.2), on the analogy of formations such as *dehonesto* and *deuirgino*. The latter is attested for the first time in the sense in question at Petron. 25.1 'cur non, quia bellissima occasio est, deuirginatur Pannychis nostra?'. Since the verb is in direct speech, it may already have been in use. *Virginitate priuauit* at Apul. *Met.* 6.23, though of a normal Latin type, was perhaps adopted by Apuleius in imitation of a favoured type of phrase in the Greek novel: cf. Xen. 2.5.7 παρθενίαν τὴν ἐμὴν ἀφανίσαι, Ach. Tat. 8.12.8 τὴν παρθενίαν ἔλυσε. The phrase *nodum uirginitatis eripere* is found 3 times in the Latin novel *Hist. Apoll. Tyr.* (pp. 2.12, 67.7, 73.5); cf. Paulus Silentiarius, *A.P.* 5.217.1 χρύσεος ἀψαύστοιο διέτμαγεν ἄμμα κορείας / Ζεύς. This expression probably derives from the undoing of the girdle.

An act subsequent to intercourse was washing (by the female). References to this were a means of suggesting that a sexual act had taken place: note Cic. *Cael.* 34 'ideo aquam adduxi ut ea tu inceste uterere'.[1]

As a consequence of intercourse the participants may be 'weary, worn out' (contrast the metaphors of 'killing, dying', above, p. 159). Verbs of wearying were sometimes substituted for *futuo* or *pedico*. For *lasso* see Tib. 1.9.55, Juv. 6.130, *H.A.*, *Maxim.* 4.7 (= *pedico*), and for *fatigo*, *Priap.* 26.3 (with female subject); cf. *perago* at *Priap.* 34.4 (also with female subject). For other words of this semantic field in sexual contexts, see *lassus* at Plaut. *Asin.* 873, Ovid *Am.* 1.5.25, 3.7.80, 3.11.13, Apul. *Met.* 2.17, *lassitudo* at Apul. *Met.* 2.17, *fessus* at Mart. 9.67.3, and *confectus* at *Priap.* 26.8. On *attriti* at Petron. 81.6, see above, p. 184.

(xxv) 'Pleasure', etc.

I move on to some 'persuasive' euphemisms.

Deliciae, 'diversions, allurements, pleasures', was a vogue usage among the youth of Cicero's day for extra-marital affairs: see Cic. *Cael.* 44 'deliciae quae uocantur'. It was deter-

---

[1] See Brandt, *Am.* 3.7.84, *Ars* 3.96.

iorating in tone. There is a note of disapproval in Cicero's remark, and the uncle of Gellius was in the habit of castigating *deliciae*: Catull. 74.1f. 'Gellius audierat patruom obiurgare solere, / si quis delicias diceret aut faceret'. Catullus, on the other hand, belonged to the group in which *deliciae* was used persuasively: note 45.24, 'uno in Septimio fidelis Acme / facit delicias', for a neutral example.[1] See further Prop. 2.15.2, Sen. *Contr.* 7.6.7, Apul. *Met.* 9.16.

Delecto was used of the pleasure which the man gives to the woman, as in a freedman's speech at Petron. 45.7 'deprehensus est, cum dominam suam delectaretur'. The idiom is both self-effacing, in that no mention is made of the fact that one of the man's motives was to obtain pleasure himself, and boastful, in that the pleasure of the female by implication reflects the virility of the man. The male orientation of the euphemism can be paralleled elsewhere in Petronius. At 75.11 *satis facio* (in a speech by Trimalchio) is a blatant boast ('ego tamen et ipsimae [dominae] satis faciebam'; Trimalchio continues, 'scitis quid dicam: taceo, quia non sum de gloriosis'). It is also appropriate to the relative social status of the participants that the *domina* should allegedly receive the pleasure, and the *seruus* merely serve as its instrument, as if his own desires were irrelevant. And at 87.1 ('rogare coepi ephebum ut reuerteretur in gratiam mecum, [id est] ut pateretur satis fieri sibi, et cetera quae libido distenta dictat') *satis fieri sibi* is hypocritical, since the *pedicator* was traditionally believed to obtain more pleasure than the *pedicatus*. What Eumolpus means is that he wishes to satisfy himself, but he has stressed the altruism of his motives. For *delecto*, see further *Rhet. Her.* 4.45, Mart. 1.34.3, Apul. *Met.* 8.7, 10.22; cf. Juv. 6.367.

For the man 'taking' pleasure, see (e.g.) the phrases containing *uoluptas* at Plaut. *Amph.* 114, Ter. *Hec.* 69, Arnob. *Nat.* 5.9. Here the role of the woman as an instrument of the pleasure might seem to be ignored. On the other hand at Hor. *Carm.* 3.6.27f. ('neque eligit / cui donet inpermissa raptim / gaudia luminibus remotis') it is the woman who gives pleasure. *Voluptas* (Lucr. 4.1263, Ovid *Am.* 1.10.35, *Met.* 4.327, Sen. *Contr.* 2.5.14) and *gaudium* (Catull. 61.110, Tib. 2.1.12, Ovid

---

[1] See the remarks of C. J. Fordyce, *Catullus, a Commentary* (Oxford, 1961), on 50.3.

Am. 3.7.63) commonly have a sexual implication.[1] See also *fruor* at Plaut. *Asin.* 918, Ovid *Am.* 2.9b.46, *Priap.* 50.5. Cf. ἀπολαύω (Luc. *Am.* 3, Heliod. 1.15.4), τέρπομαι, of the man (Dioscorides, *A.P.* 5.54.2, Meleager, *A.P.* 5.160.2) or the woman (anon., *A.P.* 5.201.2).

Vtor can be compared with *fruor*. See Plaut. *Pers.* 128 'numquam edepol quoiquam etiam utendam dedi' (here the speaker takes an earlier innocent remark in a sexual sense), ps.-Acron, Hor. *Epist.* 1.17.36 'Aristippus etiam hac fama illo perductus est, et usus Laide non etiam amore eius deuinctus est'. Cf. *usura* at Plaut. *Amph.* 108 'is amare occepit Alcumenam clam uirum / usuramque eiius corporis cepit sibi, / et grauidam fecit is eam compressu suo' (a passage which shows the physical reference of the usage). In the same play *uxor usuraria* is used of Alcmena in her dealings with Jupiter (498, 980). *Vsurarius* was employed of a slave one had the use of, but did not own (*Dig.* 7.8.14). Cf. *abutor* at Vulg. *Gen.* 19.8 (LXX χρᾶσθε), 34.31.[2] Compare χράομαι at (e.g.) Ach. Tat. 6.15.2.

(xxvi) 'Violence, corruption, defilement', etc.

A sexual act may be emotively spoken of as an act of violence or corruption, even if it is not regarded as such by its perpetrator (or even victim). Such descriptions are nevertheless euphemistic, since they do not specify the nature of the violence or corruption. The weakening of the euphemism into a means of expressing an act containing no real hostility can be seen at *CIL* IV.10694 'Iualias accepit uim hila(re). Sturnus am(ator?)' (if the reading is correct), and Petron. 140.11 'accessi temptaturus an pateretur *iniuriam*. nec se reiciebat a blanditiis doctissimus puer' (note *blanditiis*). The attitude that women enjoy sexual violence (Ovid *Ars* 1.673 'uim licet appelles: grata est uis ista puellis'; cf. ps.-Ambros. *Laps. Virg.* 12) can cause an emotive designation to be regarded as an exaggeration. Hence the designation becomes subject to weakening.

Variations of phraseology from writer to writer are due in part to variations of personal taste, and in part to the need for

---

[1] See Brandt, *Am.* 3.7.63.
[2] See *TLL* I.241.68ff.

constant changes of terminology as established expressions lose force. Whereas, for example, Terence uses the verb *uitio* 6 times (usually with *uirginem* as object), and also circumlocutions with *uitium* (4 times), Plautus employs circumlocutions with *uitium* (e.g. *Amph.* 811), but not *uitio*. Some other words and expressions are *uiolo* (Varro *Ling.* 6.80, Cic. *Fam.* 9.22.1), *corrumpo* (Ter. *Heaut.* 231, Sen. *Contr.* 1.7.4),[1] *facio, affero uim* (*Pall. inc. inc.* 2 Ribbeck, Cic. *Verr.* 1.67, Sen. *Contr.* 1.2.2; cf. βιασμός at Men. *Epitr.* 453; note too Men. *Her.* 79), *facio iniuriam* (Plautus onwards),[2] *inquino* (Petron. 25.5), *polluo* (Sen. *Contr.* 4.7, ps.-Ambros. *Laps. Virg.* 13, 39), *temero* (ps.-Ambros. *Laps. Virg.* 39). *Dehonesto* is used of a symbolic violation at Aug. *Ciu.* 7.24. *Contamino*, which is rare but classical (e.g. Sen. *Contr.* 7.6.16),[3] had a late variant *attamino* (Justin 21.3.4, Aurel. Vict. *Caes.* 16.2, ps.-Tert. *Execr.* 5). At Suet. *Nero* 35.4 ('quem cum ante mortem per uim conspurcasset: "eat nunc" inquit "mater mea et successorem meum osculetur" ') *conspurco* refers to *irrumatio*.[4] I should not claim that the above list is at all exhaustive.

Verbs meaning 'defile' and the like are not exclusively used of the aggressor's violation of an unwilling victim. In the terminology of some moralisers (e.g. Christians in late antiquity) a person who engages willingly in intercourse may 'defile himself' (see, e.g. the use of *maculo* at Cypr. *Epist.* 13.5, Aug. *Ciu.* 1.19). For the 'defilement' suffered by the partners in a sexual act, cf. Plaut. *Truc.* 381 'uerum tempestas quondam, dum uixi, fuit / quom inter nos *sordebamus* alter de altero'.[5] Conversely one who abstains from intercourse may be 'pure': note Plaut. *Asin.* 807 'tot noctes reddat *spurcas* quot *pure* habuerit'. What is considered 'impure' may vary from time to time. When Martial uses *purus* suggestively (with 'impurity' in mind) he is usually alluding to oral sex (6.66.5, 9.67.7, 14.70.2; cf. 9.63.2, in reference to *pedicatio*).

---

[1] See *TLL* IV.1056.35ff. The verb is common with *uirgo, uxor* and *matrona* as object. It is often used in prose (e.g. Seneca the Elder), but not by Cicero in this sense.

[2] See *TLL* VII.1.1670.67ff.

[3] *TLL* IV.630.82ff.

[4] See Housman, *Classical Papers*, p. 733.

[5] See *TLL* VII.1.1813.66ff., reporting E. Fraenkel. For the use of *de* here (*alter de altero*), cf. *Curc.* 51 'tam *a me* pudica est'.

(xxvii) 'Insult', etc.

Insulto is used of different types of insulting or humiliating sexual act. The anonymous senator *ap.* Suet. *Iul.* 22.2 who picked up Caesar's phrase 'insultaturum omnium capitibus' (for which see Virg. *Aen.* 8.570) made it refer to *irrumatio*: 'ac negante quodam per contumeliam facile hoc ulli feminae fore'. Cf. Arnob. *Nat.* 2.45 'insultarent uirginibus'. At Suet. *Tib.* 45 *inludo* is used exactly as *insulto* at *Iul.* 22.2: 'feminarum . . . capitibus . . . inludere'. Cf. Tac. *Ann.* 13.17 'tradunt plerique eorum temporum scriptores crebris ante exitium diebus inlusum isse pueritiae Britannici Neronem' (of *pedicatio*), 15.72 (of *fututio*). See further Min. Fel. *Oct.* 25.3.[1]

Terence's use of *ludificor* at *Eun.* 645 'quin etiam insuper scelus, postquam ludificatust uirginem . . .' may have been a rendition of ὑβρίζειν (cf. Men. *Sam.* 508). *Ludificor* achieved no currency.[2] Note Donatus' comment on the implication of the verb: 'et mire "ludificatus" potius quam "complexus est" aut tale aliquid, quod amorem indicaret'.

(xxviii) 'Harass, annoy, disturb'

This is presumably the force of *sollicito* at C. Gracchus *Orat.* frg. 27 'si ulla meretrix domum meam introiuit aut cuiusquam seruulus propter me sollicitatus est'. Cf. *uexo* at Petron. 139.1 'torum frequenti tractatione uexaui, amoris mei quasi quandam imaginem' (here the bed is treated as if it were the lover; cf. Auson. *Epigr.* 106.15, p. 351 P.), Mart. 11.81.1 'cum sene communem uexat spado Dindymus Aeglen / et iacet in medio sicca puella toro' (cf. 8.46.7, of the female 'working on' the male). In a few places *uexo* seems to suggest agitated but futile amatory activity.

(xxix) 'Disgrace'

Stuprum originally meant 'disgrace' in general, as Festus demonstrates: p. 418 'stuprum pro turpitudine antiquos dixisse apparet in Nelei carmine: "foede stupreque castigor cotidie" '. See, e.g. Naev. *Pun.* 47 (quoted by Festus) 'sin illos deserant fortissimos uiros, / magnum stuprum populo fieri per gentis'.

---

[1] For *insulto*, see *TLL* VII.1.2044.25f., and for *illudo*, *TLL* VII.1. 389.76ff.
[2] See *TLL* VII.2.1767.64ff.

But it came to be specialised of a sexual disgrace,[1] i.e. an illicit
sexual act, whether an adulterous liaison or a forcible violation
(as distinct from an act committed with a prostitute). The act
might be homosexual (Sen. *Contr.* 3.8 tit.) or heterosexual.
The word is not necessarily used of a violation perpetrated
against the will of the victim. In a context such as Sen. *Contr.*
6.8 'incesta est etiam sine stupro quae cupit stuprum', 'a
woman is unchaste if she wants sex, even if she has not had
it' (Winterbottom), or Sall. *Cat.* 23.3 'erat ei cum Fuluia . . .
stupri uetus consuetudo', it implies disapproval on the part of
the user. But often it denotes a forcible violation (e.g. Sall.
Hist. frg. 3.98, Tac. *Ann.* 14.31). The range of sexual acts
which might be described thus was unlimited: note Tac. *Ann.*
16.19 'nouitatem cuiusque stupri perscripsit'. The example at
Col. 7.6.3 shows no weakening of the evaluative sense, since
Columella is describing incestuous behaviour by a young goat:
'dum adhuc uberibus alitur, matrem stupro superuenit'. Various derivatives are attested (*stupro, constupro, stuprator*).

Probrum also tended to be specialised in this way, but the
general sense was not lost. For the general meaning, see Plaut.
Truc. 459, Cic. *S. Rosc.* 48, and for the sexual (already in early
Latin), Cato *Orat.* frg. 221 'si cum alieno uiro probri quid fecit',
Caecil. 224 'inhoneste honestam grauidauit probro', Cic. *Phil.*
2.99. The sexual sense predominates in Plautus.

For *turpitudo* of a sexual misdemeanour, see ps.-Ambros.
Laps. Virg. 21 'occulta et furtiua turpitudine constupratur' (cf.
Aug. *Ciu.* 1.19). Note too Plaut. *Amph.* 883 'ita me probri, /
stupri, *dedecoris* a uiro argutam meo!' (cf. 898; cf. αἰσχύνη at
Men. *Dysc.* 243), ps.-Ambros. *Laps. Virg.* 15 'non sorores hoc
ex te dedecus expectabant'. The 'disgrace' in the last two passages is that of the female; contrast, for example, Caecil. 224
above, where the disgraceful act is that of the male. It is
typical of such euphemisms that they may assign the disgrace
to either partner, in accordance with the outlook of the
speaker.

[1] The specialisation is already apparent in Plautus.

(xxx) *Pecco*, etc.

Pecco was used of illicit sex, as at Mart. 1.34.2 'apertis, Lesbia, semper / liminibus peccas nec tua furta tegis'. Cf. Hor. *Serm.* 1.2.63, Ovid *Ars* 2.558.[1] The example at Mart. 3.85.2 ('non hac peccatum est parte, marite, tibi') is physically more explicit than most. Various derivatives also take on a sexual sense occasionally (e.g. *peccatum* at Aug. *Ciu.* 1.18, *peccator* at ps.-Tert. *Execr.* 6). Cf. ἐξαμαρτάνω at Men. *Dysc.* 290. Sometimes even stronger language is used: note ps.-Ambros. *Laps. Virg.* 26 'furtiuum *scelus* deduxit in publicum'.

(xxxi) Names of peoples

It is a common habit to ascribe to foreign peoples different vices. Hence in Greek a number of verbs derived from proper names were coined to describe various types of sexual behaviour (e.g. λεσβιάζειν, φοινικίζειν). Latin speakers too attached vices to neighbouring peoples, as to the Oscans (Porph. on Hor. *Serm.* 1.5.62, Fest. p. 204), but they do not seem to have coined verbs like those above. But a comparable phrase is found in a speech of Trimalchio, Petron. 63.3 'a puero uitam Chiam gessi' (= 'I submitted to *pedicatio*'). The Chians were notorious for pathic behaviour. The phrase can be classified as a metonymy, since the people in question were linked with the vice. The link is in this case not one of temporal concomitance, as in most of the above euphemisms.

4. Some elliptical euphemisms

An indelicate verb or noun can be omitted (a sentence may, for example, be broken off: aposiopesis), or replaced by a pronoun, pro-verb or equivalent. I shall not deal with elliptical euphemisms systematically here, because I have discussed the matter elsewhere. The distinction between metonymy and ellipse is often a fine one; some of the euphemisms in the preceding section could be interpreted as lacking an indelicate complement (e.g. *duco, ire ad*).

---

[1] See Nisbet and Hubbard I on Hor. *Carm.* 1.27.17.

(i) *Res*

For *res* used of intercourse, see Varro *Men.* 369 'si non plus
testiculorum offenderis quam in castrato pecore in Apulia,
uincor non esse masculum ad rem'; cf. Marc. Emp. 33.73 're
peracta'.[1] The more specific *Veneris res* at Lucr. 2.173, 5.848
can be compared with Theocr. *Epigr.* 4.4 (*A.P.* 9.437) Κύπριδος
ἔργα. *Res* is so vague that it could have varying implications.
At Caes. *Gall.* 6.21.5 ('intra annum uero uicesimum feminae
notitiam habuisse in turpissimis habent rebus; *cuius rei*
nulla est occultatio, quod et promiscue in fluminibus per-
luuntur . . .') *cuius rei* certainly includes intercourse, but the
following clauses suggest that it means, rather more generally,
'sexual matters'. And at Salv. *Gub.* 7.72 ('adeo omnia paene
compita, omnes uias aut quasi foueae libidinum interciderant
aut quasi retia praetexebant, ut etiam, qui *ab hac re* penitus
abhorrerent, tamen uitare uix possent')[2] *haec res* expresses the
outward signs of prostitution.

Rem habere, 'have intercourse (with a prostitute)' is different: it is an expression from commerce (= 'have dealings with'):
e.g. Plaut. *Bacch.* 564 'tibi non erat meretricum aliarum Ath-
enis copia / quibuscum haberes rem' (cf. Ter. *Eun.* 138); for
synonymous expressions, see Plaut. *Truc.* 94 'cum ea quoque
etiam mihi fuit commercium', Ter. *Heaut.* 388 'nos, quibuscum
est res, non sinunt'.[3] Contrast Mart. 5.61.14 'res uxoris agit?
res ullas crispulus iste? / res non uxoris, res agit iste tuas' (the
adulterer is 'conducting the business' of the husband, with the
wife). Different again is Ter. *Eun.* 741f., where in the proverbial *uerba* / *res* opposition *res* is given a sexual force: 'usque
adeo ego illi(u)s ferre possum ineptiam et magnifica *uerba*, /
uerba dum sint; uerum enim si ad *rem* conferentur, uapulabit'
(cf. 740 'atqui si illam digito attigerit uno . . .').

In Greek note τὸ θεῖον χρῆμα in the Cologne fragment of
Archilochus (10).[4] At Adaeus, *A.P.* 10.20.1 ἤν τινα καλὸν ἴδῃς,
εὐθὺς τὸ πρᾶγμα κροτείσθω ('let the matter be instantly ham-
mered into shape') an expression of proverbial type has been

[1] Other examples can be found in Adams, 'Euphemism', pp.126f. See further
Heraeus, *Die Sprache des Petronius und die Glossen*, p. 34 = *Kleine Schriften*
(cited above, p. 42, n. 4), pp. 116f.; cf. Preston, p. 35, n. 57.
[2] Cited by Opelt, 957.
[3] See further Preston, p. 35.
[4] See R. Merkelbach and M. L. West, *ZPE* 14 (1974), pp. 97ff., with West *ad
loc.* (p. 105).

given a sexual implication, with πρᾶγμα suggestive of homosexual intercourse.

(ii) *Facio*

Facio ('do (it)') is frequently substituted for indelicate verbs in
Latin (cf. πράττειν at Aeschin. *in Timarch.* 160, δρᾶν at Strato,
A.P. 12.210.1).[1] Its currency in ordinary speech is shown by its
use three times in freedmen's speeches in the *Cena Trimalchionis* of Petronius of the excretory functions (47.4, 62.4,
66.2), and once of a sexual act (45.8: see below). For excretion,
see further Plaut. *Pseud.* 1178 'etiamne – facere solitun es –
scin quid loquar' (or is the reference to masturbation?). In
sexual senses *facio* was used very loosely. At Mart. 1.46.1 it
expresses the active part in homosexual intercourse ('propero,
fac si facis'), whereas at Petron. 45.8 it seems to be used of the
passive role ('quid seruus peccauit, qui coactus est facere?'
(= *pedicationem pati*)). At Ovid *Am.* 3.4.4 ('quae, quia non
liceat, non facit, illa facit') the female is subject (cf. Lucr.
4.1195), but the verb could also be substituted for *futuo* or
pedico (of the male) (e.g. Tert. *Nat.* 1.16.4).

(iii) *Factum*

At Juv. 6.271 ('cum simulat gemitus occulti conscia facti')
factum is used suggestively of a misdemeanour of a sexual
kind (cf. 279 'iacet in serui complexibus aut equitis'), but in
classical Latin the noun was not regularly specialised.[2] Later
factum (of intercourse) enjoyed a literary vogue. Note anon.,
Baucis et Traso 13 'spondet . . . / uirginis alloquium, contactus,
oscula, factum'. Here intercourse is presented as the culmi-
nating event in a scale of amatory activities, which seems to
derive from Donatus, Ter. *Eun.* 640 (quoted above, p. 185).
The terminology in the two passages is almost identical, except
that *coitus* has been replaced by *factum*. See further *Pamphilus*
695 (with a demonstrative). *Fortia facta* (with a sexual implication) at Maxim. *Eleg.* 5.136 is a military metaphor ('brave
deeds', of aggressive sexuality).

[1] See further Opelt, 951. For bibliography on *facio*, see Adams, 'Euphemism',
p. 123, n. 4. A collection of examples can be found at *TLL* VI.1.121.40ff.
[2] At Ter. *Eun.* 954 'eam istic uitiauit miser. / ille ubi *id* resciuit *factum* frater
. . .', *factum* is verbal.

(iv) *Actus*

For the verbal use of *ago* in a sexual context, see Juv. 6.58 'nil actum in montibus' ('no sexual act was committed in the mountains'). The noun *actus* usually has a specifying adjective when it is applied to intercourse: e.g. ps.-Acron Hor. *Serm.* 1.2.35 'subigitare, ut habemus in Terentio de ipso actu turpi'; cf. Apul. *Plat.* 2.6 (*uoluptarius*), ps.-Ambros. *Laps. Virg.* 22 (*ignominiosus*), Oribas. *Syn.* 1.7 Aa, p. 40.4 Mørland (*uenerius*). But at Maxim. *Eleg.* 5.135 ('non tibi semper iners, non mollis conuenit actus, / mixtaque sunt ludis fortia facta tuis') *actus* (= 'a sexual act') is not pinned down to the sexual sphere by its adjectives; cf. Arnob. *Nat.* 5.21 'redit ad prioris actus'.

5. Terminology appropriate to animals

Latin, like other languages, had sets of words for parts of the animal anatomy (e.g. *armus, pellis, corium, ungula, suffrago, gamba, corona*), for animal colours (particularly of the horse: see *Mul. Chir.* 960), and for certain animal bodily functions (e.g. *subare, catulio*; cf. the various terms indicating the noises made by different animals). The sexual behaviour of animals also attracted special terms. A list of the appropriate verbs in Greek is given by Pollux, 5.92: καὶ μὴν τὸ μίγνυσθαι ἐπὶ μὲν τῶν ἀλόγων βαίνειν, ἐπιβαίνειν, ὀχεύειν, βιβάζειν, συνδυάζειν, συνδυάζεσθαι, ἐπάγεσθαι, καὶ ἐπὶ ὄνων ἴδιον τὸ ὀνοβατεῖν.[1] It is convenient to collect the Latin material in one section, though some terms are metaphorical, others metonymies. Words proper to animals are typically transferred to humans with abusive intent (cf. βαίνω, n. 1). Examples will be given below.

Verbs of climbing had a particular applicability to mounting by animals. The first sexual example of *scando* is in a Plautine joke (*Pseud.* 23 'ut opinor, quaerunt litterae hae sibi liberos: / alia aliam scandit'), but cf. Laber. 56 (?) 'scando una exoleto patienti in catulientem lupam' (if *lupa* means 'prostitute', terminology appropriate to animals may be used: cf. *catulientem*), Col. 6.37.10 'ne femina conluctari aut admissario ascendenti

---

[1] With this last verb, compare Meleager's coinage ἀνδροβατεῖν, *A.P.* 5.208.2. For βατέω, which is not given by Pollux, see Shipp, pp. 137f. See also Shipp, pp. 126f. on βαίνω, used in classical Greek of animals mounting, but showing a tendency later to be used as an equivalent of βινέω.

auertere se possit', *ibid.* 'ut . . . facilem sui tergoris *ascensum* ab editiore parte minori quadrupedi praebeat', Apul. *Met.* 7.21 'festiuus hic amasio humo sordida prostratam mulierem ibidem incoram omnium gestiebat inscendere' (of the ass), Vulg. *Gen.* 30.41 'igitur quando primo tempore ascendebantur oues'. ἀναβαίνω is used of stallions at Hdt. 1.192.3 (contrast Aristoph. frg. 329 ἀναβῆναι τὴν γυναῖκα βούλομαι). For ἐπιβαίνω, see above. ἐπιβαίνω could also be used of boarding a ship; this use is transferred metaphorically to the male role by Antiphilus, *A.P.* 9.415.7.

Salio was used of the male animal mounting, or, in the passive, of the female mounted: for the active, see Varro *Rust.* 2.4.8 'uerris octo mensum incipit salire', and for the passive, *Rust.* 2.2.14 'neque pati oportet minores quam bimas saliri' (cf. Ovid *Ars* 2.485). The compound *adsilio* is quoted by the *TLL* only from Col. 6.37.9 'adsilientem admissarium calcibus proturbat'. *Salax* (< *salio*) was applied predominantly to animals (indicating a desire to·mount): e.g. Varro *Rust.* 3.9.5, Ovid *Fast.* 4.771, Col. 7.9.1, 8.2.9, 8.2.12; cf. 8.2.13, 8.11.5 *salacitas*. Transferred to men (or gods) *salax* was pejorative or implied sexual excess: so *Priap.* 34.1 'deo salaci'. It has so far lost its primary sense at *Priap.* 26.5 that it is used of females: 'totis mihi noctibus fatigant / uicinae sine fine prurientes / uernis passeribus salaciores'.

The possibility that *insilio* at Pompon. 40 ('et ubi insilui in coleatum eculeum, ibi tolutim tortor') refers to a sexual act must be treated with caution. It is typically the male *qui salit* (Plin. *Nat.* 10.160 refers to a popular belief, according to which female doves sometimes adopt the male role), but here it would have to be the male (*equus*) who was mounted. Perhaps the 'rider' was another male (cf. Petron. 24.4).

The frequency of *ineo* in veterinary writers and contexts is such that it must have been almost a technical term of veterinarians.[1] For the use *de hominibus*, see p. 190.

Admitto (cf. βιβάζω) was the technical term for the bringing of one animal to the other (usually the male to the female, but note Varro *Rust.* 2.2.14, 2.4.7, Plin. *Nat.* 10.180), with an implied or expressed human agent (see Varro *Rust.* 2.7.8, where the groom is agent).[2] Two common derivatives are *ad-*

---

[1] See *TLL* VII.1.1296.37ff.
[2] See *TLL* I.751.60ff. for examples.

missarius ('stallion') and *admissura*, the verbal noun for the
act of admitting the male. Occasionally a loose use of a word
of this root brings it close to the sense '*futuo, fututio*' (with the
human agent forgotten), as in the pleonastic sentence *Mul.
Chir.* 753 'nec hi admittendi non erunt ad admissuram' (=
fututionem). Cf. *Mul. Chir.* 751 'hi quidem nec admittere de-
bent, qui uno testiculo erunt' (the use of the active instead of
the expected passive virtually gives *admittere* the meaning
'*futuere*'), Veg. *Mul.* 3.7.3 'eo anno, quo admissum faciunt, non
sit ei uena laxanda' (the *admissarii* are subject of *faciunt*). At
Juv. 6.329 the cry 'iam fas est, admitte uiros' is ascribed pejoratively to women, who by implication look upon *uiri* as
mere stallions. Cf. Sen. *N.Q.* 1.16.5 'spectabat admissos sibi
pariter in omnia uiros'. There is no question here of a third
party acting as agent: 'admitted to him' = 'whom he admitted
to himself'. At Ovid *Ars* 2.732 there is a mixture of metaphors:
'admisso subdere calcar equo'. The female is spoken of as rider,
but *admisso* is appropriate to mating.[1] For *admissarius* used
derogatively of a human *fututor* (or *pedicator*), see Plaut. *Mil.*
1112, Cic. *Pis.* 69, Sen. *N.Q.* 1.16.2, *Anth. Lat.* 149.9.

Various occasional synonyms of *admitto* turn up in the veterinary language: e.g. *applico* (*Mul. Chir.* 744), *impono* (Col.
6.27.10, *Mul. Chir.* 743–5; cf. Juv. 6.334 'imposito clunem sum-
mittat asello'),[2] *mitto = immitto* (*Mul. Chir.* 752), *admoueo*
(Col. 6.37.9) and *iniungo* (Col. 6.27.3, 6.37.2).

Superuenio was used of the male animal ('cover'; cf. ὀχεύω),
without a human agent implied: e.g. Col. 6.24.3, 7.6.3. *Impleo*
was applied particularly to insemination by the male animal.[3]
For the word transferred to humans or gods, see Ovid *Met.*
6.111, 11.265, Luc. 8.409, Tert. *Ieiun.* 7.6.

It is a milder form of imagery when animal terminology of
a non-sexual kind is applied metaphorically to humans with
various types of sexual implications. *Subacta* at Hor. *Carm.*
2.5.1, as we have seen (p. 155), is a metaphor from the breaking in of animals. For *ferre iugum* (of the female role) in the
same passage, see Plaut. *Curc.* 50ff. 'iamne ea fert iugum? /
PH. tam a me pudica est quasi soror mea sit, nisi / si est

---

[1] *CIL* IV.8939 'Maritimus cunnu linget a(ssibus) IIII, uirgines ammittit' has
a different sexual use of *admitto*.

[2] For *impono*, see *TLL* VII.1.652.32ff.

[3] For examples *de bestiis*, see *TLL* VII.1.633.67ff.

osçulando quippiam inpudicior', Catull. 68.118 'indomitam ferre iugum docuit'.[1]

6. *Masturbor* and its synonyms

Various verbs used of masturbation have been mentioned already: *frico* (pp. 146 n. 1, 184), *sollicito* (p. 184), *tango* (p. 186), *tracto* (p. 186), *contrecto* (p. 186), *truso*, *trudo* (p. 146 n. 1), *tero* (p. 183), *haereo* (p. 181), *deglubo*, *glubo* (?), *rado* (?) (p. 168); cf. p. 122 on *manus fututrix*, p. 153 on *molo*, and p. 161 on *thalassionem indico manibus libidinosis*. Of these *frico* was probably in colloquial or vulgar use; it tends to have an idiomatic dative complement, and it was capable of being used elliptically (with *mentula* deleted). *Tracto* and *sollicito* were also common; it can be conjectured, but not proved, that they were more respectable in tone than *frico*. The status of *(de)glubo* and *trudo* / *truso* is impossible to determine. The other words were probably only occasional euphemisms for the act. Female masturbation is rarely mentioned. *(De)glubo* and *trudo* would have been appropriate only to the male, but the other words were probably not restricted to either a male or female object (note *frico* at *CIL* X.4483 and *tango* at Ovid *Ars* 2.713).

Various other isolated euphemisms are attested. *Foueo* was often used of embracing, not necessarily of a sexual kind.[2] At Tib. 1.6.6 ('iam Delia furtim / nescio quem tacita callida nocte fouet') the context is erotic; at *Priap.* 83.25 the verb is specifically used of masturbation: 'puella nec iocosa te leui manu / fouebit'. For *palpo* of masturbation, see Juv. 10.206 'et, quamuis tota palpetur nocte, iacebit', Arnob. *Nat.* 5.9 'palpabat res intimas'. *Digitum intingo* at Apul. *Met.* 2.7 ('beatus, cui permiseris illuc digitum intingere') is a double entendre perhaps taken from the Greek version (cf. ἐνεβάψατο at ps.-Luc. *Asinus*

---

[1] See Nisbet and Hubbard II on Hor. *Carm.* 2.5.1. I am at a loss to understand why Nisbet and Hubbard (p. 78) find 'crudity' in the imagery. The feminist (?) remark (*loc. cit.*) that 'in a male-dominated world the consequences of this view [i.e. that 'the sexual instincts of men and beasts are essentially the same'] were applied particularly to women' are also puzzling. It is admitted that the poet may see 'himself sometimes as the male animal'. The comparison is scarcely flattering to a man. In various passages cited above the man is likened pejoratively to an animal.

[2] *TLL* VI.1.1219.32ff.

6). Juvenal's 'praeputia ducit' (6.238) describes in literal terms the type of act expressed metaphorically by *excorio* (cf. *deglubo*) in the *spurcum additamentum* at Apul. *Met.* 10.21 'hastam mei inguinis niuei spurci<ti>ei pluscule excoria<n>s emundauit'. *Emundo* here can be compared with the metaphorical *exmucco* at *CIL* IV.1391 'Veneria Maximo mentla exmuccaut per uindemia tota'. It is not specified by what means Veneria achieved her result.

In addition to the above verbs there are constant circumlocutions and suggestive phrases, particularly in epigram, containing *digitus, manus* or an equivalent. It seems to have been a characteristic of popular sexual humour in Latin to allude obliquely to masturbation by such means. The 'left hand' and the *amica manus* were particularly suggestive of the act. In many cultures the left hand is regarded as the 'unclean' hand, used for sexual and excretory purposes.[1] See Lucil. 307 'at laeua lacrimas muttoni absterget amica', Ovid *Ars* 2.706 'nec manus in lecto laeua iacebit iners', Mart. 9.41.1f. 'paelice laeua / uteris et Veneri seruit amica manus', 11.73.4 'succurrit pro te saepe sinistra mihi', *Priap.* 33.6 'fiet amica manus' (contrast Mart. 11.29.1 'languida cum uetula tractare uirilia *dextra*'; here a woman performs the *tractatio*). With 'seruit amica manus' and 'succurrit . . . sinistra' above, cf. Mart. 2.43.14 'mihi succurrit pro Ganymede manus'. The phrase may have been idiomatic. For other circumlocutions in Martial, see 6.23.3 'manibus blandis . . . instes', 9.41.8 'mandasset manibus gaudia foeda suis', 11.22.6 'et faciunt digiti praecipitantque uirum', 11.29.8 'nil opus est digitis' (cf. 1.92.3), 11.104.11f. 'nec uoce iuuare / nec digitis'.

It remains to mention *masturbor*, which clearly means 'masturbate' at Mart. 9.41.7 'omnia perdiderat si masturbatus uterque / mandasset manibus gaudia foeda suis' and 11.104.13 'masturbabantur Phrygii post ostia serui, / Hectoreo quotiens sederat uxor equo' (cf. *masturbator* at 14.203.2). The etymology of *masturbor* is a mystery, though there has been some acceptance for the derivation from *man-* + *stuprare*, with the second element remodelled on the analogy of *turbare*.[2] A recent

---

[1] See Robert Hertz, 'The pre-eminence of the right hand: a study in religious polarity', transl. by R. Needham, in R. Needham (ed.), *Right and Left, Essays on Dual Symbolic Classification* (Chicago and London, 1973), p. 17, with n. 77.

[2] For a collection of etymologies, see Bader, *La formation des composés nominaux du latin* (cited above, p. 73, n. 1), p. 261, n. 25.

attempt by Judith P. Hallett[1] to derive the verb from *mas* (allegedly used in an unattested sense 'male genitalia') + *turbare* is unconvincing, and beset by mistakes of a phonological and morphological kind. Hallett's arguments against *man-* as the first element of the compound are quite unacceptable. It is not true to say (p. 303) that in compounds in which *man-* is instrumental it shows a *-u* or *-i* before the second element (cf. *manceps*, 'the one who takes in hand'); in various places Hallett seems to be under the impression that the first element of a nominal compound is inflected like the components of a sentence. There was a consonant stem *man-* (alongside *manu-*) which stands as the first element of various old compounds, regardless of its syntactic function. It is seen clearly in *mancus, mansues* ('accustomed to the hand'; *man-* here has dative function), *mantele, malluuiae* (with accusative function). Indeed in the small class of compounds which show a consonant stem directly attached to a second element, *man-* is particularly well represented;[2] *mas-* is not represented at all. If *man-* is the first element, to explain the *s-* spelling one has to posit a second element with initial *s* + consonant (such as *stuprare*). Hallett's notion that, on the analogy of *mansuescere*, a 'union of *manus* and *stuprare* should spawn *manstuprare' (p. 302) is ludicrous. In threefold groups of consonants of which the second was *s*, the normal development was for the first to be assimilated to the *s* and lost, with compensatory lengthening (e.g. *subsisto* but *subs-capio > *suscipio*).[3] The contrast *mansuescere* / *mastuprare would be perfectly regular.

Hallett adduces not an iota of evidence for *mas* = 'male genitalia'. The claim that in *emasculare* 'the connection between *mas* and the masculine member [is] notably manifest' (p. 304) is a red herring. Just as *erudio* is a derivative of the adjective *rudis*, with a prefix which derives its function from the completive aspect of various prepositional prefixes in Latin (lit. 'bring to an end the state of being *rudis*'), so *emasculare* is a derivative of the adjective *masculus* (= 'bring to an end the state of being male'). It is not a direct derivative of *mas*, and carries no notion of 'removing the *mas*'.

It is the second element of the compound which is the more

---

[1] *Glotta* 54 (1976), pp. 292ff.

[2] See Bader, pp. 14f.

[3] See, for example, P. Monteil, *Éléments de phonétique et de morphologie du latin* (Paris, 1974), p. 82.

problematical. *Stuprare* is the best candidate so far put forward, but it does not altogether carry conviction (though not for the bizarre reasons presented by Hallett, p. 299). But it is as certain as can be that *man-* furnishes the first part of the compound. The spelling *mas-* is phonetically explicable. The derivation is morphologically plausible, since *man-* was a productive formant of compounds; and it is semantically attractive, because *manus* commonly has a place in references to masturbation (see above). The problem is not solved by substituting the defensible *man-* for the indefensible *mas-*. The question can only be left open. *Mascarpio* (Petron. 134.5), which is probably an abstract verbal noun, was no doubt formed on the analogy of *masturbator / -atio*.

Masturbor could not have been a recent formation when Martial used it; otherwise its structure would have been transparent. But I am not convinced that it was a current subliterary vulgarism. The examples both of *masturbor* and *masturbatio* in Martial are in mythological contexts. If *masturbor* were a vulgarism, one might have expected it to surface in the literature rather more often, and in contexts other than these; masturbation is, after all, mentioned often enough in sexual literature. It may have been an obsolescent verb which Martial resuscitated.

7. Substitutes for *fellare* and *irrumare*

One is struck even more by the variety of substitutes for *fello* and *irrumo* than by the substitutes for *masturbor*. Some of these have been mentioned earlier: *futuo* and *lingua fututrix* (p. 122), the metaphor of 'eating' (pp. 138ff.), 'silencing' (p. 127), *haereo* and its compounds (p. 181), *tero* (p. 183), *tango* (p. 186), *contrecto* (p. 186), *capite demisso* (p. 192), *insulto, inludo* (p. 200), the implication of *purus* (p. 199), *conspurco* (p. 199), *morigeror* (p. 164 n. 7); see also p. 128 on the various ways of phrasing a threat of *irrumatio*.[1] To these expressions add Varro *Men.* 282 'ut flumen offendit buccam Volumnio', Hor. *Epod.* 8.20 'quod ut superbo prouoces ab inguine, / ore adlaborandum est tibi', Mart. 3.75.5 'coepisti puras opibus corrumpere buccas' (for *bucca* in such a context, see Varro *Men.*

---

[1] Numerous expressions have been collected by Krenkel, p. 78.

282 above, and Mart. 11.61.2), 11.46.6 'summa petas' (cf. *Priap.* 74.2 'barbatis non nisi summa petet', Auson. *Cent. Nupt.* 105, p. 216 P. 'perfidus alta petens'),[1] 11.98.23 'facias amicum basiare quem nolis',[2] Apul. *Met.* 8.29 'nudatum supinatumque iuuenem exsecrandis oribus flagitabant', *H.A., Comm.* 1.7 'ore quoque pollutus et constupratus fuit', Lactant. *Inst.* 6.23.11 'furor ne capiti quidem parcit'. Note too Donatus' interpretation of *os praebui* at Ter. *Adelph.* 215.

At Mart. 2.72.3 ('os tibi percisum quanto non ipse Latinus / uilia Panniculi percutit ora sono') *os ... percisum* probably refers to *irrumatio* (in a pun: for *os percidere* used literally of a blow in the face, see Plaut. *Cas.* 404, *Pers.* 283). The incident had occurred at a dinner party. The victim, Postumus, denied that it had taken place, but Martial declares that Caecilius, the perpetrator, had witnesses: 8 'quid quod habet testes, Postume, Caecilius?'. Taken literally the epigram has little point, but there is surely a double entendre in the last line (with *testes* also referring to the testicles). The phrase 'habet testes ... Caecilius' would mean 'Caecilius does have testicles, is after all a man' (and hence is capable of an active, as distinct from pathic, sexual act). The expression *coleos* (*et sim.*) *habere* = 'to be a man' was proverbial (Petron. 44.14; cf. Pers. 1.103). The poem gains point when it is noted that often in Book 2 Postumus is said to have a foul mouth (10, 12, 21, 22, 23). There is a similar pun on the sexual sense of *testes* at *Priap.* 15.7 'magnis testibus ista res agetur'; cf. also Mart. 7.62.6.[3]

---

[1] For 'seeking' (*peto*) a sexual part, see *CIL* XI.6721.5 'peto [la]ndicam Fuluiae', 7 'pet[o] Octauia(ni) culum', Suet. *Tib.* 44.1 'morsuque sensim adpetentes', ps.-Ambros. *Laps. Virg.* 23 'cum ad illud opus nefarium tua membra peterentur'. Also of significance in these passages is the distancing of the reference to the oral act by the avoidance of *os*. This type of euphemism is common. I have noted the following more general words or expressions substituted for *os* or *lingua*: *caput* (anon. *ap.* Suet. *Iul.* 22.2, Sen. *Ben.* 4.31.4, Mart. 2.42.2, 2.70.5, 3.81.5, 6.26.1, 14.74.2, Juv. 6.49, 6.301, *Priap.* 22.2, Suet. *Tib.* 45), *sanctissima pars corporis* (Cic. *Red. Sen.* 11), *barba* (Juv. 9.4), *uultus* (Aurel. Vict. *Caes.* 5.7), *facies* (Mart. 3.87.4, Auson. *Cent. Nupt.* 104, p. 216 P.).

[2] See Housman, *Classical Papers*, p. 733.

[3] It is worth noting the presence of *rumor* in line 6 of the poem in question ('Caecilium tota rumor in urbe sonat'). It has been pointed out by Forberg, p. 287 n.q. that Martial a number of times uses *rumor* when alluding to *irrumatio / fellatio*: 3.73.5 'mollem credere te uirum uolebam, / sed rumor negat esse te cinaedum', 3.80.2 'rumor ait linguae te tamen esse malae', 3.87.1 'narrat te rumor, Chione, numquam esse fututam'. It is possible that verbal puns were intended.

Martial sometimes uses the phrase *nil negare* suggestively, = *fellare*: see 12.79.4, and cf. 4.12.2, 11.49.12, 12.71.

This does not exhaust the methods by which oral acts were expressed in Latin. Frequently writers merely allude to the impurity, or, less specifically, the suspect character, of someone's mouth (e.g. Cic. *Har. Resp.* 11), tongue (e.g. Cic. *Dom.* 25, 47), breath (Petron. 9.6), kisses (e.g. Juv. 6.51) or saliva (Catull. 99.10).[1]

---

[1] Here is a collection (unclassified) of such passages: Catull. 78a.2, 79.4, 80.1f., Cic. *Dom.* 26, *Sest.* 111, *Cael.* 78, *Pis.* 8 (reading *osculo*), Sen. *Contr.* 9.2.11, Sen. *Epist.* 87.16, Mart. 1.94.2, 2.12, 2.15, 2.21, 2.42, 3.80.2, 3.81.6, 6.55.5 (cf. 4.43), 10.22.3, 11.25.2, 11.61.1f., 12.74.9f., Juv. 5.127f., 6.05f., 6.014–16, Suet. *Gramm.* 23.6.

Chapter Six

Conclusion

1. Sociolinguistic and contextual variation

The vocabulary of sex cannot readily be distributed into different social dialects in Latin. Basic obscenities were used by all classes. It is true that graffiti scrawled by semi-literates are full of obscenities, but members of the educated classes also made use of such words in appropriate contexts. One finds *mentula, uerpa, cunnus, futuo, pedico, irrumo* and *fello* used in much the same ways by Catullus and Martial in epigram as by scribblers on the walls of Pompeii. Augustus directed sexual abuse at Antony in the same terms as those used by the ordinary inhabitants of Pompeii (Mart. 11.20). 'Fescennines' composed by him against Pollio (Macr. *Sat.* 2.4.21) must have been couched in the same language. Various other men of distinction composed obscene or erotic verses (see Mart. 8. prooem., Plin. *Epist.* 4.14.3–4, 5.3, 7.4). There were of course circumstances in which obscenities were not tolerated by the educated, as for example in oratory and in various literary genres. But a distinction has to be made between 'vulgarisms' (lower-class usages, often displaying morphological and phonetic deviations from the educated norm) and obscenities. Vulgarisms in this narrow sense were largely alien to literary genres and no doubt to educated speech.

But it should not be assumed that in Vulgar Latin there were no special designations for the sexual parts or sexual acts. The slang and private registers of the lower classes are largely a closed book. A few possible cases of lower-class terms for the *mentula* are *strutheum, titus* and *turtur*, but the status of these is not absolutely certain. **Caraculum* and *uirga*, both of which survive in Romance, may have been current in varieties of lower-class speech, particularly in late antiquity. *Eugium, spurium* and *calo*, like *strutheum*, look like the slang of the brothel. Empty curses of the type so common in English (e.g. *fuck X, I'll be buggered*) do not find their way into literature, but they can be paralleled in graffiti (*CIL* IV. 2360 *uerpa(m) (comedam), Die Antike* 15 (1939), p. 103 *irrima medicos*). Catullus has a weakened, metaphorical use of *irrumo*, but it is possible that weakening of sexual verbs was more characteristic of popular than educated slang. Another such curse is that containing *laecasin* (used by a freedman in Petronius); it was certainly a popular borrowing, introduced from a curse which must already have existed in Greek.

It would be a mistake, of course, to assume that the sexual language of the lower classes was exclusively obscene or coarse. The euphemisms *delecto, satisfacio* and, most notably, *facio* are all found in speeches by the freedmen in Petronius, where basic obscenities are rare. But there is one coarse metaphor in the *Cena Trimalchionis* which is worthy of special mention here, because it demonstrates nicely that sexual slang tends to spread across class boundaries. The intensive *debattuo* is used in exactly the same context by Trimalchio as the similar intensives *perdepso* and *permolo* in Catullus and Horace (of sexual relations with someone else's wife). Apuleius' *dedolo* is also applied to an adulterous liaison. Intensified metaphors would undoubtedly have been employed in the coarse speech of males of all classes, often as designations for illicit sex. Other intensives seen above are *percido* and *concido*.

While there are few demonstrably lower-class sexual terms attested, some learned terms could be quoted which would not have been heard among the lower classes. We have suggested, for example, that scholastic metaphors had an artificial flavour. Various calques on Greek words in the scientific language had no place in ordinary speech. The different meanings given to *ueretrum*, as well as its distribution, suggest that it was an obscure word domiciled in scientific vocabularies. Some other learned words are *naturale, feminal, uirginal*, the metaphor of sowing, *misceo* and *furtum*.

Among the determinants of the type of sexual terminology which a writer or speaker will choose are:

(*a*) The circumstances of utterance. In the case of a literary work, the conventions of the genre were influential (see below).

The situation facing a speaker might demand a particular type of sexual vocabulary. One might expect, for example, to hear basic obscenities in invective. *Ad hoc* metaphors belong especially to jokes. The terminology appropriate to the brothel (note *struthium, eugium, calo, spurium*) differs from that of the household.

(*b*) The attitude of the speaker or writer to the sexual act in question: see p. 170 on 'persuasive designations'.

(*c*) The nature of the act itself: was it, for example, violent or mutually pleasurable?

(*d*) The sex of the speaker. Women are generally believed to be more hostile to obscenity than men, though in special circumstances, as in the bedroom or brothel (see above, (*a*)), or in smart circles in which outrageousness is deliberately cultivated (see below, (*e*)), reserve may be abandoned. One is not in a position to compare the incidence of the Latin basic obscenities in female as distinct from male speech. Women may also have special (often metaphorical) sexual terms, which they employ particularly when addressing children. *Porcus*, according to Varro, was used by women when speaking of girls.

(*e*) The sex and age of the addressee (or referent). It was a standard attitude that obscenity was unfit for the ears (and mouths) of children (Sen. *Dial.* 2.11.2, Mart. 1.35.1f., 3.69.7f., 5.2, Paul. Fest. p. 283.17ff.),[1] and it is a reasonable assumption that many speakers would have used nursery words in their presence. Languages regularly have such terms for the sexual organs of children. These may vary from family to family. Certain alleged Greek names for the penis of boys are listed by Strato, *A.P.* 12.3 (λάλου, κοκκώ, σαύρα);[2] cf. Hesych. χρυσίον· τὸ τῶν παιδίων αἰδοῖον.[3] For *porcus*, see above. At Petron. 24.7 Quartilla uses the diminutive *uasculum* as appropriate to the youthful Giton (cf. πόσθιον at Aristoph. *Thesm.* 515, of a child). And *pipinna* at Mart. 11.72.1 ('Drauci Natta sui uocat pipinnam, / conlatus cui Gallus est Priapus') was presumably a colloquial term for a boy's *mentula*. Originally

---

[1] Except on certain ritual occasions. Fescennine verses at weddings were sung especially by boys, and at the festival of Anna Perenna girls chanted obscenities: see above, pp. 4f.

[2] On λάλου etc. see L. Robert, *Noms indigènes dans l'Asie-mineure gréco-romaine* (Paris, 1963), pp. 315ff.

[3] On χρυσίον see Robert, p. 19 (especially n. 2).

it would have been an adjective meaning 'small' (cf. the vulgar adjectives *pitinnus*, *pisinnus*), used as a complement of *mentula* (expressed or understood) (cf. *pusilla* at Mart. 7.55.6). For the ellipse of *mentula* with various feminine adjectives, see p. 62.

It is sometimes suggested or implied that freeborn women should not hear obscenities or even the mention of sexual acts (Varro *Men.* 11, Ovid *Trist.* 2.303f., Mart. 5.2, 11.15.1f., Juv. 11.166, *Priap.* 8, Aug. *Ciu.* 2.4–5). A speaker at Ter. *Heaut.* 1041f. even refrains from using *scortum* in the presence of a woman: 'non mihi per fallacias adducere ante oculos . . . pudet / dicere hac praesente uerbum turpe'. But in fashionable circles such an attitude might be held up for ridicule. At 3.68 Martial states that the preceding epigrams in the book were written for *matronae*, but those which are to follow are obscene and not for the ears of a chaste woman: they are to name directly that organ (the *mentula*) which cannot be looked at by a *uirgo* without placing her hand in front of her face. But Martial's warning is not serious. In the final couplet (11f.) he suggests that the matron will now shed her previous boredom and read on with keen interest. At 3.86 he refers back to his earlier warning, and remarks that the *casta matrona* has read on against his advice. He concludes that his epigrams are no more obscene than mimes, and those are seen by women. Similarly at 11.16.9f. Lucretia is imagined as blushing at the sight of Martial's epigrams in the presence of Brutus, but reading them in his absence. And at 10.64 Martial hopes that Polla will welcome his *ioci*, despite their language. Martial obviously regarded his readership as composed of women as well as men. But he is a special case. He writes with the attitude of one deliberately flouting conventional attitudes. In less sophisticated circles it is likely that speakers would have been more reserved in the presence of women.

Public restrictions do not operate in the bedroom. Words (spoken by the woman as well as the man) were regarded as a titillating accompaniment to intercourse (see p. 7). The *nupta uerba* which, according to a speaker in Plautus, a married woman would learn to use (frg. 68 Lindsay), were perhaps the obscenities of the bedroom.

2. Generic variation

Since the remains of Latin are predominantly literary, it may be useful to expand on the conventions of various literary genres.

(i) Comedy

Compared with Old Comedy, Greek New Comedy was lexically decent, though the basic obscenities had not been eliminated entirely. κινητιάω at Men. *Dysc.* 462 probably had the same tone as βινητιάω. βινέω and its compounds are attested a few times: Men. frg. 397.11 Koerte-Thierfelder ὑποβινητιῶντα, *CGF* 138.8[1] βινεῖν, 254.1]ἐβίνησ'. λαικάζω occurs at Men. *Dysc.* 892 and Strato 1.36 Kock, λαικάστρια at Men. *Peric.* 485. References to the genitalia are scarcely found in the remains of the genre. Note, however, the fragment of the *Theseus* of Diphilus (50 Kock), quoted by Athenaeus 10.451 b, where three Samian girls attempt to answer the riddle what is the strongest thing of all; the third suggests the πέος. The word is not likely to have been Athenaeus'. Sexual double entendre is also rare (but note ἀναβαίνειν and περικαθῆσθαι at Men. *Peric.* 484, and ἔπασχον at *Dysc.* 892).[2] The alleged translation of a passage from an 'Ανεχόμενος of Menander found at *Anth. Lat.* 712, in which there is some anatomical obscenity, is no doubt spurious. Similarly the obscenity in the *Alda* of William of Blois, a work which its author claims in the preface to have descended from a Menandrian original, is medieval in spirit.[3] The Greek remains may give a slightly misleading impression of the sexual element in the genre, but it is clear that New Comedy was radically different from Old. Mild euphemisms for sexual acts, rather than obscenities or colourful metaphors, were in vogue. Such obscenities as were admitted were probably confined largely to lower-class characters.

In Terence there is no trace of the lexical obscenities or of current metaphors. He avoided mention of the sexual organs

---

[1] C. Austin, *Comicorum Graecorum Fragmenta in Papyris Reperta* (Berlin and New York, 1973). Dr D. M. Bain supplied me with information used in this paragraph.

[2] See Gomme and Sandbach, *Menander, a Commentary*, pp. 505, 270.

[3] See K. Gaiser, *Menanders 'Hydria': Eine hellenistische Komödie und ihr Weg ins lateinische Mittelalter* (Heidelberg, 1977), p. 425 n. 115.

(the highly euphemistic *gremium* at *Eun.* 585 is exceptional). Most of his references to sexual practices take the form of metonymy. Here is a selection of the semantic fields from which euphemisms are drawn: (*a*) 'violence, corruption' (e.g. *Heaut.* 231 *corrumpo, Eun.* 616 *facio uim*; cf. Men. *Epitr.* 453, *Her.* 79), (*b*) 'touch' (*Adelph.* 686), (*c*) 'be with' (*Hec.* 156), (*d*) 'lie with' (*Hec.* 393), (*e*) 'take (give) pleasure' (*Hec.* 69), (*f*) 'take' (*Adelph.* 965), (*g*) 'press close' (*comprimo*, 4 times). Terence also occasionally omits an indelicate verb (*Heaut.* 913, *Eun.* 479).

Euphemisms of all these types could be quoted from Plautus. He too avoided the lexical obscenities. But unlike Terence (and, it would seem, Menander), he was prepared to use sexual metaphors, particularly in jokes. These are both anatomical (*aratiuncula, cucumis, fundus, gladius, inferior guttur, machaera, peculium, radix, saltus, testis, uagina, uas*; cf. *rutabulum* in Naevius) and verbal (*aro, dirumpo, diuido, inforo, scando, tero*, 'marry'). It is possible that Plautus (following Naevius?) deliberately introduced to the genre the sorts of double entendres favoured in farce and mime. Given the bulk of his work, it could not be said that his sexual puns are frequent.

Primary obscenities were undoubtedly admitted in farce and mime. *Mentula, cunnus, futuo* and *culus* do not happen to occur in the fragments, but *pedico* is attested in both genres, as is *caco*; cf. Pomponius' *coleatus*, and *uerpa* (?) (Pompon. 129 Frassinetti). Martial twice likens the obscenity of epigram to that of mime (3.86.4, 8.prooem.). On the obscenity of farce, see Quint. 6.3.47. Farce and mime also made free use of metaphors (*caedo, concido, cuspis, dolo, molo, ramus, scalpo, scindo, strutheum, terminus, trua*).

(ii) Catullus and epigram

In view of the extensive remains of Greek epigram, the number of obscenities that the genre contains is very small: note πέος at Antipater, *A.P.* 11.224.1, Strato, 12.240.2, βινέω at [Meleager], 11.223.1, 2, Philodemus, 5.126.2, 4, Callicter, 5.29.1, Strato, 12.245.1, πρωκτός at Nicarchus 11.241.1, 3, Strato, 12.6.1. Cf. ξενοκυσθαπάτην at Nicarchus, 11.7.4. Figurative terminology was preferred. We have seen that Catullus used primary obscenities not only in iambics, in which he had the

220   *The Latin Sexual Vocabulary*

precedent of Archilochus and Hipponax (note πρωκτός at Hipp.
104.32 West, βινέω at Archil. 152.2, Hipp. 84.16), but also in
hendecasyllables and elegiac epigram.[1] Of the 39 examples of
mentula, uerpa, cunnus, culus, futuo and derivatives, *pedico,
irrumo* and derivatives, *fello, caco* and *peditum* (< *pedo*) in the
shorter poems, 6 are in iambics, 19 in hendecasyllables, and
14 in elegiac epigram. In epigram Catullus appears to have
innovated. He was followed by Martial and the author of the
Priapea. The sexual metaphors which he has were largely
coarse, emotive and current in slang, rather than precious in
the manner of Greek epigram: e.g. that of 'eating' (28.12f.,
80.6), 'urinating' (67.30), *caedo, glubo, penis, perdepso*; cf. the
ad hoc coinages *trabs* and *sicula*. Catullus' sexual vocabulary
was that of real life. He also employed a wide range of euphemisms, of which at least one (*deliciae*) was in vogue at the
time: cf., e.g. *attingo, gremium,* 'lie with' *et sim.* (69.8, 78.4).

Martial preferred the basic obscenities to their substitutes,
metaphorical or euphemistic. He occasionally coined a metaphor (*aluta, barathrum, Chia, leo, marisca, Symplegas*), or
adopted one from slang ('eat' at, e.g. 7.67.15, 'urinate' at
11.46.2, *dolo, percido*). A few of his metaphors were chosen as
appropriate to Priapic poems.

The author of the *Priapea* made use of the basic language of
the Latin epigrammatic tradition, but he was more Grecising
than Catullus and Martial. Greek in spirit are the Homeric
parody in 68, and the letter puzzles in 7, 54 and 67. The
metaphorical use of *ara, hortus, pares* (?) and *pratum* (?) has
a literary flavour. The verbal metaphors in the work were
chosen to stress the threatening character of the phallus of
Priapus (*caedo, excauo, fodio, percido, perforo*). Some of them
are found in Catullus and / or Martial, others were his
coinages.

Ausonius rejected the lexical obscenity of his Latin predecessors in epigram. There are isolated examples of *fello, fellator*
and *lingo*; κύσθος at *Epigr.* 82.5, p. 343 P. can be disregarded.
The Grecising preciosity of Ausonius' epigrams is illustrated

---

[1] The hendecasyllabic metre had occasionally been used in Greek epigram
before Catullus. One of the five epigrams assigned to Phalaecus by A. S. F.
Gow and D. L. Page, *The Greek Anthology: Hellenistic Epigrams* (Cambridge,
1965), II, pp. 458f. is in hendecasyllables (2946ff., = *A.P.* 13.6). On the use of
Phalaecian hendecasyllables in combination with various other metres in
Callimachus, Theocritus and Parmenon, see Gow and Page II, p. 177.

by the letter puzzle, 87, p. 344 P., and by the metaphorical use
of *Clazomenae* at 93.4, p. 346.

(iii) Satire

It has been pointed out that Horace uses *cunnus* and *futuo* in
the first book of the *Sermones*, but not thereafter. Other basic
words in this book are *caco*, *merda*, *pedo* and *oppedo* (see the
Appendix). Whether he was following Lucilius in this respect
cannot be determined. The presence of *eugium*, *muto* and *mutonium* in Lucilius, Horace's own use of *muto* in imitation of
Lucilius, and the nature of frg. 1186, are suggestive, but one
cannot be certain that Lucilius employed basic obscenities.
Horace changed his view about the propriety of such words
when he came to the second book, the lexical decency of which
set the pattern for later satire. This change of taste may also
be reflected in the *Epodes*, where there are no obscenities,
despite the conventions of early Greek iambic poetry. One
finds a few current metaphors in the *Sermones* (*permolo*, the
image of horse riding at 2.7.49f.; see further below), but Horace
did not set out to coin metaphors as a procedure of style. *Palus*
is in a Priapic context; *cauda* may be a coinage.

Juvenal did not use the basic obscenities, but neither did he
entirely avoid the coarser elements of the Latin sexual
language. The crude metaphor of 'urinating' turns up, though
only in a nominal form (11.170; cf. *uesica* = *cunnus*); it had
been used by both Horace (*Serm.* 1.2.44, 2.7.52) and Persius
(6.73). That of 'eating' also occurs, though the verbs by which
it is expressed are abnormal (and hence perhaps 'euphemistic').
In a corpus of poems in which *ad hoc* and Grecising sexual
metaphors are avoided (*penis*, *fodio* (cf. *fossa* at 2.10, used *pars
pro toto* of a pathic) and *equito* at 6.311 were no doubt well
established), *cicer* and *chelidon* in the Oxford fragment stand
out as remarkable abnormalities; they constitute an argument
against the authenticity of the piece. For the most part Juvenal favoured bland euphemisms, such as *inguen*, *testiculus*,
uenus, *genitalia*, *pars*, *coitus* (10.204), references to the position of the participants in a sexual act (e.g. 3.112, 9.26), and
to concomitant events (e.g. 6.21f.). For the mundane euphemism 'sleep, lie with', see, e.g. 4.9, 6.34, 279, 376, and for the
pro-verb *facio*, 7.240. In Juvenal's hands the sexual language
of satire became similar to that of polite prose. For drastic

effect he was, however, ready to import an occasional metaphor or striking expression (*uesica, rima, podex*). Persius, on the other hand, had shown something of a taste for *ad hoc* metaphors (*gurgulio, ualuae, filix, plantaria*; he also used *penis*).

(iv) Oratory

Orators often affected a modest silence, as at Cic. *Pis.* 71 'multa . . . recitarem, ni uererer ne hoc ipsum genus orationis quo nunc utor ab huius loci more abhorreret' (cf. *Verr.* a.pr. 14, 1.32, *Cael.* 69, *Phil.* 2.47); the commonplace is taken to extreme lengths by ps.-Quint. *Decl. Maior.* 3.6 (cf. 3.1).[1] Theoretical works urged reserve upon the orator (Cic. *De orat.* 2.242, 252, Quint. 11.1.30). Similarly Seneca advised the avoidance of obscenity both of language and subject matter in declamation (*Contr.* 1.2.21, 23).

The modest silence of the orator was to some extent a disingenuous pose. The speeches of Cicero are full of references to sexual practices, unnatural and otherwise,[2] and of sexual invective. There is also evidence that sexual jokes were fashionable in declamation. Nevertheless the orator (and declaimer) had to be euphemistic. Lexical obscenities and mildly risqué words are absent from the speeches of Cicero, and there is no evidence that they were admitted by other orators in formal speeches, although obscene invective did have a place as an undercurrent in politics (see, e.g. Macrob. *Sat.* 2.4.21 on the 'Fescennines' directed by Augustus at Pollio).

Some idea of the grossness (of subject rather than word) which must occasionally have been heard in the senate is provided by the anecdote told by Suet. *Iul.* 22.2 (where a senator alludes to *irrumatio*). Allusions to oral sexual practices are relatively common in the speeches of Cicero.[3] But the speeches to the people were more reserved than those to the senate. Nothing resembling the reference to *fellatio* at *Red. Sen.* 11 ('qui ne a sanctissima quidem parte corporis potuisset

---

[1] See R. Volkmann, *Die Rhetorik der Griechen und Römer*[2] (Leipzig, 1885), p. 504 for the commonplace in Greek; cf. R. G. M. Nisbet, *M. Tulli Ciceronis in L. Calpurnium Pisonem oratio* (Oxford, 1961), on §71.

[2] The sexual organs were subject to a more restrictive taboo. But see *nerui* at *Sest.* 16, *intemperantia* at *Red. Sen.* 11 (?), and p. 56 on expressions of the type 'quae honeste nominari non possunt'.

[3] See *Dom.* 83 and the passages collected above, p. 213, n. 1.

hominum impuram intemperantiam propulsare') is to be found in the corresponding speech to the people (*Quir.*). Implicit in the difference is an attitude that while a man can speak freely among members of his own social class, to be too outspoken before members of other classes might be embarrassing. Similarly M. Porcius Cato (of Utica) walked out of the theatre at the Floralia so that the show could go on (Val. Max. 2.10.8, Mart. 1.prooem.). The embarrassment of the people in his presence suggests that ordinary people expected greater reserve in sexual matters to be shown by leaders of old-fashioned *grauitas* than they would show themselves.

The popularity of sexual innuendo in declamation is well illustrated by Seneca's anecdote (*Contr.* 4.praef.10) about the vogue use of *officium* (p. 163); cf. *Contr.* 1.2.22–3, 4.praef.11. The grossness of these last two passages, in which *loci, libido* and *obscena* are sexually suggestive, cannot be matched in Ciceronian oratory.

In oratory sexual acts were alluded to by means of vague innuendo (see above, p. 213, n. 1 for examples), circumlocutions (e.g. Scip. Afr. *Orat.* frg. 17 'idem fecerit, quod cinaedi facere solent', Cic. *ap.* Suet. *Iul.* 49.3 'remoue ... istaec, oro te, quando notum est, et quid ille tibi et quid illi tute dederis') and by a variety of euphemisms. *Stuprum* is common. The frequency of expressions indicating corruption, tainting, the doing of violence etc. reflects the moralising stance of the orator (e.g. *uim adfero* at Cic. *Verr.* 1.67, Sen. *Contr.* 1.2.2, *uiolo* at *Verr.* 4.116, Sen. *Contr.* 1.2.7, *corrumpo, polluo* and *contamino* in Seneca). For verbs meaning 'lie with' etc. see Cic. *Cael.* 36, *Verr.* 5.63, Sen. *Contr.* 7.6.15, and for 'touch' *et sim.*, *Cael.* 20, Sen. *Contr.* 1.2.2. See further *uolutor* (p. 193), *seruio* (p. 163), *patior* (p. 190), *amo* (p. 188). Graphic metaphors with a strong anatomical implication are avoided, but vague metaphors were admissible (e.g. those of a military kind (p. 159), *ludo* (Sen. *Contr.* 1.2.22)). The orator could not afford to use recherché words or *ad hoc* coinages. Since he was dealing with real events and often speaking to an ordinary audience, he had to use current and acceptable euphemisms. Fashionable ways of referring to sexual activity surface a few times in the *pro Caelio* (*ludus* (p. 162), *deliciae* (p. 196)).

(v) Elegy

Alexandrian narrative elegy, whatever its relationship to Latin elegy, seems to have been euphemistic, but the fragments are not sufficient to allow detailed comparisons. At *Aet.* 1.frg.21.4 Callimachus uses a euphemism (παιδὶ χροισσαμ[ένη) of a type which we have seen in Latin (*tango*, etc.; cf. Theocr. 10.18). 'Touching a maiden's girdle' is another euphemism, for the amatory activities of the first night of a marriage (Call. *Aet.* 3.frg.75.45).

Ovid's *Amores* and *Ars Amatoria* are more explicit than other elegy, but both works are lexically inoffensive. The protracted account of impotence at *Am.* 3.7 is quite unlike anything in Tibullus or Propertius, but it too is euphemistic. The terms by which the organ is referred to are colourless (6 *inguinis*, 13 *membra*, 28 *corpora*, 35 *neruos*, 69 *pars pessima nostri*, 73 *hanc (partem)*). Ovid was prepared to admit anatomical double entendres occasionally, as at *Am.* 1.8.47f., 1.9.26 (*arma*), but such language is abnormal in the genre. *Membrum*, with or without a complement, is the usual word applied to the male organ (Tib. 1.4.70, Prop. 2.16.14, Ovid *Am.* 2.3.3, 2.15.25). In the *Ars Amatoria pars* in various combinations is employed of both the male and female genitalia (2.584, 618, 707, 3.804). Some substitutes for *cunnus* are *inguen* (Tib. 2.4.58), *pubes* (Ovid *Ars* 2.613), *uiscera* (Ovid *Am.* 2.14.27, = *cunnus* and 'womb'), *corpus* (Ovid *Am.* 2.14.34; cf. *Am.* 3.7.28, of the penis), and *locus* (Ovid *Ars* 3.799). Allusions to sexual parts of the body are far more numerous in Ovid than in Tibullus or Propertius.

Many of the verbal euphemisms in Latin elegy can be paralleled in Terence and oratory, and are likely to derive from the polite educated language: e.g. expressions meaning 'sleep, lie with' (Tib. 1.9.75, Prop. 1.8b.33, 2.15.16), 'spend the night', etc. (Tib. 2.6.49, Ovid *Am.* 1.8.67, 1.10.30 etc.), 'be with' (Ovid *Am.* 2.8.27), 'take pleasure' etc. (Tib. 2.1.12, Ovid *Am.* 1.10.35, 2.9b.46), *comprimo* (Prop. 2.26b.48), 'hold, join, embrace, cling' (Tib. 2.6.52, Prop. 1.13.19, 2.15.25). It has been pointed out that *uolutor* (Prop. 2.29b.36) is found in oratory and declamation.

Those metaphors which focus attention on the role of the *mentula* (e.g. *caedo* and compounds, *scindo*) are avoided. The metaphors which do occur are anatomically inexplicit and often paralleled in Greek: e.g. those of wrestling (Prop. 2.1.13, 2.15.5), rowing (Ovid *Ars* 2.731), riding (Ovid *Ars* 2.732, 3.777f.), fighting (Tib. 1.10.53, Prop. 2.15.4 and often). Cf. *ludo* (Prop. 2.15.21; note too *lusus* at Ovid *Am.* 2.3.13), *officium* (Prop. 2.22a.24), *furtum* (Prop. 4.8.34, etc.).

3. Chronological variation

The degree of sexual explicitness which is permitted in a society, at least in literature and public performances, can change drastically from period to period, as could be demonstrated from British society of the last twenty years. In the spoken language public taboos are not so influential, and in a period of public repression one would not expect the terminology of popular abuse to be much modified. In the appropriate contexts Latin speakers were equally tolerant of the basic obscenities in the Republic and early Empire. It is true that Horace turned away from obscenities in the second book of the *Sermones*, and that Ovid states that his *Ars Amatoria* is not worthy of the emperor's attention (*Trist.* 2.241f. 'illa quidem fateor frontis non esse seuerae / scripta, nec a tanto principe digna legi'). Furthermore in a few places Martial suggests that the ears of an emperor impose greater restraint on him (8.prooem., 8.1), an attitude which was at least partly due to the fact that an emperor might be expected to hold the *censura* (1.4.7). He even went so far as to present Nerva with an expurgated (?) selection of epigrams from books 10 and 11 (12.4 (5)). But Horace's change of taste was purely personal, and Martial parades various attitudes only to mock them elsewhere. Augustus himself, as we have seen, composed obscene epigrams. Martial expresses confidence that Domitian will enjoy his verses, just as he enjoyed mime and the *ioci* at triumphs (1.4; cf. 7.8.9f.). And in a dedicatory poem to his *breue opus* for Nerva he mentions the possibility that the emperor will also read the other epigrams (12.4 (5).4). That there were no public restrictions on verbal obscenity under the Empire is evidenced by the case of epigram. Mime too continued to be composed in a direct style (Mart. 1.4; cf. 3.86.4, 8.prooem.). And on various public or ritual occasions obscenities seem still to have been heard (at the Floralia, triumphs, the festival of Anna Perenna, performances of the Cadiz dancers (Juv. 11.174), and no doubt at weddings). It was only in satire that a change of fashion took place. Invective of the emperor and his associates was of course no longer a safe undertaking, but it did not have to be obscene to give offence.

Primary obscenities have a very long life, and for this reason they are often of obscure etymology. *Mentula* had no doubt been in use long before the historical period, and it lived on into some of the Romance languages (It. *minchia*, Log. *minkra*). On the other hand the complementary term *uerpa* must eventually have fallen out of use in all areas. It is attested during a relatively brief period, and it does not itself survive in Romance. It has been suggested earlier that if a primary obscenity is weakened into an empty term of abuse or imprecation, it may need to be replaced as the *vox propria* for the part or act in question. *Verpa* has an attested abusive use in which its proper force was fading (p. 13). *Pedico*, *irrumo* and *fello* may have disappeared for the same reason. *Cunnus*, *culus* and *futuo* lived on.

Words other than basic obscenities suffer a continuous process of decline and replacement. Euphemisms tend to lose their euphemistic character; they may then be dropped from the language, or live on as obscenities. We have the testimony of Quintilian that *patro* and *ducto*, both elliptical euphemisms in origin, developed an obscene tone. How long they survived in colloquial varieties of the language as offensive terms it is impossible to tell. There is a hint that a new euphemism *perficio* came into rivalry with *patro* during the Empire, but the evidence is inadequate. Certainly *patro* must have fallen out of vulgar use by the time that Theodorus Priscianus used its derivative *patratio* as a medical (and hence inoffensive) term. It is not unusual for a word which had once been coarse to be resuscitated after a gap as a recherché term. This was the lot of *penis*, *podex* and perhaps *masturbor*. The decline of old euphemisms and the appearance of new in colloquial speech cannot be adequately documented for a dead language because its remains are largely literary. A few changes can be noted in Latin. *Conquinisco* and *ocquinisco*, which may have degenerated from general into sexual terms, are confined to the Republic. *Inclino(r)* seems to have replaced them by the first century A.D. *Limare caput* was also Republican. Varro's remarks at *Ling.* 6.80 imply that *esse cum* was little, if at all, used by his day; nevertheless it continues to appear in litera-

ture. *Deliciae* was fashionable in the late Republic; so too
libido in a purely physical sense was not in use in the early
Republic. It is difficult to find examples of *tango* in late Latin,
but *contingo* is common.

The fate of metaphors is variable. Some, if used over a long
period, lose their metaphorical character (e.g. *penis* (?), *futuo*
(?), *irrumo*, *fello*, *molo*, and perhaps *iocor* and *luctor*). Others,
despite a long currency, manage to retain their imagery (e.g.
testis, *ramus*, *fodio*, *anus*). Different types of metaphors emerge
at different times, in keeping with the emergence of new objects, practices and the like which might be interpreted as
sexually symbolical. Conversely, as practices change, old
metaphors may lose their motivation and fall out of use (e.g.
datatim). Metaphors can be coined so freely that many occur
only once. But the symbolism which generates isolated metaphors may be perceived by speakers over a long period (e.g.
the symbolism of weapons, or of 'eating, feeding').

In the technical and medical languages it is possible to see
some changes. The Latin sexual vocabulary contrasts with
that of the modern languages in its lack of a fixed set of polite
technical terms for the organs of both sexes. Medical writers
display considerable variations in terminology, partly because
medical science in the modern sense, with its massive literature and need for a universally comprehensible vocabulary,
did not exist. Amateurs such as Celsus were motivated as
much by precious stylistic considerations as by a desire for
lexical precision. And the failure of Greek writers to establish
a uniform terminology had an affect on Latin writers, who
followed Greek sources closely and often merely translated
Greek terms directly into Latin. The terminology of Celsus,
who opposed *caulis* to *naturalia*, was idiosyncratic, and not
influential later. In the first century A.D. (Columella, Pliny)
genitale, *-ia* was the standard scientific term for the sexual
organs of both sexes, but it was rivalled in the later part of
the *Natural History* by *uerenda*, an equivalent of αἰδοῖον. The
author of the *Mulomedicina Chironis* made a lexical distinction between the organs of the two sexes (*ueretrum* 'penis'
contrasts with *uirginalis* 'vagina'), but like that in Celsus it
was of no further significance. *Veretrum* became the most common word for the male organ in late technical prose, but there
was no stable term for the female parts. In some works (e.g.
Anon. *Med.* ed. Piechotta, the translation of Hippocr. *Aer.*)

ueretrum (= αἰδοῖον) serves as a blanket euphemism for the parts of both sexes. *Sinus muliebris* is a common euphemism for the vagina in some late works, but its use was determined by the presence of κόλπος γυναικεῖος in its users' sources (notably Soranus, whose gynaecological work was translated into Latin by Caelius Aurelianus and Mustio). *Sinus muliebris* and κόλπος γυναικεῖος did not even oust their rivals in those writers who adopted them. In Caelius Aurelianus *ueretrum*, with or without specification, is used of both sexual organs. The inconsistency of terminology was of course caused by variations in Soranus.

4. The influence of Greek

It is not unusual for loan-words to be found in the sexual vocabulary of a language, particularly as designations for types of sexual behaviour and for the paraphernalia associated with sexual activities. Forms of perversion, as we have suggested (p. 202), tend to be ascribed particularly to foreign peoples, and those perversions may be described by a word from the foreign language in question. Various words to do with homosexuality in Latin are of Greek origin (*pedico, pathicus, cinaedus, catamitus*;[1] cf. *malacus* at Plaut. *Mil.* 668).

But the sexual organs and ordinary sexual behaviour did not attract loan-words. Although Celsus comments at 6.18.1 on the superiority of the Greek sexual vocabulary to that current in Latin, he did not introduce loan-words but instead made use to some extent of calques (e.g. *caulis, glans* and perhaps *pubes* and *orae*). Calques (of a sexual kind) are not uncommon in learned varieties of the language. Others which have been mentioned are *cicer, pecten, gemini, pares* (?), *ueretrum* (= αἰδοῖον), *uerenda, necessaria* (?), *particula, ara, pinnacula, sinus* (*muliebris*), *hortus, pratum* (?), *sedes*. Some of the Greek loan-words which we have seen (*strutheum, eugium, calo*) may have been introduced by Greek prostitutes (cf. the Etruscan (?) *spurium*). *Phallus* and *chelidon* were isolated transfers.[2] *Laecasin* must have been picked up from a vulgar

---

[1] *Catamitus* entered Latin from Greek (Γανυμήδης) via Etruscan.
[2] There are also isolated (and insignificant) examples of *balanus* (p. 72), *fisis* (p. 61) and *nymphe* (p. 98) in medical writers.

Greek curse; ordinary Latin speakers may not have ascribed
to it a sexual sense. Some other Greek words had entered the
language with non-sexual senses, before being adopted as sexual metaphors (*machaera, pyramis, thyrsus, clinopale,
palaestra*).

There is a good deal of overlap between sexual metaphors
and also euphemisms of various types in Greek and those in
Latin. Metaphors from weaponry, for example, abound in both
languages. Words meaning 'tail' were transferred to the penis
in Greek as well as Latin. The metaphor of riding was shared
by the two languages. The parallelism could be exemplified at
considerable length without difficulty. But the existence of
parallels does not in itself establish that Latin writers always
or often coined metaphors and euphemisms with Greek idiom
in mind. Sexual symbols tend to be common to many cultures,
and there is inevitably an overlap between the metaphors of
one language and those of another. Some sexual metaphors in
Latin would certainly have been imitations of Greek usage
(e.g. *hortus = culus* at *Priap.* 5.4 must have been coined with
Gk. κῆπος = κύσθος in mind), but sure examples are difficult
to find.

Given the paucity of anatomical loan-words in the Latin
sexual language, the marked presence of such words in the
short *spurcum additamentum* found in one manuscript of Apuleius, *Met.* 10.21 must be taken both as an indication of the
obscurantist tastes of a medieval delver in glossaries, and as
another proof that the piece is spurious.[1] The curious phrase
orcium pigam ('et ercle orcium pigam perteretem Hyaci fra-
grantis et Chie rosacee lotionibus expiauit') consists of ὄρχις
'testicle' along with πυγή in a Medieval glossators' sense, 'scrotum' (see Pap. *El. s.v.*, 'pyga, nates uel bursa mentula') based
on a misunderstanding of Hor. *Serm.* 1.2.133 'ne nummi per-
eant aut puga aut denique fama'.[2] *Orcis* occurs a second time
in the *additamentum*: 'et cum ad inguinis cephalum formosa
mulier concitim ueniebat ab orcibus'.[3] Otherwise in Latin *orchis* is the name of a plant or vegetable. *Cephalum* here, like
caput, is used of the glans of the penis. Another sure sign in

---

[1] On the spurious character of the passage, see the work of Fraenkel cited
above, p. 20, n. 1, and Mariotti. A text is printed by Mariotti, pp. 231f. =
p. 50.

[2] See Mariotti, pp. 232ff. = pp. 51f.

[3] See Mariotti, p. 239 = p. 58 on the text here.

the passage of a man who had a taste for glossaries is the use of *genius* = *genitale*, commented on above, p. 58, n. 3. Mariotti (p. 248 = p. 67) compares the obscenity found in the twelfth century *Alda* by William of Blois (449ff.) as a general pointer to the milieu from which the piece might have come. There is, as we have seen, a lot of obscenity in twelfth century Latin comedy from France (notably in the *Lidia*, 510ff., and the *Babio*), and descriptions of intercourse are not uncommon. But the loan-words and obscure glossators' terms in the *additamentum* make it highly unusual, though not for that reason necessarily a product of another era. *Inguen* (= *mentula*), which occurs twice in the piece, had something of a vogue in twelfth century comedy (see p. 47, n. 1). More interesting is the use of *Priapus* = *mentula* ('ganniens ego et dentes ad Iouem eleuans Priapo<n> frequenti frictura porrixabam'). Mariotti (p. 240 = p. 59) erroneously found this metaphor in Juvenal (2.95; cf. the schol. *ad loc.*) and Martial (14.70.1). In both writers it is the name of an object of phallic shape. But *Priapus* was used as an anatomical term in the twelfth century: see Vitalis of Blois, *Geta* 361 'numquam placata Priapo / semper inest rabies' (cf. 348, where *Priapus* is a manuscript variant).[1]

---

[1] The first example of *Priapus* in this sense is in a quotation at Diomedes, *GL* I.512.28 'Priapeum, quo Vergilius in prolusionibus suis usus fuit, tale est, "incidi patulum in specum procumbente Priapo" '. See *Gloss., Cod. Leid.* 191³ (see *CGL* VI, s.v. *muto*) 'muto Priapus'. Thereafter it is largely a medieval usage. For further medieval examples, see Herter, *De Priapo* p. 51 (contrast the use of πριαπίσκος of various medical instruments of phallic shape: Herter, *op. cit.* pp. 51f.).

The Vocabulary Relating to Bodily Functions

1. Defecation

A language might be expected to have a variety of words relating to defecation. There will generally be one or more crude basic terms of much the same status as sexual obscenities. In medical and polite registers euphemisms are necessary. Alongside blanket terms designating the excrement of humans and animals indifferently, a language may have a set of specialised words for the excreta of particular beasts. And the various uses to which dung can be put may motivate special terms. The Latin terminology shows variations determined by all of these factors. I begin with the crudest words.

(i) *Caco* and its derivatives

Caco, with a characteristic reduplicated form, must have begun as a nursery word,[1] but it became the basic verb for defecation, with a distribution similar, if not exactly identical, to that of *mentula*, *cunnus*, *culus* and *futuo*. It is found in hendecasyllabic poems of Catullus (23.20, 36.1, 20; the second two examples are metaphorical) and epigram (7 times in Martial, and at *Priap.* 69.4; cf. the desiderative *cacaturio* at Mart. 11.77.3), in farce and mime (Pompon. 97, 129, 130, 151, Novius 6, Laber. 66), and graffiti (8 examples are listed in the index to *CIL* IV, along with one of *cacatris* (?), 5 of *cacator* and one of *cacaturio*; I have noted 5 examples of *caco* in the Supple-

---

[1] Pokorny I, p. 521, Ernout and Meillet, *s.v.*

ments). *Caco* survives in all of the Romance languages. The example at Catull. 23.20 ('nec toto decies *cacas* in anno, / atque id *durius* est faba et lapillis') should be compared with the inscription from Ostia published by Calza, *Die Antike* 15 (1939), p. 101: '*durum cacantes* monuit ut nitant Thales'. The combination must have belonged to vulgar speech.[1] The elliptical euphemism at Juv. 1.131 'cuius ad effigiem non tantum meiere fas est' (*sc.* 'sed etiam cacare') perhaps suggests that for Juvenal *caco* was more offensive than *meio* (see below). The only verse satirist who uses the word is Horace in the first book of the *Sermones* (1.8.38 'in me ueniat mictum atque cacatum'); this is a reminiscence of an inscriptional formula (cf. *CIL* VI.13740 and Pers. 1.112, quoted above, p. 68; for *uenire cacatum* see *CIL* IV.5242). Juvenal's ellipse might be contrasted with Plautus' suggestive use of *creat* in a context in which *cacat* might have been expected (p. 138).

A freedman in Petronius also uses *caco* in a variation of the same inscriptional formula: 71.8 'ne in monumentum meum populus cacatum currat'. The presence of *caco* in Petronius marks the word as different in tone from *mentula, cunnus* and *futuo*. It is likely enough that *caco* continued to be used in the hearing of children; it might not have had the same offensiveness as the sexual obscenities. Its mild tone (relatively speaking) is confirmed by the use of some of its derivatives. The vulgar plant named *citocacia* mentioned by Isidore, *Etym.* 17.9.65 'citocacia uocata quod uentrem cito depurgat; quam uulgus corrupte citocociam uocant', would have been humorously direct, but hardly a taboo word. And Seneca twice admits the compound *concaco* in the *Apocolocyntosis* (4.3), once in direct speech and once in the narrative.[2] In the same passage one should note the circumlocution by which he avoided *culus*: 'cum maiorem sonitum emisisset *illa parte, qua* facilius loquebatur'.

Caco is also used in the veterinary work of Pelagonius

---

[1] For the adjective *durus* in this connection, see Cels. 2.7.5, *Mul. Chir.* 395, Veg. *Mul.* 2.119.1.

[2] *Concaco* is used elsewhere by Phaedrus (4.19.11), in a poem containing *caco* (25) and *merda* (25), and in the *Pactus Legis Salicae* (30.2 'si quis alterum concagatum clamauerit'); cf. *REW* 2110. On the reading *catillum concagatum* at Petron. 66.7 I share the doubts expressed by Smith, *Petronii Arbitri Cena Trimalchionis*, ad loc.; but see Heraeus, *Die Sprache des Petronius und die Glossen*, p. 17, = *Kleine Schriften*, p. 83.

(302.1, 308.1). Further evidence will be cited below to show that veterinary writers were stylistically less fastidious than medical.

(ii) *Merda*

If *merda* is of the root **smerd-*, **smord-* 'stinken',[1] its semantic development would be the same as that of *oletum facio*, lit. 'make a smell' >'*caco*' (see p. 68 with n. 2). Hence it would have deteriorated from a euphemism (metonymy) into the basest designation of excrement. In extant Latin *merda* is nowhere used exclusively of human excreta. At Hor. *Serm.* 1.8.37 (plural) the *merda* belongs to crows, at Phaedr. 4.19.25 (plural) it is that of dogs,[2] and at Anon. *Med.* ed. Piechotta 194 (plural), of the horse; cf. *ibid.* CLI (singular), of the capon. The reflexes of *merda* in Romance[3] can still be used of the dung of animals; in French the plural use (*les merdes*) so familiar in Latin is applied particularly to the excrement of birds and small animals.

Veterinary writers were prepared to use *merda* occasionally, in keeping with their tolerance of basic excretory terminology: Pelagon. 135 *merdam leporinam*, *Mul. Chir.* 268 *merdam bubalam*, 989 *merda caprina*, Veg. *Mul.* 2.8.4 *merdam bubulam*; contrast Veg. *Mul.* 2.28.6 *fimum bubalum*. The combination *merda bubula* survives as Log. *merdaula*;[4] it would certainly have been a farmers' expression, and as such emptied (by constant use) of offensive content.

Twice *merda* is attested in the vulgar expression 'to eat *merda*' (*CIL* IV.1700 'ut merdas edatis', Mart. 1.83.2 'non miror, merdas si libet esse cani'). At Mart. 3.17.6 ('sed nemo potuit tangere: merda fuit') it is metaphorical (of a cake). This example anticipates a familiar use of its reflexes (e.g. Fr. *c'était de la merde*; cf. Eng. *it was shit*; contrast Catullus' *cacata carta* at 36.1, 20). The weakening of its proper force implicit in this syntagm might in time give rise to a non-excretory sense 'rubbish, filth, dust' or the like.[5] In a technical register such a development can be seen in the use of *merda* = 'dross'

---

[1] So Pokorny I, p. 970.
[2] In this passage *merda* is used in association with *caco*.
[3] *REW* 5520.
[4] *REW* 1356, 5520.
[5] See *REW* 5520, *FEW* VI.2, p. 21.

of metal: Diosc. Lat. V, p. 209.3 'de merda ferri. scora ferri tantum potest, quantum et erugine eius, sed paulo minus' (cf. σκωρία <σκῶρ). *Merda ferri* survives as OPr. *merdafer*.[1]

Merda was obviously capable of conveying a strong note of disgust, but as a farming and veterinary term it could be used neutrally. Already in the Latin period it was showing signs of weakening in anticipation of some of its Romance uses. In poetry *merda* is confined to the first book of Horace's *Sermones*, Martial and Phaedrus (cf. *smerdalea* at *Priap.* 68.8).

(iii) *Stercus, fimus*

The polite equivalents of *merda* were *stercus* and (in Imperial Latin) *fimus*. Their distribution is as follows:[2]

	fimus	stercus
Plautus	–	2
Cato	3	25
Lucilius	1	2
Varro	1	12
Cicero	–	2
Vitruvius	–	4
Virgil	4	–
Livy	1	–
Celsus	–	16
Seneca *phil.*	–	3
Columella	25	80
Petronius	–	1
Tacitus	1	–
Suetonius	–	1
Palladius	30	67
Pelagonius	2	30
Mul. Chir.	3	74
Vegetius, *Mul.*	7	60
Vulgate	7	28
Marc. Emp.	65	56
Theod. Prisc., *Eup.*	7	11
Diosc. Lat. II	16	6
Cassius Felix	3	6

---

[1] *FEW* VI.2, p. 26.
[2] Statistics for veterinary writers were supplied by Dr K.-D. Fischer.

In the Republic and early Empire *stercus* was the standard
term in technical and formal prose, and it continued to be used
in late antiquity and survives in some Romance languages,
both in the East (Ital., Rum., Sic.) and to a limited extent in
the West (Astur. *istiercu*, Pg. *esterco*).[1] *Fimus* caught on in the
West (OFr. *fiens*, Prov. *femps*, Cat. *fems*).[2] It is remarkable for
the wide range of derivatives which it developed in late antiquity and handed on mainly to Gallo-romance and Ibero-
romance (*fimare, fimarium, fimita / femita, fimorare, fimorar-
ium*).[3] These can be compared with the comparable range of
derivatives which *stercus* already had in early Latin (e.g. *ster-
coratio, stercorare, stercilinum, stercorarius* in Cato). It will be
observed that one of the few writers in whom *fimus* outnumbers *stercus* is Marcellus Empiricus. Since he came from Bor-
deaux, his practice may partly reflect regional influence.
Stercus is glossed by *fimus* in the Reichenau Glosses (916
'stercora: femus', 3005 'de stercore: ex femo'),[4] which are a
source for early N.French vocabulary.

Stercus was acceptable in the early official / religious
language, as can be seen from *CIL* I².401 'in hoce loucarid
stircus ne [qu]is fundatid neue. . .', and from the old formula
quoted by Varro *Ling.* 6.32 'dies qui uocatur "quando stercum
delatum fas", ab eo appellatus, quod eo die ex Aede Vestae
stercus euerritur'. *Fimus*, on the other hand, to judge by its
use in Virgil, Livy and Tacitus, might have had a slightly
more literary flavour in the earlier period. But it seems more
likely that there was an early semantic distinction between
the two words.

Stercus was a very general word, which could indicate the
excrement of any animal or of humans. Lucilius was thinking
at least in part of human excreta in the comparison at 399
'praetor noster adhuc, quam spurcos ore quod omnis / *extra
castra ut stercus foras eiecit* ad unum'; for the sense 'human
excrement', cf., e.g. Cels. 2.12.2B twice. The generality of the
word can be seen at Cato *Agr.* 36 'stercus *columbinum* spargere
oportet in pratum uel in hortum uel in segetem. *caprinum*,

---

[1] *REW* 8245, *FEW* III, p. 547.
[2] *REW* 3311, *FEW* III, p. 547.
[3] See *REW* 3307–3310a, and also *FEW* III, pp. 544ff. These derivatives are
not entirely unattested in late Latin: see J. F. Niermeyer, *Mediae Latinitatis
Lexicon Minus* (Leiden, 1954–76), s.vv. *fimare, fimarium*.
[4] See H.-W. Klein, *Die Reichenauer Glossen* I (Munich, 1968).

ouillum, bubulum, item *ceterum stercus omne* sedulo conser-
uato'; cf. 161.4 'stercus *ouillum . . .* fac ingeras; . . . *aliut stercus* herbas creat'. The example at 37.2 means nothing more
specific than 'compost': 'stercus unde facias: stramenta, lu-
pinum, paleas, fabalia. . .'. Cato uses *stercus* with the following
adjectives: *caprinum, columbinum, ouillum, suillum, ceterum,
aliut* (on *bubulum* see below.)[1]

Fimus may originally have been a specialised term. Two of
the three examples in Cato are qualified by *bubulus* (40.2,
46.2), and the third (28.2 'oblinitoque fimo summas (arbores)')
is in an identical phrase to that at 46.2 ('fimoque bubulo sum-
mam taleam oblinito'); it is likely to have been used elliptically
in the same sense as the full expression ('ox, cow, dung'). Cato
does not use *bubulum* with *stercus,* if one excludes the special
case at 36, where *bubulum* is merely one of a series of adjectives and is not juxtaposed with *stercus.* A specialised sense
for *fimus* is also supported by Lucil. 1018 ('hic in stercore humi
fabulisque, fimo atque sucerdis'), where the word comes between two specialised terms (see below). Similarly the only
occurrences of *fimus* both in Varro (*Rust.* 3.16.16 'uitiles fimo
bubulo oblinunt intus et extra') and Livy (38.18.4) are accompanied by *bubulus.* Varro does not use *stercus* specifically of
ox / cow dung (the example at *Rust.* 1.2.21 is somewhat vaguer
in meaning).

By the time of Columella any original distinction between
stercus and *fimus* was probably fading. Nevertheless *bubulus*
is the only specifying adjective of its type which Columella
uses with *fimus* (5.6.8, 9.14.1, *Arb.* 3.4; cf. 9.14.2, where *fimus*
= *fimus bubulus,* and 10.82, where *armentique fimo* in verse
is presumably equivalent to *fimus bubulus*). He does not use
bubulum as an epithet of *stercus.* And at 4.8.3 ('aliquid fimi,
uel si est commodius, columbini stercoris'), where *fimus,* unspecified, is contrasted with pigeon dung, some such meaning
as 'cow, cattle manure' has to be given to *fimus* to make sense
of the contrast. Cf. Vulg. *Ezech.* 4.15 'et dixit ad me "ecce dedi
fimum boum pro *stercoribus humanis"* '. As used by Pliny the
Elder *fimus* had lost its specialised meaning (see, e.g. *Nat.*
29.106, 30.67).

I conclude that *stercus* had long been a generic term for the

---

[1] For examples, see A. Mazzarino, *M. Porci Catonis De Agri Cultura* (Leipzig,
1962), index, p. 122.

excrement of humans, birds and quadrupeds, but that *fimus* originally denoted ox / cow dung or manure. Its semantic restriction is clear in Republican Latin, but the two words overlapped by the Empire.

At a later date a distinction is drawn between *stercus* and *fimus* at *Mul. Chir.* 698: 'quodcumque iumentum ab stercore equalis [= *equilis*], quod femum[1] uocatur, collectionem in ungulam fecerit'. Here too it is *stercus* that is general, *fimus* specific (= 'stable manure'). This use of *fimus* survived in the dialect of the Morvan, France (*fien* = 'fumier d'étable').[2] It is only a small step from the original sense argued above for *fimus*, and that seen here. In a later passage of the *Mulomedicina*, and also perhaps in 698, *femus* appears to be used in a derived sense, = 'affliction caused by stable manure': 875 'malagma ad femus'; cf. 698 'collectionem in ungulam . . . famicem quod appellamus femi' (*femi* Oder, *fenici* cod.).

A few other uses of *fimus* and *stercus* are worth mentioning. In Virgil's *Georgics fimus* is used of manure (1.80, 2.347), but at *Aen.* 5.333 and 358 its sense is probably more general, = 'filth'. The tendency of *merda* to move in this direction has been noted earlier; conversely, words for 'filth' and the like are sometimes used of excrement (see below). There is a frequent overlap between words of these two general areas.

At *De Orat.* 3.164 Cicero expresses disapproval of the metaphorical expression *stercus curiae*, applied to a man: 'nolo "stercus curiae" dici Glauciam: . . . est . . . deformis cogitatio similitudinis'. With this can be compared the metaphorical use of *merda*, or more particularly of its Romance reflexes.

Stercus, like *merda* later, is used in the same sense as σκωρία at Scrib. Larg. 188.

---

[1] In this spelling the *e* must represent the open *e* which was handed on to the Romance reflexes of the word (see *FEW* III, p. 547). The *e* was no doubt due to a contamination between *fimus* and *stercus*. Words for 'excrement' were constantly contaminated phonetically both with one another and with words of similar meaning. Certain reflexes of *merda* show contamination with **fimora* (see *FEW* VI.2, p. 26). In some areas *laetamen* was contaminated with *lutum* (*REW* 4845), and *lotium* too was sometimes modified under the influence of *lutum* (*REW* 5129; see below, p. 240).

[2] See *FEW* III, p. 544. Various derivatives of *fimus* have related senses: see *FEW* III, pp. 545f.

(iv) Some specialised terms

It was mentioned earlier that a language may have a set of specialised words for the excrement of different types of animals. In Greek note ὄνις (a derivative of ὄνος, = 'ass's dung': Aristoph. *Pax* 4), βόλιτον (-ος) ('cow dung': Aristoph. *Ach.* 1026), ὀνιαῖα ('dung of the ass': Hesych. ὀνιαῖα. τοῦ ἵππου τὸ ἀφόδευμα) and σφυράδες ('balls of dung', as of the goat or sheep: Aristoph. *Pax* 790). French makes some similar distinctions: cf. *bouse* (of the cow, ox), *crottin* (of the horse, mule), *crotte* (of the dog, cat), *fiente* (of birds). There are traces of such a set in Latin. On *fimus*, see the preceding section. Cf. *muscerda*, of the *mus* (see Fest. p. 132 'muscerdas prima syllaba producta dicebant antiqui stercus murum'; cf. Varro *ap.* Plin. *Nat.* 29.106, Marc. Emp. 25.30), *sucerda* (Paul. Fest. p. 391 'sucerda stercus suillum'; cf. Lucil. 1018 quoted above), and perhaps *opicerda* (Fest. p. 390.29 opicer[da (?); if the restoration is correct, why does the word have a *p*? Was it influenced by *opilio*?). These words may be of root **sker-* (*d*-), with a false division of *mu-scerda* (*mus-cerda*) producing *su-cerda*.[1] But the etymology is doubtful. In the passage of Lucilius referred to above, *fabulus* (diminutive of *faba*) is juxtaposed with *fimus* and *sucerda*. It presumably indicated a small, bean-like pellet of dung, perhaps that of the goat. Commentators (see Marx *ad loc.*) compare *faba* at Plin. *Nat.* 19.185 'fabis caprini fimi'. The three nouns in this passage, following the generic *stercus*, look like contemporary terms of the farmyard. But both *fabulus* and the words based on *-cerda* seem to have fallen out of use by the Empire. None survives in Romance. At *Nat.* 29.106 Pliny talks of *muscerda* as an abnormality: 'praeterea, ut Varro noster tradit, murinum fimum, quod ille muscerdas appellat'.

Late Latin also had a specialised term for 'manure', *laetamen*.[2] As applied to dung *laetamen* was originally euphemistic, since in etymology it means simply 'thing for fattening, fertiliser' (< *laetus*, 'rich, fertile'). This is the force of its first occurrence, at Plin. *Nat.* 18.141 'nascitur qualicumque solo cum centesimo grano, ipsumque pro laetamine est'. Its specialisation was complete by the time of Palladius, who has it 29

---

[1] See Pokorny I, pp. 947f.
[2] In earlier Latin *stercus* and also *fimus* are frequently translateable by 'manure'.

times. On its tone, see Serv. on Virg. *Georg.* 1.1 'fimus, qui per agros iacitur, uulgo laetamen uocatur' (cf. Isid. *Etym.* 17.2.3). Sometimes Palladius has *laetamen* in a context in which Columella had used *stercus* (e.g. 3.20.2 = Col. 11.2.18); for the alternation of *laetamen* and *stercus* in Palladius, see, e.g. 10.1.2–4. His use of both *laetamen* and *stercus* no doubt reflects the current language of his day in Italy and Sardinia, in both of which he had estates. *Laetamen* survived widely in Italy and also in Sardinia.[1] *Laetare* (= *stercorare*), which Palladius has 4 times, also lived on in a few Italian dialects (and Engadine).[2]

(v) *Cunire* and some comparable words

The mysterious verb *cunire* mentioned by Paul. Festus (p. 44 'cunire est stercus facere, unde et inquinare') has been explained by J. André.[3] André argues for a phonetic alternation *incŭnare* / *inquĭnare*,[4] and establishes the existence of an intransitive *cŭnire* (=*cacare*). *Cunire* has a derivative *cuniculum*, attested at *CGL* VI.296 'cuniculum dicitur flux<us> uentris'. *Cunire* (lit. roughly = 'make filth') must be the intransitive correspondent of transitive *cŭnare*, 'defile, soil with excrement', which may be attested at *Mul. Chir.* 431 'crura sibi conabit' (with a typical vulgar spelling *o* for *ŭ*).

The association between 'filth, defilement' and excretion is a close one. Excrement is said to 'defile' or to be 'filth', and one who excretes may 'dirty himself' or 'defile' something or someone. Plautus' expression *inquinaui pallium* at *Pseud.* 1279 ('itaque dum enitor, prox! iam paene inquinaui pallium') is roughly equivalent to Eng. *soil, dirty oneself.* At *CIL* XII. 2426 *spurcitiam facere* = *cacare*: 'si quis in eo mixserit, spurcit(iam) fecerit in temp(lo) Iouis'. Cf. *Mul. Chir.* 224 'acres humores et spurcitiam corporis excludit' (cf. Veg. *Mul.* 1.43.5).[5] The association of ideas can also be seen in the following selection of passages: Hor. *Serm.* 1.8.37 'merdis caput inquiner albis / cor-

---

[1] See *REW* 4845.

[2] See *REW* 4846.

[3] See *Scritti in onore di Giuliano Bonfante* (Brescia, 1976) I, pp. 19ff.

[4] For *incunare*, see Varro, *Rust.* 3.16.34.

[5] *Spurcitia* here is not exactly synonymous with the example above. At *Mul. Chir.* 252 *expurcitia* may represent a conflation of *spurcitia* and *expurgatio*: see Oder, Index, p. 369.

240   *The Latin Sexual Vocabulary*

uorum', Col . 8.5.19 'plumulaeque . . . detrahendae, ne stercore
coinquinatae durescant', 8.7.2 'ne stercore coinquinentur', Isid.
Etym. 11.1.133 'ex ipso enim sordes stercorum defluunt'. *El-
uuies* (lit. 'filth *et sim.* to be washed away') is sometimes used
of excrement (e.g. Lucil. 645, [Aurel. Vict.] *Epit. de Caes.* 9.18),
as is *caenum* (*CGL* IV.217.1).[1] The contamination of *laetamen*
(and *lotium*) with *lutum* (see p. 237 n. 1) is of course comparable in type with the phraseology illustrated above; it is illuminated by Auson. *Epigr.* 106.9, p. 351 P. 'luteae Symplegadis
antrum', where the anus by implication contains *lutum*.

(vi) *Foria* and its derivatives

Foria is attested in two forms, as a neuter at Nonius p. 163 L.,
where it is glossed as *stercora liquidiora*, and as a feminine at
Varro *Rust.* 2.4.5, where it is a disease (unspecified) of cattle.
The two forms are given separate lemmata in the *TLL*, but
with little justification.[2] The variation of gender is of no consequence. *Foria* must have been a subliterary vulgarism = 'diarrhoea, liquid excrement', and it survived as (e.g.) Fr. *foire*.[3] The
disease of cattle might have been some sort of flux. The issue
is confused by Pelagonius' peculiar remark, 183.1 'ad eos quibus membra deficiunt, *quod mulomedici foria appellant*'. He
was not thinking of diarrhoea, as is made clear at 183.2 'quibus
membra aut sole nimio aut labore deficiunt nec stare possunt,
. . . ne dolorem uentris sperans [= *putans*] medellas et curas
strofo praebeas'. The clause 'quod mulomedici foria appellant'
may be an interpolation, as suggested by Vollmer at *TLL*
VI.1.1055.23f. Dysentery or diarrhoea might well cause weakness (e.g. *Mul. Chir.* 431). The interpolator may have misunderstood *foria* as meaning 'weakness' from a passage in which
weakness was mentioned as a consequence of *foria*.

Foria had various derivatives. *Conforio* at Pompon. 64 ('conforisti me, Diomedes') survives as Rum. *cufurì*. *Foriolus* at
Laber. 66 ('foriolus esse uidere: in coleos cacas') has an obvious
enough tone in the context. Both words clearly refer to diarrhoea, and both were vulgar. Cf. Schol. Juv. 3.38 'forirę est pro
deonerare uentrem' (cf. *CGL* V.296.12). The intransitive use

---

[1] See *TLL* III.98.79ff.
[2] See Fischer, *Pelagonii Ars Veterinaria*, p. 110.
[3] See *REW* 3438, *FEW* III, p. 711.

of *forire* should be compared with that of *cunire*; *conforire* was transitivised by its prefix. The one word of this root which may have achieved some respectability was *forica*, 'privy' (Juv. 3.38, *CGL* V.296.11).

A more polite expression for 'diarrhoea' was *fluxus uentris* (e.g. Hipp. *Aer.* 3, p. 7.1, translating διαρροίας).[1] Cf., e.g. *uentris effusio* at Theod. Prisc. *Eup.* 2.101, p. 200.3. *Diarrhoea* itself is sometimes used in medical works (e.g. Theod. Prisc. *Eup.* 2.37, p. 136.12).

(vii) Miscellaneous

(a) 'Sit'
For a typical euphemistic allusion to defecation, see Mart. 11.77.2 'die toto sedet'. The proverbial expression at Sen. *Apoc.* 10.3 ('tam facile homines occidebat quam canis adsidit') probably refers to defecation rather than to a bitch urinating; the euphemism was obviously a familiar one in ordinary speech. It was taken over into the medical language. *Desideo* is used by Celsus and Scribonius Largus,[2] and *adsellor* (based on the syntagm *ad sellam ire*) is common in later medical and veterinary works.[3] The abstract *assellatio* sometimes comes close to the concrete sense *stercus* (e.g. Cass. Fel. p. 130.13 *assellatio uentris humida*). Contrast ps.-Theod. Prisc. *Addit.* p. 304.13 'cum *sellas* perfecerit, intret balneum', where *sellas* is virtually equivalent to a verbal noun (= *assellationem, deiectionem*). Cf. *urina* = **urinatio*, below. p. 248.

(b) Deicio
Deicio was an old Latin euphemism, found first in Cato (e.g. *Agr.* 158.1 'aluum deicere hoc modo oportet, si uis bene tibi deicere'). The elliptical expression *aluum deicere* ('cast down (the contents of) the intestine') was obviously idiomatic (cf. 158.2); it referred to purging rather than to natural excretion. One effect of this, and perhaps similar, phrases was to cause *aluus* to take on a derived sense, '*stercus*, stool': e.g. Cels. 2.6.12 'aluus quoque uaria pestifera est' (cf. 3.18.18). *Deicio*

---

[1] See further *TLL* VI.1.985.22ff.
[2] See *TLL* V.1.695.79ff.
[3] See P. Flobert, *Les verbes déponents latins des origines à Charlemagne* (Paris, 1975), p. 232.

shows a weakening of sense, 'purge' > 'excrete normally' by
the time of Celsus: e.g. 2.12.2B 'si stercoris odorem *nihil de-
iciens* aeger ex spiritu suo sentit'. For *deiectio*, see, e.g. Cels.
1.3.25. Note the pleonasm at Cass. Fel. p. 127.10 *frequenti
deiectione assellationis* (with *assellationis* concrete in meaning:
see above).

(c) 'Withdraw'

The euphemism of 'going' or 'withdrawing', either for an unspecified purpose and to an unspecified destination (sc. *ad
sellam*), or to a place and for a purpose which, though they
may be specified, are euphemistically described (e.g. Eng. *go
to the toilet*), is probably familiar in most languages. Note Gk.
ἀποπατέω at (e.g.) Aristoph. *Eccl.* 326, and cf. ἀφοδεύω,
ἀφόδευμα, ἄφοδος. There was no well established euphemism
of this type in Latin, but note Plaut. *Curc.* 362 'dico me ire
quo saturi solent', Sall. *Hist.* frg. inc. 3 '*profectus* quidam Ligus
ad requisita naturae' (commented on by Quintilian, 8.6.59),
Amm. 23.6.79 'nec stando mingens nec ad requisita naturae
secedens'. With this use of *secedo* should be compared *secessus*
= 'privy' at Vulg. *Matth.* 15.17 'non intelligitis quia omne,
quod in os intrat, in uentrem uadit, et in secessum emittitur'
(ἀφεδρών is translated). *Secessus* also tended to take on the
sense 'excrement'.[1] At Vindic. *Epit. Alt.* 27, p. 479.8 ('sed
malum signum est exigua *meando* libido') *meando* is probably
not elliptical (sc. *ad sellam*), but a misspelling of *meiando*
(*-i*?). *Meiere* developed a first conjugation variant (p. 245).

(d) *Excerno, excrementum*

Excerno, which is used first of excretion by Celsus (e.g. 2.4.9
'praeter haec periculum ostendit id quod excernitur, si est
exiguum . . .'),[2] is a calque on ἐκκρίνω (L-S-J, *s.v.* 4; cf.
ἀποκρίνω at *Hipp. Berol.* 46.1 quoted below). The derivative
excrementum is used from Pliny the Elder onwards,[3] of any
type of bodily secretion (e.g. at Tac. *Hist.* 4.81, *Ann.* 16.4, of
the mouth and nose). Note Cael. Aurel. *Acut.* 1.114 'excre-
menta uentris (Graeci scybala dicunt)'.

[1] Svennung, p. 120.
[2] See *TLL* V.2.1227.21ff.
[3] *TLL* V.2.1283.47ff.

(*e*) 'Expel' and the like
Numerous verbs of this general semantic area are used euphemistically of urination and defecation and also vomiting, particularly in technical prose. It would be pointless to distinguish here between the first two senses.

For *emitto*, see Sen. *Epist*. 2.3 'cibus . . . qui statim sumptus emittitur' (cf. Veg. *Mul*. 1.17.4 'emittere lotium'). This verb and some other compounds of *mitto* obviously had some currency in technical registers. Compare, for example, Hipp. *Aer*. 9, p. 19.24 'demittunt facile urinam' with the Greek διουρεῦσι ῥηιδίως, and *Mul. Chir*. 395 'duriorem uentrem facit et remittit stercus durum' with *Hipp. Berol*. 46.1, *CHG* I, p. 220.11f. ἀφοδεύων σκληροτέραν ἔχει τὴν κοιλίαν, καὶ ἀποκρίνει μικρά, καὶ φυσᾶται ἡ ἕδρα (cf. *Mul. Chir*. 482 'quidquid remittit').

Egero is particularly common in the Empire and later Latin: e.g. Cass. Fel. p. 117.2 'urinae egerendae delectationem patiuntur' (*delectatio* = *desiderium*).[1] For *egerenda* = 'excrement', see Macrob. *Sat*. 7.4.17 'et inde uia est egerendis'. *Egestio* is used both as a verbal abstract (e.g. Aug. *Serm*. 243.7.6), and in a concrete sense, = 'excrement' (e.g. Cass. Fel. p. 122.5 'est autem dysenterica passio intestinorum causatio cum ulceratione, ex qua excluditur egestio sanguinolenta aut fellita'.

With the use of *excludo* in this last passage, cf. Hipp. *Aer*. 9, p. 21.4 'limpidas manat, excluditur', = τὸ καθαρώτατον διιεῖ καὶ ἐξουρέεται.[2]

Cf. Theod. Prisc. *Eup*. 2.31, p. 129.7 'expositis scybalis',[3] Marc. Emp. 31.49 'quod et libidines *offerendi* et conatus reprimet'.[4]

(*f*) 'Needs of nature', etc.
This type of expression has been seen above (*c requisita naturae*). Cf. ps.-Acron Hor. *Serm*. 1.6.109 'uas, in quo exoneratur uenter, . . . inuentum ad exquisita naturae', *Liutprandi Leg*. 125 'puellam liberam *sedentem ad necessitatem corporis sui* . . . ubi ipsa femina *pro sua necessitatem* nuda esse uedetur'.

[1] For *egero*, see *TLL* V.2.244.7ff.
[2] See *TLL* V.2.1271.51ff.
[3] Similarly for *depono*, see *TLL* V.580.5ff. Cf. Svennung, p. 109 (*pondus depono*). With this use of *pondus*, cf. *exonero* at, e.g. Plin. *Nat*. 10.126, ps.-Acron Hor. *Serm*. 1.6.109, and expressions such as *H.A.*, *Hel*. 32.2 'onus uentris auro excepit' (cf. Mart. 1.37.1 and Citroni *ad loc.*).
[4] On *conatus* (*conatio*), see Svennung, p. 109 n. 3.

244   *The Latin Sexual Vocabulary*

(g) Probrum

Sexual intercourse is often described as a 'disgrace', as we
have seen. It is an extraordinary form of euphemism when the
excretory functions are spoken of in the same terms of moral
disapproval: but see Plin. *Nat.* 33.152 'eademque materia et
cibis et *probris* seruiat'.

(h) Farciminalis

Another isolated usage is *farciminalis* = *stercus* at *Mul. Chir.*
229 'cum haec tamen causa euenerit, per anum farciminalis
sero uenire solet'. It is a derivative of *farcimen*, which indicated a 'stuffed gut' (i.e. a type of sausage). *Farciminalis* denotes that with which the gut (still in the body) is stuffed.

(i) Some Greek words

A foreign word from the sexual or excretory spheres can be
euphemistic, because its impact on readers may be less im-
mediate than that of a native word. When dealing with bodily
functions Cicero sometimes adopted Greek medical terms,
which he seems to have written in Greek script: *Att.* 10.10.3
'δυσουρία tua mihi ualde molesta; medere, amabo, dum est
ἀρχή', *Fam.* 7.26.1 'sane δυσεντερίαν pertimueram', 7.26.2
'tanta me διάρροια adripuit ut . . .'. Later medical writers introduced σκύβαλον from the Greek medical language as a term
for excrement: e.g. Theod. Prisc. *Eup.* 2.25, p. 122.12 'coacti
scybala uel urinas . . . excludere' (cf. 2.28, p. 125.20, 2.29,
p. 126.16f., 2.31, p. 129.7, Oribas. *Syn.* 1.19 La, p. 67.4
Mørland, *Mul. Chir.* 230, Veg. *Mul.* 1.47.2.

At *Mul. Chir.* 139 ('dare etiam bibere pusillum non contin-
uum et intermittentem producere caute et bolutationes et urinam prouocare') *bolutationes* (= 'defecation') may be due to a
conflation of βόλιτον and *uolutare*.[1]

On *facio*, see p. 204, and on *facio oletum*, p. 68, n. 2.

---

[1] See Oder, Index, p. 330, s.vv. *bolutare, bolutatio*. The examples of *uolutare*
at 148 and 433 are also quoted by Oder in this connection, but the second case
is highly dubious.

2. Urination

(i) *Mingo* and *meio*

It is not easy to separate these two verbs in Republican and early Imperial Latin. Do the perfect *mixi* and supine *mictum* belong to *meio*, or are they parts of *mingo*, without the nasal infix? Were they perhaps borrowed by *meio* from *mingo*? Were there historically two distinct perfects, *mixi* / *minxi*, or were scribes responsible for adding (or subtracting) *n* haphazardly? Manuscripts are often split between *mix-* / *minx-* or between *mict-* / *minct-* (e.g. Catull. 99.10, Hor. *Serm.* 1.2.44, 1.3.90, Mart. 3.78.1). In the infectum *meio* is attested for the first time in Catullus (97.8 *meientis*). *Mingo* may occur for the first time in the Republican orator Titius, but it is not in the infectum (frg. 2 *it minctum*, quoted by Macrob. *Sat.* 3.16.16 with a nasal infix). Most of the Republican and Augustan examples of the two (?) verbs, whether meaning 'urinate' or 'ejaculate', are in the perfect or supine (Catull. 39.18 *minxit*, 67.30 *minxerit*, 78b.2 *conminxit* (a conjecture), 99.10 *commictae*, Hor. *Serm.* 1.2.44 *perminxerunt*, 1.3.90 *comminxit*, 1.8.38 *ueniat mictum*; cf. *CIL* IV.4957 *miximus*). From this period onwards the infectum *meio* becomes common enough (Hor. *Serm.* 2.7.52 *meiat*, Pers. 1.114 *meiite*, 6.73 *inmeiat*, Petron. 67.10 *meiere*, Mart. 11.46.2 *meiere*, 12.32.13 *meiebat*, Juv. 1.131 *meiere*). The infectum *ming-*, however, does not appear until the fourth century (see below).[1] It is not impossible that *meio, mixi, mictum* was the original verb, and that *mingo* was a late back-formation from the perfectum formed on the analogy of those verbs which lost a nasal infix in the perfectum. Late scribes might have added the nasal infix haphazardly in the perfectum and supine in Republican and Augustan writers.

In late Latin a first conjugation variant *meiare* made an appearance (e.g. *Mul. Chir.* 399; for the perfectum, see Diosc. Lat. II, p. 207.1 *meiauerit*), perhaps under the influence of *cacare*. *Meiare* survives in the Romance languages (e.g. Sp. *mear*, Pg. *mijar*).[2]

---

[1] On the problem of *meio* / *mingo*, see F. Sommer, *Handbuch der lateinischen Laut- und Formenlehre*²⁻³ (Heidelberg, 1914), p. 500, J. B. Hofmann, *Glotta* 29 (1942), pp. 41ff., Ernout and Meillet, *s.vv.*

[2] *REW* 5468.

Mention of urination may not have been under such a strong taboo as that of defecation (unseemly though the act may have been considered by some: see Amm. 23.6.79), and there is no word attested in Latin which seems to have been quite as offensive as *caco*.[1] *Mingo* (in late Latin) was a direct verb, in that it had no other more basic meaning than 'urinate'. But though it is by no means common in literature, it was not an outright obscenity. It is admitted in various works from which basic obscenities were excluded. Apart from one possible case in Titius and another in Juvenal (3.107), there are certain examples in Ammianus (23.6.79), the *Historia Augusta* (*Quad. Tyr.* 14.5; cf. *Hel.* 32.2 *minxit*), medical writers (e.g. Cass. Fel. pp. 113.19, 117.2; see below on Vegetius) and the Vulgate (6 times). The failure of *mingo* to survive in the Romance languages shows that it did not have a popular character, at least in the late period. The supine *mictum* leaves traces,[2] no doubt because the expression *ire (uenire) mictum* was idiomatic (see Titius frg. 2, Hor. *Serm.* 1.8.38), but it is not certain whether this is the supine of *meio* or *mingo*.

Meio was a more popular word, but its distribution is not the same as that of *caco*. Unlike *mingo*, it survives in Romance. Its relatively low status, at least in late Latin, is shown by Vegetius' use of *mingo* in contexts in which the more vulgar *Mulomedicina Chironis* has *meio* (e.g. Veg. *Mul.* 1.46.1 = *Mul. Chir.* 228, Veg. *Mul.* 2.79.1 = *Mul. Chir.* 460).[3] Nevertheless *meio* is admitted by Persius and Juvenal (see above), both of whom avoid *caco*. At Juv. 1.131 *meio* is used in a context in which *caco* is merely implied. Similarly in the *Mulomedicina Chironis meio* is admitted but *caco* avoided, even though defecation is often mentioned. *Meio* was obviously a sub-standard word, but it was not subject to such a rigid veto as *caco*.

(ii) *Lotium* and *urina*

Lotium began as a euphemism (lit. 'liquid for washing', < *lauo*). It would have developed the sense 'urine' from the custom of employing urine as a liquid for washing clothes and

---

[1] It is of course impossible to determine the tone of *pišare* in our period, if it was in existence. It survived throughout the Romance-speaking world (*REW* 6544).

[2] *REW* 5563.

[3] See further *TLL* VIII.604.54f.

other objects (see Isid. *Etym.* 11.1.138 'qui humor uulgo lotium dicitur, quod eo lota, id est munda, uestimenta efficiantur'). Something of the etymological force of *lotium* is still apparent at Catull. 39.21 (of urine used for cleaning the teeth).

The distribution of *lotium* and *urina* is as follows:

	lotium	*urina*
Cato, *Agr.*	10	–
Varro, *Rust.*	–	2
Cicero	–	1
Catullus	1	1
Celsus	–	88
Seneca, *phil.*	–	1
Columella	2	19
Petronius	1	–
Juvenal	–	2
Suetonius	1	4
Apuleius	2	2
Palladius	1	34
Pelagonius	8	13
Mul. Chir.	37	23
Vegetius, *Mul.*	22	27
Vulgate	–	2
Marc. Emp.	35	74
Theod. Prisc., *Eup.*	2	11
Diosc. Lat. II	4	22
Cassius Felix	–	27

In Cato *lotium* is the standard word, but by the end of the Republic and early Empire (Varro, Cicero, and most notably Celsus) *urina* was clearly the polite term. One must assume either that Cato deliberately admitted a colloquial word (156.7 'quibus aegre lotium it' looks like a colloquial idiom; cf. 127.1 'lotium facere'), or that *urina* was not yet established in the educated language. *Vrina* is a puzzling word. The verb *urinor* means 'dive' (Varro *Ling.* 5.126), and *urinator* 'diver'. The relationship between these derivatives and *urina* = 'urine' is obscure. Perhaps *urina* originally meant 'water'; [1] hence *inurinare*, 'dive (into water)' (Col. 8.14.2). Whatever the case, *urina* = 'urine' may have become established as a technical

[1] See Ernout and Meillet, *s.v.*

term because it was associated with οὖρον and οὐρέω, both medical terms. As the educated term *urina* did not survive into the Romance languages except as a learned loan-word. But *lotium* is well represented.[1] Some of its reflexes mean 'urine', but others are more general (e.g. Apul. *lottsu*, 'mud'). *Lotium* tended to be contaminated phonetically with *lutum*, and a semantic contamination would also have taken place. For the association of the two words, see Pelagon. 155 'lutum de uia, id est ex lotio cuiuslibet equi factum' (cf. Veg. *Mul.* 2.79.22). Isidore's description of *lotium* as vulgar is certainly accurate for the period from the late Republic onwards. Hence it is noteworthy that in veterinary works (including that of Vegetius) *lotium* is abnormally frequent. In agricultural Latin *lotium* may have lost any vulgar of offensive tone which it had in other varieties of the language (cf. *merda*). The specialised meaning 'urine of the cow' which one of its Romance reflexes has (Val.-ses. *lots*) must reflect its currency among farmers. It may already have been a farmers' term as used by Cato.

There is an example of *lotium* in a freedman's speech in Petronius, in an expression with a proverbial ring (57.3 'qui non ualet lotium suum'). That at Suet. *Vesp.* 23.3 is in direct speech following *urina* in the narrative. In the Scholia to Juvenal at 6.312 Juvenal's *urinam* is glossed with *lotium*. The derivative *lotiolentus* at Titin. 137 would suggest that there was a coarse element in the vocabulary of the *fabula togata* which was missing from that of *palliata*. Excretion, including urination, is an occasional source of jokes in Plautus, but explicit terminology is avoided (*Curc.* 362 and *Pseud.* 1279 have been quoted earlier; cf. *Curc.* 415f., *Most.* 386, *Pers.* 98).

Vrina had acquired no corresponding verbal noun *urinatio*, because of the sense attaching to *urinor, -atio*. Hence *urina* itself (in the genitive) often behaves as a verbal abstract, as at Cels. 2.1.8 'urinae difficultas, quam στραγγουρίαν appellant', Cass. Fel. p. 115.14, etc. It was a more normal semantic development for an abstract noun to become concrete in meaning, as at Cass. Fel. p. 116.18 'sanguinolentus minctus aut saniosus'. *Minctus* is a few times used by Cassius Felix as a verbal noun (note p. 113.11 *minctus difficultate*), as is *minctio* by the author of the *Mulomedicina Chironis*[2] and by Vegetius

---

[1] *REW* 5129.
[2] See Oder, Index, *s.v.*

(e.g. *Mul.* 1.50.1). Gerund / gerundive expressions were also employed (e.g. Cass. Fel. p. 116.2 'initio urinae excludendae'). The Greek words *dysuria*, *stranguria* and *ischuria* were well established in the Latin medical language (*stranguria* from Cato onwards: *Agr.* 127.1), and the use of one of these might sometimes save a Latin writer from the need to select a Latin verbal noun or equivalent.[1] Cicero's choice of the Greek form δυσουρία at *Att.* 10.10.3 has been noted earlier.

3. *Pedo* and its alternatives

Pedo 'fart' (of root *pezd-, alongside *perd-, seen in Gk. πέρδο-μαι) has numerous Indo-European cognates as well as Romance reflexes (e.g. OIt. *pedere*, OFr. *poire*). The noun *peditum*, used by Catullus at 54.3, also lived on into the modern languages (e.g. It. *peto*, Fr. *pet*).[2] *Pedo* is not the sort of word one would expect to find in polite literature, but it occurs in the first book of Horace's *Sermones* (1.8.46; cf. *oppedo*, with a dative complement, at *Serm.* 1.9.70), and in Martial (6 times). According to Cicero, the innocent word *intercapedo* contained a *cacemphaton*: *Fam.* 9.22.4 'non honestum uerbum est "di-uisio"? at inest obscenum, cui respondet "intercapedo" '. See further Garg. Mart. *Curae Boum* 12 'intestinum enim mouit ut pedere non cesset'.

Words of this root had an onomatopoeic origin, and the same is true of *uissire* (a *cacemphaton* contained in Cicero's *diuisio* above). The implication of *uissire*, with its lack of a plosive consonant, is well illustrated by the inscription published by Calza, *Die Antike* 15 (1939), p. 102 'uissire *tacite* Chilon docuit subdolus'. *Vissire* rarely surfaces in recorded Latin, but it survives in Romance,[3] along with various derivatives (*uissi-nare, uissio).[4]

A less offensive substitute for *pedo* was the more general verb *crepo*. *Crepo* was employed in a speech by Cato (frg. 73), in reference to a controversy concerning the ill-omened character of farting: 'serui, ancillae, si quis eorum sub centone

---

[1] For more basic, non-abstract references to such afflictions, see Cato, *Agr.* 122 'si lotium difficilius transibit', 156.7 'quibus aegre lotium it'.
[2] *REW* 6358.
[3] *REW* 9382.
[4] *REW* 9380, 9381.

crepuit, quod ego non sensi, nullum mihi uitium facit. si cui
ibidem seruo aut ancillae dormienti euenit, quod comitia pro-
hibere solet . . .'. The same topic is touched upon by Martial
(12.77), who also uses *crepo*: 11 'sed quamuis sibi cauerit cre-
pando, / compressis natibus Iouem salutat'. *Crepo* is also used
in this way by Plautus in a pun at *Poen.* 610: 'fores hae fecerunt magnum flagitium modo. / ADV. quid <id> est flagiti?
CO. crepuerunt clare. ADV. di te perduint!'. For farting as a
flagitium, see Mart. 12.77.7 'post hoc flagitium misellus Ae-
thon . . .' (cf. *uitium* in the passage of Cato above). Jupiter is
said by Martial to have been offended by the action. Plautus
does not use offensive terminology in his puns, nor indeed is
Cato likely to have done so in a speech. Cf. Plaut. *Men.* 925f.
'enumquam intestina tibi *crepant*, quod sentias? / MEN. ubi
satur sum, nulla *crepitant*; quando essurio, tum *crepant*'. For
crepitus uentris, see, e.g. Suet. *Claud.* 32.

Crepitus had long overlapped, and been associated, with
strepitus (e.g. Plaut. *Amph.* 1062). Occasionally *strepitus* is
used as an equivalent of *crepitus* in our sense: e.g. Petron.
117.12 'tollebat subinde altius pedem et strepitu obsceno simul
atque odore uiam implebat' (cf. Min. Fel. *Oct.* 28.9, *Mul. Chir.*
38, 464).

In medical Latin flatulence is usually described by means of
circumlocutions containing (e.g.) *inflatio* (Cels. 2.3.6, 4.23.2),
spiritus (Cels. 2.12.2B, 4.19.1), *uentus* (*Mul. Chir.* 231), *uen-
tositas* (Theod. Prisc. *Eup.* 2.84, p. 186.10). Cf. πνεῦμα (L-S-J,
s.v. II.3). For an expression of this type in non-technical Latin,
see Plaut. *Aul.* 304f. 'etiamne opturat inferiorem gutturem, /
ne quid *animai* forte amittat dormiens'; cf. perhaps *Curc.* 314–
16 (*uentum facere*).

Addenda and Corrigenda

p. 20: Pompon. 40. I print Frassinetti's text (34). O. Ribbeck, *Comicorum Romanorum praeter Plautum et Syri quae feruntur Sententias Fragmenta*[3] (Leipzig, 1898) prefers *coculeatum* (Buecheler). The *codd.* at Non. pp. 7, 150, and 267 L. are split between *coleatum, cocleatum, clocleatum, culeratum, culenarum.*

p. 22: For κέρας, see R. L. Hunter, *ZPE* 41 (1981), pp. 20f.

p. 22: Novius 80. I quote the fragment in the form which it has in Festus. Ribbeck[3] has <*ut*> *otiosi* (Buecheler), Frassinetti (79) 'quid ego facerem otio si rodebam rutabulum'.

p. 27: Plaut. *Cas.* 912 'profecto hercle non fuit quicquam *holerum*' would have particular point if vegetable-names were commonly used of the male organ in jokes. The passage is full of agricultural terminology: see W. T. MacCary and M. M. Willcock, *Plautus Casina* (Cambridge, 1976), 914n. on *grandis* and *calamitas.*

p. 35: On φλέψ, see Hunter, *ZPE* 41 (1981), p. 21.

p. 37: I would no longer subscribe to the interpretation of *bracchia macra* at *Priap.* 72.4 tentatively suggested here.

p. 38, with n. 2: I am no longer convinced by this interpretation of Cic. *Sest.* 16.

p. 39: On δέλτα see now D. M. Bain, *LCM* 7.1 (January 1982), pp. 8f.

p. 43: I take *peculium* to mean 'penis' not 'anus' at Plaut. *Pseud.* 1188 because of the expression 'femina summa sustinent'. The 'thighs' (*femina*), the 'top of the thighs' (see Juv. 6.423), the 'space between the thighs' *et sim.* are often spoken of in Latin as the site of the genital organs (see pp. 51, 93), but not, as far as I know, of the *culus.* Harpax would thus be abused as a man who sold his *mentula* (cf. Mart. 1.58, 9.63, Juv. 9.136), whereas at 1181 he was abused as a pathic. In invective a man may be labelled both a *pathicus* and *pedicator*: see Cic. *Cat.* 2.8.

p. 45: Pompon. 86. The interpretation of this fragment is extremely doubtful; Ribbeck³ prints 'farinam insipui concussi condepsui'. If *partem* had an anatomical sense, it would only be object of the first two verbs; there would have to be a pause before *condepsui*.

p. 57: With *uenus*, cf. Theod. Prisc. *Eup.* 2.33, p. 131.11 'hi etenim frequenter *usum* erigere *uenerium* consuerunt'.

p. 57: For *surgo*, see Ovid *Am.* 2.15.25, Mart. 12.86.2, 12.97.9 (cf. Apul. *Met.* 7.23).

p. 57, sect. v: Buecheler, *RhM* 18 (1863), p. 400, = *Kleine Schriften* I, p. 347 may have been right in suggesting that *stator* indicates the *mentula* at *Priap.* 52.3: 'iam primum stator hic libidinosus / alternis et eundo et exeundo / porta te faciet patentiorem' (for *libidinosus*, cf. 63.14). It would be used in its etymological sense ('the one who stands'; cf. *sto* at Mart. 2.45.1, 3.75.1, *Priap.* 73.2), and would thus be an *ad hoc* 'descriptive' designation. But *statores* ('orderlies') might have a crude virility (Petron. 126.5), and various other extraneous characters (and an *asellus*) are introduced in 52 to punish the thief.

p. 62: For *sexus*, cf. Cass. Fel. p. 174.11.

p. 65: J. Knobloch's view (*RhM* 112 (1969), pp. 23ff.) that *salaputium* was inoffensive (= 'little chap') is no more compelling than any other interpretation hitherto proposed. Knobloch sees in the second element the same root as in *pusus, putus, pullus* etc., but his argument (pp. 26f.) that *sala-* is a 'lallende Wortverlängerung' (with dubious affiliations) carries no conviction. The fact that *Salaputis* (*-ium?*) was a *cognomen* (see Knobloch p. 27, quoting *CIL* VIII.10570) does not of course establish the inoffensiveness of *salaputium* (cf. p. 63 on *Penis* and *Mutto*).

p. 68: The text and interpretation of *Priap.* 50.6 remain unclear to me. For *pares* ('equal') as an epithet of *testes*, see Col. 6.29.2 (Pelagon. 2).

p. 83: Laber. 25. I quote the fragment in a form close to the paradosis (Non. p. 154 L. 'an concupisti eugium scindere'). Bothe suggested *concupiuisti*. Ribbeck made a radical transposition.

p. 84: Matthew of Vendôme, *Milo* 68*d* contains a verbal (agricultural) metaphor, not a nominal.

p. 88: For doubts about this interpretation of *uter* at *Mul. Chir.* 224, see Fischer, *Pelagonii Ars Veterinaria*, p. 106.

p. 90: On *sinus* and κόλπος see now P. Migliorini, *Prometheus* 7 (1981), pp. 254ff.

p. 93 n. 3: Cf. Mart. 3.81.1 *femineo . . . barathro*.

pp. 95, 224: *Viscera* at Ovid *Am.* 2.14.27 could equally well be interpreted as meaning 'foetus' (cf. the use of *uterus* and *uenter* mentioned on p. 102). For *uiscera* = 'womb', see Quint. 10.3.4.

p. 97: At Jer. *Epist.* 84.5.3 it is a question whether *membra* individually are resurrected. *Coitus* must be given a concrete anatomical sense. If Jerome were talking of male and female parts, he would have mentioned those of the male first, to judge by the rest of the passage. Since *uulua* comes first, I assume that he has used the female body for this illustration.

pp. 111f.: G. Neumann, *Würz. Jahrb.* 6a (1980), p. 174n.6 suggests *apsculare* for *apoculare*. But would a vulgar compound have contained the archaic *abs-*, unless it were very old?

p. 114: For a convincing (non-sexual) interpretation of Εὐρώτας see now A. Cameron, *GRBS* 22 (1981), pp. 179ff.

p. 114: For the active participant in a sexual act described as 'burning' the passive, cf. *CIL* IV.1840 'Maria urit, fellat bene'. The metaphor on the coins is akin to that of 'striking'. Verbs of burning readily develop a metaphorical use of 'burning' with blows (Hor. *Epist.* 1.16.47).

p. 116: For *cunnus* = *culus*, see *CIL* IV.8898 'Popilus canis cunnu linge Reno' (cf. 8843).

p. 127: For the joke of 'silencing' someone, see also Min. Fel. *Oct.* 28.10 'homines malae linguae etiam si tacerent'.

pp. 137f.: The overlap between κινέω and βινέω may have arisen because κινέω came to be used as a phonetically suggestive substitute for the direct verb.

pp. 141, 172: Pompon. 151. The text is that of Frassinetti (150). On *has* see his note *ad. loc.*

p. 143 n. 1: For *finis* see also *Priap.* 26.4 'sine fine prurientes', with which should be compared Mart. 11.81.4 'sine effectu prurit utrique labor'. Cf. William of Blois, *Alda* 467 'crebros in fine salientis senserat Alda / uirge singultus'.

p. 144: With *effectus* at Mart. 11.81.4, cf. Petron. 140.9 'cum ergo res ad effectum spectaret'.

p. 144: According to H. D. Jocelyn, in F. Cairns (ed.), *Papers of the Liverpool Latin Seminar Third Volume* (Liverpool, 1981), pp. 279f., *propero* at Mart. 1.46.1 means 'I am in a hurry to do something elsewhere'. But this rare idiomatic use could only be given to the word in the presence of clear contextual pointers. There is no hint in Mart. 1.46 of another task, extraneous to the epigram, to which Hedylus is to move on. In various words in the poem sexual intercourse is by implication likened to spatial motion (*expectare*, *uelocius*, *ibo*, *retentus*), and these are the pointers by which *propero* must be interpreted. It is certain that *propero* could have the implication 'perform a physical act quickly, come quickly to a physical climax' of one sort or another. That is the sense that *ne properem* must be given, on any interpretation of the epigram, in line 4 (where Jocelyn would have to give *propero* two different meanings). It is also the sense of *propero* in the inscription from Ostia, whether the writer had in mind defecation or ejaculation; there too other words relevant to spatial motion are used. And it is the sense that the verb has at Ovid *Ars* 2.727 (*ad metam properate*). This last expression, like *coitum patrare*, is an expansion of an elliptical usage of the spoken language.

p. 146: *Cecidit* at Petron. 21.2 is unlikely to refer to *pedicatio* performed by the *cinaedus*. The usage is analogous to that of *distriuit* at 24.4 (of the motions of the *cinaedus* astride his supine victim). *Extortis clunibus* must mean 'with his own *clunes* twisted apart'. In both passages the *cinaedus* employs his *clunes* and *basia*.

p. 151: For 'digging', see also Plaut. *Cas.* 455 '†ecfodere hercle hic uolt, credo, uesicam uilico' (of homosexual assault: see MacCary and Willcock *ad loc.*). The notion that penetration might reach the bladder throws light on Juv. 1.39 (see pp. 91f.). For this type of exaggeration, see *Priap.* 6.6, 25.6f., 51.4, Auson. *Cent. Nupt.* 127, p. 217 P.

pp. 156f.: With *labor*, etc., cf. *laboriosus* at Petron. 92.9, of a man whose endowments cause him much *labor*.

pp. 159f.: Cf. *facere nuptias* at Plaut. *Cas.* 486; for the various senses of *nubo*, see also Jocelyn, *Papers of the Liverpool Latin Seminar Third Volume*, pp. 277f.

p. 162: It is not made explicit here that both *lusus* and *ludus* could have a sexual sense.

pp. 167f.: Intercourse may, of course, be 'stolen' or 'taken': e.g. Plaut. *Cas.* 891 'cupio illam operam seni surrupere' (here intercourse with a woman is 'stolen' from another male), Petron. 86.4 'si ego huic [dormienti] abstulero coitum plenum et optabilem', 100.1 'etiam cum uoluerit aliquid sumere, opus anhelitu prodet'.

p. 168: For a financial interpretation of *glubo* and *rado*, see H. Tränkle, *Mus. Helv.* 38 (1981), pp. 245ff.

p. 173: For χαλάω, see also ps.-Luc. *Asinus* 9.

p. 176: With Mart. 12.75.1, cf. *Priap.* 68.27 'ad uetulam tamen ille suam properabat', and also Plaut. *Cas.* 889–90 'enim iam magis adpropero, magis iam lubet in Casinam inruere'.

p. 179: *Coitus* could also be scanned as trisyllabic at Lucr. 1.185, Stat. *Theb.* 10.796 and Juv. 10.204, but in all of these places a disyllabic scansion is also possible. If *cŏĭtus* existed, it would be a recomposition (see F. Sommer, *Handbuch der lateinischen Laut- und Formenlehre*[4], revised by R. Pfister (Heidelberg, 1977), p. 96; cf. p. 67 on the phonetics of *coetus*), but I am now inclined to doubt the authenticity of the trisyllabic form. Even the spelling *coitus* could be a scribal invention.

p. 180: For the feet in intercourse, see also Plaut. *Cas.* 465 'hodie hercle, opinor, hi conturbabunt pedes'.

p. 181: Hipp. *Hom.* 3 should read Hipp. *Nat. Hom.* 3.

p. 185: With the stages of *amor* at Don. Ter. *Eun.* 640, cf. Petron. 109.2 'non amplexum, non osculum, non coitum uenere constrictum'.

p. 187: Cf. *pertracto* at Petron. 24.7.

p. 188: With *libido* and *uenus*, cf. *uota* of intercourse in Petronius (11.1, 86.5, 94.5; cf. 87.8 'quod uoluerat accepit').

p. 190: For *omnia* with a sexual implication, see also Petron. 11.2, 130.5.

pp. 193f.: For *uolutor*, see also [Cic.] *Inu. in Sall.* 1.3, quoted below.

p. 196: For other expressions comparable with *uirginitate priuauit* in the Latin novel, cf. Petron. 9.4 'coepitque mihi uelle pudorem extorquere' (spoken by Giton, and hence scarcely of deflowering; used thus the phrase is a 'persuasive' euphemism intended to imply that the speaker was more chaste than was really the case), 112.1 'pudicitiam eius aggressus est'.

p. 198: *Iniuria* as it is used in the *Satyricon* has the appearance of a homosexuals' vogue term for *pedicatio* of a boy (cf. 79.9, where the word was deleted by Müller, and 133.1; note too 133.2 'iurauit . . . sibi ab Ascylto nullam uim factam').

p. 200: For *uexo*, cf. Aug. *Ciu.* 6.9 'ne Siluanus deus per noctem ingrediatur et uexet'.

p. 204: With the idiom *fac si* . . . ('do it if . . .') in a homosexual context at Mart. 1.46.1, cf. Petron. 87.5 'si quid uis, fac iterum'.

p. 205: Laber. 56. Ribbeck's *scando* (for *scinde*), printed in the first edition of *CRF*, is attractive in the context, provided of course that a sexual act was being described. In his third edition Ribbeck preferred 'scinde una exoleto <huic> patienti <hanc> catulientem lupam', and he is followed by M. Bonaria, *Romani Mimi* (Rome, 1965), no. 70.

p. 206: For *salax* transferred to men, see also Catull. 37.1 *salax taberna* (= *taberna salacium*: Kroll), Petron. 43.8 'noueram hominem olim oliorum, et adhuc salax erat', *Priap.* 56.5 'mandabo domino tamen salaci'; cf. Hor. *Serm.* 1.2.45 *caudamque salacem.*

p. 208: To the verbs listed add *agito* (p. 144).

p. 209: With Mart. 11.104.11f. cf. *CIL* X.4483 'diciti adiuuabunt prurigin[em]'; *adiuuo* here should be compared with *iuuare* in Martial.

p. 235: The generality of *stercus* is also illustrated by its use = 'contents of the stomach': e.g. Pelagon. 88 'tolles illi uentrem et sic, quomodo est cum stercore suo, inuoluis illum . . .' (cf. 138.1).

p. 237: For the metaphorical use of *stercus*, see also Sen. *Apoc.* 7.5.

p. 237 n. 1. The contamination of *lutum* with *lotium* and *laetamen* is illuminated by *facias lutum* at Afran. 199 ('non usque quaque idoneum inuenias locum, / ubi derepente cum uelis facias lutum'), which may refer to urination (cf. Pelagon. 155, quoted at p. 248) or defecation (cf. *luteae* at Auson. *Epigr.* 106.9, *lutulentus* at [Cic.] *Inu. in Sall.* 1.3 quoted below). The passage of Afranius was drawn to my attention by H. D. Jocelyn.

p. 238: With *fabulus* and *faba*, cf. Catull. 23.21 'nec toto decies cacas in anno, atque id durius est *faba*'.

p. 240: With *luteae* at Auson. *Epigr.* 106.9, cf. perhaps *lutulentus* at [Cic.] *Inu. in Sall.* 1.3 'itaque nihil aliud studet nisi ut *lutulentus cum quouis uolutari*'.

p. 243, sect. *f*: Compare the use of *officium* at Hippocr. *Aer.* 9, p. 21.9 'perhibet [*sic*] officium urinae' (= κωλύει οὐρέειν).

p. 247: For *lotium* used with its etymological force, see also Cato *Agr.* 157.11, Pelagon. 56, 294, 348, 448.2.

Index

1. Latin

2. Greek

268   *Index*

3. General

abstract (for concrete), 55, 57,
  69–70, 97
'adjoining parts', 47–51, 91–2
aggression (sexual, verbal), 6, 77,
  124, 128, 130, 133–4
agricultural imagery, 23, 24–5,
  26–9, 82–5, 113–14, 152–5, 157
'altar', 87
amulets (phallic), 49, 63
anatomical metaphors, 33, 35–8, 98
animal metaphors, 29–34, 82
animals, terms appropriate to, 50,
  69, 101, 104, 108, 155, 167, 205–8
Anna Perenna, 5–6, 7, 225
apotropaic obscenity, 4–6
Apuleius, 21, 29, 57, 58, 86–7, 93,
  94, 149, 150, 157, 158, 159, 192,
  196, 208–9
[Apuleius], *spurcum additamentum*,
  20 n.1, 47 n.1, 58 n.3, 72 n.1, 73,
  142, 187, 209, 229–30
Archilochus, 11, 220
architectural metaphors, 17 n.1
Arnobius, 36, 53, 55 n.5, 62, 64, 67,
  68, 69, 75, 86, 137, 151, 179, 193
Atellane farce, 3, 14, 20, 23, 28, 66,
  77, 123, 140, 141, 147, 149, 152–3,
  175, 219, 231, 240
Augustine, 5, 17, 36, 42, 64, 91, 188
Augustus, 11 n.3, 26, 65, 121, 123,
  214, 225

Ausonius, 19–20, 25, 28, 30, 34, 39,
  74, 76, 85, 89, 92, 95, 112, 114,
  119, 135, 136, 139, 148, 151, 152,
  153, 159, 168, 172, 220–1

'bag', 75, 87–8
'bark', 74, 168
'be with', 177
Biblical parody, 24–5
birds, 31–3
'body', 46, 69
botanical metaphors, 26–9, 72, 74,
  76
'bow, bow string', 21–2
brothel slang, 32, 83, 173, 215
'burst', 51, 150, 151
buttocks, 47, 115, 149

cacemphata, 28, 97, 249
Cadiz dancers, 194 (with n.2), 225
Caesar, C. Iulius, 11 (with n.3), 23,
  128, 132, 200, 203
calques, 14, 26–7, 28, 29, 45, 53–4,
  59, 62, 68, 72, 76, 84, 90, 99, 100
  n.1, 108, 113, 181, 228, 242
castration, 46, 49, 69, 70 n.1
Catullus, 2, 10–12, 13, 21, 23, 26,
  29, 32–3, 46, 47, 51, 62, 64, 65,
  77, 81, 110, 119, 120, 123, 124,
  125, 127, 128, 129–30, 131, 132,
  133, 134–5, 138, 139, 142, 145–6,